Buffy the Vampire Slayer FAQ

Buffy the Vampire Slayer FAQ

All That's Left to Know About Sunnydale's Slayer of Vampires, Demons, and Other Forces of Darkness

David Bushman and Arthur Smith

APPLAUSE
THEATRE & CINEMA BOOKS
An Imprint of Hal Leonard LLC

Published in 2017 by Applause Theatre & Cinema Books
An Imprint of Hal Leonard LLC
7777 West Bluemound Road
Milwaukee, WI 53213

Trade Book Division Editorial Offices
33 Plymouth St., Montclair, NJ 07042

All images are from the authors collections unless otherwise noted.

The FAQ series was conceived by Robert Rodriguez and developed with Stuart Shea.

Printed in the United States of America

Book design by Snow Creative

Library of Congress Cataloging-in-Publication Data

Names: Bushman, David, 1955- author. | Smith, Arthur, 1971- author.
Title: Buffy the vampire slayer FAQ : all that's left to know about Sunnydale's
    slayer of vampires, demons, and other forces of darkness / David Bushman and
    Arthur Smith.
Description: Milwaukee, WI : Applause Theatre & Cinema Books, 2017. |
    Includes bibliographical references and index.
Identifiers: LCCN 2017016600 | ISBN 9781495064722
Subjects: LCSH: Buffy, the vampire slayer (Television program)
Classification: LCC PN1992.77.B84 B87 2017 | DDC 791.45/72—dc23
LC record available at https://lccn.loc.gov/2017016600

www.applausebooks.com

To Joss (even though he never granted us an interview),
and to all the Potentials out there.

Contents

Acknowledgments

L ike Buffy, we have our Scoobies, and here's where we thank them. True, we weren't slaying vampires, hell goddesses, or sociopathic geeks (well, maybe some sociopathic geeks), but those are metaphors anyway, and we parried demons of our own: unheeded e-mails, unlisted phone numbers, and—the biggest bad of all—deadlines.

Scott Ryan, co-host (with David Bushman) of the *Big Bad Buffy Interviews* podcast and a gifted gabber and valued friend, participated in most of the original interviews included herein; Loretta Ramos, gifted at just about everything, opened seemingly impenetrable doors for us through her Buffyverse connections. We are grateful to both, more than we can express.

Research of the kind that went into writing this book involves long, lonely nights, but happiness is finding a new or forgotten detail, or making connections never made before. We thank Franck Boulègue, John Dorsey, Simon Fleischmann (whedonverse.net), Marisa Hayes, John Thorne, and of course Jane Klain of the Paley Center for Media for all their assistance in this endeavor (Jane even tracked down the elusive Marcia Shulman's phone number).

We also thank the following for their assistance in arranging the interviews that appear in this book: Dianne Busch, Lea Carlson, Lee Dinstman, Beth Fleisher, Theresa Fortier, Anna Gand-Sislyan, Wendy Greene, Amy Hartman, Tom Hill, Eva Lu, Dax Stokes (*The Vampire Historian* podcast), and Melissa Zukerman.

On the subject of interviews: the following people were extremely generous with their time and insights. We had a ball talking to them, and wish we could do it all over again: Jeanine Basinger, Dean Batali, Gail Berman, Nicholas Brendon, Cynthia A. Burkhead, Chris Claremont, Andrew J. Ferchland, Tracey Forbes, David Fury, David Greenwalt, Thomas Dana Hill, Georges Jeanty, Fran Kuzui, Kelli Maroney, Clinton McClung, Elizabeth Miller, Douglas Petrie, Marcia Shulman, David Solomon, Dacre Stoker, Kristine Sutherland, Kristy Swanson, Stephen Tobolowsky, and Rhonda Wilcox.

Buffy raised the bar for genre television.

We are fortunate that so many superb *Buffy* websites live in cyberspace, and while we can't single out every one, we do especially tip our hats to BuffyWorld, which has transcripts and shooting scripts for every episode of the series, an invaluable resource.

Thanks to Photofest and Jerry Ohlinger's Movie Materials for most of the images we collected, plus Clinton McClung (again) and the very gifted artists Tim Shay and Aaron Minier.

We thank Laurie Starr for her help with transcripts, and Peter Tartara for all of his support and ideas, plus all of our colleagues at the Paley Center for Media, especially Ritty Burchfield, Rebekah Fisk, Katy Jacobs, Megan Marcus, Barry Monush, Ellen O'Neill, Caroline Quigley, Rebecca Paller, and James Sheridan.

Arthur thanks Jenny, who Slays him every time, and Owen, a Watcher in training if ever there was one.

Last, David thanks Mariam, Alex, and Scout, with whom he has spent so many days and nights in Sunnydale, both metaphorically and not, laughing, tearing, and slaying demons.

Art by Aaron Minier

Introduction

What's left to say about *Buffy the Vampire Slayer*?

By our estimate, approximately 73 percent of the Internet is devoted to praising, parsing, and perpetuating all things *Buffy*. The impact of the character and the show on popular culture is self-evident, as the Slayer established an irresistible new archetype: an empowered young woman who could kick ass and take names (there are dozens of examples, for better and worse, but we can essentially thank Buffy for *The Hunger Games*). BTVS is famously studied at universities, as its narrative richness, formal daring, and identity politics offer endless opportunity for interpretation and analysis. The Buffyverse is *beloved*, and has been catalogued exhaustively; if you want to know the name of the forgotten drone-pop band that played The Bronze in a given episode, you don't need to come here for that information. It's a mouse click away.

Still, it is our hope that there is more to say. The relationship between the *Buffy* viewer and the show is an intensely personal one; the fully dimensional characters and emotional intensity of *BTVS* make the audience feel invested and participatory on a profound level. Everyone's *Buffy* experience is different; here, then, is ours, our opinions, our takes on the people and their stories, our sense of what the show means and why it matters (and our dumb jokes). We hope that the *Buffy* fan who investigates this book will find ideas to challenge, perspectives to argue with, insights that hadn't occurred before—basically we'd like to be one-half of the deepest-dive geek-out conversation possible about this extraordinary creation with you, dear reader.

Did we get Xander wrong? Is Season Four your favorite? Did they get the mustard out? Join us as we descend into the Hellmouth to refresh your memory on the rules of lycanthropy, relive favorite moments, and compare Monsters of the Week—*Buffy FAQ* is an invitation to re-engage, rigorously but irreverently, with Joss Whedon's monumental achievement. We can't think of a better way to pass a chilly moonless night, safe at home, keeping the demons at bay.

You Think I Don't Watch Your Movies?

Buffy the Vampire Slayer: The Film

In the beginning Joss created the movie, and it too was titled *Buffy the Vampire Slayer.* So how'd that work out? Note that the bulk of this book is about the TV series. Released on July 31, 1992, the film nested in theaters for five weeks, grossing $14.2 million, so about $148 million less than the year's top grosser, *Batman Returns*—a *much* pricier film than the $9 million *Buffy,* to be fair. Still, 20th Century Fox had anticipated boffo b.o., as they say at *Variety,* propelled by teen heartthrob co-star Luke Perry of *Beverly Hills, 90210* and by an anomalously ambitious promo campaign for such a low-budget picture, including billboards and newspaper ads across the country and a clever "Buffy Home Slayer" kit distributed to press as swag. Fox even bumped up the release date from late summer after viewing the dailies, positioning the PG-13 film as an alternative to the Summer Olympics for teen girls who had better things to do than watch the country's first-ever Dream Team—including Michael Jordan, Larry Bird, Charles Barkley, and Magic Johnson—sweat profusely while running up and down a wooden floor. Joe Roth, chairman of 20th Century Fox Film Corporation, later told *Newsday,* "We thought we had a campaign that really worked, and obviously we didn't. . . . I took my son and his ten-year-old friend to see it. On our way out, the ten-year-old said to me, 'This is a movie for adults, but there's no way they would know that.' I offered him a job."

The Gene-and-Roger crowd? Strictly splitsville. Naysayers included the *Chicago Tribune*'s Gene Siskel, who called it "a blown opportunity to update the vampire film," adding that titular star Kristy Swanson "plays the bland title character in a script that offers little more than tired gags about teenage girls being preoccupied with shopping and makeup." And in this corner— Jack Mathews of *Newsday*: "'Buffy the Vampire Slayer' is as intentionally silly as it sounds, and as cleverly crafted by novice screenwriter Joss Whedon and

Stakeout: Buffy (Kristy Swanson) makes her point to watcher Merrick (Donald Sutherland), though Merrick (and reportedly Sutherland, too) preferred hearing himself talk.

20th Century Fox/Photofest

director Fran Rubel Kuzui. It's about the freshest comic breeze to blow into theaters since this stalest of movie summers began." Many critics purred over the cheeky dialogue, now known as "Joss-speak" or "Slayer Slang" (the title of a 2004 book on the subject by Michael Adams), though Janet Maslin of the *New York Times* referenced it then as "state-of-the-art Val-speak," or Valley Speak, after the San Fernando Valley dialect of the seventies, popularized by fourteen-year-old Moon Unit Zappa's monologue on her father Frank's 1982 hit single "Valley Girl." Fox script reader Jorge Saralegui had another name for it: "neo-surf speak."

Sample dialogue, delivered by Swanson as Buffy: "Does the word 'duh' mean anything to you?" "Excuse much! Rude or anything?"

Whedon's mentor Jeanine Basinger, Corwin-Fuller professor of film studies at Wesleyan University, noted the uniqueness of Whedon's writing voice from the start: "I ask my students to write an essay about *Rear Window* after they have seen it for the first time as a final exam in my Hitchcock class, and I still have Joss's—I save them, of course. And Joss's was brilliant. If you read it you would not even write the book. You would just say, 'It's more than we can do.' The first thing it says is, 'They thought it couldn't hurt them.' Who, as a student, sits down with a blue book for a teacher like me, because I'm very demanding and I'm very tough, and begins to write an essay on *Rear Window* with the sentence 'They thought it couldn't hurt them'? You see what I'm saying? And the rest of it is just as brilliant, but I mean he can compose, in class, under those exam circumstances, he's already writing an elegant piece of analysis in his own voice, from a very particular point of view—a point of view that has so thoroughly understood the film that he begins where it takes many critics and scholars four years to get. That's exactly the problem: they thought viewing couldn't hurt them. That's exactly the issue, at the highest level. He not only has it, he starts with it, and he puts it in his own voice."

Critics also alluded to the film's feminist slant—soon to become another Whedon trademark—most of them approvingly, though Dave Kehr of the *Chicago Tribune* bemoaned the hard sell: "Kuzui has imposed a heavily block-lettered feminist message on the movie, suggesting that Buffy discovers her empowerment as a woman by driving huge, phallic stakes through the hearts of her enemies."

Truth be told, Whedon wasn't thrilled with the film either, even though he had scripted it himself based on an original idea. Kuzui had directed one previous feature, *Tokyo Pop*, a $1.7 million independent film released in 1988, praised by the *New York Times* as "a wedding of American and Japanese youth cultures as seen through a fun-house mirror," with "rhythm and zing." Maybe so, but when your director and screenwriter conflict over their visions for a film, trouble lurks. Typically, in the film world—though not in TV—the director prevails, and so Kuzui did. "I know, ultimately, that it's my world, but it's Fran's movie," Whedon told *Fangoria* magazine in an interview *before* the movie was released, foreshadowing troubles ahead. "It's very frustrating, but that's called being a writer in Hollywood."

Origins

A Night Alone, Whedon's 1986 film project at Wesleyan University, has been christened the proto-*Buffy*, which makes sense, since it's about a high school coed who discovers that her prom date is a vampire—not exactly your garden-variety nightmare date, though a pretty nifty metaphor for it. "I have a lot of successful students, and their work is totally different, and I'm proud of that," says Basinger. "They are allowed to create on their own. Michael Bay made a senior film here also, which by the way won the prize for best senior film. It was exceedingly well-made. They were in a class together with me, and Joss or Michael would kill me if I ever let anyone see either of those films."

Four years later, while story editing at the ABC sitcom *Roseanne*, Whedon began scripting *Buffy* in earnest, though at the time it was called either *Martha the Immortal Waitress* or *Rhonda the Immortal Waitress*, depending on which version of history you believe. "Just the idea of some woman who seems to be completely insignificant who turns out to be extraordinary," Whedon says in "Buffy the Vampire Slayer: Television with a Bite," a featurette on the sixth-season DVD. "I was raised by an extremely strong woman, and uncompromising and fun and funny, and I wanted to make a somewhat low-key, funny, and feminist horror movie." Now comes the famous "dark alley story": Whedon had served time as a video-store counter jockey, partaking freely of the inventory, including low-budget B-movies like *Assault of the Killer Bimbos* that, judging by their titles, promised female empowerment, but didn't deliver.

"I've always been a huge fan of horror movies, and I saw so many horror movies where there was that blonde girl who would always get herself killed," Whedon says in first-season DVD commentary. "I started feeling bad for her. I thought, you know, it's time she had a chance to take back the night. And so the idea of *Buffy* came from just the very simple thought of a beautiful blond girl walks into an alley, a monster attacks her, and she's not only ready for him, she trounces him" (there's literally a scene about thirty minutes into the film where Buffy traps and stakes a vampire by deliberately leading him into a dark alley).

One film that didn't disappoint, and wound up influencing *Buffy*: *Night of the Comet* (1984), which "actually had a cheerleader in it, with a title that would actually make people take it off the video store shelves, because it has to sound silly and not boring." (Years later, *Comet* would get a hat tip in *Angel*, the *Buffy* spinoff, when one character remarks, "This is incredibly creepy," and another responds, "Only in a post-apocalyptic, *Night of the Comet* way.") Buffy, he explained, "was the name that I could think of that I took least seriously. There is no way you could hear the name Buffy and think, 'This is an important person.'"

Whedon wanted to make a "crappy, low-budget B-movie" (as he told Ken Plume in a 2003 interview), in the vein of horrormeister George Romero (*Night of the Living Dead*, the seminal 1968 zombie pic) or films like *The Amazing Colossal Man* (1957) and *Attack of the 50 Foot Woman* (1958); Kuzui, not so much. She was a martial-arts-film buff who palled around with Quentin Tarantino and John Woo, and had just been unceremoniously dumped as director of *Cool Runnings*, a feel-good film about the Jamaican national bobsled team at the 1988 Olympics ("I got told that they had decided that it was a *guy's* story, and they better have a man direct the film, okay?" Kuzui told journalist David Morgan in 1992), and by golly she wanted to make a funny film, albeit one with lots of martial arts and a kick-ass female hero in it, which is exactly what she did, much to Whedon's chagrin. (Kuzui has cited *Sailor Moon* and Woo's *The Killer*—which she required everyone in the crew to watch before shooting—as major influences on *Buffy*, along with spooky comedies like *Abbott and Costello Meet Frankenstein*.) Between Kuzui's reimagining of his vision and the blithe butchering of his script on set by actor Donald Sutherland (who played Buffy's Watcher, Merrick), Whedon became so despondent that he stopped showing up.

While pre-promoting the film, Sutherland had told *Newsday*, the Long Island newspaper, that when he first signed on for the role, he was too embarrassed to pronounce the title of the film aloud. One night at dinner, Roland Joffé and Jake Eberts, the director and producer of the 1992 film *City of Joy*, asked him what he was working on, and Sutherland replied, "'Uh, a film for Fox.' 'What film?' 'Fran Kuzui's new picture.' 'Well, what's it called?' I finally had to write it down on a piece of paper and hand it to them. They fell on the floor laughing."

Whedon elaborated on his issues with Sutherland in unusually strong terms in a 2001 interview with Tasha Robinson of *The A.V. Club*, even calling the actor "a prick": "I pretty much eventually threw up my hands because I could not be around Donald Sutherland any longer. It didn't turn out to be the movie I had written. They never do, but that was my first lesson in that. Not that the movie is without merit, but I just watched a lot of stupid wannabe-star behavior and a director with a different vision than mine—which was her right, it was her movie—but it was still frustrating. Eventually, I was like, 'I need to be away from here.' . . . [Sutherland] was just a prick. The thing is, people always make fun of Rutger Hauer [for his performance as Lothos, the big baddy]. Even though he was big and silly and looked kind of goofy in the movie, I have to give him credit, because he was there. He was into it. Whereas Donald was just. . . . He would rewrite all his dialogue, and the director would let him. He can't write—he's not a writer—so the dialogue would not make sense. And he had a very bad attitude. He was incredibly rude to the director, he was rude to everyone around him, he was just a real pain. And to see him destroying my stuff. . . . He's a great actor. He can read the phone book, and I'm interested. But the thing is, he acts well enough that you didn't notice, with his little rewrites, and his little ideas about what his character should do, that he was actually destroying the movie more than Rutger was. So I got out of there. I had to run away."

While Whedon and Kuzui have minimized their creative conflict in recent years, *Cinefantastique*'s March 1998 issue included incendiary comments by Kuzui: "Joss's screenplay had Buffy just roaming around, sticking stakes through vampires' hearts. There was no humor, and absolutely none of the martial arts that you saw in the final film." She further stated that Whedon "had written the character of Buffy as being so stupid and empty, she was totally unbelievable. I said to Joss, 'You can't have this doltish seventeen-year-old girl just going in and spearing vampires. It simply isn't going to hold up for an entire movie.'" Whedon responded to the comments in the March 1999 issue of the same magazine: "I talked to Fran right after the article [was published] and we had a big laugh about it. I'm being constantly quoted as saying how much I hated the movie . . . which I didn't, and both of us are sort of used to it. We've been set against each other in the press before, so it was no big deal."

Why didn't Whedon just direct the movie himself? Well, he wasn't there yet. All those mega-success stories—*Toy Story*, *The Avengers*, and, of course, the TV *Buffy*—were yet to be. Whedon's only professional writing by 1992 was for *Roseanne* and the original television version of *Parenthood* (not the later, far more successful Jason Katims iteration), and the only directing credits he had to his name were, well, none. The *Buffy* script was shopped to every major studio in Hollywood and "turned down across the board," Whedon told *Fangoria*. Kuzui, meanwhile, had visited her friend Howard Rosenman, production co-president at Sandollar (owned by country music superstar Dolly Parton and her manager, Sandy Gallin) to vent about *Cool Runnings*; he tossed the red-covered *Buffy* script on the table in front of her and asked if she wanted to direct. Um, yeah? (She wound up sending him a garlic pizza with a note reading, "You're on!") Kuzui may not have been amped by vamps, but like *Tokyo Pop*, *Buffy* was a about a young woman struggling with her identity. *Buffy* "isn't really about vampires at all," she told the *Orange County Register*, but rather about "learning to be yourself and accept yourself. And I think every teenage movie is about that."

Kuzui and Whedon chatted by phone; each was impressed with the other. Kuzui, Whedon told *Fangoria*, "understood exactly what the movie was about emotionally. She was more interested in character than set pieces. To her, the script wasn't just a bunch of gags." But, he added—big "but" coming—"she wasn't as interested in making a horror movie as I was, so the film is a lot lighter than I intended." He spent a year rewriting to accommodate notes from Kuzui and others. Among the most significant revisions: Amilyn, Lothos's henchman, "came from working with Fran," Whedon told *Fangoria* in 1992. "We felt we needed a little kick to offset Rutger's villainy, a character that was genderless and raceless." Joan Chen, who had just wrapped up work on the TV series *Twin Peaks*, which, like *Buffy*, was cast by Johanna Ray, was originally given the role, but later bowed out, reportedly for financial reasons, and Amilyn was limned instead by Paul Reubens (Pee-wee Herman)— just his second film (after *Batman Returns*, released a month earlier) following his 1991 arrest for indecent exposure after being caught masturbating in an adult theater in Sarasota, Florida, and his subsequent retreat from the public eye. Whedon called the casting a "stroke of genius." (Kuzui's original choice for the role was Hong Kong actor/singer Leslie Cheung, star of Woo's 1986 crime thriller *A Better Tomorrow*, who told her of course he'd act in her film—as long as he was the leading man; Joan Chen had been Cheung's date to the premiere of Kuzui's *Tokyo Pop* in 1988.)

Meanwhile, Kuzui and her husband, Katsusuke (Kaz), an international film distributor who ran Kuzui Enterprises, had optioned Whedon's script and ponied up for rewrites, but now contracts needed to be signed if shooting was to start on time. Kaz Kuzui bet the house—literally—that the film would not just be made, but would recoup his investment, borrowing a million dollars. Fran Kuzui then approached her friend Susan Cartsonis at Fox, who bought in as domestic distributor; Spelling Entertainment first grabbed international rights, then backed out, leaving the whole kit and caboodle to Fox, a major Hollywood player.

Vampire Chic

For reasons above our pay grade (though academics had plenty to say about it, trust us: repressed fears of sexuality, repressed fears of death, repressed fears of sexuality causing death; this was, after all, the age of AIDs, just as Bram Stoker's *Dracula* was published in 1897, a time when syphilis killed thousands, including, possibly, Stoker himself), Hollywood was infested with vampires in the early nineties (we get it, but here we refer only to the celluloid kind). Fox fast-tracked *Buffy* to capitalize. In 1992 alone, *Buffy* was joined by *Sleepwalkers*, *Innocent Blood*, *Tale of a Vampire*, and of course the legendary *Samurai Vampire Bikers from Hell*, along with Francis Ford Coppola's monster-budgeted ($40 million) *Bram Stoker's Dracula*; a year later came *Love Bites*, *Dracula Rising*, and *To Sleep with a Vampire*, and a year after that *Interview with the Vampire: The Vampire Chronicles*, Neil Jordan's adaptation of Anne Rice's bestselling novel, starring Brad Pitt and Tom Cruise. Writing in the *New York Times* in April of that year, Pat H. Broeske said, "Vampires, a veritable staple of the horror genre, have historically materialized in B movies and more recently direct to video quickies. Now the genre is getting a shot of fresh blood with some high profile projects from major studios."

Plus, as referenced earlier, jittery Hollywood studios were shuffling their decks to counter-program the Summer Olympics, which, for the first time, included participation by stars of the National Basketball Association. Two weeks before *Buffy*'s release, Rosenman told the *Wall Street Journal* that the film ("very, very hip . . . and comic," he called it) was targeted at girls as young as twelve: "I think that kids want to go to air-conditioned theaters to see hot

Vested Interest: The movie *Buffy* didn't shutter any theaters (as far as we know), but audience response was tepid, and Whedon wasn't a huge fan either.

movies. . . . You put in a Luke Perry, and it's all over. They go!'" Fox was ada-
mant about a PG-13 rating, somewhat anomalous for a vampire flick, "mainly
because it's a kid's story," per Kuzui, who acknowledged that she was afraid,
following the *Cool Runnings* debacle, that "the same thing would happen to
me" on *Buffy*. Fox, touting the film as a "tongue-in-cheek horror/comedy,"
and even a "romantic comedy," brimmed with confidence: "We really have
our summer kind of scheduled around *Buffy*," marketing president Andrea
Jaffe told the *Los Angeles Times*, which in May reported that *Buffy* was "already
creating a buzz around town," and cited the film as among a "handful of giant
Slayers" stalking blockbuster summer releases like *Lethal Weapon 3*, *Far and
Away*, *Alien 3*, and *Batman Returns*. Early ads depicted a cheerleader from the
waist down holding a wooden stake in one hand and pompoms in the other,
with the tagline, "She knows a sucker when she sees one"; in a later campaign,
Swanson gripped a stake as Perry peered over her shoulder, with a tagline
reading, "Pert. Wholesome. Way Lethal."

Only Whedon—who merited just a single line in the studio's two-plus-page
press release ("The screenplay is by Joss Whedon")—seemed to raise red flags.
Buffy wasn't a parody, he insisted to *Fangoria*. "It's not a spoof of the vampire
genre. It's a movie that takes itself seriously. It's true to its narrative; it's not
some modernist thing that invites you to laugh at a bunch of funny film
conventions." Yet he conceded that the film was "definitely different from the
movie I was going to make. As I said, it's much lighter, and it's geared toward
a younger audience than I originally intended. That's pretty much based on
the fact that it's more of a comedy now than a horror film."

On opening weekend, *Buffy* was clobbered by *Death Becomes Her*, a big-
budget black comedy starring Meryl Streep, Goldie Hawn, and Bruce Willis,
which gobbled up $12 million, versus *Buffy*'s "weak" (*USA Today*) $4.5 million
over 1,959 screens (that's $2,305 per, for all you math geeks). Commercially
the movie never recovered; in a summer-box-office wrap-up piece headlined
"Why Three Didn't Live Up to High Hopes," the *L.A. Times*' Robert W. Welkos
reported that even in a summer of multiple major-studio busts (including *Far
and Away*; *Honey, I Blew Up the Kids*, and *Alien3*), *Buffy* was one of three films
(along with *Diggstown* and *Cool World*) most often mentioned in Hollywood
"when it comes to hopes being dashed."

Let's give critics their due: many noted the discord between Whedon's
vision and that of Kuzui and the studio, none more eloquently than *Newsweek*'s
Charles Leerhsen: "The film's basic problem is that it fails to create what
might be called the vanilla-fudge effect, the delicious swirling of the scary
and the funny that marked, say, 'Abbott and Costello Meet Frankenstein.'
As a comedy, 'Buffy' is a horror show, and vice versa." The *Chicago Tribune*'s
Kehr seemed to channel Whedon's thoughts in his homage to B movies,

writing that "the age of innocence in teenage exploitation films produced such classics as 'High School Confidential,' 'I Was a Teenage Frankenstein' and 'Hot Rods to Hell.'" Kehr's lament was that Buffy was "relatively slick, well-produced and very much above it all," rather than "stupid, cheesy and into it." As for Kuzui, Kehr added, "[T]he movie is a joke we are all meant to be in on, but it's a joke that never yields more than contemptuous sniggers."

Ouch.

Kristy Swanson

FAQ: Can you talk about the character of Buffy and the evolution she goes through over the course of the film? A lot of people focus on the early Buffy and say she's ditzy, but she goes through a tremendous evolution, and she seems like a completely different person by the end.

Kristy Swanson: Yeah, you can say she's kind of ditzy, but I looked at her more as like a typical teen. I tried to make her as normal as possible. She cares about her friends, and her cheerleading, things like that, and then to be told by this guy Merrick that she's the Chosen One, like how ridiculous is that? She basically is constantly fighting the fact that she is the Chosen One, and she just doesn't want to face it.

FAQ: Did you ever meet Sarah Michelle Gellar and have a conversation with her about the character?

KS: I did meet her several years later. There was someone making a movie that wanted her and me. I forget the name of the project and I don't think the movie ever got made, but we did get to meet, but we never talked about Buffy. In a way they're almost two totally separate things, the movie and the TV show. They were so different from each other. The look of it, the feel of it. I never really watched the series but I saw the very first episode, and I was impressed with it, I thought it was cool, it just was, like—the movie was more bright and colorful and—I don't want to use the word "bubblegummy," but it just seemed more lighthearted, and then when I saw the pilot it just had a different feel and tone, a little darker and a little grittier.

FAQ: We were hoping to see you make an appearance on the TV show. That would have been so cool.

KS: I know, a lot of people say that to me, and I agree, but I don't think anybody from the movie was ever in the TV show.

FAQ: Were you aware of any of the tension that existed between Joss and Fran or Joss and Donald Sutherland?

KS: No.

FAQ: Really? Because Joss has said that he wished that Donald Sutherland had not changed the dialogue as much as he did.

KS: Prior to filming, Donald and I had a lot of rehearsal time—just he and I, and Joss and Fran, just going over scenes and stuff. I know that Donald is an incredible—I mean, I got along awesome with him, I loved working with him, he was incredibly supportive, and always energetic to make the scenes great, and he's very much the kind of actor that, he wants to bring his own thing into it, and I did see him doing that, but I don't remember there being any conflict over it.

FAQ: Was it intimidating at all to work with him?

KS: No, I wasn't intimidated, I was genuinely excited. . . . I remember there was one scene we did out in the alleyway, and we were shooting a lot at night, the whole movie, and it was really late at night, and they had wrapped him and they were going to shoot the reverse of the scene—my side of it—and they were letting him go early and he said, "No, I'm going to come back. You guys call and let me know when you're going to shoot that. I'm going to come and be off camera for Kristy, because it makes a difference. I don't want her to have to read the scene with somebody else off camera. I want to be there." So he came back in the middle of the night to shoot that scene with me.

FAQ: What do you think of the film? Are you proud of it? Is there anything you wish you had done differently?

KS: I do wish I could have done the cheerleading dance again, because I was like one beat off from everybody else. I didn't have as much rehearsal time as the other girls did, so I was sort of flailing on the choreography with that. But yeah, I'm super proud of it. I was proud of it at the time that we were making it, I had a great experience making it, I learned a lot, I got to work with great people, and we were having a good time. You never know if your movie's going to be successful or not. You make it, and then you release it. Who knows what's going to happen? But it's turned itself into this cult classic, which is awesome, and then when they came out with the TV series I was just tickled, I was like, "God, that's so great," because I like strong female characters, and I thought, "What a great thing for a TV series because now all these young girls can watch TV every week and see this strong girl."

FAQ: Anything we haven't covered? We'll give you the last word.

KS: Well, the Funky Chicken was not in the script. That came from me. Fran was saying, "We need some cheers. We gotta do some cheers from the sidelines, other than the dance we do at the beginning. We need some cheerleader cheers." And my cousin Erica was one of the cheerleaders in my squad, and she was a real cheerleader, so I went to her and said, "What's that one we used to do when we were kids, with the 'Firecracker, firecracker, boom, boom, boom?'" And she said, "Yeah, that." So we were rehearsing it and then I said, "And there's that Funky Chicken we used to do when we were kids," and she goes, "Yeah, let's show Fran and Joss that," so we showed them the Firecracker and the Funky Chicken and they said, "The Funky Chicken, it's in the movie! Let's do it!"

Night of the Comet

Night of the Comet, you say? Never heard of it? Probably not, unless you're a fan of cult films. Penned and helmed by Thom Eberhardt (best known today for, well, *Night of the Comet*), the film (original title: *Teenage Comet Zombies*) was released on November 16, 1984, and starred Catherine Mary Stewart and Kelli Maroney as Valley Girl *sestras* who—thanks solely to being in the right places (meaning steel-encased rooms) at the right time—survive an apocalyptic smash-up between a prodigious comet and Earth, instantly eradicating most of the planet's population and spawning a race of ravenous flesh-eating zombies unlucky enough to soak in the celestial dust. The cheerleader frequently cited by Joss Whedon as a model for Buffy Summers is sixteen-year-old Samantha (Sam) Belmont (Maroney), who, along with her older sister Reggie (Stewart), mixes it up with not only the walking undead, but also evil (natch) scientists who are themselves infected (though not yet turned), and whose ethical code of conduct apparently doesn't preclude experimenting on healthy survivors in their urgent race for a cure (the sole egghead with a conscience is played by erstwhile Warhol It Girl Mary Woronov).

Night of the Comet scored mixed reviews—critics labeled it everything from "entertainment junk food" (*Newsday*) to a "good-natured, end of the world B-movie" (*New York Times*)—but the film was a surprise hit (Hilary Roberts of *Screen International* called it "this year's pre-Christmas sleeper"), reaping $3.5 million on 1,098 screens in its opening weekend (ruddy enough for third place) en route to a $14.4 million total domestic gross over the course of its forty-two-week release, and has endured as a cult hit ever since—the kind that podcasters and Internet-based film buffs love to minutely deconstruct. Even naysayers huzzah the film's feisty heroines, applauding their intellect, sociolect (in, like, a Valspeak sort of way—familiar much, *Buffy* fans?), and pluck, including their kick-ass proficiency with M20 submachine guns.

Like *Buffy*, *Night of the Comet* functions on dual levels—as both straight sci-fi/horror mash-up (Eberhardt prefers "adventure") and as parody (among the terms critics coined at the time were "new wave comedy" and "punk sci-fi parody"). The theatrical trailer released contemporaneously treats the film like an adolescent fantasy ("The night the teenagers ruled the world," proclaims the voice-of-God narrator), citing lines like "Hey, I'm sorry if the end of the world makes me a little nervous" and this exchange between two characters: "The burden of civilization is on us." "Bitchin', isn't it?" In one famous scene, Reggie and Sam boost their spirits with a shopping spree at the abandoned Bullocks Wilshire department store, set to "Girls Just Want to Have Fun" (tagline for the 2007 DVD release: "They came, they shopped, they saved the world.")

Night of the Comet didn't break any banks to make, which—of course—is half the fun (at least); the budget was somewhere between $700,000 and $750,000, and the producers' parsimony is splattered all over the screen; note, for example, that buildings are seen from the middle up, since there wasn't enough money to hire people to clear the streets (in one scene, Eberhardt inadvertently captures window washers toiling on a building, but couldn't afford to reshoot). In fact, the only reason the film is set at Christmas time is because it was shot in November, and the budget couldn't cover the cost of hiring people to go around pulling down Christmas decorations. Most hilarious ramification of the cut-rate economics: late in the film, Reggie is sneaking around the scientists' underground lair in a nearly pitch-black scene, searching for something; according to Eberhardt's DVD commentary, the segment is completely improvised because his studio time had expired and technicians were tearing down the set around them, having already packed up most of the lights. No one, including Catherine Mary Stewart, had any idea what Reggie was looking for. Oh, and all that smoke that inexplicably appears in the scene? Easy to explain: "The set is heavily smoked," Eberhardt says, "because half of it is missing."

B-movies are the best.

Kelli Maroney

FAQ: Joss Whedon has talked about the influence of *Night of the Comet* on *Buffy* because he was looking for examples of films where young women were empowered and didn't need some male to come to their rescue . . . Specifically, he's mentioned your character—you're a cheerleader, you're blonde—all of which you can see later with Buffy Summers. Were you aware of that?

Kelli Maroney: I'll tell you what: I was walking down Hollywood Boulevard when the movie (*Buffy the Vampire Slayer*) came out, and I saw the billboard for it on the side of a bus, *Buffy the Vampire Slayer*, and I went, "That's me! They ripped me off, that's me!" [laughing]. It's the first thing I thought.

FAQ: So then did you go see it?

KM: I never saw the movie, no, but I love Joss Whedon, I love his sense of humor . . . . What I love that people take away from *Night of the Comet* is that Samantha is fun.

FAQ: Thom has talked about the guerilla nature of the filming because the budget was so low. Did you have any sense of this when filming?

KM: Oh, yeah. I remember when we were downtown when we'd break for lunch—mind you, it was probably one o'clock in the morning—homeless people assumed we were a soup kitchen and got in line with us. I'm in my rollers and my bathrobe and we're all just lining up at the food truck and they lined up right with us. And the whole reason that I say, "See, that's the problem with these things; Daddy would have gotten us Uzis" is because Thom wanted Uzis, but they weren't in the budget, so when the guns came they were MAC-10's. He was furious, because they jam. And sure enough, [they jammed on] every single take. And we did not have the luxury of—we had to be on time—we did not have the luxury of having the guns jam and doing retake after retake after retake. In low-budget movies, one take, one for safety, moving on.

Machine Gun Kelli: Cheerleader/Buffy prototype Maroney aims and fires in *Night of the Comet*.

FAQ: Did you have to do any training to learn how to fire those guns? Was that difficult?

KM: Yes, they took us out to a gun range and they taught us how to shoot with real guns. . . . Anyway, that day that we were shooting the car scene and the gun is jammed and jammed and jammed and this is going on for some time now, and Thom had had it, and he just said, "I'm not gonna cut if that gun jams again. Just deal with it." And I said, "Just deal with it?" And he goes, "Yeah, and say something." And I go, "Say something?" Because I was so afraid to make anybody mad. I didn't want to make it seem like I was criticizing production. And he said, "I'll tell you. Say, 'You see, that's the problem with these things. Daddy would have gotten us Uzis.'" Meaning him—*he* would have gotten Uzis. And so sure enough it jammed, and sure enough I said—because I knew they would just cut it if they didn't like it—so I said the line and I just walked on, and that's the scene that people really love about the movie.

FAQ: You said you didn't see the movie *Buffy*; did you watch the TV show?

KM: I saw some of it. I saw enough to know, to really get what he meant when he said that about Samantha. When I saw his work I went, "Oh, my gosh, of course. I totally get it." And I was hoping—he didn't say that right away when *Buffy* came out, but a couple of years later he started to say it in interviews and everyone said, "Well, why doesn't he give you a guest spot on *Buffy* or something?" and I went, "I don't know!"

FAQ: Did you ever reach out to him?

KM: I have no idea if he got this or not but somebody said, "Why don't you send him a picture of Samantha?" because I do the autographed-picture thing, and I don't know if he got it or not, but it was just my way of saying thank you for saying that because it meant a lot to me. I was blown away. Because that is true: I saw the thing on the bus and I went, "Oh, my God, that's me!" What an honor to inspire somebody, to do that, because *Buffy's* given everyone so much joy.

2

I Died Twice

The Second Coming

Buffy's underwhelming box-office performance put the kibosh on plans for a sequel, surely a good thing given director Fran Kuzui's plans for it: "I wanted to make the sequel in Hong Kong, and make it even more of a martial arts movie than *Buffy*." Woo-hoo. However, the home video clicked, perching in the top twenty on *Billboard*'s rental chart for two months, and was re-released in 1995 under the 20th Century Fox Selections banner. Gail Berman, at Sandollar Productions, which owned the rights with Kuzui, came up with the idea of adapting it into a TV series, and asked Whedon, still under contract, if he was interested in scripting, possibly expecting him to say no, since he had, in the interim, built a lucrative career script-doctoring big-budget films like *Twister* (1996) *Speed* (1994), and *Waterworld* (1995), and earned an Academy Award nomination for *Toy Story* (also 1995).

"They approached me because they more or less had to—I was under contract to them," Whedon told *Cinefantastique* in March 1998. "I guess they thought I would just pass this thing by, but I was so intrigued by it, the whole thing just started to snowball." Two networks—NBC and FOX—passed, but Berman persisted, and the WB, just two years old at the time, ordered a "presentation," rather than a full-fledged pilot, a then-not-uncommon means of saving money. The result, also Whedon-directed, runs twenty-five minutes and thirty-four seconds, and has never been released on DVD (and never will be as long as "there is strength in these bones," according to Whedon, responding to a question from IGN Film Force in 2003), though a bootlegged copy has long been viewable on YouTube.

As Gail Berman recalls:

> You see this very few times in your career, your life as a creative person or creative executive. Joss had that vision thing, and he had it probably in a more sophisticated and excellent way than maybe anybody I've ever worked with, ever in my career. So this was about getting out of his way, and helping others get out of his way.

Cast Away

To run the national talent search, Berman flew in New York casting director Marcia Shulman, well known for her work on independent films, including *Living in Oblivion* (1995) and *The Ambulance* (1990), though her post-*Buffy* credits would include *Dawson's Creek* and *Felicity*, so count Katie Holmes, Michelle Williams, and Keri Russell among her many discoveries (Russell read for the role of Buffy, and Holmes was Shulman's first choice for the role, but was too young given all of the anticipated night shooting).

Shulman, who had never met Whedon, recalls their first encounter as "obviously great," as the two bonded over classic movies. "These characters he had created were to me very timeless, so in the meeting I said to him, 'I feel these actors, but they're all dead, and I was mentioning people like Ed Wynn, just crazy, dead people, and one of the people I mentioned to him was this actor Franklin Pangborn. And I said, 'You probably don't know him. He was always sort of like the butler in Fred Astaire movies and sort of the Tony Randall of his time.' And Joss said, 'I can't believe you're saying Frank Pangborn, because when I wrote the movie I made a reference to Franklin Pangborn and they made me take it out of the movie because no one would know what that meant.'. . . I think Joss was very excited to talk to someone who had a sense of cinema history, and we could talk in prototypes, and I think that was when I really sensed that we had a great connection." Whedon knew his film history; again, from his Wesleyan film professor Jeanine Basinger: "Joss really loved the work of the Hollywood master filmmakers. Joss really saw in the Hollywood cinema of the Golden Era, he saw the ability to tell visual stories cinematically—not just photograph them, not just make them theater, but he understood what a cinematic story was. He loved Howard Hawks, he loved Alfred Hitchcock, he loved Nicholas Ray, he loved John Ford, he loved Raoul Walsh, all the classics of Hollywood cinema. He, I think, particularly liked Nicholas Ray, and that makes a lot of sense, because Nick's work had a kind of lyrical energy to it, full of imagination and tender and touching feelings for young people, and Joss is a person who sees the humor in teenage adolescent situations—the ironic humor of being suspended between youth and maturity, but he is never cruel about it. He has respect for the process you go through as a teenager lurching desperately toward maturity. Nicholas Ray's work also often has that feel to it." *Rebel Without a Cause* (1955), a groundbreaking film about troubled suburban youths, is Ray's best known work.

The WB granted them enormous freedom, according to Shulman, "so most of the time it was just Joss and I in a room. I would meet people first, and for most of the roles I would read a lot of people." Especially challenging:

finding actors comfortable with "Joss-speak." Shulman adds, "And then every character has their own voice *within* Joss-speak, and you either got it or you didn't, but one of the things that was really hilarious—and I'm sure agents put their two cents into this—is that every time somebody would read in a breakdown that they were a vampire, you wouldn't believe how people prepared for the role. I mean I would have fifteen-year-old kids coming in doing Nosferatu imitations." Shulman wanted actors who "got that they were just who they were, and that they happened to be doing those things [slaying vampires, or playing vampires] was secondary."

Anthony Stewart Head holds the distinction of being the first actor chosen, as Giles, on day one of casting. Most problematic: Angel, who doesn't appear in the presentation, but does in the first episode. Shulman's challenge was to find "something like the most mysterious, charismatic, amazing—it was just like every superlative—the most fascinating man on the face of the Earth, basically. And agents are calling me and saying, 'Good luck with that.'" It wasn't just the pressure of matching the description; most agents were unwilling to send over their most charismatic clients for so small a part. Whedon couldn't grasp her obsession, since the role was miniscule. Eventually, an associate of Shulman's called her to say, "I don't know this guy from Adam, but he walks his dog in front of my apartment in Hollywood, and I'm telling you he looks like the guy that you're describing." That was David Boreanaz, who, at this point in his career, had only a handful of tiny parts, with credits like "Dinner Guest" and "Security Guard," on his résumé, though he had guested as a character named Frank in an episode of *Married . . . with Children*. Shulman didn't even read him—they met and talked about Italian food—before parading him before Whedon, who wasn't immediately impressed, so Shulman pulled in Gail Berman, and together the two of them convinced him.

Buffy, too, was a challenge. Whedon and Shulman were intent on *not* evoking the film character, portrayed by Kristy Swanson, not because of any dissatisfaction with the actress, but because they "felt even at that point that the Valley Girl thing had run its course, that it would feel like a dated character, like Sean Penn's Spicoli [in *Fast Times at Ridgemont High* (1982), itself released a full ten years before the *Buffy* movie]. We felt Buffy was a warrior, a feminist, a really strong, intelligent woman." Shulman had known Sarah Michelle Gellar for over ten years, from New York, and considered her a "no-brainer" for Cordelia, a character she calls similar in some ways to Kendall Hart Lang, Gellar's Daytime Emmy–winning role on *All My Children*. Two factors changed her mind: one, Shulman was now looking for someone who projected similar intelligence and strength to Holmes's, and two, the casting team was struck by Gellar's star quality, convincing them she could carry the show.

Soap, No Radio: Sarah Michelle Gellar and Rudolf Martin in a scene from ABC's daytime sudser *All My Children*.   *ABC/Photofest*

Hard Times, Come Again No More

David Solomon, who edited the presentation and later became a producer/director on the series—one of the very few behind-the-scenes creative people to be with the project from the start—remembers the shoot as "difficult," lasting four to five days. According to Solomon, Whedon

> had a lot of people who were not really focused on what he wanted, because he was pretty new at this and they thought they would push him around a little bit, and I'd say it was kind of an unfortunate thing for him. He came out fine, he can be a tough guy—I mean in a good way. He stood up for what he wanted. If you're fans of his you know that nobody's got a vision like this guy. Nobody ever has or probably ever will. It's a remarkable thing. So even in his beginnings he could still see exactly what he wanted. He wasn't sure how to get it there, but he could see it very clearly. Everybody who was around him could see it. . . . They all realized the same thing we all realized, which is that he may need a little help because he's just getting into this, but this is clearly the smartest guy anybody's ever met, and he'll figure this out by the end of the day.

Whedon may not care for the presentation, but there's no disputing its historical significance, as a draft of what would become one of the most storied, and studied, programs in television history, making his refusal to release it (as well as his *Buffy*-prototype film at Wesleyan) especially frustrating. Some changes made by the time the series premiered on the WB are relatively minor—there's no theme song, the title font is different, Sunnydale High School here is named Berryman High, and Buffy is brunette instead of blonde. However, key "Welcome to the Hellmouth" characters, like Joyce Summers, Angel, and the Master, are all MIA, and two significant roles were recast: Principal Flutie, played here by Stephen Tobolowsky and later by Ken Lerner, and, more crucially, Willow, the role that eventually went to Alyson Hannigan but is here limned by Riff Regan.

Shulman says Regan was deliberately hired because she was less glamorous looking than other members of the cast—"the feeling was that we should have people in the cast of all shapes and sizes," to reflect real life, "but ultimately she just didn't embody the character as well as every other cast member did." Hannigan came in later, and won the part with her reading, because "[t]here was something so optimistic about her. . . . I think for all of these characters, Joss was inspired by the actors and the actors were inspired by Joss, because I think Alyson's reading was what Joss had in mind, but he either didn't know it or couldn't articulate it, and when she came in it was like, 'Yes! That's exactly it!' And that's why I brought her to him, because I saw it, and it was unspoken."

Tobolowsky's story is a bit more complicated. Here's his version. Bear in mind that there are certain chronological inconsistencies, in that *Blue Skies* aired in 1994 and *A Whole New Ballgame* in 1995, both before the *Buffy* presentation was shot. *Mr. Rhodes*, another show Tobolowsky starred in, aired in 1996–1997, which makes the timing right, but it was an NBC show, and Barry Kemp wasn't involved. Notified of this in a follow-up communication, Tobolowsky said that may be so, but he could only comment on it as he remembered it, and to be fair, 1996 was a long time ago.

FAQ: How did you get involved in the pilot that never aired?

Stephen Tobolowsky: I believe I was working in Canada at the time, and I wanna say I was shooting the movie *Mr. Magoo* (1997). . . . I was coming back, and I was going to be under contract to ABC, to do a show called *Blue Skies*. Barry Kemp, who did *Coach*, was going to be the executive producer. And I got a call from Joss—Whedon—through my agent saying that he wanted me to play the principal in the *Buffy* pilot, and I didn't know what to do because as an actor you always want to say yes to work, especially if it's something that seems like it's gonna be kind of fun, but I was under contract to ABC, and Joss said, "Don't worry about it, we'll just go shoot the pilot, we don't even know if the pilot is going to be picked up." And so, when I came back to Los Angeles, the week before I started *Blue Skies*, I shot the *Buffy* pilot. We shot out in the wilds of Los Angeles. I think we were out in Torrance County, and we shot at a real high school. . . . It was a lot of fun. I was thrilled to hear that the show got picked up. And wouldn't you know it, *Blue Skies*, the show I was in, was canceled after eight shows, nine shows [authors' note: eight shows were produced, seven of which aired], and *Buffy* went on for years and years and years. But, of course, I was replaced as the principal. The big question I didn't know is that later I read some interview with Joss and he said I was replaced because I was no good, was the essence of the answer, but I was actually under contract for another show and couldn't shoot anything else, but that does not mean that those two facts are mutually exclusive. I could have stunk up the joint. Joss could have replaced me anyway.

FAQ: You have to be the only actor in Hollywood who wouldn't jump at the chance to attribute that to the fact that you were under contract to another show.

ST: One thing you have to understand about a pilot: Right now, you guys are looking at the pilot with the advantage of hindsight, in that you know what the show became. When you're doing a pilot you don't know what a show is. So it's quite possible that a performance could be incorrect, or outside the bounds of what the creator felt the logic of the show was or what the tone of the show was, and "We don't want that. We want something different." For example, I didn't know what *Buffy the Vampire Slayer* was at all. You listen to the title and if you don't know what it was you think—you know what the movie was beforehand, and it was campy and kitschy, and goofy, I mean just combining the word "Buffy" with "Slayer," right there you have cognitive dissonance, like, "This has got to be a joke." I kind of played it tongue-in-cheek, like the whole thing was kind of goofy, and the script kind of supported that too, so it could have been that they wanted a change of tone, and a lot of times what a writer or producer will do is, it's kind of the opposite of football and basketball: when something goes wrong with a football team you fire the coach. That's the first thing you do. But in TV, if something is kind of wrong, you fire an actor. You get rid of him and you say, "Well, that was the problem." Do you watch *Westworld*? Well, sometimes you need a blood sacrifice. But I really don't know the true story. I just know the physical true story is I was under contract at ABC, and I not only was under contract at ABC for that show, but I ended up immediately afterward doing Barry's next show, which replaced *Blue Skies*, called *A Whole New Ballgame*, which I believe was canceled after ten [authors' note: seven] shows, so I did a total of nineteen shows, which is almost a full season, for Barry under that contract. So even if Joss didn't fire me for being bad, if that's what he did in fact, I couldn't have done *Buffy*.

FAQ: If it makes you feel any better they killed off Principal Flutie in the first four or five episodes.

ST: Oh, you're kidding! I thought they killed him in, like, the second season.

FAQ: No, they brought in Armin Shimerman to replace Ken Lerner, because they did kill him off. It's interesting that in the two iterations of the principal—Flutie, whom you created and then Ken Lerner went on to play, and Snyder, as played by Armin Shimerman—they're two different representations of the authority figure. Yours is clueless, but not mean-spirited or oppressive.

ST: And I think what you describe are the two perfect archetypes of the way people see—it goes back hundreds of years, that archetype. In the plays of Molière, for example, they always had a character which they called the Adraste, and the Adraste was the old person who was there to thwart the love of the young people. He was the one who was supposed to stop youth from making itself heard. So, in dramaturgy, in writing, for hundreds of years, you have had this character, the Adraste, who will stand in the way of young people. And that Adraste in Molière's plays fall into the two categories. They will either fall into the category of the person without a clue, in his funniest comedies, and then you have the authoritarian figure who is just harsh, who will punish, who will do anything to keep the young people from having a say in the world.

Not Ready for Prime Time . . . Yet

In May 1996, when the WB announced its fall lineup, *Buffy* wasn't on it. However, four months later, the network ordered thirteen episodes of the series and announced it would debut in the spring, as a midseason replacement for *Savannah*, a second-year nighttime soap, which was canceled. The two-hour series premiere, "Welcome to the Hellmouth" and "The Harvest," both Whedon-scripted, aired at 8:00 p.m. on Monday, March 10, 1997.

Many years ago a flamboyant, stogie-chomping film producer named Joseph E. Levine appeared on the ninety-minute late-late-night show *Tomorrow* with Tom Snyder, who asked him how he got his start in showbiz. Levine spent all of about five minutes recapping, sat back, folded his arms and said, "And the rest is history."

"Well, Joe," Snyder told him, "you better start telling me some of that history, because I have eighty-five minutes to fill."

Here, then is the rest of the history of *Buffy the Vampire Slayer* . . .

The WB: We Are Young

Buffy gave the frog legs.

Lame, but true. *Buffy* helped put the WB, a fledgling, two-year-old network (or "weblet," as *Variety* used to call it), and its mascot, Michigan J. Frog (a character first introduced in the 1955 Merry Melodies cartoon *One Froggy Evening*), on the map, especially with adolescents who, in 1997, were ready to graduate from preteen Nickelodeon shows like *Clarissa Explains It All* and FOX's sudsy *Beverly Hills, 90210*, and *Party of Five*. Early on, the WB was a loose aggregate of stations, even without affiliates in every major market, so that *Buffy*—passed over by the network in the fall of 1996 but inserted as a midseason replacement the following March—was labeled a hit despite averaging just 3.7 million viewers a week (versus 20.5 million for *ER*, the season's top-rated show), ranking 144th among all prime-time series, mostly because it resonated with the WB's targeted audience of twelve-to-thirty-four-old viewers, salivated over by advertisers (by 1998 the WB was branding itself "the network for young adults"), though critical praise was certainly another factor. Buoyed by these results, the WB loaded up on teen-appeal dramas, including *Dawson's Creek*, *Felicity*, and *Charmed*, all premiering the following season, and *7th Heaven*, which had bowed in 1996 but enjoyed a ratings jolt the following season, from 3.2 million viewers a week to 5.8 million. (*7th Heaven* wound up running ten

Bond, Deep Bond: Giles's (Anthony Stewart Head) emotional connection to Buffy (Sarah Michelle Gellar) winds up costing him his job in season three.

seasons on the WB and one on its successor, the CW, making it the network's longest-running show at the time.)

The WB, co-owned by Warner Bros. and Tribune Broadcasting, held vast sway over teen culture during this time, cross-pollinating its TV properties and stars with Warner's recording artists and Time Warner's hugely popular print publications (like *People*, *Entertainment Weekly*, and *Time*). Often-cited example: Paula Cole's recording of "I Don't Want to Wait," which served as the *Dawson's Creek* theme song. Plus, as TV critic Joyce Millman pointed out, WB on-air promos "were things of softcore beauty, slo-mo shots of Sarah Michelle Gellar (*Buffy*), Jessica Biel (*7th Heaven*), Scott Speedman (*Felicity*), and the rest of the doe-eyed and tousle-haired WB stars striking dreamy poses to evocative trancy ballads by little-known Warner Bros. recording artists."

Buffy and *Dawson's Creek* will forever be interlocked in TV history, first because the WB moved *Buffy* to Tuesday nights on January 20, 1998, as a lead-in for the brand-new *Dawson*, to create a much-touted "New Tuesday" night of programming (WB research had uncovered remarkably light crossover viewership between *Buffy* and its previous lead-in, *7th Heaven*). Plus, the two shows ended their runs within a week of each other in 2003, though *Buffy* by then had moved on to UPN, after five seasons, due to a contract dispute with the WB. Millman commemorated these era-ending expirations with a column headlined in the *Portland Phoenix* "Hail and Farewell: 'Dawson's Creek,' 'Buffy' and the Soul of the WB," in which she argued that while *Buffy* was the superior show "in any universe . . . it was Dawson who won the battle for the soul of the WB—assuming that a network that made its reputation on a cartoon frog and a seemingly endless supply of pretty young actors and actresses has a soul." The marrow of her thesis was that as *Buffy*'s reputation soared, it began to attract older, more sophisticated viewers, which didn't exactly thrill the network's core advertisers, who were ponying up big bucks to rope in teenage girls—the key reason the WB allowed *Buffy* to jump to UPN. "In the end," Millman wrote, "*Buffy* didn't leave much of a mark on the network it helped make. Instead, *Dawson's Creek* became the blueprint for the WB teen dramas to come."

Gail Berman

FAQ: Is it true that you at some point talked about *Buffy* being a half-hour *Power Rangers*–type show?

Gail Berman: We talked about it being a half-hour or an hour, we referenced *Power Rangers* and the Pink Power Ranger being a Buffy-esque kind of character. We never talked about it as an afternoon show, but I think what [Joss] was referencing was when originally it might have been a syndicated show.

FAQ: And why did you make the decision to move from syndication to network?

GB: Because I felt that Joss's burgeoning career would allow for a potential FOX buy or WB buy. Even though we pitched it to FOX first and then NBC, we really pitched it to NBC to work on the pitch. We didn't think NBC was ever going to buy it.

FAQ: One place where you sort of take on heroic proportions in this story as it's told is that you knew how to navigate network TV, and that this was a tough sell, and you had the savvy to do it and also the perseverance to get it done. Was it as difficult as it sounds?

FAQ: I actually thought FOX would buy it, to be perfectly honest. We pitched it to [executive vice president of programming] Bob Greenblatt, and I was shocked when Bob Greenblatt called me and passed, and I did something that I'd never done before: I actually called him back, as we were about ready to go to NBC, and I said, "Really? You're gonna pass on this? I just think it feels like such a FOX show," and he said that's just not the mandate they had at that time. Whatever their then-mandate was, they didn't feel like this was part of it. I was surprised by that. The reason we went to NBC next was I thought maybe there was something off in the pitch and that maybe just another rehearsal would do well. I knew we were pitching to [senior vice president, primetime programming] Jamie Tarses. I knew she would never buy anything like this. It was way off the mark for them. But I did have a suspicion that the WB might like something like this. It's a young-person show; they had mostly at the time urban-oriented programming. They seemed to be somewhat female-skewing, and I felt like this kind of thing might have a shot there, and [programming executives] Susanne Daniels and Jordan Levin were there, I just felt like they might have a good feeling for this, and not only was I right about that, but they did in the room. They got it immediately. Joss's pitch was impeccable, and they got it.

FAQ: Did you leave the room with a deal?

GB: We left the room knowing that they wanted him to write a script, and we would subsequently do a deal with them. That was a lot more complicated, because the rights were a very complicated situation.

FAQ: At that point it involved FOX and the Kuzuis [Fran and Kaz]?

GB: No, it was more complicated than that, because our, Sandollar, television deal was then at Disney. FOX didn't actually have rights to the television show, but they were going to argue that they did. Warner Bros. Television was very interested in doing the show, which obviously was good for the WB. The problem would then come down to FOX threatening to sue over the fact that FOX wouldn't be the studio, based on some inconsistencies in the original contract. Basically FOX's position was this was a sort of negative pickup deal and TV was included, and other people thought TV wasn't included. So rather than have a lawsuit, it turned out Disney wasn't interested in the project, so our first look at Disney became a nonissue, and Warner Bros. and FOX fought it out a little bit and FOX ultimately prevailed and the show went to the WB, but the studio was 20th Century Fox.

FAQ: And what about Fran and Kaz? Could they have stepped in at some point and said they wanted creative control?

GB: Before we did the pitching, there was a wooing process of Fran and Kaz, so by the time I went to see Joss, I believe, if my memory serves me correctly, Fran had gotten on board. It was not easy because there were definitely issues between the two of them, but Fran did come on board, and Fran and I became friends and good partners throughout the run, and she was good to her word throughout and was never an obstacle and only a help.

FAQ: So, you had somewhat of a difficult time selling this—

GB: Well, think about it. I was not the most popular girl around when I was running around with a show called *Buffy the Vampire Slayer* based on a movie that had been around several years earlier that had not fared well. It did not make me, like, "Wow, she has the hot property this week." In fact, in some circles I looked ridiculous.

FAQ: Is it true that you ran into interference over the title?

GB: [Laughs] Susanne and I still argue about it. The WB wanted to change the title—and this is not unusual, by the way. Networks try to change titles all the time. I can tell you all about the attempts by FOX Broadcasting Company to change the title of *Malcolm in the Middle*. This was like that. So we made the presentation, the show was finally picked up, it's a long story, but when the show was getting ready to be marketed, the network came to us and said, "We want to change the name. We want to call it *Slayer*," which sounded like a bad metal band. . . . It was, to me, and this was a really hard argument to make, it was crazy to change the name. And yet from the network's perspective, which was not crazy, the movie had failed, so why are we doing something based on a movie that did not perform well in theaters?

FAQ: So what was the counterargument? Why not change it?

GB: Because the name is what the show is, that's what the show is, and in a world where things were starting to get ever, where there was ever more content . . . name identification is a good thing, not a bad thing. Well, it's bad if it represents something that did not succeed, and my point was,

"No, it's not when it represents exactly what this is," and so we prevailed ultimately, but this was not easy. It was very difficult.

FAQ: So why bring in Marcia Shulman, a casting director from New York?

GB: I knew Marcia, I knew how good she was, and I knew that we needed somebody who would take this thing really seriously. It was a presentation on the WB, so it wasn't going to be getting the hot names for anything, plus it was very late in the season when we got the order, so instead of going to a casting director who was somebody who was not amazing, I knew an amazing casting director in New York who had done some really unique things and had great talent but wasn't a run-of-the-mill person here or like the fiftieth on the list who might be available. This was somebody who was first-rate but was coming from a world with a different knowledge of a different talent pool. It might have seemed odd, but it didn't seem odd to me.

FAQ: Were you nervous during this presentation process? What did you think when you first saw it?

GB: Well, I was completely panicked, because everybody around was panicked. FOX was panicked, Joss was not panicked. It was the first time he ever directed anything, and that was part of the reason that he wanted to do this. I said, "You direct it. You get what this is so much, you should direct it." It just seemed very logical to me at the time. This was his vision. It was a completely unique vision and he was, I thought, a great talent. And I thought he should direct it. And I thought Marcia should cast it.

FAQ: When you saw the presentation, what were your thoughts?

GB: I liked it a lot. I thought we had something very unique. And by the way, Joss's direction was really good, especially given the fact that he was really—if you think about what this was, it was a presentation, which is sort of the bottom of the list of things, it wasn't a first-class pilot, it was ordered late in the season, people didn't know him as a director, he wasn't the Joss Whedon we know today, so 20th was sort of giving us a lot of the bottom of the barrel. He had a very difficult time, and so much was on his shoulders, just directing this presentation, because it certainly wasn't the A-list project. . . . It was terribly difficult. Let's put it this way: when you love your director, and you love your project, people really go the distance for you. You can tell the difference. . . . I thought Joss did a great job—and we didn't get picked up. What can I say? That happens all the time.

FAQ: When they didn't pick you up, did they say maybe midseason?

GB: Yes, but I can't tell you how many times I've had that happen, so that doesn't necessarily mean it's so. I just believed in it so much, and I think Susanne and Jordan did too, and they had their work internally, or as I like to say, "*7th Heaven* got picked up, so God beat out the vampire at that moment," but they were committed to getting it ordered, and they did.

FAQ: What role did David Greenwalt play in the series?

GB: We needed a showrunner, because Joss had never done that before, and that was very *de rigueur* for the network, and we went looking for an available showrunner, somebody that got this and whom Joss liked and who was interested in doing this, and David's name came up. These are always hard marriages to make, when the creator has another person step in in a sort of supervisory capacity, but that's just never the way it really, ultimately happens. Joss was beyond a showrunner. Joss was the total vision, and visionary, and what David did so uniquely and so beautifully was just found his comfortable place in that the two of them became quite a marriage, and in some ways the student became the teacher and the teacher became the student. They started to talk like each other, that is David started to acquire Joss-speak, and they were a very, very tight match, and it was a very special marriage, and of course we would learn, and David would learn, Joss didn't need somebody else, but they worked so well together. And then of course David would go off to do *Angel*. Look, I've seen it not work, too. This is one where it was brilliantly executed by both men.

FAQ: Speaking of *Angel*, do you remember how you decided there would be a spinoff, and who would leave the main show to be in it?

GB: Well, the WB wanted a spinoff. I mean, they were so excited they wanted a spinoff, like, the next day. They wanted a spinoff so quickly. We didn't quite see it that way. But it just happened very quickly, and it was hard in some ways, because Buffy and Angel were such a strong relationship. It almost seemed impossible that there could be another relationship in Buffy's life that could be that strong, but of course Spike would come along.

FAQ: We were going to save that for our last question for you. Which shipper are you?

GB: I'm an Angel girl. Are you kidding? I'm always Team Angel, no matter what, Team Angel.

FAQ: Are you? Why?

GB: Because, it's Buffy and Angel forever! . . . I'm a romantic, a total, total romantic, and that relationship, I think maybe, to date, is one of the best relationships I've ever seen on television. I remember when Joss was pitching Buffy losing her virginity and what happened and I was, like, "It can't be! It can't be!"

FAQ: One thing we've read is that when *Buffy* became popular with critics, and academics, it started to draw an older audience, older than teens, and that was one reason the WB was prepared to let it go, because they were less interested in attracting those types of viewers than they were in their core audience of *Dawson's Creek* and so on. Is that true?

GB: No, that had nothing to do with it. The only thing that this had to do with was money. WB did not want to have to step up to a very significant new license fee now that the contract had concluded. . . . That was [WB chief exec] Jamie Kellner's decision, and it would be the end of the WB, this decision, because once they decided that they were not going to pay for their big hit show an increased license fee, why would anyone else ever bring a show there? And that was the beginning of the end of the WB. And that is why it went to UPN.

FAQ: We talked to Fran Kuzui. Clearly the name that was going around when everyone was talking about a new *Buffy* film back in 2009 was Fran, that it was Fran's idea to do this, and Fran came right out and said to us, "I'm not doing a new *Buffy* unless Joss Whedon tells me he wants to do a new *Buffy*." That's not what the press was reporting at the time. Everybody seemed to think to do a new *Buffy* without Joss Whedon was, to quote Sarah Michelle Gellar, the dumbest idea she ever heard. What do you know about it? Will it ever happen?

GB: No. My understanding is that there will never be another version of the show that doesn't include Joss's vision. It's certainly not something that I would work on. And everyone knows that. And I'm assuming that Fran feels the same way. If there will ever be another life for this it will be because Joss wants it to happen or Joss is the leader of it happening and he either passes the baton to someone who he feels creatively can handle that or he does it himself, period, that's it.

3

You're the Slayer and We're, Like, the Slayerettes!

Scoobies

The idea of this band of kind of outcasts being the heart of the show and sort of creating their own little family is very much the mission statement. To me, high school is so much, I think, for almost everyone, that band of, you know, "We few people that nobody really understand exist on a level that they don't," and your friends seem so terribly real to you and everybody else seems so fake and strange.

—*Joss Whedon, DVD Commentary*

I don't take orders. I do things my way.

—*Buffy Anne Summers (Sarah Michelle Gellar)*

Buffy Summers originated as a concept—the subversion of a genre trope, the "little blonde girl who goes into a dark alley and gets killed in every horror movie," according to creator Joss Whedon—and, over the course of seven seasons, evolves into not just a feminist icon, but a richly textured, profoundly conflicted character whose superheroism never obscures her humanity. Buffy craves normalcy—dating, shopping, cheerleading—but, knowing "what goes bump in the night," she accepts the futility of that desire. She embraces her destiny, but on her terms, firing the Watchers Council; romantically engaging with not one vampire, but two; and refusing to shun family and friends because that's what Slayers are supposed to do. She cherishes life, yet inflicts death. A beacon of light to others, she is prone to deep, dark funks herself. She has no use for handbooks, rules, or traditions, relying instead on emotion, instinct, and a resolute moral compass, in the process injecting the role of Slayer with unprecedented power and integrity. All this, plus scoring a 1430 on her SAT—not too shabby, considering that she test-prepped in the cemetery in between dusting vampires.

Over the course of the series, viewers meet two other Slayers, in addition to Buffy (a function of Buffy's momentary expiration in the season one finale, at the hands of the Master), and each, in her own way, serves as a warning against what Buffy could have become, but didn't, through a combination of

First Edition: Scooby Gang, early years.

circumstance, upbringing, and willpower. First, Kendra Young, "raised to be a human weapon," as writer/producer Marti Noxon puts it in her DVD commentary, representing "just how rigid and straight and uptight a Slayer would have been without friends and family around her." Kendra shuns emotions, as weakness; Buffy embraces them, as "total assets." Kendra chides Buffy for treating slaying as a job—she herself sees it as "who you are"—but Buffy refuses to let outside forces define her. Next, Faith Lehane, Buffy's shadow self, who reduces the rules of slaying to "Want, take, have." Lonely, emotionally damaged, Faith has no moral bearings; she and Buffy start off as friends, and for a time Buffy finds her apparent disregard for consequences intoxicating, but they eventually devolve into mortal enemies.

Buffy arrives in Sunnydale—fresh from her slaying days in Los Angeles, which resulted in her expulsion from school and a two-week stay in a mental hospital, plus possibly contributing to her parents' divorce—a reluctant vampire hunter, insisting to Giles that "I've both been there and done that, and I'm moving on," reversing course only when Willow's life is threatened. No turning back from there, though Buffy continues to pine for a life of normalcy. "Now is the time that you should train more strictly, you should hunt and patrol more keenly, you should hone your skills day and night," Giles tells her. "And the little slice of life that still belongs to me from—I don't know, seven to seven-o-five in the morning—can I do what I want then?" she responds.

As David Fury explains:

> What made the show work, for me, and the whole premise of *Buffy* from the get-go, from the movie on, was the idea that you have very normal desires in high school, to meet a guy, or a girl, and have a relationship, and have a future ahead of you. To have your future already predetermined was just a terrible weight on her, so I think a large part of the progression of the show was Buffy really coming to terms with what she is, and recognizing, "This is what I'll always be, and I'm never gonna get a break from it."

As a high schooler, Buffy never stops worrying that slaying consumes her identity. Needing a teacher recommendation, she approaches Miss Moran, from Contemporary American Heroes, from Amelia Earhart to Maya Angelou (meta much?), "the class that changed my life," but the teacher doesn't even remember who she is. "I'm, like, a nonperson," Buffy says, a theme reinforced when Cordelia, miffed at Buffy for challenging her for homecoming queen, questions why she would even bother running when she's the Slayer. "Because this is all I do," Buffy replies. "This is what my life is. You couldn't understand. I just thought . . . homecoming queen. I could pick up a yearbook someday and say, 'I was there. I went to high school. I had friends, and for one moment I got to live in the world,' and there'd be proof—proof that I was chosen for something other than this." And yet, in "Helpless," when Buffy is stripped of her powers through subterfuge by the Watchers Council, she panics, asking Angel: "If I'm not the Slayer, what do I do? What do I have to offer? Why would you like me?"

Angel's response—that he loved her *before* she became the Slayer—puzzles her. "Why?" she asks. "'Cause I could see your heart," Angel responds. "You held it before you for everyone to see. And I worried that it would be bruised or torn." This is Buffy's single-most defining characteristic—for better and for worse: her passion—for friends, boyfriends, family, justice—gives her intensity, fire . . . on good days. "A Slayer with family and friends; that sure as hell wasn't in the brochure," a still-evil Spike says in "School Hard," after being bested by Buffy (and Joyce, who clobbers him on the head with an axe) in a rumble. However, there's a flip side, and it isn't pretty: because of her fervency, and her refusal to shut herself off completely, Buffy experiences the horrors of her trade with raging intensity, leading to melancholia, self-doubt, and sometimes, as in a huge chunk of season six, even self-loathing. "The hardest thing in this world," she tells Dawn at the end of season five, just before leaping to her death, to spare her sister and save the world, "is to live in it."

Buffy's burden is unrelenting. She alone is the chosen one (though, technically, there's Kendra, and later Faith, which doesn't always help). Only Buffy can kill Angel, her great love, in season two, when he's on the verge of destroying the world. In season seven, after Anya has wiped out an entire fraternity as an act of vengeance, Buffy decides she has to be killed, and she's the one who's going to have to do it, despite Xander's remonstrance. "At some point, someone has to draw the line, and that is always going to be me," Buffy says. "You get down on me for cutting myself off, but in the end the Slayer is always cut off. There's no mystical guidebook. No all-knowing council. Human rules don't apply. There's only me. I am the law."

David Greenwalt recalls of the show's star:

> Sarah loved notes. She wanted an important person, like Joss or me, to be there watching—all the time if possible, much of the time if not, but she wanted notes. And when I was directing you could walk up and give her eight or nine notes, and *bam!* She'd hit every single one of them in the next take. It was like, "Whoa!" It was like driving some high-performance Ferrari.

Buffy's despair threatens to overwhelm her in season six, when she's plucked from heaven by one of Willow's spells and loses her will to live. "I was happy," she tells Spike. "Wherever I was, I was happy, at peace. I knew that everyone I cared about was all right. I knew it. Time didn't mean anything. Nothing had form. But I was still me, you know? And I was warm. And I was loved. And I was finished, complete." Now, not so much: "I was torn out of there, pulled out, by my friends. Everything here is hard and bright and violent—everything I feel, everything I touch. This is hell. Just getting through the next moment, and the one after that, knowing what I've lost." This is the whole point of "Once More with Feeling," that season's venerated musical episode, with songs about "going through the motions" and "Why can't I feel?"; this same theme is tackled in "Normal Again," also from season six, in which Buffy hallucinates (we *think*) that in reality she is in a mental institution, and that everything that has ever transpired in Sunnydale is merely a figment of her imagination. Tempting as it is—her mother and father are still together, vampires don't exist, nor do her responsibilities as a Slayer—Buffy ultimately rejects that unreality (again, we *think*), inspired by Joyce's misdirected appeal to, of course, her heart: "You've got a world of strength in your heart. I know you do. You just have to find it again. Believe in yourself."

Buffy's twisted (secret) sixth-season relationship with Spike—who, at this juncture, has a chip in his brain, but still no soul—which ends in attempted rape, is clearly an act of desperation, to feel *something*, but there's no disputing Buffy is drawn to darkness, a fact that Spike never stops harping on, whether taunting Riley as "white bread" or baiting Buffy as a "creature of the darkness, like me. Try on my world. See how good it feels." Even Dracula, who encounters her in the fifth-season opener, having come to Sunnydale to see what all the fuss is about, senses it, telling Buffy her power is "rooted in darkness. You must feel it."

As the Slayer, Buffy *is* part demon, but she resists it—in season seven she even rebuffs the Shadow Men when they seek to boost her power with a fresh dose of essence of demon, to prep her for the coming battle with the First Evil, refusing to become less human, lashing out at them as "weak" and "pathetic" for "violating" the First Slayer. This is Buffy, locked in eternal conflict: life versus death, light versus dark, freedom versus responsibility, humanity versus superhumanity. In the end what we admire most about her is that she will make the decision on her own terms, and with all her heart.

In David Fury's view,

> Joss is clearly Buffy. I mean, Joss, he gravitated toward, or thought he was, Xander, as an outsider, but he comes from so within, and he's a fervent feminist, girl power, all those things, and there's part of me that thinks, and a lot of us have discussed it, if he didn't actually backtrack in some interview, and I feel like he did, that he said, "Actually, I'm Buffy." If he didn't say it, I will say it. He was more Buffy, because he had that strength and desire for being very female centric. In his heart he's

a sixteen-year-old girl. He had a very strong mother, a brilliant, smart mother who affected him and infused in him this feminist streak. The stories were always, "What's the Buffy of this story?" It was never, "What's the Xander of it?" That would be a different show.

X-Phile: Buffy Summers, Kitty Pryde, Chris Claremont, and the X-Men

If there's a bigger influence on Buffy than Kitty, I don't know what it was. She was an adolescent girl finding out she has great power and dealing with it.

—Joss Whedon

Joss Whedon has often cited Kitty Pryde, member of the mutant superhero team the X-Men, as a primary inspiration for the character of Buffy Summers (although we must point out that Willow Rosenberg also possesses some of Kitty's key traits: Jewishness, prodigious computer skills). Parallels abound: Kitty, like Buffy, is an ordinary teenage girl who, through an accident of birth, finds herself dealing with strange powers and terrifying responsibilities that turn her mundane suburban existence upside down. Kitty is recruited into superhero-dom by a bookish, vaguely British mentor figure, with whom she has a frequently strained relationship, and who sets her against various monsters, literal and figurative.

Like Buffy, Kitty is a relatable teen, bright and sociable, interested in boys and dating but not defined by such concerns. Also like Buffy, she initially struggles to summon the courage necessary to face the horrific circumstances she so often encounters. Kitty's evolution, from smart and determined but underconfident neophyte to seasoned, hyper-competent mainstay of the team was, for comics, unusually nuanced; attribute this sensitivity to legendary *X-Men* scribe Chris Claremont, chief architect of the *X-Men* franchise and co-creator of Kitty Pryde. Claremont had a reputation in the comics industry for his progressive attitudes toward characters, pushing for greater representation in terms of gender and race. Other hallmarks of Claremont's work—distinctively colorful, literate dialogue, a focus on the emotional lives of his characters, playful digs at pop culture, and a deft melding of genre tropes and engrossing soap opera—clearly made an impression on young comics fan Joss Whedon (in fact, Willow's descent into madness and apocalyptic power surge after Tara's murder explicitly reference Claremont's epochal "Dark Phoenix" saga, a foundational text in modern comics).

After the conclusion of *BTVS*, Whedon was invited by Marvel Comics to script a new X-Men series (*Astonishing X-Men*), bringing him full circle; to no one's surprise, Whedon put Kitty front and center and wrote the hell out of the character, giving her, in the person of the haughty, hypersexualized teammate Emma Frost, a

Cordelia-like sparring partner who precipitated much hilarious banter between the two. In addition to providing more classic Whedon snark, their relationship helps position Kitty as a fully realized and mature woman, confident, compassionate, and no longer remotely naïve about the horrors of the world . . . she's basically Buffy at the end of series. In fact, Kitty, in Whedon's X-Men run (which, by the way, sold like fury and won an Eisner Award), becomes a teacher to a new generation of mutants, echoing Buffy's eventual role as a trainer of Potentials. Finally, at the end of Whedon's arc, Kitty sacrifices her life to save the world, which is nothing if not a signature Buffy move.

We spoke to Chris Claremont about the Kitty/Buffy connection, and about his thoughts on the series. (Spoiler: he's a fan.)

FAQ: Are you aware of Joss Whedon citing Kitty Pryde as inspiration for Buffy?
Chris Claremont: Yes.

FAQ: How do feel about that?

CC: It's intensely flattering. I've admired Joss's work from the beginning, so I guess it's a natural circle.

With Sarah Gellar, you watched her evolve, from season to season, and that's the gift you can get from the right actor in an ongoing TV series because as they grow up, you grow up with them.

As a writer, I generally find adults boring. Their patterns are set. When you have adolescents, anything is possible, and you can almost justify any indulgence in terms of character change, evolution, screw-ups, you name it.

FAQ: You are known for putting female characters front and center.

CC: Some of my best friends who are women are some of the bravest people I know. If I know people like that, why shouldn't I put them [in my work]?

FAQ: Can you tell us about the origin of Kitty?

CC: So, here we have the X-Men working out of Charles Xavier's School for Gifted Youngsters, and there are no gifted youngsters. So, John Byrne and I decided we wanted to go back to the basics and present Xavier and the readers with someone who was not experienced with their powers, not at all used to the life—literally she woke up one morning and fell through the floor of her room.

My intent [in] writing the book was that every year or so [to] present a character to give new readers an easily accessible entry point. Quite frankly, at the time I was really unthrilled by the predominant number of kid sidekicks, none of whom were like kids. They were like midget versions of the grownups.

The trick was to show by doing: What's happening to Kitty? How does she feel about it? Where she gets pulled into the conflicts, like . . . what are her parents supposed to do? So, it became a sequence of natural steps. And by the same token, being thirteen, being full of (if you'll pardon the expression) piss and vinegar, and trying in her own mind and heart to live up to the A-plus-level characters she is surrounded by, she tries to overcompensate every which way. Sometimes [she] gets it right, sometimes gets it wrong, but at the same time Charles Xavier has to deal with the fact that Kitty is unlike the five kids that came to his school back in X-Men #1.

We were trying to go out of our way to present her as a kid. She was not fully formed. She is kind of weird looking and occasionally not attractive, because when you're thirteen, that's the life. The idea was to give readers a fresh perspective, not simply on the team, but on the life.

Here you have a kid at thirteen facing the fact that superheroing isn't always an adventure. Sometimes it is a horror, and she's got to deal with it.

FAQ: What was your reaction to Whedon's Astonishing X-Men run?

CC: I was so pissed. The first thing I asked for when I got Extreme X-Men was to get Kitty back, because I was tired of not seeing her done right. And then Joss beat me to it.

FAQ: Did he get her right?

CC: [Pause] Yeah. Damn it [laughter]. He got them all right.

One of the things that made me watch that damn series every week was that Buffy made mistakes. She was not perfect. With Buffy you could go in any direction and find a plausible rationale for it.

The thing that makes BTVS so cool as a series to watch was the sense of risk. There were consequences to actions. The ridiculously outrageous concept of having Buffy die—and then when you shift to the new network, bringing her back—and when she gets back she's really pissed. Willow thought she was doing the heroic thing, and it was the worst thing she could have done.

FAQ: What did you think of Dark Willow—who was a pretty clear homage to Dark Phoenix?

CC: Really? I hadn't noticed [laughter].

FAQ: What do you most respond to in BTVS, as a fan and creator yourself?

CC: I loved the singalong episode . . . I hate to say it, I listen to the damn thing while I'm writing, feeling incredibly jealous.

The frustratingly neat thing about Joss's work is that you bond with the characters. Any idiot can do "A giant comes to New York and wants to eat the planet." Once Jack [Kirby] did it, who cares? The thing that has you turning the page is Reed Richards shaving: "Ben, we must look our best." It's Thor getting into the back of a taxi cab and having a moment of conversation with the driver . . . the thing is, you find, the more fantastical the concept, the more necessary it is to find moments of recognizable reality to lock it in to the audience. If we weren't involved in Buffy's life, with Giles, with Xander, with Willow . . .

In a context of, she's saving the world, she's being a superhero, responsible for not only taking care of the town but, by implication, everything—let's face it, it's a Hellmouth, you walk down the wrong set of stairs and you're in a very dark place—but she's still holding on to, "Why does my guy have to be a vampire?" It was as much about life as it was about the crazy stuff.

The neat thing about Buffy was it danced along this ridiculously thin border between adventures, demons, madcap stuff going along—but at the same time, each season Sarah's a year older, we learn more, we deal with consequences, we carry the memories of what's happened . . . on the one hand it's, like, wackadoo adventure story, but on the other hand, he's telling you the story of a young woman growing up. And it's not always smooth sailing, and she's got to carry the memory and the consequences of all the actions that occur around her, were committed by her, from then on.

Willow Danielle Rosenberg (Alyson Hannigan)

Buffy Summers is the protagonist of *BTVS*—as the titular heroine, it would be awkward if she weren't—but perhaps no character on the show evolves as much over the course of the series as Willow Rosenberg. We first encounter Willow as a socially invisible high school sophomore, puppyish-ly devoted to her oblivious best (and pretty much only) pal, Xander Harris, and exemplifying the dictionary definition of "wallflower." The series ends with Willow as a confident, assertive, frighteningly powerful witch, secure in her identity and courageous in the face of apocalypse. Which is all well and good, but as Willow's eldritch abilities increase, so do her arrogance, impulsivity, and temper . . . which makes Willow pretty fascinating, and arguably *BTVS*'s most richly dimensional character.

Like her soulmate, Xander, teenaged Willow endures an unhappy home life, though her parents' brand of abuse tends more to chilly judgment and emotional detachment than the chaotic desperation of the elder Harrises. Preternaturally brilliant, Willow possesses dazzling computer skills, matched only by her paralyzing timidity. A natural target for Cordelia Chase's mean girl attentions, Willow skulks around Sunnydale High in her painfully unhip wardrobe just trying to keep her head down, until Buffy's arrival shakes up her cloistered, drab existence.

After Buffy rescues Willow from a vampire attack, the hero-struck girl dedicates herself to the demon fighting cause, bringing Xander along to form the first iteration of the Scooby Gang under the Watchful eye of Rupert Giles. Willow contributed to the team mostly through her research and computer-hacking skills—and, it must be said, contributed to the plot all too often as victim to be rescued, as Hannigan's vulnerable, emotionally affecting performance was a surefire generator of audience sympathy and concern. Even at this stage, though, Willow is more than a delicate flower or damsel in distress;

Red Alert: Willow (Alyson Hannigan) and Oz (Seth Green): such a great couple, except for that werewolf thing.

she's funny, and sharply perceptive, and her budding close friendship with Buffy makes sense, despite their surface differences. Willow grounds Buffy and offers supportive emotional intimacy, while Buffy inspires and gives a sense of mission to Willow. Most importantly, they get each other's jokes.

Willow also develops a close relationship with Giles. They're nerds of a feather, geeking out over magical research, and the elder Watcher serves as unofficial mentor to the budding witch. It's a sweet, father/daughter dynamic, which will make their later estrangement all the more wounding. Willow's slow emergence from her shell is further aided by her romantic relationship—her first—with the werewolf Oz, whose respect, affection, and support do wonders for her self-esteem, until she fools around with Xander behind his back and is found out, breaking Oz's heart. An early indication of Willow's less than purely angelic nature?

Willow's dark side is literalized when a wishing spell transforms Sunnydale into a vampire-ridden carnage pit (well, more than it is usually), complete with a vampire Willow, who projects a bored, offhand cruelty and salacious interest in attractive women, which is an interesting foreshadowing. Vamp Willow gave Hannigan a juicy opportunity to play against type (she's wonderfully sinister and sexy), but it also set the stage for the future cracks in Willow's good-girl persona.

After a traumatic breakup with Oz (he forgave the infidelity, but his lycanthropic issues drove him to wander to the Far East in search of a cure), Willow meets Tara, a fellow witch-in-training, and the pair quickly go from research partners to giggling besties to passionate, devoted lovers. Much has been made of *BTVS*'s progressive portrayal of a lesbian relationship (per David Greenwalt: "They [the network] did try to have me talk Joss out of making Willow gay, and I said, 'You are joking, right?' First of all, I'm not gonna talk him out of anything under any condition. Second of all, every time we have one of these conversations I'm going into his office and reporting the conversation we had, because I always thought my job was to serve the creator of the show's vision and style and I wasn't going to be some busboy for the network"), and deservedly so—their partnership is functional and productive (and adorable; see: Miss Kitty Fantastico), but not perfect. Willow keeps the relationship on the downlow to the extent that it hurts Tara's feelings, and Tara gets up to some potentially fatal magical mischief in an effort to hide her past from her new paramour. The most serious cracks appear when Willow begins "abusing" magic, provoking Tara's justifiable concern. Willow's response is chilling: she magically erases the problem from Tara's mind, a shocking violation that indicates Willow's escalating corruption, as she commits the profound betrayal almost as an afterthought.

When Giles confronts Willow about her recklessness and hubris after the witch successfully resurrects the dead Buffy, her response is an icy threat—she's losing it, and she soon spirals into a devastating magical addiction. She recovers, and wins Tara back (the more sensible Wiccan had ended their romance as an act of tough love), but she's nearly unrecognizable as the shy, unassuming, innocent sidekick of seasons past. She's now a mature, complicated woman, who must reconstruct herself and her life after blowing it all up. In other words, she's more relatable and dimensional than ever before, and Hannigan's total commitment to her performance makes the transition utterly compelling and believable.

Sadly, Dark Willow reappears upon the tragic event of Tara's murder: grief-maddened, Willow gives full head to her dark powers, which at this point are sufficient to crack the planet in two like a china plate. Xander talks her down from ending the world, but she flays Warren Mears, Tara's accidental killer, alive, which certainly puts the Dark in Dark Willow. Shattered after the ordeal, Willow travels with Giles to England for recovery and rehabilitation. She returns to Sunnydale for the final confrontation with the First, and proves her might again by magically activating all of the potential Slayers in the world to join the fight. Willow develops a new relationship with Kennedy, an activated Potential, but seems conflicted about it.

And that's where we leave her: conflicted. Good witch or bad witch? The simplest answer is "both," because she's human . . . and no other character on *BTVS* embodies the messiness, weakness, contradictions, and hard-won grace of that unfortunately terminal condition like Willow Rosenberg.

Alexander Lavelle Harris (Nicholas Brendon)

Alexander, a.k.a. Xander, the Zeppo, is a founding member of the Scoobies. Steadfast Xander Harris serves as a key audience identification point: largely hapless, usually confused, and completely unequipped (on the surface) for hero-dom, wisecracking, good-natured Xander is easy to root for, and to see ourselves in.

And maybe see Joss Whedon in? People have often speculated about which *BTVS* character is "really" Joss, and Xander is a leading candidate. Effortlessly witty, unhappy in high school, encumbered with an unusual nickname ("Xander" from Alexander, "Joss" from Joseph), passionately devoted to the strong female figures in his circle; the connections are there for those who care to make them.

Unique among the Scoobies, Xander has no special powers, skills, or connections to the supernatural; we meet him as a socially awkward, motor-mouthed quipster suffering through the indignities of high school, the pathologically shy Willow Rosenberg practically his only friend. From his first moments on screen, Xander feels fully realized, as Nicholas Brendon's offbeat charm, unassuming good looks, and flawless comic timing coalesce into an instantly likeable, recognizable fellow: the class clown and secret romantic, always underestimated—particularly by himself.

Writer/producer David Fury on Xander:

> Xander's the Everyman. He's the audience's vessel into the stories often, because his friends were exceptional, they all became exceptional, they didn't necessarily start out that way. Willow was a very powerful witch, and Oz is a werewolf, and Dawn is the Key, and then there's Xander, just this guy in the middle of it all who loves his friends, but he's powerless, he doesn't have their power and it makes him extra brave. He is arguably the bravest character on the show, even though he often acts like Lou Costello meeting Frankenstein.

The product of a fractious, miserable home life, Xander, upon meeting Buffy, has failed to distinguish himself academically, athletically, or socially, and seems fatalistically resigned to a dreary, unsatisfying future. The arrival

Meetup: Xander (Nicholas Brendon) runs into Buffy (Sarah Michelle Gellar) on his skateboard during her first day at Sunnydale High.   *WB/20th Century Fox/Photofest*

of Buffy Summers shocks Xander into active participation in the world around him, initially because of his instant crush on the Slayer, and later due to the sense of purpose he derives from aiding her mission. The evolution of his feelings for Buffy, from puppyish infatuation to a profound brother/sister bond, is one of the series' most satisfying emotional arcs, as Xander time and again accesses the better angels of his nature through Buffy's example and demonstrates unshakeable loyalty to her. (Nicholas Brendon told us: "In season seven, Joss came up to Sarah and I, he's like, 'I'm toying with the idea of having Buffy and Xander together on the show. What do you guy's think about that?' And we were like, 'Cool.' And then he did the exact opposite. I don't think Joss ever wants his characters happy in love, to be honest with you.")

It is loyalty, in fact, that most strongly defines Xander, for good and ill; he doesn't hesitate to sacrifice himself for his loved ones, but he also holds a hell of a grudge (see: Angel; Spike). When he, Giles, and Willow magically bind their essences to Buffy's during her fight with the cyborg Adam, they are each positioned as aspects of a single being: Giles, the mind; Willow, the spirit; Buffy, the hand; and Xander, the heart. This is astute: Xander is indeed the heart of the Scoobies, representing the fragile humanity that heroically pits itself against powerful agents of evil despite the seeming hopelessness of the situation. It is precisely Xander's lack of conventionally heroic attributes that distinguishes him as the most courageous of the group; he's got no real resources, but throws himself into the fight anyway, out of pure love for his friends.

His love for the ladies is another story. Xander's love life is its own kind of Hellmouth: His overpowering attraction to Buffy barely registers on the Slayer. He attracts the attentions of a predatory insect woman and an ancient Incan mummy girl. Beautiful Cordelia Chase takes special pleasure in mocking and belittling him in public—and bewilderingly begins hooking up with him in private, protesting her shame and disgust every step of the way. When Xander and Willow—the witch had long carried a torch for her constant pal—surreptitiously begin smooching in stolen moments, they are caught by Cordelia and Willow's boyfriend, Oz, resulting in an accident that horrifically injures Cordy and leaves Xander a guilt-ridden mess. Wild child and rogue Slayer Faith takes his virginity one night on a lark, then, later, nearly rapes and kills him. Then there was the vengeance demon: Anya (Emma Caulfield), summoned by Cordelia's pain over Xander's betrayal, instead likes what she sees, and proclaims her amatory interest in the shocked Mr. Harris. As Anya is now a very attractive mortal woman, he goes along with it. *Ulp.*

Xander and Anya's tumultuous relationship—exacerbated by his passive defeatism and her obliviousness to human mores—was a roller coaster for viewers, alternately touching (these two oddballs found and appreciate each other!), maddening (they did bicker a lot), disturbing in some of its implications (Xander often seemed embarrassed by, if not outright contemptuous of, some of Anya's peccadillos), heartbreaking (Xander's courage finally fails him at the altar), and tragic (the spurned Anya loses her life in the series' final apocalyptic battle). Brendon and Caulfield generated tremendous chemistry as the mismatched lovers—they are among *BTVS*'s straight-out funniest performers, and their interactions were absurdist little duets of quirky delight, when they weren't tearing your heart out.

Xander's insecurities about his usefulness to the team, his own potential, and his future prospects would recur throughout the series, throwing his rapid-patter comic image into poignant relief when the façade came down. He never seems to realize the depth of his courage, or the centrality of his contributions to Buffy's mission. This lack of self-esteem leads to his breakup with Anya at their wedding, precipitating her return to vengeance demonhood and all manner of mayhem; ironically, the Scooby with the biggest heart is unable to love himself, and this is his greatest weakness.

Still, this failing is more than compensated for by his empathy, insight (Caleb takes out Xander's eye during a fight, as Xander "sees everything"—the resulting eyepatch is quite dashing on the lad), and moral clarity. Xander alone is able to pull Dark Willow back from the brink of world destruction after Tara's death—proving an average, well-intentioned guy can save the world, provided he possesses the necessary courage and heart.

Cordelia Chase (Charisma Carpenter)

Over three seasons of *Buffy* and four-plus of *Angel*, Cordelia undergoes radical transformations. Not that this is a good thing . . .

Cordelia starts off, in "Welcome to the Hellmouth," a shallow, vain, solipsistic bully (albeit a very funny one—Kristy Swanson's film Buffy, but on 'roids), and by the time of her death, midway into season five of *Angel*, has mutated through an array of iterations, some of them staggeringly ill-advised, including Scooby member, spurned lover, poor little poor girl, semi-demon, Team Angel matriarch, higher being, love interest of both Angel and his son, Connor (gross), and, finally, host vessel to a parasitic deity who, in effect, gives birth to herself. Even the *Angel* writers (some of them, at least) acknowledge losing sight of who the character was, before David Fury finally rescued her with his script for "You're Welcome," an episode from the fifth season, in which Cordelia finally, mercifully, passes on. The episode "allowed me to send off Cordelia as the one we loved—the Cordelia that was loved in the beginning gets to go away, because before she went away, we disliked her, the whole pregnancy thing, it just wasn't working," Fury says. "I have to say, Joss was always very emotionally connected to these episodes. He'll be weeping as he writes. He'll watch them, he'll direct them, and he'll tear up, and I always thought that was kind of, 'Okay, that's sort of the sixteen-year-old girl again,' but when I did 'You're Welcome' and I did the scene between Cordelia and Angel at the end, before he gets the call and finds out she died, *I* was crying, *I* was weeping, I was doing exactly what Joss does, and I was like, 'Okay, I get it now.' I was really touched by it."

It took Lear (the King, not Norman) four acts to figure out that Cordelia was the noblest of his daughters, but we were hip to Cordelia Chase from the start. Cordy had, as writer Jennifer Crusie phrases it in "The Assassination of Cordelia Chase," a "keen intelligence and a fixity of purpose that makes her almost invincible." Never was there anything deceitful about Cordy, as Buffy discovers in "Earshot," when she can read minds and discovers that, among the Scooby gang, only Cordelia says exactly what's on hers. Similarly, in "Halloween," while all the other characters transform into the persona of their enchanted costumes, reflecting identity crises they are enduring at the time, Cordelia is exactly who she always is (sure, she shopped at a different Halloween store, but that's the point).

Seat of Powerlessness: Mean queen Cordelia (Charisma Carpenter), villain magnet.

Yes, of course Cordelia can be considerate of feelings, as long as they're her own; in "Killed by Death," an exasperated Giles, hardly prone to insulting students, refers to her as "Homerically insensitive," a characterization Cordelia would easily dismiss if she were to hear it, believing that "tact is just not saying true stuff; I'll pass." (Our favorite Cordelia Chase-ism, from season two's "Passion": after Angel has transformed into Angelus, Cordelia realizes that she had once invited Angel into her car, meaning an open invitation for Angelus as well. When Giles announces that he has discovered a spell to revoke the invitation to a vampire, Cordy responds: "Oh, thank goodness. I actually had to talk my grandmother into switching cars with me last night.") Fury once joked about publishing a coffee-table book titled, "The Wit and Wisdom of Cordelia Chase."

The Wit and Wisdom of Cordelia Chase

"I just am not the type to settle, you know? It's like when I go shopping. I have to have the most expensive thing, not because it's expensive, but because it costs more."

"Guys from our grade, forget about it, they're children. Y'know? Like Jesse. Did you see him last night, following me around like a little puppy dog? You just wanna put him to sleep. But senior boys, they have mystery. They have . . . What's the word I'm searching for? Cars!"

"I'm not saying that we should kill a teacher every day just so I can lose weight, I'm just saying when tragedy strikes, we have to look on the bright side."

"Buffy—love the hair. It just screams street urchin."

"So, can I go now? She doesn't need this many stakes. I mean, if this guy Spike is as mean as you all said, it should be over pretty quickly."

"Oh, God. Is the world ending? I have to research a paper on Bosnia for tomorrow, but if the world's ending, I'm not gonna bother."

"Ooo, again, I strike the nerve. I am the surgeon of mean."

Cordelia had her posse (the Cordettes, including ditzy Harmony Kendall), but was far too sharp and impertinent to bend her will to a flock of sheep (hence, while initially succumbing to peer pressure to dump Xander Harris, she eventually rebels, though in classic Cordy style: "I'll date whoever the hell I wanna date, no matter how lame he is"), and in Scoobyland she was always the odd woman out, which is usually what happens when you keep deriding everyone in your circle as losers.

Still, dig below the surface and there's more to Cordy than meets the eye (not that there's anything wrong with what meets the eye, either). Charisma Carpenter, commenting in the March 1998 issue of *Cinefantastique*, said Cordelia was "popular on purpose. And she's misunderstood. She obviously had a bad relationship with her mom. She is always reaffirming her importance, either with her looks, her wardrobe, or her words. Some of Cordelia's bravado and nastiness is used to cover up what I see as her vulnerability." As director/producer David Solomon put it, "She had a sweet sort of sad thing about her, like she's so beautiful she should be given everything, but she's not being given everything. She's suffering on the inside."

Signs surface early on: in season one's "Out of Mind, Out of Sight," in which invisible girl Marcie Ross targets Cordelia for vengeance, out of resentment, Cordy exhibits unexpected introspection, telling Buffy being "so cute and popular" doesn't mean she isn't lonely: "I can be surrounded by people and be completely alone. It's not like any of them really know me. I don't even know if they like me half the time. People just want to be in a popular zone. Sometimes when I talk, everyone's so busy agreeing with me they don't hear a word I say." So why work so hard at being popular? Buffy asks. Cordelia's response: "It beats being alone all by yourself." Still, in the end, Cordy calls the Scoobies a "social leper colony" and sashays off with a popular boy. Hey, character development takes time.

An episode later, in "Prophecy Girl," Cordy performs perhaps her first selfless act of the series, rescuing Willow and Jenny from an army of vampires, and in the season-two premiere intervenes after witnessing Buffy's "bad girl" behavior in front of Xander, Willow, and Angel at The Bronze, counseling Buffy to lose the Joan Collins "'tude . . . because pretty soon you're not gonna even have the loser friends you've got now."

Cordelia's romance (if you can call it that) with Xander—described by Whedon in the March 1999 issue of *Cinefantastique* as an "I hate you but I'm wild about your hormones relationship"—ends badly, with Cordelia victimized; her suffering crescendos in "Lovers Walk" when she (and Oz) burst in on Willow and Xander, hoping to rescue them from Spike, but instead find them canoodling, and when she tries to make a run for it falls through a collapsing stairway, impaling herself on a metal rebar below. Soon after, she learns that her father has been fingered for tax fraud, meaning her family loses everything; she's forced to get a job, at formalwear outlet April Fools, and still can't afford a dress for senior prom (Xander winds up buying it for her). College too is out of the question—nothing but the best for Cordy; hence her move to *Angel*, set in L. A., where she hopes to become an actress.

In the early days of *Angel*, Cordelia is at least recognizable as the girl from Sunnydale, even if older, wiser, and more self-aware. For example, in one first-season episode she finally finds an apartment she loves and, in danger of losing it, tells Angel such an outcome would mean she's still being punished.

"For what? Angel asks.

"I don't know. For how I was? For everything that I said in high school, just 'cause I could get away with it? And then it all ended, and I had to pay."

The transformation is gradual, but certainly the mind-splitting visions from the Powers that Be that Cordelia inherits from Doyle are instrumental, as Wesley, who undergoes a reinvention of his own, points out to Angel: "Our Cordelia has become a very solitary girl. She's not the vain, carefree creature she once was. Well, certainly not carefree." Cordelia—whose single-most defining characteristic in *Buffy* was self-absorption—"knows and experiences the pain in this city, and because of who she is, she feels compelled to do something about it," Wesley adds.

By the conclusion of season three, Angel and Cordelia are in love, which is bad enough, but on the way to profess her feelings she is waylaid by a demon and catapulted to a higher realm, from where she appears for several episodes as a glowing, disembodied head, pleading to be rescued.

The metaphor is hard to ignore.

Daniel "Oz" Osbourne (Seth Green)

Daniel "Oz" Osbourne, the man behind the curtain, is a tough read: taciturn, Delphic, unflappable (or nearly so, since, in the end, he is super flappy, after discovering that Willow and Tara are a thing). Oz is a recurring or regular presence in seasons two and three, but leaves abruptly six episodes into season four ("Wild at Heart") to address certain existential crises, like the fact that three nights out of every month he's a werewolf (nipped on the finger by cousin Jordy, also a lycanthrope), he has just ripped out the throat of another werewolf (Veruca, lead singer of a local rock band), and he was on the verge of mauling Willow, his girlfriend, before Buffy stepped in to save her. He appears in the series just twice after that, both times in season four: once in "Restless," the dream episode, and once in "New Moon Rising," returning to Sunnydale to woo Willow, revealing that during his sabbatical he had visited Tibet and learned to conquer the beast in him, God help him, with such New-Agey tools as herbs, chants, meditation, and copious amounts of magically delicious Lucky Charms, or some sort of charms anyway. All fine and good, but this is Sunnydale, home of the Hellmouth, not woo-woo Tibet, so once Oz gets a whiff of Willow's relationship with Tara, and then gets an actual whiff of Willow on Tara, the big bad wolf is back, and soon Oz is following the yellow brick road right out of town (intertextual allusions: exhausting).

All this *mishigas* was necessitated by the fact that Seth Green wanted out, to focus on films, which we'll say no more about out of admiration and respect (interestingly, according to Green, he was the only regular in the series who had acted in the film version of *Buffy*, though his brief, "awful" performance didn't survive the cutting room). But for most of his two-plus seasons on *Buffy*, Oz was a way-cooler cat than that—"ironic detachment guy," Willow calls him—who, in one Halloween episode, slaps a "God" nametag on his shirt and walks around as himself and totally gets away with it ("somebody just so cool that he would see just how cool Willow was even if she was wearing a big Eskimo outfit—in fact *because* she was wearing a big Eskimo outfit," according to Joss Whedon, who modeled the character on someone he knew at Wesleyan).

Oz was brilliant, but epically unmotivated, to the point where he had to repeat his senior year of high school because of so many incompletes, and he refused to go to summer school to make up the credits; lead guitarist for Dingoes Ate My Baby, a favorite at The Bronze, Oz was, by his own admission, not a "work-of-any-kind person," and his one overriding ambition was to master the E-flat diminished ninth chord—"a man's chord; you could lose a finger." When it comes to sarcasm, nobody's in Oz's league except for Cordelia, but while Cordy leaves no room for misinterpretation, Oz opts for subtlety; he compliments the exceedingly dense Larry Blaisdell, for instance, on mastering the single entendre.

In season two's "Halloween," Oz and Cordelia engage in what some might describe as conversation, but we prefer to call it perfection:

Cordelia: Are you guys playing tonight?

Oz: Yeah, at the Shelter Club.

Cordelia: Is Mr. I'm-the-lead-singer-I'm-so-great-I-don't-have-to-show-up-for-my-date-or-even-call gonna be there?

Oz: Yeah, y' know, he's just going by "Devon" now.

Cordelia: Well, you can tell him that I don't care, and that I didn't even mention it. And that I didn't even see you. So that's just fine.

Oz: So, what do I tell him?

Cordelia: Nothing! Jeez! Get with the program. (Walks off in a huff.)

Oz: Why can't *I* meet a nice girl like that?

Of course, Oz *does* meet a nice girl, though nothing like that: Willow Rosenberg. Fans, believing Willow should be with Xander, were slow to embrace the relationship. In his DVD commentary for "Innocence," Whedon comments that at this point in the series, fans were "not loving Oz," so he specifically wrote the exchange between Willow and Oz waiting in the van for Xander and Cordelia "as the scene that would make them love Oz, because it's the scene that makes Willow love Oz." In it, Willow angles for their first kiss, which seems likely at first, though ultimately Oz demurs, telling her, "To the casual observer, it would appear that you're trying to make your friend Xander jealous or even the score or something. And that's on the empty side. See, in my fantasy, when I'm kissing you, you're kissing me. It's okay. I can wait."

Willow and Xander do eventually hook up, permanently fracturing Xander's relationship with Cordelia when they're discovered, though Oz is so cool he actually chooses to forgive Willow. Oz himself later strays, with Veruca, his fellow werewolf; the triangle was supposed to last through most of season four, but Whedon and team had to adjust when Green made known his wish to ankle.

Anya Christina Emmanuella Jenkins (Emma Caulfield)

Anya Christina Emmanuella Jenkins, a.k.a. Anya Emerson; Anyanka, Patron Saint of the Women Scorned; and, originally, in ninth-century Scandinavia, Aud. Odd is right.

Anya's (for efficiency's sake we'll stick with that appellation) strange, long life took a turn for the weird when she—up until that point a mildly eccentric rabbit farmer in ninth-century Scandinavia—resorted to dark magic to exact revenge on her philandering husband, Olaf. Successfully transforming the oaf into a literal troll, Anya attracts the attention of the demon D'Hoffryn, who, impressed by the girl's raw talent, makes her an offer: become a vengeance demon and gain immortality, doling out vengeful wishes (powered by a magic amulet) to aggrieved ladies. She takes the job, which comes with the impressive title "Patron Saint of the Women Scorned," and spends happy centuries administering curses to deserving men and comparing notes with peer/frenemy Halfrek. So powerful and dedicated was Anya to her work that one of her spells set off the Russian Revolution of 1905.

In present day Sunnydale, when Cordelia Chase discovers that Xander (then her boyfriend) has been secretly hooking up with Willow, her fury summons Anya to the Hellmouth. She adopts the form of pretty high school student Anya Emerson and manipulates Cordy into voicing her fondest desire: that Buffy Summers had never come to Sunnydale, thus sparing

Cordelia the indignity of becoming involved with a group as déclassé as the Scoobies. Done.

The granting of Cordelia's wish results in a sort of *It's a Wonderful Life* riff, if that film had been directed by John Carpenter rather than Frank Capra. Sunnydale, unprotected by the Slayer, is transformed into an apocalyptic demon free-for-all, complete with vampire versions of Xander and Willow. Giles manages to suss out what's going on and destroys Anya's amulet, reversing the spell and restoring Sunnydale to normal (well, "Sunnydale normal," anyway). D'Hoffryn, angry at his protégé's failure, strips Anya of her demon powers, leaving her a mortal teenaged girl with no friends and a hell of a CV. And that's where the character gets interesting.

After making herself scarce for a few months, Anya returns to Sunnydale, for the last reason anyone could expect: she has developed a mad crush on Xander, and the two quickly fall into a passionate, if fractious, relationship. What makes this development so delightful is Anya's peculiar, awkward, and often infuriating personality. New to mortal-hood, not to mention social norms and civilized behavior, Anya speaks with complete candor at all times, frequently inadvertently deeply offending her colleagues with her honest, unsolicited observations. Further, her lack of social graces of any kind and unwavering literal-mindedness reliably frustrate and annoy the other Scoobies, to great comic effect. Our favorite pairing is Anya with Giles, who hires her at The Magic Box due to her financial acumen and lives to bitterly regret it every day henceforth.

Emma Caulfield is wonderful as Anya, deftly playing the erstwhile demon's confusion and obliviousness with crack comic timing and, in well-judged moments, moving poignancy, as when she struggles to understand her feelings and behavioral expectations following Joyce's death. She is at her most heartbreaking—and terrifying—when Xander develops cold feet before their wedding, driving Anya to resort to sex with Spike for solace, which neither Xander nor Buffy particularly appreciate. She reassesses and decides to retake her position as vengeance demon. She's lost a step, though; her time as a human has taught her empathy, and her heart's not really into vengeance any more. After going too far and slaughtering a group of frat boys, Anya is horrified by her actions and again gives up her demonhood, losing friend Halfrek in the process.

D'Hoffryn again sacks Anya, disappointed with her new merciful disposition, and the now twice-ex-demon resolves to figure out her feelings and priorities independently, away from the whole mess. Because Anya is caring, brave, and loyal as well as awkward and tactless, she ultimately decides to rejoin the Scoobies and aid them in their battle against the First Evil, but is killed in battle. "That's my girl," the crushed Xander remarks, "always doing the stupid thing." Damn, it's getting dusty in here.

The introduction of Anya breathed new life into *BTVS*, as she filled the considerable void left by the departing Cordelia; she's as funny as Cordy, but in a different way (her spontaneous invention of the incongruously frou-frou moniker "Anya Christina Emmanuella Jenkins" when questioned by the Watchers Council is a fine example), and her "blank slate" personality afforded rich opportunities for character development and growth. Her heroic death rivals Joyce's passing for the series' most emotionally traumatic moment . . . who knew we'd come to love this aggravating, troublesome, sour-tempered weirdo so deeply? Joss Whedon did, and Anya stands as one of his most reliably entertaining and touching characters.

Tara Maclay (Amber Benson)

Still waters run deep. Painfully shy, hiding behind a lank curtain of hair and baggy wardrobe, Tara Maclay was a powerful witch in wallflower's clothing. Sensing a kindred spirit in fellow Sunnydale freshman Willow Rosenberg—the two first meet at a lame campus wannabe-wiccan conclave—Tara, herself the daughter of a powerful witch, begins practicing the craft with Willow in earnest, with impressive results: during the attack of the ghoulish Gentlemen, the pair join hands to telekinetically shift a soda machine across the room to block a door. Yes, there's a metaphor at work here—together, Willow and Tara are stronger than they are apart. Which is the foundation of a romantic relationship, which is what Willow and Tara are moving toward, much to Willow's initial surprise.

The Tara/Willow love story was a milestone in gay representation in mainstream media, but its function on the show was never to merely stir up controversy or preach tolerance; the romance emerges organically from the characters' interactions and chemistry, and though Buffy is (surprisingly) a bit put off by the development at first, not much of a fuss is ever made of the fact that this is a partnership between two women. The affection, respect, and common interests shared by the couple make their pairing feel inevitable, and their relationship is easily the healthiest and most functional romantic alliance in the group (not that the competition is very stiff).

Tara evolves a tremendous amount during her arc on the series, becoming visibly more confident and assertive as her relationship with Willow progresses and she becomes more integral to the Scooby Gang. A visit from her backward family, who had fraudulently convinced her that she was part-demon, explains a lot about Tara's meek, retiring nature—and her rejection of them and assertion of her independence marks a sea change

Grounded: Tara (Amber Benson) was often a voice of reason among the Scoobies.

in the character, as Tara's stammer recedes (it flares up under stress), her sartorial choices begin to reflect a new confidence in her appearance, and her delightfully naughty sense of humor bubbles to the surface. Amber Benson is a great match for Alyson Hannigan—the two share a certain shy-girl sweetness, but Benson's tremulous, aching vulnerability highlights Willow's growth from the blanching milquetoast of seasons past, and her maternal warmth and level-headedness help to balance Willow's spikier, more impulsive side.

In fact, Tara's sensible attitude toward magic—which respects the threat of devastating consequences inherent in spellcasting—drives a wedge between the two. Willow, whose rapid mastery of (and dependence on) the dark arts devolves into a dangerous addiction, prompts Tara to break off the affair. Displaying admirable character, Tara continues to aid the group, and her connections, particularly with Buffy and Spike, grow deeper, as Tara's fundamentally kind and compassionate soul makes her a natural sounding board and trusted confidant. Willow eventually mends her ways and the pair blissfully reunites for a time . . . until Tara is felled by a stray bullet meant for Buffy, fired by the series' most loathsome antagonist, the toxic nerd Warren Mears.

Tara's death brings about the second manifestation of Dark Willow, who shockingly flays Warren alive and nearly brings about the apocalypse with her grief and rage-fueled magical retaliation. The level of this response felt appropriate, as Tara by this point had emerged as the kindest, most empathic, and gentlest of the Scoobies, assuming to some degree the maternal role vacated by Joyce (Tara and Willow acted as surrogate parents to Dawn after Buffy's death in season five, in a development that felt entirely natural). Tara treated all with respect and consideration, and her death at the hands of the grotesquely selfish and petty Warren Mears stung like an insult to the very notion of human decency.

We choose to remember Tara at a happier moment: rapturously, passionately enmeshed with her true love Willow, hovering in midair in intimate bliss, singing "I'm Under Your Spell." Conventional wisdom holds that seasoned musician Anthony Stewart Head is the "Once More with Feeling" musical episode MVP, but it's Amber Benson's pure, bell-like voice in amatory celebration that moves us every time.

Also, she had a cat named Miss Kitty Fantastico. Tara rules.

Dawn Summers (Michelle Trachtenberg)

How do we solve a problem like Dawn, a.k.a. the Key? Introduced, with no explanation, as Buffy's sister in season five, Dawn threw *BTVS* fans into a tizzy: Buffy, Joyce, and indeed all of the Scoobies acted as if Dawn had always been

Kid Sister: Dawn (Michelle Trachtenberg) materializes out of thin air (or, more precisely, mystical energy) to join the Scoobies in season five.

around, and the show audaciously waited to explain the situation for several episodes before revealing that Dawn was, in fact, an entity known as the Key, a magical energy construct that could open portals between dimensions. A mystical order of monks disguised the Key as an adolescent girl and magically implanted memories of Dawn in Buffy's (and her circle's) minds.

So . . . why did they do that? Well, an exiled hell goddess known as Glory sought the Key to enable her return to her home dimension, thereby dooming our own, and the monks figured the Slayer would fight extra hard to protect a loved one. They're correct: even after learning the truth about Dawn's nature, Buffy and the others find their emotions for the girl are real, and they henceforth consider Dawn a full, actual member of the family. Buffy goes so far as to sacrifice her life for Dawn's to thwart Glory, and she does so without hesitation.

For a being constructed from magical energy, Dawn sure seems like a human kid—she's surly, permanently aggrieved, resentful of being treated like a child; she even takes up shoplifting and sneaking out at night. Some less charitable viewers might feel moved to describe the younger Summers as "excruciatingly annoying." Spike, though, dotes on the girl, developing a fatherly protective feeling toward her, and after Buffy's death, Tara and Willow move in to act as loving, de facto guardians.

Too often, Dawn functions as a plot device, stupidly bumbling into trouble and requiring rescue, but Trachtenberg makes her feel like a real, albeit exasperating, person. Her shining moment comes during the final battle with the First Evil: Xander drugs her to take her out of Sunnydale to safety, only to be tased by the furious teen when she awakens. She drives them straight back into the apocalypse. Because, Key or not, she's a Summers.

4

I Just Wanna Be a Big Snake

Big Bads

The Master (Mark Metcalf)

True, he's master of his domain, but his domain is a rank underground lair with crummy views, no gym membership, and spotty Wi-Fi, so, understandably, he's dying to vacate (although the rent is very reasonable). Though the Big Bad of season one, the mighty Vampire King suffers from dermatologist-proof bad skin and halitosis ("fruit-punch breath," Buffy calls it), and all in all has a pretty harsh year. Yes, he kills Buffy (as prophesied in the Pergamum Codex), but he has a terrible time escaping that underground prison, and once he finally does it doesn't take the resuscitated Slayer long to convert him into a rack of un-undead bones. Plus, Buffy is so much wittier, as the following dialogue attests:

> *The Master* (to Buffy): You're dead.
>
> *Buffy*: I may be dead, but I'm still pretty, which is more than I can say for you.

According to Giles, the Master is a "very old, very powerful vampire" (sired by the demon lord Archaeus, if you want to bring the canonical comics into it) who came to Sunnydale sixty or so years earlier hoping to pry open what Spanish settlers referred to as the "Boca del Infierno"—roughly translated, the Hellmouth, or portal to the demon world. Fatefully, Mother Nature outmastered the Master, as an earthquake swallowed up half the town, including the King of Vampires himself, who has remained imprisoned underground "rather like a . . . cork in a bottle" (Giles again) ever since. He spends the entire first season hatching grand schemes to bust out—a Harvest here, an Anointed One there, yada yada—and though he finally succeeds, the

Fruit-Punch Breath: The Master (Mark Metcalf) was not only a soulless killer, but also, according to Buffy, had bad breath.   *WB/20th Century Fox/Photofest*

celebration is fleeting. "Will you laugh when my hell is on Earth?" he taunts Buffy. "You're so amped up about hell," she replies, just before slaying him. "Go there." While most vampires turn to dust when staked, the Master, for reasons never made clear, leaves behind his skeleton, which the Anointed One later attempts to use in a Revivication Spell, hoping to bring his mentor back, though that scheme, too, is thwarted by Buffy.

Until his death, The Master is Grand Poohbah of the Order of Aurelius, a venerable (aren't they all?) vampire cult that worshipped the Old Ones, pure-breed demons that once ruled the Earth, which also included Darla (whom The Master sired), plus, by extension, Angel, Spike, and Drusilla, and everyone they sired, though not all of them were practicing Aureliusists, which is a term we just made up.

The Master's real name is never revealed on screen, but "Welcome to the Hellmouth" identifies him as Heinrich Joseph Nest (note the Nazi ring to it), "the most powerful of vampires," roughly six hundred years old, in the shooting script. Original plans called for a beard and long hair, but actor Mark Metcalf, who had portrayed ROTC psycho Douglas C. Niedermeyer in *Animal House* and the Maestro in *Seinfeld*, suggested the bald look, as an homage to *Nosferatu*, F. W. Murnau's 1922 unauthorized film adaptation of Bram Stoker's *Dracula*.

Mayor Richard Wilkins III (Harry Groener)

Maybe Donald Trump *could* gun someone down in the middle of Fifth Avenue without consequence, but can he transform into a giant reptilian demon at high school graduation and chow down on rampaging seniors? *That's* impressive. Well, gosh and golly gee, Mayor Richard Wilkins III is like a demented iteration of Jefferson Smith (Jimmy Stewart in *Mr. Smith Goes to Washington*, as if you didn't know), unfailingly genial and polite (though Buffy seems to grate on him, especially that time he tries to smother her with a pillow), a germaphobe who loves moist towelettes, *Family Circus*, Faith Lehane, and himself. Things he doesn't love: mixed metaphors, Marmaduke ("unsanitary"), swearing, and Scoobies—understandable, given that they're trying to kill him. The shooting script for season three's "Homecoming," the mayor's debut episode, describes his face thusly: "It couldn't be more unassuming. One feels this man has not raised his voice in years, and although he is mild enough in demeanor, one hopes he won't."

Background: According to "The Glittering World," David Fury's contribution to the canonical 2002 graphic novel *Tales of the Slayers*, Wilkins arrived in California over a century earlier, and founded Sunnydale following the death there of the Navajo Slayer Naayéé'neizghání (say that three times fast, or even once). "Do you have any idea what you'll be calling the new town?" a padre asks him. "Something real cheery sounding," Wilkins replies. "I was thinking Happydale. Or Sunny Acres. What do you think?" Gee, how about Satan's Gulch?

Located atop the Hellmouth, Sunnydale was overrun with demons, but Wilkins brokered a deal: the demons get free, bountiful supplies of food (by which we mean humans), plus periodic tributes, like the sacrifice of newborn babes; Wilkins gets a hundred years of life without aging, followed by ascension to pure demonhood (his demon of choice: Olvikan). Or, as Faith explains it to Buffy: "Mayor's got it wired, B. He built this town for demons to feed on, and come graduation day he's getting paid." So, good for the mayor, bad for everyone else: typical politician.

There are many, many advantages to this, but, as Wilkins counsels Buffy and Angel during the course of a "fatherly" lecture, also complications: "I just don't see much of a future for you two. I don't sense a lasting relationship. And not just because I plan to kill you." Wilkins, who is on his third iteration—he just keeps reinventing himself, as his own son or grandson, to hide the lack of aging—speaks from experience, if not from the heart: he married a woman named Edna May back in "ought-three" (1903, we're assuming), and remained with her until her death, by which time she was "wrinkled and senile and cursing me for my youth." Poor guy.

Wilkins is perturbing on so many levels, but his relationship with Faith is especially creepy, though also, strangely, sweet. The bad-girl Slayer surrenders to the dark side in the late stages of season three, applying for a job with the mayor after she has mistakenly staked a human and tried to pin the blame for said transgression on Buffy, deepening her rift with the Scoobies. The mayor, who apparently never had any children (unless you count himself), is pleased as punch about his new hire, and though he buys her an apartment, clothes, and a PlayStation, he will not stand to be called "Sugar Daddy" ("Now, Faith, I don't find that sort of thing amusing. I'm a family man.").

In the end this "human weakness," as Faith herself describes it to Buffy in a portentous dream, proves the mayor's fatal undoing, an ironic denouement for someone who couldn't wait to shed his mortal skin. After Wilkins ascends to pure demonhood during the Sunnydale High graduation ceremony, Buffy taunts him into chasing her into the school, brandishing the knife that the mayor had presented to Faith as a gift, and that Buffy had used to stab her during a fight, crowing over how she had "stuck it in her gut. Just slid in her like she was butter." The livid mayor, who by this point has transformed into the giant, serpentine Olvikan, pursues, until they come to the library, which has been rigged to explode with diesel fuel and fertilizer. The mayor's last words, before being blown to bits: "Well, gosh."

Adam (George Hertzberg)

There is a certain species of annoying human who is quick to correct those referring to Mary Shelley's stitched-together-from-corpses literary creation as "Frankenstein"; "Actually," this type of annoying human will condescendingly intone, "Frankenstein was the mad scientist's name; the monster is called Adam."

And so is Maggie Walsh's (herself no slouch in the mad scientist department) crowning achievement—and ultimate doom. The Initiative's 314 Project, which proposed the creation of cybernetic demon super-soldiers (solid plan) produced season four's Big Bad Adam, a grotesque fusion of human, demon, and machine parts powered by a uranium core. Not surprisingly, ol' ugly proves himself a devastatingly effective killing machine . . . a bit surprisingly, he demonstrates this coldblooded lethality by impaling his creator with a repurposed Polgara Demon arm spike upon his activation. He reanimates her as a semi-sentient zombie assistant later, but still, clearly a bad seed.

So, Adam likes to kill—and talk. And talk. A compulsively philosophizing monologist, Adam is consumed by identity issues, as his mix-n-match biology precludes any obvious allegiance to man, demon, or machine. Adam's struggle to define himself and his place in the world cleverly echoes the themes bedeviling the Scoobies in season four as they adjust to college and young adulthood—but Whedon himself has conceded that Adam is the series' "most boring" Big Bad, perhaps due to the character's "tell, don't show" style of presentation. Adam really likes the sound of his own voice, and his actions are largely off screen or indirect, as when he sends Spike to sow dissension within the Scoobies' ranks.

Adam also seems to lack a clear motivation—he more or less plans to continue the Project 314 agenda, creating an army of monstrous super-soldiers to . . . take over the world, or something. This fuzzy, vague sense of goals and future direction may be intended as a humorous comment on our heroes' similar sense of rudderlessness in season four, but it's not a particularly dynamic villainous arc.

Visually, Adam impresses, his patchwork cybernetic form reminiscent of Marvel Comics' unnerving cyborg hero Deathlok. He's tricked out with an impressive array of ordnance, both military and hell-spawned, and is practically indestructible. Adam, then, also represents institutional hubris (a real Whedon bugbear), as the Initiative harnesses forces beyond its understanding to forge an unstoppable weapon that it can't control. Paging Dr. Oppenheimer.

More than a physical match for Buffy, Adam merrily sets about his plans, bringing his "brother" Riley (Walsh had also technologically augmented her favorite commando, but, sadly, forgot the personality chip) into the fold via voice-activated mind control, which is kind of funny to watch.

Adam is finally taken out by Buffy after she, via an enjoining spell, melds her essence with those of Giles, Willow, and Xander, enabling her to draw on the strengths and skills of each to counter Adam's attacks. Finally, she rips the uranium power source from his chest, killing him. And we never saw him again.

Psych!

Adam's pre-Project 314 human form appears to Buffy in a dream, cryptically explaining that no man alive can remember his original name . . . which foreshadows his later appearance as an incarnation of the First.

The First = Adam, get it? (*Sigh.*) That's what we're saying. No offense to George Hertzberg, who does some very droll work as the soliloquizing science project, but in the end, Adam is just kind of lame.

Glory (Clare Kramer)

Glory, a.k.a. Glorificus, the Beast, the Abomination, and Hell Bitch, was an exiled hell god who had been thrown out of her old dimension by rivals who feared her tremendous power and influence. Consigned to Earth, in the form of a pretty, vivacious young woman, Glory had a single agenda: find the Key that would return her home. Aided by sycophantic demon minions, opposed by Dagon Monks and the Knights of Byzantium, Glory tore a swath through Sunnydale looking for the Key, knowing only that it was incarnated in human form.

Eventually, after much mayhem, Glory discovers that Dawn Summers is her quarry, and she sets in motion the blood ritual that will open the dimensional barrier allowing her to return to her presumably awful old stomping grounds—a process that will doom Earth, not that Glory gives a tin fart in a high wind. Buffy manages to subdue Glory (aided by a god-smashing troll hammer) and then sacrifices her own life to close the portal, saving Dawn and the world. Giles ends Glory's threat forever by killing her human host body, belonging to the friendly hospital intern Ben Wilkinson (Charlie Weber).

(Oh yeah—Glory shares a body with a mortal man. They take turns in the driver's seat, each unaware of the other's activities while in their dormant state. A spell prevents humans from remembering these transformations, much to Spike's aggravation and our amusement. It's weird.)

Glory is perhaps the most serious threat yet seen in a Big Bad—in terms of strength, she far outpaces any Slayer, vampire, or demon around, and

Glittering, Glistening Glorificus: Hell hath no fury like a banished hell goddess (Clare Kramer).

though Dark Willow is able to cause Glory some degree of pain with a magical assault, it's ultimately akin to shooting an elephant with a BB gun. Glory handily trounces Buffy in their first few encounters, and seems to harbor no weaknesses—aside from her need to psychically feed on human brains once in a while, which leaves her victims slobbering basket cases.

She's a nasty piece of work, but fun; Clare Kramer is a firecracker in the part, dispensing acid snark and mean girl arrogance along with the butt-kickings. She gleefully revels in violence, and sadistically enjoys torturing victims for information. Perhaps her most monstrous quality is her selfishness and self-absorption, as she blithely dooms our world to apocalypse almost as an afterthought . . . we're just in her way.

After a season of lip-smacking, consequence-free cruelty, it's enormously satisfying to watch Buffy beat the tar out of Glory with her enchanted hammer, assisted by Xander with a well-placed wrecking ball. Glory had no interest in the Slayer, or ruling the world, or in anything beyond her immediate concerns. She's a spoiled child, essentially, with the power of a juggernaut and the looks of a femme fatale. Yikes.

The Trio: Warren Mears (Adam Busch), Andrew Wells (Tom Lenk), and Jonathan Levinson (Danny Strong)

What kind of supervillain triumvirate operates out of their leader's mother's basement? The Trio kind. Uber-geeks Warren Mears (he of the creepy sex-bots), Andrew Wells (brother of hellhound-unleasher Tucker), and Jonathan Levinson (mystical mischief magnet) pettily argue over obscure sci-fi references, obsess over *Star Wars* action figures, and futilely lust after sexy babes; in short, they are the Internet, toxic nerds drowning in childish trivia and sexual frustration. And they're funny, at first—watching these beta males puff themselves up into comic book archvillains is inherently absurd, and the three actors seem to understand their stunted characters on a molecular level.

But there is a sinister side to wounded masculinity manifested as fanboy-ism run amok: rabid misogyny and threats of violence, which Warren fully embraces. A true psychopath, Warren exercises his rage by an escalating objectification of and need to dominate women; his first project was an android sex toy, followed by a mind-controlling device to turn living women into sex slaves for the Trio—and that's flat-out rape. Warren fully embraces evil when he kills his ex-girlfriend and pins the murder on Buffy. He then attempts to take out the Slayer with a handgun, and very nearly succeeds, killing Tara in the process.

Andrew, as the weakest of the Trio, generally goes along with Warren's increasingly depraved agenda, but Jonathan, grateful to Buffy for saving his life (and being an essentially decent person) turns traitor and assists the Slayer. Not that this spares him from Dark Willow's wrath after Tara's murder—after torturing Adam and flaying him alive (he so had it coming), she sets her sights on his minions, who are able to escape to Mexico in the confusion of Dark Willow's almost-apocalypse.

Back in Sunnydale, Andrew, under the influence of the First, kills Jonathan as part of a failed magical ritual intended (so Andrew believes) to elevate the Trio members to godhood, but later changes his colors to become a sort of adjunct Scooby and help prepare the activated Potentials, ultimately training to be a Watcher.

The Trio represents a prescient glimpse of a now sadly familiar trope: the angry neckbeard Internet commenter spewing resentment and chauvinist rage from the anonymous security of his parents' basement. And there's really nothing very funny about that at all.

The First Evil

The personification of evil itself, older than any man or demon, the First Evil seems completely undefeatable. Working through agents—including the psychotic preacher Caleb, the mutilated demon Bringers, and a mind-controlled Spike—the First Evil worked to end the Slayer line by eliminating all of the world's potential Slayers as well as Buffy, thereby leaving our world supernaturally undefended.

The First habitually took on the appearance of its victims' deceased loved ones and played mind games with its targets, favoring psychological attacks over brute force. When brute force was warranted, it sent out the diabolically strong Caleb or dagger-wielding Bringers.

After Buffy and her crew manage to defeat the First Evil's vampire army and seal the Sunnydale Hellmouth, the entity is presumed "scrunched" by Willow. We doubt it.

Caleb (Nathan Fillion)

Whedon is evidently a fan of the 1955 film *Night of the Hunter* (and considering his education, that's likely); Caleb strongly calls to mind Robert Mitchum's terrifying villain from that movie, as he is also a loquacious, murdering, sexually screwed-up, defrocked priest. Nathan Fillion brings his planet-sized charisma to the role of Caleb and is legitimately terrifying as the overwhelmingly strong, completely mad serial killer in thrall to the First Evil;

Buffy (Sarah Michelle Gellar) battles a Turok-Han, übervamp minions of the First Evil.

he tosses Buffy around like a rag doll, and his demonic malignancy is palpable. Caleb sets the Bringers against the Potentials and bombs the Watchers Council, taking out most of them—he's very, very dangerous, and very, very crazy. Buffy finally kills the rabid misogynist in appropriately symbolic fashion, cleaving him vertically from the groin up. *Ulp.*

Face of Evil: Defrocked priest/serial killer Caleb (Nathan Fillion), servant of the First.   *Art by Tim Shay*

5

Whenever We Fight, You Bring Up the Vampire Thing

Vampires

Y ou've heard of them, right? Big, ugly, undead things with sharp teeth, yellow eyes, bumpy foreheads? *Buffy* posits an inverted Genesis, in which sentient life begins not in some Edenic garden, but in hell on Earth (though *Angel* eventually suggests a slightly altered genesis, if you can take Jasmine at her word). As Giles explains it, pure-breed demons known as "Old Ones" walked the Earth for "untold eons," making it "their home, their—hell." For reasons never made clear in the television series, these demons eventually "lost their purchase on this reality," Giles says. "The way was made for mortal animals, for man. All that remains of the old ones are vestiges, certain magicks, certain creatures." Hello, vampires. According to Watcher lore, the last purebred demon to leave this dimension fed off a human, mixing their blood, creating the first vampire (patient zero, if you will). This being pre-Internet, vampirism spread not by meme, but through the exchange of blood—biting alone doesn't do it; rather, the vampire and her victim have to feed off each other. "And so they walk the Earth, feeding, killing some, mixing their blood with others to make more of their kind, waiting for the animals to die out and the old ones to return," Giles exposits.

Team Whedon cherrypicked from among traditional vampiric tropes, keeping those that suited their purposes, chucking those that didn't, tossing in a few new ones of their own. Angel tells us later in season one that "when you become a vampire, the demon takes your body. But it doesn't get your soul. That's gone. No conscience, no remorse" (unless, of course, you're a vampire with a soul, due to a gypsy curse). Buffy phrases it this way in season two's "Lie to Me" to Billy Fordham, who's terminally ill and hoping to become a vampire himself: "You die, and a demon sets up shop in your old house, and it walks, and it talks, and it remembers your life, but it's not you." This bit of genius forges a bond between vampire and Slayer—both part human, part demon, a fact Spike never stops harping on. "Vampires are a paradox," Adam tells Boone in season four. " . . . Demon in a human body. You're a hybrid, natural and unnatural. You walk in both worlds, and belong in neither." Slayers too, which may explain Buffy's taste in men.

Buffyverse vampires can't fly or shapeshift, but like Dracula and many other prominent vamps in pop culture, they are reflectionless in mirrors and incapable of entering private homes without an invite. Whedon's vamps tend to run in tribes, like the Order of Aurelius, commanded by the Master in season one, and El Eliminati, a dueling cult loyal to the demon Balthazar in season three. WVD (weapons of vampiric destruction; we coined it!) are fairly standard stuff in the Buffyverse, like wooden stakes, garlic, fire, decapitation, holy relics, etc., though vamps here can withstand sunlight as long as it isn't direct.

Vexing question: Can Buffyverse vampires—the soulless kind—love? They're half-human, after all. In season one, Darla says to Buffy, "Do you know what the saddest thing in the world is? . . . To love someone who used to love you," a reference to her feelings for Angel. But in the *Angel* episode "Dear Boy," Angel rejects the notion that he and Darla were ever in love: "I couldn't feel that with you, because I didn't have a soul."

What then of the Spike-Drusilla *amour fou*? In season two's "Surprise," the Judge, a demon who sniffs out humanity in others and then burns it out of them, tells them: "You two stink of humanity. You share affection and jealousy." And Spike's initial pursuit of Buffy, which precedes the restoration of his soul (though succeeds the chip implantation in his brain)? Is it love? Lust? Or, in this kingdom of passion, is the ruler obsession?

According to David Fury:

> I was probably the most vocal having difficulty with [Spike loving Buffy], the most vocal being pro-Spike was Marti [writer/producer Marti Noxon]. I think Marti was loving the idea of the Spike-Buffy love story, and I was often too much of a logic police kind where I'm going, "Wait a minute, didn't we say they're soulless creatures? How could Spike be in love with Buffy if he has no soul?" I would argue that he has a chip in his head, it's the only thing that's keeping him from being a serial killer. There was no morality to Spike, despite the fact that he started to become part of the crew and was fighting demons. The fact of the matter is that's the chip, that's not Spike. This guy was artificially being a good guy only because he loves to kill things and the only thing he's allowed to kill without feeling pain are demons, are vampires, so there was a morality issue for me, which I guess is stupid in the long run. Joss saw much more gray area than I did. I guess that's my simple-mindedness.

But then I wound up writing some of those episodes, including "Lies My Parents Told Me," which was a big episode in terms of their relationship. I also wrote "Crush," so suddenly I'm writing those kinds of episodes, and what I had to do was I had to justify it in my own mind, and what I initially decided was that Spike was an anomaly—that, somehow, he maintained some small part of his soul.

So, we got into a lot of debates about it, but that being said, it didn't matter what the audience thought. In other words, Joss really wanted to play this out, and Marti certainly did too. She just thought it would be an interesting place to go, so I had to throw out my logic, and that's probably why I didn't write "Fool for Love." I was having a hard time reconciling in my mind how to make this work, and then Doug Petrie wrote a great, brilliant episode and I thought, "Oh, *that's* how you make it work."

Angel/Angelus/Liam (David Boreanaz)

Angel is one of the great romantic heroes of television, but, let's face it, also a mess, a volatile compound of three monumentally damaged elements. The guy should come with a warning sticker: "Highly combustible; handle with care." Over three seasons on *Buffy*, and five on the spinoff series *Angel*, he is mostly the valiant white knight, the vampire with a soul, adoring lover of Buffy Summers, a "unique force for good in a troubled world," as one advocate phrases it, with *mostly* being the operative word. In the second half of *Buffy*'s second season, with his soul having temporarily vacated the premises, he is unconscionably (literally) brutal and cruel, and he endures some perilous moments in the aphotic zone in *Angel*, as well. Even on the best of days being Angel is an ordeal: he's perpetually wracked by guilt over all the many, many atrocities he committed as a vampire; denied romantic fulfillment, at the cost of being transformed back into that vampire; and consumed by the Sisyphean task of winning a redemption he is convinced is forever beyond his grasp.

Buffy "shippers" love to argue over the relative merits of Angel and Spike, who, in the later seasons of the series, has his own soul restored and emerges as a rival for Buffy's affection. Spike himself can't resist reminding his "Yoda" that while Angel's soul was forcibly restored, by a gypsy curse, Spike won his back voluntarily, "because I knew it was the right thing to do. It's my destiny" (Angel's retort: "Really? Heard it was just to get into a girl's pants"). Even as soulless vampires, Spike and Angel approached life (undeath?) from vastly different perspectives: for Spike, it was fun times; Angelus reveled in the cruelty of it.

"For a demon, I never did think that much about the nature of evil," Spike says. "No, just threw myself in. Thought it was a party. I liked the rush. I liked the crunch. Never did look back at the victims."

Relapse: Angel (David Boreanaz) had a hard time making friends, maybe because of this irritating habit of reverting to his evil self, like in the second half of season two.
WB/20th Century Fox/Photofest

Responds Angel: "I couldn't take my eyes off them. I was only in it for the evil. It was everything to me. It was art. The destruction of a human being."

Yes, twisted and disturbing, but Angel's obsession imbues him with a depth just beyond Spike's reach, no matter how soulful he ultimately becomes. Spike is intoxicating; Angel, Byronic. So it is that in the first-season *Angel* episode "In the Dark," Angel smashes the Gem of Amara with a brick, even though it renders him invincible, after watching his first sunrise in two hundred years.

"I did a lot of damage in my day, more than you can imagine," he explains.

"So, what, you don't get the ring because your period of self-flagellation isn't over yet?" responds Doyle, the half-demon sent by the Powers That Be to assist him. "Think of all the daytime people you could help, between nine and five."

"They have help," Angel says. "The whole world is designed for them, so much that they have no idea what goes on around them after dark. They don't see the weak ones lost in the night, or the things that prey on them, and if I join them, maybe I'd stop seeing too."

Arguably, Angel's most torturous ordeal unfolds in *Buffy*'s season-three Christmas episode, "Amends," in which we discover that his return from the hell dimension to which he was dispatched at the conclusion of season two (long story, but keep reading) was engineered by the First Evil, not for any noble purpose, but with the intent of goading Angel into killing Buffy, and thus reverting to Angelus—sort of a two-for-one deal. The pressure to embrace evil becomes so onerous that Angel loses faith in himself, and climbs atop Kingman's Bluff to await the sunrise, and his own death. Buffy follows, desperate to save him. Convinced of his own weakness, Angel says, "It's not the demon in me that needs killing, Buffy. It's the man." Only a miraculous snowfall during a Sunnydale heat wave shakes Angel from his despair.

So who is the man? In the beginning, Angel was Liam of Galway, Ireland, born in 1727. We have no clue what he was like as a child, but as a young man he was a drunken, whoring scoundrel with colossal Daddy issues (interesting how many men in the Buffyverse do), mostly because Daddy was a colossal jerk. At the age of twenty-six, after yet another night of drunken brawling, he's lured into a dark alley by the vampiress Darla, who tells him, "I could show you—things you've never seen," just before taking a chunk out of his neck, then offering him a sip of her own blood. Liam likes. Angelus is born.

So here we have identity number two: a legendarily cruel vampire, which we know because everyone keeps telling us. Darla: "Before you got neutered you weren't just any vampire. You were a legend. Nobody could keep up with you, not even me." The Master: "He was the most vicious creature I ever met. I miss him." Angel himself: "For one hundred years I offered an ugly death to everyone I met. And I did it with a song in my heart." We know, for instance, that the first thing Angelus does upon becoming a vampire is kill his own family, including his little sister, whom Liam loved. He "signed" his victims by carving a Christian cross into their left cheek. Still, nothing compared with what he did to Drusilla, Spike's eventual sire, who, writer-producer Marti Noxon says in her DVD commentary, "represents to Angel the epitome of his bad behavior. She is one of his greater works of art." Angel tells Buffy that Drusilla "was pure and sweet and chaste."

"And you made her a vampire," Buffy says.

"First I made her insane," Angel replies. "Killed everybody she loved. Visited every mental torture on her I could devise. She eventually fled to a convent, and on the day she took her holy orders, I turned her into a demon."

Angelus roams the Earth for over 130 years, sometimes accompanied by "Whirlwind" teammates Darla, Drusilla, and Spike, sometimes not, creating death and destruction everywhere he goes, until 1898, when he feasts on a young Romani, "beautiful, dumb as a post, but a favorite among her clan." Payback *is* a bitch: the clan elders "conjured the perfect punishment for me," Angel explains. "They restored my soul. . . . When you become a vampire the demon takes your body, but it doesn't get your soul. That's gone. No conscience, no remorse. It's an easy way to live. You have no idea what it's like to have done the things that I've done, and to care."

Hence, identity number three: Angel, vampire with a soul. No more feasting on humans, for starters (vermin and animal blood: still kosher). This isn't like giving up carbs. All that guilt, for starters. No Vampires Anonymous. No family or friends to comfort you (especially if you've already slaughtered them). Angel endeavors at first to hide this transformation from Darla, but the woman wasn't born yesterday (off by about two hundred years, actually); she banishes him, repulsed by his "filthy soul," but Angel refuses to let go, tracking Darla to China two years later, during the Boxer Rebellion, hoping to convince her Angelus is back, but she tests him, demanding that he feast on a new-born babe. Instead, Angel takes the infant and runs. Next up: a century of aimless, solitary wandering, until at last he's paid a visit by Whistler, friendly neighborhood demon, dispatched by unnamed powers (more than likely the Powers That Be) to reorient Angel, or, more colloquially, give him a kick in the pants: "You could become an even more useless rodent than you already are, or you can become someone, a person, someone to be counted."

Whistler whisks him away to Hemery High School in L.A., where together they observe from a distance as Buffy Summers is informed by her Watcher, Merrick, that her destiny awaits. "She's gonna have it tough, that Slayer," Whistler tells him. "She's just a kid. The world's full of big, bad things."

Angel, smitten (with Buffy, not Whistler), finds his purpose: "I wanna help her. I want . . . I wanna become someone."

Whistler warns him: "This isn't going to be easy. The more you live in this world, the more you see how apart from it you really are."

That's our Angel—always without, never within. Still, he follows Buffy to Sunnydale, and eventually becomes a champion for good, fighting alongside her in the cosmic war against evil, falling hopelessly in love with her, and vice versa. Angel is deep, mysterious, devoted. He gives her a Claddagh ring, tells her to "wear it with the heart pointing toward you. That means you belong to somebody." He loved her from the moment he first saw her, he tells her, even before she was the Slayer. "I could see your heart. You held it before you for everyone to see. And I worried that it would be bruised or torn. And more than anything in my life I wanted to keep it safe . . . to warm it with my own." That Angel: a man of few words, but silver-tongued. In the face of defeat, he reassures her: "We never will [win completely]. That's not why we fight. We do it because there's things worth fighting for."

We all know where this is leading, right? Midway through season two, Buffy and Angel have sex, which sounds like a good thing: they're in love, Buffy is preternaturally mature for her age, Angel is over 270 years old—they should know what they're doing. One ginormous complication, however: the gypsy curse includes an out clause: if Angel experiences even a moment of true bliss, he reverts to Angelus. ("It's like something out of Fitzgerald," says Winifred "Fred" Burkle, in *Angel*. "The man who can have everything but love.") Newly revived, after a century of dormancy, Angelus erupts, snapping Jenny Calendar's neck, torturing Giles, emotionally tormenting Buffy, threatening her friends, maneuvering to engineer the end of the world, all with unbridled arrogance and glee (this is a guy who once responded to the Master's comment that "we do not live amongst the human pestilence" with the retort, "I'll be honest: You really couldn't with that face, now could ya?"). Plus he kills Willow's goldfish. The devil is in the details.

As season two concludes, Buffy dispatches Angelus to that hell dimension, in order to save the world (she does that a lot), but tragically he is converted back into Angel just moments before she plunges in the sword, thanks to a Willow spell (she meant well). The next season he miraculously reappears on Earth, courtesy of the First Evil, and while each tries like the dickens to resist the other, it ain't happening, because, well, Buffy and Angel forever! Except not, because Buffy's mom pays Angel an unprecedented visit, encouraging him to leave Sunnydale once and for all, though preferably not for a hell dimension this time, so that Buffy can get on with her life without him. Naturally, Angel does the right thing and moves on, though not before surprisingly showing up at the Sunnydale High senior prom in a tuxedo for a last dance with Buffy, in a scene that makes grown men and women cry, no matter how many times they've seen it, though of course this is only hearsay.

And so move on Angel does, to Los Angeles, and five seasons of *Angel*, in which all of this happens: he becomes a private eye, working with fellow *Buffy* alum Cordelia and Wesley; he runs into Darla, whom he had killed in season one of *Buffy*, but who is resurrected as a human; he sleeps with Darla, but doesn't revert to Angelus because he experiences perfect despair, not perfect bliss; he refuses to turn the tables on Darla by siring her, even though she is dying of syphilis and begs him to; he tries (and fails) to kill Darla and Drusilla by setting them on fire; he and Darla miraculously have a human son, Connor, who hates him so much that he tries to kill him; he tries to smother Wesley with a pillow, for kidnapping Connor to protect him from Angel, who, Wes is convinced, will try to kill the boy; he averts multiple apocalypses (yawn); and he makes peace with Spike, eventually fighting alongside him like Butch Cassidy and the Sundance Kid, to embrace an analogy favored by the writers.

He even returns as Angelus, though just briefly, and intentionally this time, to shed light on a demon known as the Beast. Worrisome, but not nearly as egregious as this: he falls in love with Cordelia, who, by this point in *Angel* (end of season three), is barely recognizable as the girl we knew in *Buffy*. Nothing against character development, but some things are sacrosanct, and the surgeon of mean should have been one of them.

Still, let's not hold it against him. Life isn't easy for our existential hero, who fights "the good fight" not because he expects to win, but because his conscience allows him no alternative, in the face of all the unspeakable horrors he has seen—even committed. The world is harsh. All Angel can do is his best, in his bid for redemption. He isn't perfect, but he tries.

Timeline

> How few days go to make up a century.
>
> —*Count Dracula*

The intertwined stories of the Fab Four, or Whirlwind—Angel, Darla, Drusilla, and Spike—unfold over five centuries and two television series (*Buffy* and *Angel*), beginning with the Master's siring of Darla in 1609, but the timeline can be confusing because events are never presented in chronological order.

This is where we come in.

You're welcome.

1609   The Master sires Darla in the Virginia Colony (*Angel*: "Darla").
1753   Darla sires Angelus in Galway, Ireland (*Buffy*: "Becoming").

1760   Darla introduces Angelus to the Master in London (*Angel*: "Darla").

1764   In England, Darla and Angelus murder the wife and infant son of vampire hunter Daniel Holtz, and turn his young daughter into a vampire (*Angel*: "Lullaby").

1771   Holtz traps and tortures Angelus in the sewers of Rome, before he is rescued by Darla (*Angel*: "Offspring").

1773   Holtz makes a deal with Sahjhan, a demon, to be transported into the future to kill Angelus and Darla, showing them no mercy (*Angel*: "Quickening").

1860   Angel sires Drusilla in London (*Buffy*: "Becoming").

1880   Drusilla sires Spike in London, completing the Fab Four/Whirlwind (*Buffy*: "Fool for Love"); Darla temporarily leaves Angel for the Master (*Angel*: "Destiny").

1894   The Fab Four travel to Rome, where, for better or worse, they encounter the Immortal (*Angel*: "The Girl in Question").

1898   Kalderash gypsies curse Angelus in Romania, restoring his soul (*Buffy*: "Becoming").

1900   Angel briefly reups with Darla, Drusilla, and Spike in China during the Boxer Rebellion, but refuses to kill a newborn baby as demanded by Darla, splintering the group again; Spike kills his first Slayer (*Buffy*: "Fool for Love"). Eventually Darla returns to the Master, and Spike and Dru venture out on their own.

1932   The Master, having come to Sunnydale hoping to open the Hellmouth, is buried underground by an earthquake (as related in *Buffy*: "The Harvest").

1977   Spike kills his second Slayer, Nikki Wood, on a New York City subway train (*Buffy*: "Fool for Love").

1996   Angel, stumbling through the streets of Manhattan chasing a rat for food, meets Whistler, a friendly demon, who whisks him away to Hemery High School in Los Angeles, where they spy on Buffy; Angel finds a purpose in life: assisting the Slayer (*Buffy*: "Becoming, Part 1").

1997   Buffy moves to Sunnydale (*Buffy*: "Welcome to the Hellmouth); Angel dusts Darla (*Buffy*: "Angel"); Spike and Drusilla arrive in Sunnydale (*Buffy*: "School Hard"); Buffy drowns momentarily, activating a new Slayer, Kendra Young, but is revived by Xander and goes on to kill the Master (*Buffy*: "Prophecy Girl").

1998   Angel deflowers Buffy, and Angelus resurfaces (*Buffy*: "Surprise"/"Innocence"); Drusilla kills Kendra (*Buffy*: "Becoming, Part 1"); Buffy sends Angelus to hell (*Buffy*: "Becoming, Part 2), though he is eventually returned to Earth, as Angel, likely by the First Evil (*Buffy*: "Faith, Hope + Trick"); Spike and Drusilla flee Sunnydale (*Buffy*: "Becoming, Part 2").

1999   Angel moves to L.A. (*Angel*: "City Of").

2000   Wolfram + Hart resurrects Darla, as human (*Angel*: "To Shanshu in L.A.");
        Drusilla sires Darla (*Angel*: "The Trial").
2001   Vampire Slayer Daniel Holtz arrives in modern-day L.A. (*Angel*: "Offspring");
        Darla gives birth to Connor, stakes herself through the heart (*Angel*:
        "Lullaby").
2002   Spike's soul is restored (*Buffy*: "Grave").
2003   Spike burns to dust as the Hellmouth collapses during the epic battle with
        the First (*Buffy*: "The Chosen"), but is resurrected from an amulet and winds
        up in L.A., fighting alongside Angel (*Angel*: "Conviction").

Spike (James Marsters)

Fool for Love

Spike, a.k.a. William the Bloody, a.k.a. William Pratt, was the gift that kept
on giving. Originally intended to appear only in a limited arc of episodes, the
punk-rock vampire Spike proved such a compelling character that the writers
kept bringing him back, ultimately elevating the sardonic bloodsucker to one
of *BTVS*'s central figures, a psychologically complex, morally compromised
bundle of fascinating contradictions who has arguably inspired the most
passionate following in *Buffy* fandom. Spike was introduced to provide some
comic relief after Cordelia's departure, and he does so brilliantly—Marsters is
one of the deftest deliverers of Whedonesque snark on the roster—but as the
series progressed and his character evolved, he revealed surprising depths,
and Spike riveted attention whether cracking wise, nursing a broken heart,
committing terrifying violence, or struggling against his divided nature.
Spike is a Protean, wild card anti-hero with a quick wit and lethal cheekbones;
who could possibly resist?

Spike's entire presentation is distinctive: usually clad in black, wrapped
in a leather duster (a trophy taken from New York Slayer Nikki Wood), his
hair close-cropped and peroxided. Visually, Spike is a dead ringer for MTV-
era Billy Idol, a sneering bad boy punk pin-up, and he also strongly recalls
Kiefer Sutherland's cool kid vampire from the 1987 cult film *The Lost Boys* in
look and manner. Slangy, working-class (an affectation, per his aristocratic
human life), witheringly perceptive, dangerously sexy and delightfully rude,
Spike, as wonderfully portrayed by the versatile James Marsters, was a character rich in narrative possibilities: a Spike scene could be scary, funny, disturbing, erotic, or tragic (or some combination of those), and he is never less
than compulsively watchable.

Proto-Spike? Kiefer Sutherland (Donald's son) as David, a vampire, in the 1987 film *The Lost Boys*.

Born William Pratt (a classic horror reference: William Pratt was the given name of Frankenstein monster actor Boris Karloff) in Victorian England, pre-vamp Spike toiled in deserved obscurity as a would-be poet (his later monstrous appellations "William the Bloody" and "Spike," in fact, date from this time, as references to the painful experience of listening to his work). A simpering, cossetted mother's boy, Spike is routinely humiliated by his privileged peers and cruelly rejected by the object of his desire, Cecily Addams (most likely Halfrek, in disguise), but after a chance encounter with the vampire Drusilla, who transforms him into a vampire companion (she was bored and lonely), Spike renounces his existence as a milquetoast and gains a reputation as a particularly fierce, vicious killer, cutting an international swath of mayhem in the company of Dru and the other members of the Whirlwind pack, Angelus and Darla.

From the outset, Spike was different from most vampires; while those afflicted typically retained only echoes of their human personalities, William Pratt's signature traits—passionate romanticism, finely tuned sensitivity, and steadfast loyalty—seemed to remain fully intact, as Spike regarded his relationship with Dru as a true love for the ages, despite her infidelities and general contempt for such pitifully human sentiments as "love." Spike demonstrated utter devotion to Drusilla throughout their association, even during periods of outright abuse doled out by his mad beloved. Spike also differed from his fellows in that notions of "evil" held little interest for him; whereas Angelus loved the elaborate, prolonged, sadistic torture of his victims, Spike committed violent acts solely for the adrenaline rush. More reckless than the typical vamp, Spike liked to have something on the line when he fought, hence his fascination with Slayers.

Famous for his savagery in battle, Spike cemented his reputation as a heavy hitter with the killings of two Slayers, one in China during the Boxer Rebellion, and one in 1970s New York. Besting a Slayer was a euphoric experience for Spike—he likened it to "dancing," and upon his inevitable

Poser: Will the real Spike (James Marsters) please stand up?

arrival in Sunnydale, he developed an immediate fascination with Buffy Summers. Spike was in town looking for his old partner Angelus, whose blood he required to restore an ailing Drusilla. This plan goes poorly, and Spike is seriously wounded in the ensuing conflict, spending months confined to a wheelchair enduring the abuse of Angelus and Drusilla, who delight in mocking the unmanned demon. Spike's ability to take punishment in the name of love would recur as a defining character trait.

He eventually recovered, going on to bedevil Buffy and the Scoobies in ways big and small, leaving Sunnydale for a time and returning again in the company of former Sunnydale cheerleader/vapid vampire Harmony Kendall, whom he treats rather poorly. Captured by the paramilitary organization the Initiative, Spike is implanted with an electronic chip that effectively neuters him, making him unable to harm humans without experiencing intense pain—and here the next, transformative chapter in the saga of Spike the Conflicted Vampire begins.

Now encumbered by a sort of artificial conscience (could we say soul?) Spike begins to, painfully, integrate himself into the Scooby Gang, amusingly alternately sharing quarters with Giles and Xander, who both bear him a particular antipathy. It's a strictly practical arrangement—the Scoobies protect Spike from the Initiative in return for information and added muscle in fights after learning his chip has no problem with hurting demons. Despite himself, Spike seems to benefit from the company and sense of shared purpose, and though he colludes with the Initiative's secret weapon Adam the Amazing Cyborg to destroy the Scoobies (again nothing personal: Adam promises to remove the chip in trade), he ultimately sides with Buffy and the Scoobies in a showdown.

Spike's continued presence in the Scoobies' orbit after these events was difficult to explain; Spike himself had not yet realized that he had fallen deeply, hopelessly, completely in love with Buffy, his natural enemy, who continues to express her contempt for the undead killer in no uncertain terms. Spike being Spike, he takes it, continuing to offer Buffy support and understanding through the ordeal of her mother's death (Spike and Joyce had previously evinced an amusing and touching personal connection during his rampaging days) and becoming paternally protective of Dawn, withstanding unimaginable torture to protect her identity from Glory. Moved at last by Spike's undeniable devotion, Buffy grants Spike a measure of respect and appreciation before sacrificing her life to save the world.

Traumatized and adrift after her resurrection, unable to feel reconnected to the living, Buffy begins a sexual relationship with Spike (having died himself, he's in a unique position to understand her ennui), in a desperate attempt to feel something (and punish herself for her perceived sins). It's a violent, bruising union: their first time together literally brings down the house around them. While Buffy appears to use the relationship as self-flagellation, Spike revels in the attention, though he laments the one-sidedness of the arrangement. Indeed, Buffy subjects Spike to outright emotional and psychological abuse during their affair, eventually breaking it off after becoming consumed by shame. Devastated, he attempts to rape her—and, failing, flees, unable to live (well, you know) with himself after committing such a loathsome act against his beloved. He travels to Africa, where he undergoes a series of brutal trials. His reward: the reinstatement of his soul.

And this is key: unlike Angel, whose soul was a curse, Spike, a soulless demon hybrid, fought to gain his back, driven by love and remorse, emotions creatures of his ilk are not supposed to possess or understand. Spike's ability to overcome his fundamental nature through the power of love is swooningly romantic—like something William Pratt might sentimentally set to verse. Spike returns to Sunnydale in very shaky mental shape, compelled by the First Evil to again murder and terrorize—but an old nursery song his mother used to sing brings him back to himself in time to join the right side of the fight. That is very sweet, and very Spike, and he finally earns redemption by sacrificing himself to destroy the Turok-Han army and seal the Hellmouth forever. Sunnydale itself is razed as collateral damage, which he would probably find funny.

No rest for the wicked: after the conclusion of *BTVS*, Spike ghosted over to *Angel*, where he haunted the staff at Wolfram + Hart for a while before being returned to corporeal form and, you guessed it, ambivalently assisted in the fight against evil. He's continued to appear in the comics, too popular—and just too damn much fun—to ever stay down for long.

Darla (Julie Benz)

Four-hundred-year-old matriarch of the Fab Four of Buffyverse bloodsuckers—comprising also Angelus, Drusilla, and Spike—Darla is the first vampire depicted in the series, the first to kill in the series (alas, poor Chris Boal, we knew him not at all), and the first character of any kind to pronounce a line of dialogue ("Are you sure this is a good idea?" . . . not!), all helpful if you are ever competing in a Buffy/Angel trivia contest, but what you really need to know about her is this: she's both the sire of Angelus and the inadvertent precipitant of the gypsy curse that restores his soul, and thus indirectly responsible for so much of both the good and the evil that unfold over seven seasons of the series—even though Darla herself appears in just three first-season episodes before being dusted by Angel (plus two flashbacks in subsequent installments). She figures far more prominently in seasons two and three of *Angel*: resurrected at the end of season one by the cosmically evil Los Angeles law firm (an entire category unto itself in the L.A. yellow pages) Wolfram + Hart, with the specific aim of rebooting Angelus, she blows that assignment spectacularly, but does—incredibly, since vampires are technically, you know, dead, and thus supposedly incapable of creating, you know, life—bear Angel a son, Connor, and, in her single act of virtue over the course of the two series, stakes herself in a dark, rain-drenched alley (what is it with Whedon and blondes in alleys?) in order to spare Connor's life. Explanation: as Connor grew inside her, Darla absorbed his soul, so that she was actually capable of loving the unborn baby inside of her. However, Darla was frightened about what would happen once the child was born; would she revert to her old, soulless self, and thus despise—perhaps even kill—her own child?

And why wouldn't she? Darla was an uncommonly sadistic vampire sired and mentored by one of the most uncommonly sadistic of them all, the Master, leader of the Order of Aurelius, an elite cult of vampires (don't even think of applying with sub-1500 SAT scores) that worshipped the Old Ones, waiting for "that promised day when we will arise! Arise and lay waste to the world above!" (Master-speak). Pre-vamp, she was a popular prostitute, though that career comes to a premature end when she contracts a fatal bout of syphilis. Darla is visited on her deathbed in colonial Virginia by the Master, disguised as a priest, whom she originally mistakes for Death (not exactly a supermodel, our Master), but who rather grants her the promise of immortality. Over a hundred years hence (1753), she encounters a strapping young rascal by the name of Liam on the streets of Galway, Ireland, luring him into a dark alley, where she sires him, rechristening him Angelus. The two of them wreak havoc across the globe, leaving a trail of death and destruction everywhere, in the process siring numerous other vamps, including Drusilla, who in turn sires Spike; the four of them create this sort of supergroup of legendarily cruel bloodsucking fiends (known among some fans as The Whirlwind, after a comment made by Darla), though also racking up an impressive list of enemies, including vampire hunter Daniel Holtz, killing his wife and infant son and turning his young daughter, Sarah, into a vampire, whom Holtz himself then burns to death.

The foursome finally fractures in the year of our Lord 1898, when, in Borsa, Romania, Darla presents Angelus with a young female member of the Kalderash tribe, whom Angelus tortures, drains, and kills, which the rest of the clan doesn't appreciate, so much so that they inflict Angelus with a curse, restoring his soul and hence his conscience, making it impossible for him to go on brutally murdering innocent people just for the fun of it, or even to satisfy his appetite. For once, a great band doesn't break up over creative differences.

Angel, still crazy for Darla after all those years (the feeling had been mutual, as Darla demonstrated a century earlier, choosing Angelus over the Master), tries at first to hide the transformation, but Darla's no dummy; repulsed by his "filthy soul," she reacts in her signature way—slaughtering (with assistance from Spike and Drusilla) the Kalderash after they refuse to undo the curse. Two years later, Angel tracks Darla to China, during the Boxer Rebellion, promising her he's still the legendary Angelus, but Darla subjects him to a test: kill a newborn, the child of missionaries, or face eternal exile. Thankfully he chooses the latter, thus sealing his ostracization from the group. With the exception of a brief encounter in Budapest in 1901, it is another ninety-seven years before Darla and Angel meet again, in Sunnydale, Angel now fighting alongside vampire Slayer Buffy Summers and Darla back with the Master.

In the presence of the old man, Darla's no longer the imperious, elegant doyen she was back in the day, with a taste for the finer things in death, which explains why she's cribbing in a dank underground lair, dressing in skirts and knee socks. Still, not exactly checking her ego at the door, our Darla, as she demonstrates in "Harvest," part one of the premiere episode, when she takes a nip out of poor, pathetic Jesse McNally, whom she's supposed to be saving for the boss man. She's champing at the bit to take on the Slayer—even before knowing of Angel's infatuation with her—but the Master, perhaps in a vote of no-confidence, since he treasures Darla and would hate to lose her, farms that assignment out instead to a trio of ancient vampire warriors (The Three), though he does throw Darla a bone by allowing her to dust them once they fail miserably at that assignment.

Lest you infer that Darla is all brawn and no brain, she devises a sophis-ticated scheme to win back Angel, hoping to trick Buffy into believing that he attacked Joyce Summers, Buffy's mom, so that Buffy would go after him, forcing him to kill her in self-defense. Unfortunately for Darla the play goes horribly awry, so she winds up going after Buffy herself, which goes even worse, and ends with Angel dusting her.

Dead, undead, dead again . . . what is it with this chick? Darla returns not in *Buffy*, but in *Angel*, nearly three years later, resurrected by Wolfram + Hart—but human, not vampiric. So what else is back? That would be Darla's syphilis, meaning she's dying, meaning she wants Angel to turns the tables and sire *her*. Happening? Not. Angel even convinces Darla to embrace her humanity, even though it will end in death, but Wolfram + Hart has other plans, so summons Drusilla to do what Angel refused to do: sire Darla. So, undead again. The dynamic duo are soon up to their old tricks, massacring a roomful of Wolfram + Hart lawyers, recruiting an army of demons to conquer LA, yada yada. Angel, fed up with the both of them, sets them on fire, but guess what? They survive again. Angel descends even deeper into darkness, and he and Darla have sex, with Darla hoping to break the curse—she seems to be the only one of the two of them who believes they were in love. The next morning, Angel—*not* Angelus—explains that what he experienced was not true happiness, but true despair.

Somehow—something to do with a series of "miracles" orchestrated by a higher being known as Jasmine, but no need to go there—Darla becomes pregnant; at first, she wants nothing to do with the child, but is physically incapable of aborting it, no matter what she tries. Finally, she returns to Daddy in L.A., and for the first time in either series we begin to see traces of a new Darla, different even from the human we glimpsed on her deathbed hundreds of years earlier. Once, she even says thank you! (to Cordelia, for helping her to a seat). What's happening is that she is absorbing her baby's soul. Kind of late in the game, though, as by this time Darla, Angel, and the unborn baby are being tracked by Holtz, another in a seemingly endless array of time travelers, who has one thing on his mind: revenge, whether Darla and Angel have acquired souls or not. Holtz chases them into an alley during a violent rainstorm; Darla, to save the baby, stakes herself, and the boy (later named Connor) is born. Let's not blame Darla for the likelihood that *Angel* would have been vastly better if he never had been. What does matter is that Darla finally wins redemption and, at long last, love.

Drusilla (Juliet Landau)

Stone-cold crazy Dru is the only member of the Fab Four/Whirlwind who never has her soul restored (at least not in the two TV series, which is all we care about here). That's the bad news. The good news is . . . well, there is no good news. Crazy Dru wreaks death and destruction everywhere she goes, which is terrifying enough, but her mad ramblings imbue her with an additional layer of inscrutability, making her more frightening in some ways than even flamboyantly cruel creatures of the night like Angelus and Darla. Some members of the Dru crew make allowances for her because of her chronic, bent devotion to Spike (the Judge, a demon who sniffs out humanity in demons, claims she and Spike "stink" of it), but we're unconvinced; she's the Daisy Buchanan of the Buffyverse, helplessly self-absorbed and deeply unworthy of her acolyte's devotion. What foul dust floats in the wake of her dreams.

Still, let's be fair: Drusilla is as much victim as scourge. Once—late nineteenth century, more specifically—she was prim, proper, and chaste, a young woman residing in London, devoutly Christian but deeply troubled by her "gift": the ability to see into the future. Yup, she got the shining. Sadly, she encounters Darla, who introduces her to Angelus, who becomes obsessed with converting this vestal virgin into his personal "masterpiece," because he is just that demonic. Knowing Dru's prescient visions mean she will foresee everything he does to her, Angelus decides to go wild, butchering her entire family before her eyes. When Dru flees to the convent of the Sisters of Mary, Angelus tracks her down and massacres the nuns too, also right in front of her, tipping Drusilla over the edge.

Even by vampire standards, the new and unimproved Dru is completely batty, conversing in oblique ramblings that scream incoherence, yet have a logic all their own. She's like a demon toddler, hosting tea parties with her blindfolded china dolls (including Miss Edith, her personal fave) one minute, toying with real human victims the next. In 1880 she sires William the Bloody, an awkward, infatuated poet freshly humiliated and scorned by the object of his desire; William in turn (pun) becomes Spike, and together the two of them—modeled after Sid Vicious and Nancy Spungen—embark on a world tour lasting over a hundred years—longer even than the Grateful Dead (another friend of the devil), and a lot bloodier. In 1997, they invade Sunnydale, hoping the mystical energy from the Hellmouth will heal Drusilla, weakened from her encounter with an angry mob of humans in Prague.

When first met, in season two, Drusilla is like the frail relative who never leaves her bedroom, though her cruelty is undiminished. She preys on children, savors torture (Angel and Giles are among her victims), and exhibits classic, Queen-of-Hearts-like signs of volatility. When Angelus resurfaces later in the season, Drusilla shamelessly savors his advances, even knowing (enjoying?) how agonizing it is for Spike, his longtime (and we do mean longtime) rival—to the point where Spike secretly allies with Buffy to vanquish Angelus and flee Sunnydale with a drugged Drusilla in tow, though she eventually leaves him anyway, first for a chaos demon, then for a fungus demon, convinced he is carrying a torch for Buffy, which he is: if there's one thing Dru is good at, it is seeing. Also, killing, though, like when she slices Slayer Kendra Young's throat, or, in *Angel*, when she and Darla slaughter a roomful of Wolfram + Hart attorneys (sure they were lawyers, but still).

Drusilla plays for team Big Bad in season two of *Angel*, summoned to the City of Angels to re-sire Darla (now human, and dying of syphilis) once Angel refuses to, which goes swimmingly. The two femmes fatale then team up to assemble an army, hoping to turn LA into a playground for demons (ha ha), which goes less swimmingly, especially when Angel sets them both on fire, but they survive, and Drusilla makes one last trip back to Sunnydale to woo

Punked: Spike (James Marsters) and Drusilla (Juliet Landau) were modeled after Sex Pistol Sid Vicious and girlfriend Nancy Spungen.

Spike, though by this point he is head over heels in love with the Slayer, so Drusilla takes off for parts unknown, never to be heard from again (in either of the TV series).

Absalom (Brent Jennings)

Absalom is the apoplectic vamp who spearheads the doomed early-season-two movement to revive the Master by uniting his bones with the blood of those present at the time of his blessed demise (Giles, Willow, Cordelia, and Jenny Calendar). Unlike the biblical Absalom, this one boasts neither beauty nor charm, either before or after Buffy slays him. Chutzpah, yes: "Your day is done, girl," he tells Buffy. "I'll grind you into a sticky paste and hear you beg before I smash in your face." Her reply, just before setting him ablaze: "So are you gonna kill me or are we just making small talk?"

The Anointed/Collin (Andrew J. Ferchland)

When first met Collin is just an eight-year-old boy on the bus. Collin's bus is attacked by vampires, who kill five passengers, including his mom, and bring the youngster back to the Master's underground lair, where he is anointed, well, the Anointed, rising from the ashes of five dead souls, destined to become the Master's great warrior and lead the Slayer into hell (sadly for Buffy, this is prophesied to happen on the evening of the thousandth day after the Advent of Septus, so on the very night of a really hot date at The Bronze with Owen Thurman, leading her to instruct Giles: "If the apocalypse comes, beep me"). On the plus side, Collin never had to worry about homework again. According to Joss Whedon, the Anointed One was originally anointed Big Bad for season two, but logistical problems—including Andrew Ferchland's growth spurt over the summer hiatus—nixed that plan, and the character was killed off in "School Hard," the third episode of the season, by Spike, who had already nicknamed him "The Annoying One," a sobriquet gleefully embraced by many fans of the series.

Andrew J. Ferchland

FAQ: Was it difficult or easy for you to settle into that eerie, very calm, sort of chilly, understated approach?

Andrew J. Ferchland: It wasn't that hard. . . . I looked at him as very powerful, perhaps cocky, perhaps somewhat arrogant. I don't know if it necessarily portrayed itself that way. He has a power within him that does not show. He's a tiny human with this massively anointed demon inside him, a grossly disproportionate amount of power for his size. So, I looked at him almost like an imperial officer, that he was a commanding presence, that sort of calmness to him but at the same time a sweetness because of this child exterior that he has.

FAQ: As a sci-fi and FX and makeup fan, were you disappointed that you never got to transform into the vampire face?

AJF: Yeah, I have to say I was, kind of. I understand the necessity of not transforming me. I couldn't say with certainty, but I think they probably didn't do it for production reasons.

FAQ: Production reasons?

AJF: When you're a child actor you have to abide by child labor laws and also union laws. And when I was that age, I couldn't tell you the exact amount of hours that I could work, but I do know they were required to school me—I had to have a certain number of hours of schooling a day, which have to be charted and marked by your teacher and also your social worker, and say you have to have three hours a day, so whether or not you shoot that day you still have to get your three hours in, so there's that, and at the same time you're only allowed to be on set for a certain amount of time as well, and being in the makeup chair also counts as being on set, so it would have taken way too long and they wouldn't have been able to shoot enough time on set. So, I totally understand why they didn't do it. But I would have loved to have gotten the whole vamp transformation. I did actually get teeth made, though. It never aired, but we did shoot a scene with the teeth in and the teeth out. When I was revealed there was a shot where I showed my teeth. Back when I was doing that—of course, when you're a young actor you lose teeth all the time through childhood, and when you're an actor you can't *not* have teeth, so you have to get "flippers"—they're called flippers, they're like false teeth that you put into your mouth, and you have to learn how to talk with them in, so I had some experience with what the special FX department did. I went into their "monster house" and they made the same thing, just like the mold you get from the dentist, they put it in your mouth and they let it sit for a good four or five minutes and pop that sucker out and you show up later and they've got teeth made for you. And they did the same thing for the vampires, except they were fangs.

FAQ: Do you think your character has gotten a raw deal with the nickname "The Annoying One"? Is that frustrating to you? Or do you take that with a grain of salt?

AJF: Oh, I think it's the greatest thing ever. I find it absolutely hilarious. It happens a lot with characters who are child actors and children on shows. I mean, you look at Wil Wheaton on *Star Trek: The Next Generation*, or another prime example would be *The Walking Dead*, with Carl, it's like, "Oh, get the kid out of here." People don't want to watch kids, I guess. I kind of embrace that. I think it's funny.

FAQ: What about working with Mark Metcalfe [the Master]? What was that like?

AJF: Oh, it was great. I honestly don't know what he looks like as a human being.

FAQ: Is that really true?

AJF: Pretty much, yeah. I'm trying to jog my memory to remember what he looks like out of costume and I think I only met him once out of costume the entire first season.

FAQ: Have you seen *Animal House* or the Twisted Sister video and gone like, "Oh, that's him!"

AJF: No! I've seen *Animal House*, but I didn't even know Mark was in it.

FAQ: He's the ROTC guy.

AJF: Oh, that's *him*? Oh, that's hilarious.

Big Ugly (Gregory Scott Cummins)

Another Order of Aurelius vamp vamping for top prize post-Master's demise, by promising to kill Buffy—"It'll be the greatest event since the Crucifixion!" Spike has no patience at all for this guy's delusions of grandeur, and neither does Buffy, who dusts him during an encounter at The Bronze. Not exactly the Second Coming, but we enjoyed it.

Boone (Rick Stear)

A vampire enlisted by Adam for the cyborg's army, Boone finds new purpose when Adam motivates him to overcome his fear of religious objects through will alone. This Tony Robbins–esque pep talk inspires Boone to attack a church, where he is promptly destroyed by Buffy (in Faith Lehane's body, long story). Amen.

Andrew Borba (Geoff Meed)

Cuddly Andrew Borba was a religious zealot/psychotic who was suspected of committing double homicide and was riding on the same bus as Collin when it was stormed by vamps from the Order of Aurelius in the season-one episode "Never Kill a Boy on the First Date." As a result, Borba is sired into a vampire, and his charming background misleads the Scoobies into originally believing him to be the Anointed One.

Carl (Adam Gordon)

The "rebellious" leader of Justin's vampire pack, Carl proudly flouted tradition and hunted on Halloween. He also annoyed Spike, who ended him with a crossbow.

Charlotte (Robinne Lee)

A fiercely bloodthirsty vampire, sired by Spike while he was controlled by the First. She attacks Spike when he declines to join her on a hunting outing, and he kills her. Patience, lady!

Christy (Dawn Worrall)

A distaff vampire member of Justin's little gang. Cute bangs.

Claw

It's not nice to fool the Master, as this ostracized vamp finds out first-hand, which admittedly is a shameless pun. After displeasing his boss, the Claw severs his own hand as penance, replacing it with a metal claw. In season one's "Teacher's Pet," Buffy spies him stalking the She-Mantis Miss French, observing that he is afraid of her, information she eventually leverages to track her to her lair and rescue Xander. Claw's infamy is short-lived, as he is dusted by the Slayer, though we wonder if the metal claw survives.

Dalton (Eric Saiet)

If vampires were a mob gang, Dalton would be the dweeby accountant off in the corner cooking the books. We're pretty sure he's the only demon ever to appear on *Buffy* wearing glasses. He plays for Team Spike, charged with deciphering the du Lac Manuscript, which delineates certain spells and rituals, including one that will restore Drusilla to full health, but is written in archaic Latin. How to put this nicely? Dalton is a screw-up, once to the point where Drusilla breaks his glasses and threatens him, though Spike reminds her, "He is a wanker, but he's the only one we got with half a brain. If he fails, you can eat his eyes out of the sockets for all I care." Dalton also plays a role in the demonic scheme to unleash the apocalypse by reassembling the Judge, who winds up burning Dalton to death, just because he loves books, which the Judge considers un-vampirely, much to Dru's delight.

Count Dracula (Rudolph Martin)

Yep, *that* Count Dracula. Mr. Transylvania. He never drinks ... wine. He does visit Sunnydale to see what all of this Slayer fuss is about, and finds himself attracted to Buffy's "darkness" and power, which he feels rival his own. The charismatic Count dazzles the Scoobies in short order: Anya fondly reflects on the high times she and Drac used to have while hanging out in centuries past; Willow, despite her exclusive attraction to women, finds him "sexy"; an easily enthralled Xander Renfields all over the place, eating bugs and cheerfully doing his master's dark bidding; and Buffy herself invites the Prince of Darkness into her bed for a little late-night snack. Spike is immune to Dracula's thrall—they have had a longtime disagreement over a loan of eleven pounds, and Spike resents the older vampire's celebrity status. Dracula also has some unique powers, including shapeshifting and various mental abilities. Still, Buffy manages to regain her senses and banish Dracula from Sunnydale (staking him proves a merely temporary reprieve), and all returns to "normal," though Xander amusingly continues to harbor a helplessly subservient connection to him. The soap opera–handsome Rudolf Martin had previously appeared with Sarah Michelle Gellar on *All My Children* (of the night?).

Eddie (Pedro Balmaceda)

Buffy meets this nice, literate young man, a fellow freshman at UC Sunnydale, on her first night at school, and perhaps feels a romantic spark as they commiserate about being newly away from home. She meets him again a few nights later, under less pleasant circumstances: freshly sired as a vampire by Sunday, Eddie attacks the Slayer and is summarily dusted. Moral: Don't assume the people you meet your first week of university will be your lifelong pals.

El Eliminati

Pathetic, five-hundred-year-old cult of dueling vamps who loved to go around flashing their jeweled swords (nothing Freudian there). As their ranks kept thinning, they demonstrated that they were not only overrated warriors, but also very poor judges of character, hitching their star to the blubbering Balthazar, who just can't seem to win a war.

Glenn (Charles Duckworth)

Another obnoxious teen vamp buddy of Justin's, killed by Giles. You're doing the Lord's work, Rupert.

Julia (Julie Michaels)

This vamp doesn't say much—half of what she says is meaningless anyway—but she does purloin the du Lac manuscript from the Sunnydale Library in season two's "Lie to Me." Plays for Team Spike/Drusilla.

Justin (Kavan Reece)

Poor Dawnie. Her first kiss is from Justin, a vampire (though she's initially unaware of this fact) who plans to sire her. We guess this sort of thing is kind of a Summers Girls tradition, but it's definitely a drag. In his teenage boy persona, Justin is attractive and warmly open with Dawn, but there are primal, monstrous urges just below the surface. In other words, a pretty typical adolescent male.

Kakistos (Jeremy Roberts)

This ancient, hoofed vamp arrives in Sunnydale in season three along with his lieutenant, Mr. Trick, in pursuit of not Buffy but Faith, unaware even that there are two Slayers in town. Kakistos (Greek for "worst of the worst") is out to settle a score with Faith, who disfigured him (though, really, how can you tell?) during an earlier battle, after he had killed her Watcher, which has left the ancient one apoplectic with rage, plus apparently famished: "The Slayer, I'm going to rip her spine from her body, then I'm going to eat out her heart and suck the marrow from her bones." None for us, thanks. In the end Kakistos is dusted by Faith, though it takes a Costco-size stake to do it.

Harmony Kendall (Mercedes McNab)

The most vapid of Cordelia Chase's mean girls coterie, Harmony was made a vampire by one of Mayor Wilkins's henchmen. As a vampire, Harmony seemed utterly unchanged from her human self, as unthinkingly cruel and self-obsessed as ever. She hooks up with Spike, who barely tolerates her, for a time, launching a spectacularly unsuccessful bid to become Buffy's new "Big Bad." Blessed with a certain low cunning (and blonde bombshell sex appeal), Harmony does okay for herself overall, taking a job at Wolfram + Hart in the final season of *Angel*, after the fall of Sunnydale, and, eventually, in the canonical comics, launching a career as a reality television star—hey, she's already a shallow, rapacious ghoul. It's a lateral move.

Lean Boy (Andrew Palmer)

This vamp's big moment comes in season two's "School Hard," when he argues with Big Ugly over who will succeed the Master as the leader of the Order of Aurelius. And the answer is . . . none of the above.

Lenny

Vampire Lenny doesn't need a weatherman to know which way the wind blows. Originally one of Spike's minions, Lenny winds up on Team Mayor, and is dispatched to "welcome" his old boss back to Sunnydale in season three's "Lovers Walk." If asked to fill out his performance review, we would likely go with "failed to meet expectations," since he is dusted by Spike.

Luke (Brian Thompson)

Luke's no saint, trust us. Rather, he's the lucky vamp who gets to serve as the Master's vessel, whose feedings are supposed to infuse the big cheese with strength enough to bust out of his underworld prison. Sure he's fearsome and strong, but in the final analysis he's just a moron, as demonstrated when Buffy tricks him into believing that the sun has risen (nine hours early), districting him just long enough to drive a stake through his cold, cold heart. Luke is played by Brian Thompson, who returned to the show in season two as the Judge.

Lyle + Tector + Candy Gorch (Jeremy Ratchford + James Parks + Lee Everett)

Dumb and dumber Texas brothers who carved out their reputation by massacring an entire Mexican village in 1886—*before* becoming vamps—Lyle and Tector Gorch are, as Giles phrases it, "not among the great thinkers of our time." Less charitably, they're complete idiots, and as stupid as Lyle is, Tector is even stupider, which explains why he is the one devoured by the Mama Bezoar in "Bad Eggs," while Lyle lives to fight another day. Which he does, returning to Sunnydale with his new bride, Candy, in season three's "Homecoming" as a contestant in Mr. Trick's SlayerFest '98. This customized version of Richard Connell's "The Most Dangerous Game" features Buffy and Faith as the intended prey (although, due to a case of mistaken identities, it winds up being Buffy and Cordelia instead). If there's ever an apocalypse we want to be standing next to Lyle Gorch, because he survives yet again, which is more than we can say for Candy, staked to death with a spatula by Buffy. Lyle is, of course, furious, but flees in fear at the wrath of Cordelia, who, on the warpath for being inconvenienced on the night of the homecoming dance, scolds him as a "redneck moron" and "needlebrain."

Maria (Emily Kay)

Another vampire girl who hung out with Justin and who, like her pal Christy, had really nice hair for a dead person.

Mort (Brian Turk)

A big, ugly galoot of a vampire (we never see his human visage), Mort was the squeaky wheel in Harmony's crew, questioning his mistress's strategy and ultimately attempting to take over her gang. He meets an undignified end, staked by Buffy with Harmony's unicorn figurine.

Anne Pratt (Caroline Lagerfelt)

William Pratt's solicitous, devoted mother. William Pratt? That's what Spike was called before he became a vampire (also, we note, Boris Karloff's real name). After, he transformed his mother as well—ultimate mama's boy move—but Vampire Anne was cold, mocking, and, *ahem*, inappropriate. Spike dusts her in the course of a really uncomfortable family disagreement.

Sandy (Megan Gray)

The comely Sandy, patron of The Bronze, caught Vamp Willow's eye and was subsequently bitten and turned—though we learn of this fate only years later, when the undead vixen hits on Riley Finn at Willy's Bar. Riley initially rejects her, but later engages her in a twisted arrangement in which he masochistically allows her to bite him. Then he kills her. Riley was going through some stuff, but come on, man.

Shempy the Vamp (Paul Greenberg)

This hapless stooge of a vamp (unnamed on screen but referred to in the script as "Shempy") lives up to his nickname when, after discovering the Buffybot is a mere decoy of the dead Slayer, he tries to parlay the information into membership in the demon biker gang the Hellions. They just kill him instead—Shempy indeed.

Sunday (Katharine Towne)

UC Sunnydale's resident undead Mean Girl, Sunday was the alpha of an on-campus nest of vamps who had hunted students since the early 1980s. Sunday certainly embodies that era, with her New Wave styling and air of Bret Easton Ellis entitled ennui. Sunday actually gets the better of Buffy in combat—it's rumored the vampire was originally conceived as a fallen Slayer—but when she breaks Buffy's Class Protector Award, our heroine rallies to angrily dust her with a broken tennis racket. Game, set, match. Fun fact: actress Katharine Towne is the daughter of legendary screenwriter Robert Towne (*Chinatown*).

Thomas (J. Patrick Lawlor)

Another of the Master's minions; though appearing in just the premiere episode of *Buffy*, the "young and stupid" (per Darla) Thomas holds two key distinctions. One, his abduction of Willow persuades Buffy to resume slaying, and two, he's the first vampire she kills, more to protect Willow than to comment on his appalling fashion sense, which she compares to the DeBarges's.

The Three

Oh, unholy trinity! This trio of "unusually virile" (Giles) warrior vamps, brethren of the Order of Aurelius, are dispatched by the Master to slay the Slayer in the first season's "Angel." Of course they all fail, and offer their own lives as penance. The Master is unmoved, opining that their deaths would bring him little joy, then watches as Darla smites them, adding, "Of course, sometimes a little is enough."

Tom (Mace Lombard)

Sunday's senior vampire lackey, Tom was a luckless fellow: after he spent decades in the dubious company of stoner vamp Rookie (Mike Rad) and gluttonous vamp Dav (Shannon Hillary), and the other one, Jerry (uncredited),

Buffy and crew take out his abusive master and off-putting colleagues. Tom escapes . . . and runs straight into the warm, caring arms of the Initiative. There, he warns an imprisoned Spike to avoid the poisoned blood rations (they're "spiked," ha ha) and helps the peroxided predator escape—but Spike double-crosses him, leaving him to die at the hand of Initiative soldiers. Tom, ya shoulda picked better friends.

Mr. Trick (K. Todd Freeman)

This flashy third-season vamp liked to wear red, like Santa, and had an affinity for the comic-strip Great Dane Marmaduke ("Nobody tells Marmaduke what to do"), which is all-around ironic because a) he was neither chubby nor jolly, but rather a svelte, cold-blooded (literally) killer and b) someone was *always* telling him what to do. Trick was a super-slippery capo who slithered from boss to boss—he starts off with Kakistos, the hoofed vampire who arrives in town seeking vengeance against Faith, but bails the minute he smells trouble, telling a colleague: "If we don't do something the master could get killed. Well, our prayers are with him." After a brief interlude of independence during which he indulges his theatrical impulses by organizing SlayerFest '98, Trick is recruited by the mayor without the slightest hint of resistance. It is while in service of Hizzoner that he is dusted by Faith, whose place at the Mayor's side she then takes. His last words: "Oh, no. No, this is no good at all." Personally, we weren't really troubled by it.

Vincent (Alex Skuby)

A member of the El Eliminati vampire cult and acolyte of the demon Balthazar, Vincent would be just another forgettable bloodsucker in *Buffy* lore if not for a single scene, in which he splits Mayor Wilkin's head vertically by half with his sword. Unfortunately for Vincent, the mayor is fresh off his dedication ceremony, meaning he is invincible for the one hundred days leading to his ascension to full-fledged demon, so his bifurcated head simply pieces itself back together, and poor dumb Vincent is staked in the back by the mayor's henchman Mr. Trick.

Holden Webster (Jonathan M. Woodward)

A former Sunnydale High student-turned-vampire, Holden engages Buffy in a discussion about relationship issues in the course of a prolonged fight. He makes some insightful observations, but Buffy stakes him anyway.

Whip (Emmanuel Xuereb)

A sleazy vampire who ran the bitey-bordello in which Riley Finn paid to be bitten. Buffy slays Whip with a flaming beam before burning his whole sordid operation to the ground.

Zack (Dave Power)

Justin the Vampire Boy's jerky vampire buddy. Giles impales him on a tree branch, which is sweet.

6

It May Be That We Are All That Stands Between Earth and Utter Destruction

Watchers + Slayers

Watchers

Rupert Edmund Giles (Anthony Stewart Head)

Tweedy, reserved, archly droll and painfully British, Rupert Giles, a.k.a. Ripper, is a rebel in librarian's clothing. Giles was a third-generation Watcher, charged with overseeing the Slayer Buffy Summers. Giles's cover was his post as the librarian of Sunnydale High, which meant that, in addition to Buffy, students Willow, Xander, Cordelia, and Oz had occasion to cross his transom, and his domain, the library—amusingly devoid of students not employed as monster killers—provided a handy headquarters for the nascent Scooby Gang. Giles, as the unquestioned authority on magic, demonology, and vampire lore, was often tasked with delivering large chunks of exposition, and serving as a comic foil for his young charges, his English fuddy-duddy-ness contrasting sharply with the Scoobies' Southern Californian élan.

But Giles contains hidden depths: We and the Scoobies learn, as the series progresses, that stammering Rupert was once known as Ripper, a violent criminal who had catastrophically dabbled in dark magicks before taking up the mantle of Watcher. More shocking still, it transpires that Giles possesses rock star musical skills and the sexual prowess of a stevedore (as per Joyce Summers). It is this messy, complicated, reckless emotional side that makes Giles, the very picture of genteel repression, such an interesting character, and such a perfect mentor for Buffy, who similarly prioritizes personal feelings and relationships over her sacred duties as a Slayer. Giles and Buffy are kindred spirits, and their growing mutual respect and father/daughter affection and devotion provide *BTVS* with its strongest emotional through-line.

Giles began life in England as the scion of an upper-class family that included two Watchers—his father and grandmother—who expected young Rupert to continue in the family business. An intellectual genius and brilliant student, Giles dutifully trains as a Watcher until a combat exercise goes awry, killing his fellow apprentices (and nearly Giles himself) before their elders intervene. Sickened by the Watchers Council's carelessness, Giles drops out of the Watchers Academy and Oxford University to pursue a life of petty crime and magical mischief. Finding a like-minded crowd of necromantic ne'er-do-wells, including wingman/future nemesis Ethan Rayne, Giles—now calling himself "Ripper"—shifts his attentions to stealing cars and meddling in forbidden mystical forces. When the group summons a powerful demon called Eyhgon, one of their number is killed by the beast, and Giles carries the shame of this arrogant folly with him from that time forward.

Chastened, Giles completes his Watcher studies and makes for Sunnydale, California, where newly activated Slayer Buffy Summers awaits his instruction. Or so he expects—Buffy, in reality, proves to be an exasperating free-spirit, disdainful of rules, tradition, or discipline, more sun-kissed party girl than grimly dedicated defender of humanity. Unsurprisingly, the two clash often, as Buffy bristles under Giles's expectations and Giles despairs over Buffy's improvisatory, intuitive approach to demon fighting. But Buffy soon proves her mettle, and Giles begins to appreciate his charge's unconventional approach. They also begin to bond emotionally, as daughter of divorce Buffy comes to rely on Giles's paternal concern, and Giles develops protective, fatherly feelings for the Slayer, which will have a profound effect upon their "professional" relationship.

Giles also befriends Buffy's "Scooby Gang," tolerating Xander, barely tolerating Cordelia, and doting on Willow, who shares Giles's advanced intellect and fascination with magic. He begins a romantic relationship with computer science teacher/techno-pagan Jenny Calendar, an aggressively modern knockout who teases the stuffy Giles unmercifully, driving him to clean his glasses ever more furiously in embarrassment. Turns out Jenny is also in Sunnydale on a secret mission: she's a descendant of the Gypsy clan that cursed Angel with the reinstatement of his soul and is in town to keep tabs on the brooding vampire. This ends very badly, as Angel, once again evil (long story), brutally kills her. This occasions our first glimpse of Giles's rather alarming dark side, as he, in response, bludgeons Angel with a baseball bat and burns down his lair.

Switcheroo: Sarah Michelle Gellar was originally pegged to play Cordelia, but eventually got the role of Buffy. How'd that work out?

Life in the Hellmouth goes on: Giles briefly becomes Watcher to Faith Lehane, failing to make much of an impression on the rogue Slayer before her defection to the dark side. Ethan Rayne blows into town to wreak havoc with his enchanted "band candy," which regresses adults who eat it back to mental adolescence. Giles and Joyce Summers are affected and embark on an evening of raising hell and making love. Twice, to Buffy's eternal chagrin. He first seriously breaks with Watchers Council protocol when he takes on the Master—an ancient, impossibly strong vampire—singlehandedly, in an attempt to foil a prophecy that foresaw the Master killing Buffy in combat. Giles is relieved of his post as Watcher after interfering in Buffy's "Cruciamentum" ritual, in which a de-powered Slayer must vanquish a demon foe; Giles again intervenes to save Buffy's life, and is fired by the Watchers Council for his emotional overinvestment in the Slayer. His replacement, Wesley Wyndham-Pryce, proves himself a by-the-book company man, earning him the contempt of Buffy and the Scoobies (briefly excluding Cordelia, who thought the creep was cute for a second), who effectively ignore him. Giles continues in his capacity as Watcher (unofficially), but loses his other job—librarian—when the school is destroyed in the conflict with the mayor. Guy can't catch a break.

Adrift, unemployed, and increasingly alienated from the college-consumed Scoobies, Giles mulls a return to England, but decides to stay after Buffy renews her commitment to training and understanding her nature as a Slayer. He takes over The Magic Box, the local Wiccan supplies store, and, hey presto, new headquarters! He also buys a nifty sports car and enjoys a romantic liaison with his old friend (and stunning beauty) Olivia Williams— for a minute there, everything's coming up Giles. Ah, but this is Sunnydale; after Ethan Rayne returns to temporarily transform him into a demon, after Spike becomes his unwilling houseguest, after assorted other indignities, and, most importantly, after Buffy sacrifices herself to save Dawn, he's had enough, and sets sail for Old Blighty.

Until news reaches him of Buffy's resurrection, which understandably brings him right back . . . and into direct conflict with Willow, whose reckless use of serious magic to bring back the Slayer horrifies the reformed spellcaster. His anger and disappointment with his magical mentee—and Willow's unrepentant hostility in response—drives a wedge between the two, and Giles again returns to England.

It's Willow who brings him back again. Grief-stricken by Tara's murder, Willow nearly unleashes a magical apocalypse, and Giles returns to face her, armed with the combined might of an English coven of witches. It's extremely upsetting to watch them tear into each other, and even more upsetting when Giles loses the battle. Xander is able to avert disaster with a vulnerably emotional Hail Mary, and Giles, physically and emotionally exhausted by the conflict, again goes home to England, with Willow in tow, to recuperate.

He's back again to aid in the fight against the First, which is ultimately successful. Post the destruction of Sunnydale, Giles works with the activated Potentials as a mentor, unsurprisingly, and gets into all manner of continuity headaches in the comics as he is killed, brought back, de-aged, etc. But we are primarily concerned here with the TV Giles, brought indelibly to life by Anthony Stewart Head. Head handled the comedy and drama of the series effortlessly, quick with a quip and able to shift from stammering charm to steely gravitas on a dime, and his musical ability was one of the show's most delightful secret weapons. His paternal connection to Buffy and Willow yielded richly nuanced and emotionally potent stories and character development, and Giles's relative age and experience provided a more mature perspective on the fantastical goings-on in Sunnydale that deepened the storytelling and helped elevate the piece above the level of a frivolous (if masterfully executed) supernatural teenaged adventure.

And the man looks damn good in tweed.

Wesley Wyndam-Pryce (Alexis Denisof)

Wesley, dispatched to Sunnydale by the council to watch over Buffy and Faith after Giles's firing in "Helpless," is of minor importance in *Buffy*, appearing in just nine, third-season episodes as an officious buffoon, but emerges as deeply textured and consequential once he makes the move to *Angel* ten episodes into season one. In the end—and, sadly, we mean that literally—Wes is as bookish and brilliant as ever, but also highly competent, confident, and, when necessary, ruthless, with a cool, new blow-dry haircut and roguish wardrobe—completely unrecognizable from his *Buffy* days.

When writer-producer David Fury first pitched "Helpless," to Whedon, "Giles gets fired by the council at the midway point and then gets rehired at the end. It didn't occur to me how I suddenly affected the mythology of the series. I was thinking when I pitched it, 'Well, Giles has to get his job back, because Buffy needs her Watcher,' but one of the things Joss loved about the pitch was Giles getting fired: 'Great! This'll give us a chance to bring in somebody else.' And I was feeling upset, because I'm going, 'I don't want to get Giles fired,' but I did."

Fury admits he was "never sure about Wesley" during the character's *Buffy* arc, finding him "arch and buffoonish" (Whedon once wrote a stage direction for the character that read, "Thinks he's Sean Connery; is George Lazenby").

Prom Night: Watchers Giles (Anthony Stewart Head) and Wesley (Alexis Denisof), looking their spiffiest for Sunnydale High's senior prom.

Douglas Petrie scripted Wesley's first episode, "Bad Girls," originally envisioning a Michael J. Fox–George Stephanopoulos–type character: "young and arrogant and way too college-educated, who thought he knew everything, but an American. And once Alexis stepped into those shoes it ended any conversation about what Wesley is or isn't; it became his." Although born in America, Denisof spent thirteen years in London, and is Shakespearean-trained.

As Petrie recalls:

> At the end of season three, when the big fight breaks out at the school and the mayor transforms into this giant creature and they have to blow up the school, during the final fight, Joss said, "All right, Wesley, you've

been such a punk, we've really put you through the ringer. We've really made you such an incompetent boob, let's give you a moment during the fight, let's give you a moment of true heroism," and Alexis just instantly said, "That's great, thank you so much, but can I just be knocked unconscious instantly?" And we just thought that was the funniest thing in the world, because no actor ever says that, and we went there and he gets knocked unconscious instantly. So many other actors would have been, like, "Oh, finally, it's my moment to be a badass and be cool," and he was like, "No, let me be Wesley."

In *Buffy*, Wesley's ineptitude is truly staggering. He arrives having battled vampires only twice in his career, both times "under controlled circumstances, of course."

"No danger of finding those here," says Giles.

"Vampires?" asks Wesley.

"Controlled circumstances," answers Giles.

He's instantly dislikeable, and not just because he's replacing Giles. He spouts useless aphorisms like, "Remember the three key words for any Slayer: preparation, preparation, preparation," and admonishes his predecessor as an embarrassment for his deep emotional attachment to Buffy—so full of himself he's obviously covering up an Everest of insecurity (Daddy issues; what else?). Once the action kicks in, he's even worse: a sniveling coward before roly-poly demon Balthazar; summoning the council to apprehend Faith after eavesdropping on a conversation between Buffy and Giles—exactly the wrong thing to do, with dire consequences; and voting against the motion to swap the Box of Gavrok for Willow, held hostage by the mayor—committing the ultimate sin in Scoobyland, heartlessness, triggering Buffy's rebuke: "Are you made of human parts?"

Only Cordelia isn't instantly chafed by Wesley; still smarting from Xander's betrayal, she dubs him "Giles, the next generation," and practically flings herself at him—better yet, delete "practically." Wes is flattered, but as inept at romance as everything else, plus conflicted, since Cordy is, after all, a teenager—and a student. At senior prom, he can't decide whether or not to ask her for a dance, so Giles tells him, "For God's sake, man, she's eighteen. And you have the emotional maturity of a blueberry scone. Just have at it, would you, and stop fluttering about."

Multiple factors trigger Buffy's third-season rebelliousness—the events of "Helpless," when she is deceived by the council, and the arrival of Faith among them—but make no mistake: Wesley (Buffy calls him a dork) plays his part; the tipping point comes when he reports that the council won't help find a cure for Angel, who's been pierced by a poison arrow, because "[i]t's not council policy to cure vampires." When Buffy responds that the council "can close up shop; I'm not working for them anymore," Wesley screams mutiny, but truth be told, by this point he has thawed, and by the following episode, the season-ending "Graduation Day, Part 2," he defies his bosses, staying on to enlist in the war against the mayor (even if, as Petrie reminds us, he is knocked out instantly).

Wesley never returns to *Buffy*, but he shows up in L.A. in episode ten of *Angel*; having been cut loose by the council for ineptitude (though somehow Quentin Travers gets away with it), he's now, proudly, a "rogue demon hunter," though equally inept at that. Wesley sticks around for the duration of the five-season *Angel*, however, and over time becomes an infinitely darker and deeper character, until, in the final episode, he is fatally stabbed in the stomach by demonic sorcerer Cyvus Vail.

Ironically, Wesley was initially summoned to *Angel* because, as Petrie phrases it, "[T]here were feelings in the upper echelons of the creative end of the show that it was too dark, that there wasn't enough of a comic element, and that the mix of the dark and the light is partly what had made *Buffy* so successful, and that *Angel* had a chance to do that in a different way. . . And so Wesley seemed to be an obvious character to be able to bring that." And yet, by the conclusion, Wes had become, arguably, the darkest character on the show; even one demon member of the Circle of the Black Thorn admires him as "intriguingly unstable." According to Petrie, "At one point, we felt we had been so successful in taking Wesley down this dark place that there was this talk about whether to just go ahead and make him the Big Bad, let him go all the way and maybe or maybe not retrieve him."

In the end, Petrie says, the writers decided it would be "more interesting and more suitable, and I think the right decision, to keep him just a hair's breadth away from completely disappearing to the other side." We couldn't agree more.

Blair + Hobson (Dominic Keating + David Haydn-Jones)

Basically interchangeable clock-punchers at the Watchers Council, except that Hobson is apparently the more sadsack of the two, since Blair winds up feeding on him. These two worker bees were supposed to guard cannibalistic serial killer-turned-vampire Zachary Kralik in anticipation of Buffy's Cruciamentum (don't ask, but see the relevant entry) on the occasion of her eighteenth birthday, but good help is hard to find, especially at Watchers Council rates. Kralik breaks free and sires Blair, and the two of them feast on Hobson. There must be more civilized ways to lunch with a co-worker.

Collins (Alistair Duncan)

The leader of the Watchers Council Special Operations Team, Collins displays rationality and a willingness to strike a deal, which means the Watchers Council probably fired him when he returned to England.

Bernard Crowley (None)

Nikki Wood's Watcher in 1970s New York, appearing only in the canonical comics, specifically in a flashback in season nine.

Lydia (Cynthia Lamontagne)

A Watcher who accompanied Quentin Travers on his trip to Sunnydale to evaluate Buffy. Tweedy, proper, and buttoned-up, Lydia exuded a sexy librarian sort of vibe, and seemed a bit inappropriately fascinated by Spike. She died, when Caleb's bomb detonated and took out the Watchers Council.

Merrick (Richard Riehle)

Buffy's first Watcher, Merrick was a huge deal in the film *Buffy*, portrayed by Donald Sutherland, one of Joss Whedon's least favorite people in the world. In the TV series he appears just briefly, in a flashback in the second season's "Becoming," when Whistler drags Angel to Los Angeles to encourage him to devote the rest of his interminable life to fighting evil, beginning with helping Buffy (it works). The only non-Summers character to appear in both the film and the TV series, Merrick also figures prominently in "The Origin," a three-issue comic book miniseries adapted for Dark Horse in 1999 by Christopher Golden, Dan Brereton, and Joe Bennett from Whedon's original screenplay for the film. In an Internet chat room, Whedon stated that "The 'Origin' comic, though I have issues with it, CAN pretty much be accepted as canonical. They did a cool job of combining the movie script (the SCRIPT) with the series, that was nice, and using the series Merrick and not a certain OTHER thespian [Sutherland] who shall remain hated."

Nigel (Kris Iyer)

Another of Quentin Travers's Slayer evaluation team. A particularly snotty and officious fellow, he aggravates Buffy into throwing a sword at him, which barely misses. Death catches up to Nigel later in the form of Caleb's Watcher-decimating bomb blast.

Robson (Rob Nagle)

Watchers Council member and Giles's close friend. Badly wounded when he and his trainee, Nora (she doesn't make it), are attacked by Bringers, but he survives. Tough dude.

Gwendolyn Post (Serena Scott Thomas)

Gwendolyn Post's Etiquette: First, abuse the dark arts, so you're booted from the Council. Second, head for Sunnydale, in search of the Glove of Myneghon, a mystical artifact with great power. Third, go rogue, posing as Faith's Watcher. Fourth, incapacitate Giles and Angel. Fifth, purloin the glove. Sixth, pontificate about your accomplishment ("I have the glove, and with the glove comes the power!"). Seventh, summon forth lightning, so you can fire it at Buffy and Faith. Eighth, die, when Buffy cuts off your arm.

Smith (Kevin Owers)

The somewhat reasonable and least bloodthirsty member of the Watchers Council Special Operations Team, Smith nonetheless blithely opens fire on both Faith and Buffy, because the Watchers Council is a bunch of jerks.

Quentin Travers (Harris Yulin)

Statesmanlike, authoritative Quentin Travers was director of the Watchers Council and a frequent protocol-driven thorn in Buffy's side. Travers came to eventually respect Buffy's resolve and abilities, despite her disregard for the rules. Cold, ruthless, and imperious, Travers also had little patience for Giles's "sentimental" emotional attachment to his Slayer, an attitude shared by most Watchers and further evidence of Giles's unorthodox approach to his job.

Weatherby (Jeff Rickets)

The most fanatical member of the Watchers Council Special Operations Team sent to assassinate Faith Lehane. A real spits-while-he-talks true believer and deeply unpleasant man.

Sam Zabuto (None)

Kendra Young's never-seen Watcher. Zabuto seemed to have a much easier job than Giles, since Kendra paid strict attention to the Slayer Handbook, while Buffy didn't even know there was one, and probably wouldn't have read it anyway.

Shadow Men

Three African shamans who, in the prehistoric era, imbued a young girl with demonic powers, creating the First Slayer. In effect they were the First Watchers, and their affiliation would eventually evolve into the Watchers Council.

Slayers

> In every generation there is a chosen one. She alone will stand against the vampires, the demons, and the forces of darkness. She is the Slayer.

The following Slayers are either seen or referenced in the TV series (in addition to Buffy, of course):

Sineya, a.k.a. the First Slayer (Sharon Ferguson)

In prehistorical Africa, a group of shamans known as the Shadow Men imbued a young girl with demonic essence, transforming her into a supernatural warrior against evil. This was Sineya, the First Slayer.

Sineya periodically appeared to Buffy as a sort of spirit guide, offering obscure wisdom such as "death is your gift." Sineya's existence was horribly circumscribed by her identity as the Slayer—cut off from her humanity, she lived in exile, shunned and feared by those she was sworn to protect (so she was also the first X-Man).

Xin Rong (Ming Liu)

The Slayer active during the Boxer Rebellion at the turn of the twentieth century in China, Xin Rong was killed by Spike—but not before permanently scarring his eyebrow with her sword. Dying, she asks the vampire to tell her mother she's sorry, but Spike fails to understand Chinese. Probably for the best he didn't swing by for a visit.

Korean Slayer (None)

In season one's "The Puppet Show," Sid, the Demon Hunter, mentions that he knew a Slayer in the 1930s: "Korean chick. Very hot. We're talking muscle tone. Man, we had some times." She is never identified by name or spoken of again.

Nikki Wood (April Weeden-Washington; K. D. Aubert)

A Slayer active in 1970s New York, Nikki, like Xin Rong, was killed by Spike. A Pam Grier–esque badass, Nikki, also like Xin Rong, contributed to Spike's signature look: he takes her leather jacket as a trophy and rocks it for decades. Nikki's son, Robin, eventually turns up in Sunnydale as the high school's new principal, continuing his mother's legacy as a vampire killer and intent upon revenge. April Weeden-Washington played Nikki in her debut appearance; K. D. Aubert played her subsequently.

Kendra Young (Bianca Lawson)

Kendra, activated when Buffy is momentarily drowned by the Master in the season-one finale, arrives in Sunnydale about midway into the second season, in "What's My Line," and let's just say she and Buffy aren't a match made in heaven, or even above the Hellmouth. As writer/producer Marti Noxon explains on her DVD commentary, Kendra is "completely unable to socialize, the epitome of someone who was raised just to be a weapon." If Faith is Buffy's dark side, Kendra represents "just how rigid and straight and uptight a Slayer would have been without friends and family around her." Buffy, a balance of instinct, emotion, and reason, is the happy (sometimes) medium between the seething, impetuous Faith and the dutiful, unpliable Kendra. When Kendra advises Buffy to report to Giles for orders, Buffy sets her straight: "I don't take orders. I do things my way." Born and raised in Jamaica, Kendra has known of her calling since she was very young, when her parents "gave me to my Watcher because they believed they were doing the right thing for me—and for the world." Kendra shuns emotions as weakness; Buffy embraces them as assets. Eventually, these two Slayers make their peace, work together, and appreciate the unique bond they share. Kendra returns to Sunnydale at the end of season two, warned by her Watcher that trouble is brewing, and even gifts Buffy with her favorite stake, Mr. Pointy, as the latter heads for a showdown with Angelus. Sadly, the return engagement isn't a hit with everyone, particularly Drusilla, who slits her throat. Given that Kendra's

Forever Young: Jamaican Slayer Kendra Young (Bianca Lawson), *right*, grew up to be righteous. *Photofest*

death leads to Faith's activation, and that Buffy's death at the end of season five fails to generate a new Slayer, we apparently can assume that the line of succession had passed from Buffy to Kendra to Faith. The good die Young, and Young died good.

Faith Lehane (Eliza Dushku)

Faith is one of the most complex and fascinating characters to appear on *BTVS*. A Slayer, activated by Kendra's death, Faith comes to Sunnydale fleeing the vampire who killed her Watcher. It's not the first time she's been left hanging: neglected and abused by her shiftless Southie parents, Faith entered the game as damaged goods, and her emotional and psychological instability leads to considerable mayhem and trauma for both herself and the Scoobies.

Aggressive, sarcastic, and strikingly attractive—her sultry, dark good looks and unfettered sexuality throwing Buffy's blonde, all-American girl-next-door appeal into sharp relief—Faith comes on as the archetypal Bad Girl, a rock and rollin' free spirit seemingly unfazed by her burden of destiny. She enjoys killing, and her wild, impulsive fighting style makes up in ferocity what it lacks in finesse. Faith implies a long familiarity with such vices as promiscuity and substance abuse and projects a withering coolness that Willow in particular finds abrasive. In short, she is Buffy's Bizarro reflection, the Dark Slayer, a glimpse of what Buffy might have been without her emotional connections to friends and family. And for a while, the two Slayers make a dynamite combo, fire and ice, passion and control, complementary killers in the demon war.

For a while. Faith's personal demons (a far more urgent threat than the literal hellspawn who routinely threaten her life) eventually emerge as she begins to resent Buffy's "golden girl" status and feels increasingly alienated from the other Scoobies. Her trust issues are further exacerbated by the betrayal of her ostensible new Watcher, Gwendolyn Post, and when she accidentally kills a human being during a mission, she burns her bridges with her companions by blaming Buffy for the killing and assaulting Xander in her hotel room when he attempts to reason with her (she had earlier taken his virginity, seemingly as an afterthought).

Faith's downward spiral ends at the mayor, as she joins forces with the diabolical politician, forming a deep daughter/father bond with Wilkins, who sincerely seems to care for her (bizarro-world version of the Buffy-Giles bond). Their relationship queasily skates the line between touching and creepy as his support and affection both help repair Faith's self-esteem and render her pliable to his evil, murderous requests.

Rogue One: Bad-girl slayer Faith Lehane (Eliza Dushku) was never *really* five by five.

When Faith shoots Angel with a specially treated, vampire-killing arrow, Buffy gets right down on her now hated rival's level: the only antidote for Angel is Slayer's blood, and Buffy comes calling on Faith to collect. In the ensuing donnybrook, Buffy critically stabs Faith with Faith's own knife, but the Dark Slayer evades capture by falling onto a passing truck. She spends the next few months in a coma, and when she awakes it is most assuredly on the wrong side of the bed.

Consumed by her lust for vengeance, Faith goes after Buffy con gusto, attacking Joyce and temporarily switching bodies with Buffy, causing all sorts of trouble (for example, having sex with Buffy's in-the-dark boyfriend Riley).

Still, there is much potential for goodness in Faith. While "borrowing" Buffy's form and life, Faith begins to reassert her heroic nature and it becomes clear that so much of her rage and violence stems from deep self-loathing. Freed from being "Faith," she is able to act compassionately and remember her old righteous sense of mission.

Reeling, unsure of herself, Faith makes her way to Los Angeles to develop a tortured relationship with Angel (déjà vu), alternately trying to kill him at the behest of Wolfram + Hart and begging the vampire to kill her in punishment for her sins. We said she was complicated.

Faith eventually rehabilitates completely (well, as close as she's going to come), reuniting with the Scoobies to face the First Evil and serving the newly activated Potentials in a leadership role. That career transition goes less than smoothly, as she and Buffy vie for control of the Slayers, but she shows amazing growth when she cedes leadership back to La Summers after leading a raiding party directly into a deadly trap. She still has attitude to burn, but Faith is back on the side of the angels. After the end of the series proper, Faith is depicted in the comics as a continuing work in progress, endeavoring to keep the new Slayers on the straight and narrow.

It's a fitting resolution for the mercurial character. Her evolution can be seen as a mirror of Buffy's, as hard-won wisdom slowly leads to maturity; Faith's path is just a little rockier. Faith brings a lot to *BTVS*: she's unpredictable and charismatic, which helps keep things exciting, and she's riveting in her dramatic scenes, conveying rage and wounded vulnerability in equal measure. And that contradiction is at the heart of her appeal: for all of her crimes, Faith is really just hungry for love and acceptance, and cursing her name while simultaneously aching for her sadness makes for a compellingly complicated audience/character relationship.

And it doesn't hurt that Eliza Dushku, the actress playing Faith, combines dazzling sex appeal, an impressive emotional range, and a whip-smart delivery perfectly suited for *BTVS*'s witty dialogue. Faith's status as a fan favorite is a no-brainer—she's the dangerous, sexy Han Solo to Buffy's Luke Skywalker, and Dushku brings indelible brio and nuance to the role. Dushku would reteam with Whedon for the series *Dollhouse* . . . which has much to recommend it, but what we would really love to see is a Faith spin-off. She's a corker. Five by five.

Potentials

When the Shadow Men created the First Slayer, they baked into their magic some rules: when a Slayer dies, a replacement is chosen from a large pool of "Potentials," adolescent girls with dormant Slayer abilities who served as understudies to the currently living Slayer.

Buffy and Willow, with the help of the scythe, ended that tradition, simultaneously "activating" the full powers of all the world's potential Slayers in an effort to counter the superior might of the First Evil. All well and good, but the vast majority of these girls were living ordinary, teen-aged lives, finding themselves completely unprepared to take on the responsibilities of Slayerdom.

Buffy recruited them and gave them a crash course in demon killing, but many of the inexperienced girls died horribly in the conflict, and all had a difficult time adjusting, but the gambit was ultimately successful and the First Evil was defeated (though Sunnydale was leveled).

Following this epic battle, many of the Potentials continued to train and fight, organized into international cells overseen by Buffy, as depicted in the canonical comics. The Potentials we meet on TV include:

Kennedy (Iyari Limon)

Brash, beautiful, and gay, Kennedy catches Willow's eye and the two date for a time. In the comics, Kennedy would later work as a bodyguard, which makes sense.

Molly (Clara Bryant)

Crossbow-wielding Cockney, killed by Caleb.

Annabelle (Courtnee Draper)

Officious, British, and first of the Potentials to die.

Nora (Linda Christopher)

Watcher Robson's protégé, killed by Bringers.

Shannon (Mary Wilcher)

Attacked by Bringers and stabbed by Caleb upon her arrival. Welcome to Sunnydale.

Colleen (Rachel Bilson)

Sexy Slayerette who erotically haunts Xander's dreams. Bilson would go on to star on *The OC*, where she erotically haunted Seth Cohen.

Caridad (Dania Ramirez)

Fancied by Xander, Caridad was damn tough, surviving numerous attacks and dangerous missions in the stand against the First Evil.

Dianne (Miranda Kwok)

Killed by Caleb at the Vineyard.

Rona (Tauvia Dawn)

Cynical, defeatist, and self-interested, Rona is kind of a downer. She survives the final battle despite serious injuries.

Eve (Amanda Fuller)

Killed by the Bringers before even getting the chance to meet Buffy. Harsh.

Chloe (Lalaine Vargas)

Emotionally unstable and vulnerable Chloe was persuaded to commit suicide by the First Evil, prompting Buffy to double down on the mission.

Violet, a.k.a. Vi (Felicia Day)

Geek culture goddess Felicia Day portrayed Vi, who started out painfully shy and awkward but grew into one of the most formidable physical combatants among the Potentials.

Chao-ahn (Kristy Wu)

A Potential and Chinese national who consistently mistook Giles's overtures of friendship for threats.

Amanda (Sarah Hagan)

A shy, sweet, bullied swing band enthusiast, Amanda was also somewhat darkly and violently inclined. So no surprise she shared a strong bond with Faith. Killed by a Turok-Han.

Dana

Dana is unique in the Buffyverse: the only Potential who appears on *Angel*, but never on *Buffy*. In season five's "Damage," Dana is a super-powered young psycho who escapes from an institution in Los Angeles, determined to wreak vengeance on the man who killed her family and kidnapped and tortured her over fifteen years earlier. Sadly for Spike, her twisted mind somehow becomes convinced (falsely) that he is the culprit, and she winds up cutting off his hands as retribution (though they are eventually reattached). This leads to profound soul-searching for Spike, who tells Angel, "The lass thought I killed her family. And I'm supposed to what, complain? 'Cause hers wasn't one of the hundreds of families I *did* kill?" Sounds a lot like Angel to us, but that's what you get for joining his show.

History of the Slayer

The following Slayers appear in 20th Television-produced "History of the Slayer" promos airing on The WB in 1997, in anticipation of the premiere of *Buffy the Vampire Slayer*. One of these aired immediately before the two-hour premiere of the series on March 10, 1997, after this disclaimer: "The following two-hour world premiere is rated TV-PG and contains action scenes which may be too intense for younger viewers." However, these Slayers have not appeared in any Joss Whedon script, and therefore are not considered canon:

Abigail Cole: Plymouth Colony, Massachusetts, 1625. Puts an end to mysterious deaths "attributed to some unknown animal."

The Boston Slayer (unidentified by name): Boston, Massachusetts, 1845. A "quiet young woman" who arrives in town following a series of grisly murders at the Boston Shipyards.

Lucy Hanover: Virginia, 1866: Sets up camp in a graveyard following the serial disappearances of Civil War widows.

Belle Malone: Dodge City, Kansas, 1888. Arrives in town following forty deaths under suspicious circumstances.

The Oklahoma Slayer (unidentified by name): Oklahoma Territory, 1893. A blacksmith who passes through town following savage attacks claiming the lives of seventeen homesteaders.

Florence Gilbert: Virginia City, Wyoming, 1897. Twenty years old when she arrives in town following a string of bizarre murders.

Arabella Gish: Brooklyn, New York, 1912. Puts an end to the Brooklyn Boarding House Murders, which claimed the lives of twenty-three citizens.

The Chicago Slayer (unidentified by name): Chicago, Illinois, 1927. Arrives in town following the mysterious murders of forty-one people in the Union Station area.

Tales of the Slayers

The following Slayers appear in the canonical graphic novel *Tales of the Slayers* (2002) and the canonical comic books *Tales of the Slayers: Broken Bottle of Djinn* (2002) and *Fray* (2003)—all Whedon–approved—and thus deemed canonical:

Sineya/The First Slayer: See above, under TV Slayers. Here Sinyea appears in the Whedon-scripted prologue, which also includes a reference to the Shadow Men, the Watchers Council prototype that created the Slayer.

The Unnamed Slayer in "Righteous," also scripted by Whedon, in rhyme, and set in medieval England; accused of witchcraft by ungrateful villagers and burned at the stake.

Claudine, in "The Innocent," set during the French Revolution and authored by Amber Benson (Tara).

Elizabeth/Edward Weston, in "Presumption," a little transgender action from Jane Espenson, set in early nineteenth-century England.

Naayéé'neizghàni ("Monster Slayer"), the Navajo Slayer in David Fury's "The Glittering World," who slays the vampire who killed her Watcher, but is herself mortally wounded.

Anni Sonnenblume, fourteen-year-old Slayer in Rebecca Sinclair's "Sonnenblume," set in Nazi Germany.

Nikki Wood, who also appears in the TV series, is the focus of "Nikki Goes Down!" scripted by Doug Petrie.

Melaka Fray, Slayer of the future, appears in the Whedon-scripted "Tales" in *Tales of the Slayers,* and also in her own comic-book series, also written by Whedon and titled simply *Fray.*

Rachel O'Connor, in "Broken Bottle of Djinn," scripted by Espenson and Petrie, and set, after a brief prologue in modern-day Sunnydale, in 1937 New York, where Rachel is recruited by the feds for undercover work involving a Nazi agent.

So, Who Do You Kill for Fun Around Here?

Welcome to Sunnydale

Residents, visitors, and landmarks. Abandon hope, all ye who enter here.
—*Dante's Inferno*

Joyce Summers (Kristine Sutherland)

Joyce Summers—Buffy's mom, and later Dawn's as well—is unique in the Buffyverse, the only Scooby parent who takes an active interest in her child's life. Joyce is a deliberately flawed creation—Whedon described her on DVD commentary as "like Giles, somebody who's clearly still searching in her own life, who doesn't have all the answers"—and, for almost two full seasons, is handicapped by her apparent obliviousness to Buffy's secret life as a vampire Slayer, leading to multiple parental edicts that are ludicrously out of touch with reality ("I know—if you don't go out it will be the end of the world"), yet there is never any questioning her profound love for her daughters and her courageous determination to protect them. This is hilariously demonstrated in "School Hard" when an army of vamps crashes Sunnydale High on Parent-Teacher Night and Joyce comes to Buffy's rescue by bopping a still-evil Spike over the head with an axe, admonishing him to "get the hell away from my daughter," and not so hilariously in season three's "Prom," when she essentially tells Angel that he and Buffy have no future together, and that if he really loves her he will leave Sunnydale and let her get on with her life.

Joyce is defined, more than anything, by her momness; Marcia Shulman, who cast the pilot and first four seasons, says, "We really wanted a warm mom in the middle of all this craziness." She hovers over not just her own offspring (including Dawn), but all the Scoobies, each coping with serious mommy issues of his/her own: it's practically a requirement for the club. Hot cocoa, hugs, advice, Christmas dinner—Joyce is an endless well of empathy even for Spike; once they bury their "School Hard" brawl, they connect like old chums, especially over *Passions*, the supernatural daytime soap. When asked about her role, Kristine Sutherland insisted:

> I enjoy playing mothers. I really do. Most of my career has been playing mothers, and I think that some other actresses might feel limited by that or typecast and want to break out of that mold. I think being a mother is the most fascinating thing in the world. And there's a million different kinds of mothers. And every mother has to deal with an individual child, and so a mother has to be one thing to one child and to another child has to be entirely different. So, for me, the range within a mother is absolutely fascinating. My own mother had mental illness. She was bipolar and I loved her very much, but it was very hard. Her life was very hard. And so, I think part of my joy in playing mothers is exploring what a mother should be, could be.

Still, not talking Carol Brady. Arriving in Sunnydale a middle-aged, single parent, Joyce must carve out a new life for herself, both personally and professionally, in the wake of a busted marriage and her daughter's expulsion from high school in L.A. after burning down the gym (during an epic battle with

Generation Gap: Joyce (Kristine Sutherland) and Buffy (Sarah Michelle Gellar) didn't always see eye to eye, but they sure loved each other.

vampires, though, of course, Joyce doesn't know that). She gets little-to-no help from ex-hubby Hank, and her ignorance of Buffy's secret identity leads to multiple mother-daughter conflicts, a metaphor for the popular teen notion that parents can't possibly understand what they are going through.

Kristine Sutherland went through a complicated, challenging process in coming to terms with "clueless Joyce":

> A lot of people have asked me, "How did you do that? How did you be so dumb? How could you make that work?" I had to figure out early on how to always be Joyce, but sometimes I was playing a facet of all mothers. So there were times I had to do things that were out of character. But I also understood that in the context of the show we were seeing Joyce through Buffy's eyes . . . I understood that there was this filter going on. The audience was seeing Joyce and her actions through Buffy's eyes as a teenager. I would have what was real to me as Joyce and then there would be that extra filter. Because we don't see our parents for who they are when we're teenagers.

One of the most poignant scenes in the series (and Sutherland's personal favorite) occurs at the conclusion of "Innocence," when Buffy, devastated that Angel had transformed into the soulless Angelus immediately after taking her virginity, returns home for a quiet seventeenth-birthday celebration with her mom, who asks how she celebrated the day. Replies Buffy: "I got older." Joyce looks tenderly into her daughter's face and says: "You look the same to me." Joyce strokes Buffy's hair; Buffy leans over and rests her head on her mother's shoulder.

FAQ: Tell us your thoughts about those two season-two episodes, "Surprise" and "Innocence."

Kristine Sutherland: When I first read those scripts, I was like "Oh, my God," this is that guy I dated in junior high school!" That's what he did to me. And some of the other women on the crew who were older, we were talking about it, like, "Don't you remember that guy who did that to you? You allowed him in and you had some sort of intimacy with him and then he, like, freaked out and ran?" It was so amazing that Joss knew that, and that's why I think parents and people who are older can watch *Buffy* and get something out of it on a whole different level, whereas at a young enough age you're just seeing a story of the vampires and the Romani curse and not understanding the relationship stuff. That's one reason people love to watch it and re-watch it. As they get older they see and find different things in it.

FAQ: There's a scene in that episode in the mall where Buffy kills the Judge with the rocket launcher. And Joss said that after that was shot, he was jumping up and down because he was so happy. But then he says the scene you shot the next day, with you and Buffy on the sofa in the living room with the cupcake because it was her birthday, made him a thousand times happier, that you guys did such a beautiful job with what he wrote. Do you remember anything about filming that scene?

KS: I would have to say that was my favorite scene in the entire series, just off the top of my head. As fun as "Band Candy" was, that scene on the couch, there's so much unsaid. And that, to me, was sort of the epitome of their relationship. Joyce knows everything that's important to know about what's happened to her. She doesn't ask her, she's just there for her. Wouldn't you love to know, don't you want to know as a parent, who hurt my child, but you know that that's theirs and you can't ask, but you feel their pain. You went through all that pain yourself. You know what it's like. You're devastated that your child's been hurt so badly. I think Sarah did an amazing job with that. There was so little dialogue. Everything about it was just so spectacular. That was my happiest scene ever.

FAQ: That's such a beautiful moment when you look at her and say, "You don't look any different to me."

KS: Yeah, yeah. And she knows what she's really saying, which is, "You're going to be OK."

Buffy finally shares the truth with Joyce at the conclusion of season two; ironically, the revelation leads not to conciliation, but confrontation, with Joyce suggesting all sorts of alternate possibilities, including that Buffy is in need of psychiatric help (a foreshadowing of our discovery in season six that Buffy actually had spent "a couple of weeks" in a mental hospital in L.A., after sharing her vampire visions with her parents). Buffy's response—"Open your eyes, Mom. What do you think has been going on for the past two years? The fights, the weird occurrences. How many times have you washed blood out of my clothing, and you still haven't figured it out?"—certainly suggests the possibility that Joyce has all along known something was amiss, but was suppressing suspicion. When Buffy interrupts this exchange to head off to save the world (again), Joyce forbids her from leaving: "You walk out of this house, don't even think about coming back!" According to Kristine Sutherland, this was the hardest scene she ever had to play on *Buffy*, because, as a mother herself, she couldn't conceive of issuing such an ultimatum to her daughter under any circumstances.

FAQ: Did you ever have a situation where you thought Joyce was called on to do something that was out of character for her?

Kristine Sutherland: Yes. Everything that I had to do that was difficult was somewhat manageable except for telling Buffy that if she walked out that door she couldn't come back. That was so painfully hard to do because I just couldn't imagine that Joyce would really say that.

FAQ: So, was there a conversation that you had about that?

KS: No.

FAQ: So, you just did it?

KS: You got that script and you had to do it, word perfect. I knew this was something that had to drive the plot forward and my job was to try to do it to the best of my abilities, but it was very hard. It didn't feel right. All I could justify was that she did it in the heat of the moment, the way we sometimes say things we don't really mean. We feel we don't have enough power, so we try to grasp some sort of power by making some sort of giant pronouncement.

FAQ: So, there was never even in your thought while you were trying to reconcile it that you would go to the writer or Joss and say, "This just doesn't feel right to me."

KS: Mmm—no, no. . . . But it was hard, because I, as a mother, would never do that. And Joyce definitely had so much of me in her. It was one of those really wonderful times when you get a character and you feel like it fits so much like a glove.

This turns out to be a transformational point in their relationship: Buffy does indeed leave, averts another apocalypse, and, taking Joyce at her word, hops on a bus to Los Angeles, leaving Sunnydale and the slaying life behind, without informing anyone. As season three opens, Joyce, distraught over her missing daughter, lashes out at Giles, blaming him for having "taken her away from me." When Buffy finally returns, at the season-opener's conclusion, their relationship is redefined once again; Joyce even volunteers to accompany Buffy to the cemetery at night to witness slaying in action (you know, like watching your daughter's soccer games). Joyce spends much of this season worrying about her daughter's future, encouraging her to go away to college and enjoy life as any normal teenager would, leading, finally, to her confrontation with Angel.

In lighter news: season three isn't all *sturm und drang* for Joyce; in the hilarious "Band Candy," charmed chocolate bars transform Sunnydale's adults into raging-hormone teens; we find out Giles likes Cream and Joyce likes Seals and Crofts, but also that they like each other, since they have sex (off-camera) . . . twice . . . on top of a police car, which Buffy discovers—to her horror—much later on in the season, in "Earshot," when she can read minds, and Joyce clearly doesn't even want to be in the same room with her. This Joyce-Giles flirtation was another "shipping" that divided viewers—some wanted to see them together, others, like Buffy, were horrified by the idea of it. Sutherland herself believes Joyce was attracted to the Watcher, but also jealous of his relationship with Buffy, and would have liked to have seen the writers tackle it further. But, she says, "I knew in my heart they would never get together, because it just would not have worked for the story. As unexpected as Joss could be, and the curveballs that he throws at people, I don't see how he could ever have made that work. It would just be so fundamentally strange for them to get together."

Joyce appears in just four episodes in season four, as Sutherland moved to Italy with her husband and young daughter, but returns for season five, in which the character develops a brain tumor and, in one of the most acclaimed episodes of the series ("The Body"), passes away. The tumor reorients Joyce's mind, awaking her to the knowledge that Dawn is not really her child (but, rather, the human embodiment of a mystical key unlocking the gateway between dimensions). Fearful that death is encroaching, Joyce tells Buffy: "No matter what she is, she still feels like my daughter. I have to know that you'll take care of her, that you'll keep her safe. That you'll love her like I love you."

RIP, Joyce.

FAQ: What was it like filming that scene in the living room, where Buffy finds your body?

KS: It was amazing. . . . When she walks in the room and I'm laying there and I hear her go "Mom?" I couldn't cry because I was supposed to be dead. I kept saying, "I'm so sorry, you guys, I'm so sorry, you guys" because I just couldn't stop crying. It brought up every ounce of grief of life. Grief is like that. And I had lost my own father when I was twenty-eight. So it was very personal for me.

FAQ: If I remember correctly, she starts with "Mom" and then goes into "Mommy."

KS: Yes, exactly. And then the sort of fantasy part when she tries to revive me and the medics come and lift me up and put me into the ambulance. It was a really very sort of bizarre experience. I had an emergency appendectomy a couple of years ago. I live in New York and I knew that I was really ill and I couldn't stop shaking and I took a cab to the hospital. And the cab driver kept saying, "Why didn't you call an ambulance?" I was, like, "I've already done that and I'm never doing that again. It was too traumatic. I'm taking a cab."

Dr. Stanley Backer (Richard Herd)

The mad Dr. Backer was a lightning rod for controversy, thanks to his unorthodox practices at Sunnydale Memorial. But his notion of burning the virus out of sick children by inoculating them with megadoses of the same virus in season two's "Killed by Death" was a stroke of genius, so much so that it got him bumped off by der Kindestod, the demon who was rather fond of sick children, since he depended on them for nourishment.

Kevin Berman (J. Evan Bonifant)

Dawn's middle school crush, a kind and sensitive kid who treats Dawn with sympathy and understanding during an intimate conversation. Obviously, never seen again. Sorry, Summers women. Not in the cards.

Timothy Blane (Andrew Reville)

A surly employee of the ever popular Doublemeat Palace.

Chris Boal (Carmine Giovinazzo)

The cool thing about Chris is that he is the first person to die on *Buffy*, thanks to Darla, with whom he breaks into Sunnydale High one night in the cold open to the pilot episode, "Welcome to the Hellmouth," likely thinking he is in for an evening of delights. A former Sunnydale High student, he is never mentioned by name in the series, but is so identified in a deleted scene from the original, unaired pilot.

Brie (Melanie Simmons)

Sultry brunette Bronze patron magicked by Amy into lusting for Willow, which, uncool, Amy. Total Warren Mears maneuver.

Lance Brooks (Brandon Keener)

R. J. Brooks's older brother. A former alpha jock (and Xander Harris bully) gone to seed, working in a pizza joint and living in his mother's basement—the fate oppressed high school nerds traditionally imagine for their academically uninclined tormentors.

Chantarelle/Lily Houston/Anne Steele (Julia Lee)

This young lassie occupies a unique place in the Buffyverse, guesting on five episodes over two shows—twice in *Buffy* and thrice in *Angel*—and going by three different names, each an alias, since she rejected her birth name long before we meet her. Anyone who plays this kind of name game is likely to be hauling around a trunk full of baggage, and so Chantarelle/Lily/Anne is. But the good news is that by the time of her two appearances in season two of *Angel*, she has metamorphosed into an extremely confident, constructive member of society, operating a shelter for wayward teens in Los Angeles—not bad for someone whose first appearance, in "Lie to Me" (season two, *Buffy*), is as a wacked-out vamp votary looking to get nipped so she can "ascend to a higher level of consciousness." By the time of her next appearance, in "Anne," the season-three opener of *Buffy*, Chantarelle has rebranded: she's now Lily, homeless and penniless in L.A., where she runs into Buffy, who has fled Sunnydale herself and is waitressing at a diner, and enlists her in the search for her missing boyfriend. At the end of this episode, Buffy, having by now saved Chantarelle once and Lily once, heads back to Sunnydale, leaving the troubled woman with both a new moniker (Anne, Buffy's middle name) and the remainder of the lease on her apartment. Happily, we can report that Anne makes the most of this new opportunity, turning her life around by the time we next meet her, in *Angel*. The shelter she runs is unfortunately bankrolled by the evil law firm Wolfram + Hart, and while Anne is unaware of the nature of her benefactor until Angel breaks the news to her, she finally is compelled to choose between accepting the firm's "blood money" and risking the financial stability of her shelter. She initially refuses to do anything to harm the shelter, but ultimately winds up participating in Angel's scheme to embarrass W+H at a charity fundraiser, and in the end gets to have her cake and eat it too when the money is stolen and delivered by Angel to her, bloodstained, just in case anyone misses the point.

Christine (Amy Hathaway)

A spurned bride with a cheating fiancé, Christine would have been perfect vengeance fodder for Anya, if Anya could have stopped complaining about her own ruined wedding long enough to notice.

Cleo (Jessa French)

Sunnydale hairstylist tasked with salvaging Buffy's impetuous self-administered haircut. She does her best.

Diana (Nicole Hiltz)

An attractive woman who hits on Xander at a bar after he breaks up with Anya. Xander, ever self-defeating, turns her down.

Diego/Marvin

A Sunset Clubber who appears in "Lie to Me" as a nitwit vampire worshipper whose seriousness is further undermined by his outfits, which Buffy calls dorky and Ford says make him look like a "ninny."

Duncan (Nathan Burgess)

A crooked Sunnydale cop who attempted to capitalize on Sunnydale's evacuation in the face of the First.

Deputy Mayor Allan Finch (Jack Plotnick)

No relation (that we know of) to Atticus Jem, and Scout, Allan Finch is, as the Shins say, "barely a vapor" (his favorite comic strip is "Cathy"), but he has hitched his wagon to a very dark star (Mayor Wilkins), and, ironically enough, it is only when his conscience apparently compels him to unhitch and narc on his boss that he finally pays the price, as he is staked to death when Faith mistakes him for a vampire. His death is a hugely significant development in the arc of season three, rupturing Faith's relationship with the Scoobies, who, as a general rule, don't believe in staking humans.

Mrs. Finkle (Bonita Friedericy)

Cordelia's overlord at April Fool's, a Sunnydale clothing store, Mrs. Finkle is, by all indications, a stern and disapproving person, and "so has it in" for Cordelia, according to another salesgirl. Beyond that we neither know nor care much about her.

Samantha Finn (Ivana Milicevic)

Demon hunting wife of Riley Finn. Sam accompanies Riley on his return to Sunnydale. She's beautiful, accomplished, highly competent, and nice, so Buffy wants to hate her but can't, instead feeling (we assume) a deep, deep sense of pity.

Billy "Ford" Fordham (Jason Behr)

Buffy's elementary school crush back in L.A., Ford pops up unexpectedly, claiming that his dad has been transferred to Sunnydale in "Lie to Me," which is exactly what he's doing to Buffy (though it is actually Buffy who speaks the words of the episode title, after asking Giles if life ever gets easy). In reality, Ford has been diagnosed with brain cancer and given six months to live, so is determined to become a vampire, dealing with the devil (Spike, really) to hand over Buffy in exchange for eternal undeadness. Come on, Ford, surely you've a better idea? Ford does indeed deliver Buffy to Spike and remains bitter and unrepentant to the end, though of course Buffy escapes, and saves a whole bunch of Ford's fellow cult members in the process. Ford is rewarded for his treachery by getting his wish: he becomes a vampire, but is staked rising from the grave by Buffy. The cemetery scene is one of the great ones, especially if you're into the whole Buffy-Giles father-daughter thing: "Nothing's ever simple anymore," Buffy says. "I'm constantly trying to work it out—who to love, or hate, who to trust. And it's just like the more I know, the more confused I get."

Replies the G-man: "I believe that's called growing up."

Frank (Garrett Brawith)

Frank was a bully who liked to pick on Warren Mears—so, a bully with good taste—who is assaulted and nearly killed by Warren during the Trio's reign of terror.

Frank (Daniel Hagen)

Social worker Doris Kroeger's nonplussed supervisor. Bears a passing resemblance to Giles.

Gina (Marion Calvert)

An aged employee of the Doublemeat Palace, and possible glimpse of a grim future for Buffy.

Anthony Harris (Michael Harney; Casey Sander)

A drunken, unemployed, abusive bigot, Xander's dad represented all of Xander's fears for his own future and prompted the younger Harris to call off his wedding, for fear his marriage would deteriorate like that of his parents'.

Carol Harris (Jan Hoag)

Xander's zaftig, much-married cousin, who took a fancy to Krelvin, the demon, at Xander's nuptials. Apparently at least somewhat tolerant and open-minded, Carol is one of Xander's less objectionable relations.

Jessica Harris (Lee Garlington)

Xander's abused, neurotic, unhappy mother. Poor cook. Poor lady.

Rory Harris (Steve Gilborn)

Xander's uncle. A bigoted jerk like his brother, Rory distinguishes himself with his love for inappropriately young girls, a sophomorically cruel sense of humor, and his devotion to taxidermy. First-class family, those Harrises.

Inga (Chanie Costello) and Ilsa (Julie Costello)

Twin Nordic bombshells who shared the magically augmented Jonathan Levinson's mansion and . . . *assisted* him in some undefined manner. *Ahem.*

Dr. Isaacs (William Ford)

A physician attending to Joyce Summers. Bedside manner like a toaster oven.

Jordy + Maureen + Ken

The reason Oz is a werewolf. Toddler Jordy, Oz's mentioned-but-never-seen cousin, is himself a werewolf, who, in human form, takes a nip out of Oz while the latter is tickling him. Jordy's mom, Maureen, also never seen, is aware of her son's identity issues and confirms them to Oz. Jordy's dad, also never seen: Ken.

Mrs. Kalish (P. B. Hutton)

Anyone ever wonder what happened to real-estate values in Sunnydale once the Summers moved in at 1630 Revello Drive? The good news is Mrs. Kalish, Buffy's neighbor, never has to worry about that again. The bad news is she's dead, smote by Order of Taraka assassin Norman Pfister, who was simply looking for a comfy place to pass the time while waiting for his real-target, Buffy, to come home.

Kaltenbach (John O'Leary)

Bait and switch! Kaltenbach was an eccentric old recluse who gave people the creeps—a former toy designer, he apparently made a terrible "mistake" and lost his job, though he maintains a curiously intense reverence for children. Skeeze Factor: ten out of ten, but it transpires he is a sincere, benign sweetheart, so it kind of sucks when teen dream vampire Justin kills him.

Dr. Aaron Kriegel (Randy Thompson)

Dr. Kriegel treated Joyce Summers, mercifully allowing her to convalesce at home and later reassuring Buffy that Joyce's death was likely quick and painless.

Doris Kroeger (Susan Ruttan)

A social worker assigned to check in on Dawn, Ms. Kroeger is horrified by the apparent chaos and unsavory atmosphere of the Summers home and threatens to remove Dawn to foster care. Buffy, temporarily invisible courtesy of the Trio, addresses the problem by pranking the poor woman at work, making her seem mentally unstable and thus removed from the Summers case. It's a funny sequence, but the poor woman was just trying to do her job.

Ms. Lefcourt (Joy Demichelle Moore)

A teacher at Dawn's middle school, Ms. Lefcourt was mildly flummoxed by the overly literal Buffybot at a parent-teacher conference. She seems pretty on the ball, and again Dawn's educational experience looks a lot more pleasant than Buffy's ever was.

Linda (Lisa Jay)

A human victim of Spike's, she was seduced and killed while Spike was under the influence of the First.

Lisa (Rae'ven Larrymore Kelly)

Dawn's middle school pal. Lisa seems supportive and invested in Dawn's happiness, lending her a sympathetic ear and rooting her on as she flirts with Kevin Berman. Dawn has a lot to be angsty about, but she evidently has at least one cool friend, which is not bad for junior high.

Beth Maclay (Amy Adams)

Tara's sour, reactionary cousin Beth resents her witchy relation, threatening to reveal the (untrue) secret of Tara's half-demon nature and reading her the riot act when she refuses to return home to a life of servitude and isolation. This unpleasant young lady is portrayed by none other than future multiple Academy Award nominee Amy Adams, who here gives a real master class in hatefulness.

Donny Maclay (Kevin Rankin)

Tara's foul-tempered, ill-mannered, creepy backwoods brother, and further evidence that the Maclay clan (excluding Tara) sucks rocks.

Mr. Maclay (Steve Rankin)

Tara's disapproving, taciturn dad is a real piece of work: he convinced both his late wife and daughter that they were demons, all the better to dominate and control them . . . a canny metaphor for the ways in which psychological abuse is internalized and self-sustaining.

Mothers Opposed to the Occult (MOO)

Joyce Summers–founded civic organization dedicated to avenging the deaths of two young children discovered in a playground one night and believed to have been slaughtered by witches. The irony, however, is that the MOO-ers are themselves unknowingly acting as agents of an occult force, that being the demon who disguised himself as the youths in order to create an atmosphere of paranoia and persecution. Bad MOOS!

Munroe (Justin Shilton)

A corrupt Sunnydale police officer (there are Sunnydale police officers?!) who tried and failed to kill Faith during the evacuation of Sunnydale. His punishment was a severe beating from same.

Bob Munroe (Brian Reddy)

Sunnydale Police Chief Bob Munroe redefines the term "rogue cop," since it doesn't usually involve working in cahoots with a one hundred-plus-year-old mayor on the precipice of becoming a full-fledged demon. Munroe appears in just a couple of second-season episodes, both times to huddle with Principal Snyder, possibly the only equally odious *human* in town, in the aftermath of some supernatural catastrophe at Sunnydale High, clearly establishing that he (and Snyder) is cognizant of the Hellmouth, and threatening to tattle on the pygmy principal to the mayor if he doesn't come up with some sort of plausible deniability.

Nancy (Kaarina Aufranc)

Nancy, frustrated with her "spineless" boyfriend, gets vengeance demon Anya's attention, who turns said boyfriend into a ravenous, wormlike Sluggoth Demon. The demon eats Nancy's dog, but she seems consoled by a romantic interest in Xander—until various Scooby antics wig her right out of contention. Poor Xander.

Phillip Newton (Glenn Morshower)

Doomed Cassie Newton's belligerent, alcoholic father—who, in a Whedon universe of bad dads, surprisingly conveys real love and concern for his daughter.

Billy Palmer (Jeremy Foley)

In "Nightmares," twelve-year-old Billy Palmer is beaten into a coma by a psycho little league coach who blames him for a loss. That in and of itself is horrific enough, but this being the Hellmouth, Billy's astral projection crosses over from the nightmare world in which Billy is trapped into the real world, hauling the nightmare world along with him, so that everyone's worst fears are realized: Buffy's rejected by her dad, attacked by the Master, becomes a vampire; Giles can't read; Willow has to perform an opera; Xander is attacked by a clown, etc. And Cordy? Bad hair day.

Pat (Nancy Lenehan)

Friendship has benefits, though if it's with one of the Summers women you might want to be careful. Pat (last name unknown) is an insufferably friendly woman who provides great solace to book-club mate Joyce Summers during Buffy's sojourn to L.A. at the end of season two/beginning of season three. She's rewarded for this kindness by being killed by zombies, and turning into a zombie herself, and finally being killed again, this time as a zombie by Buffy, who shoves a shovel into her eyes.

Janice Penshaw (Amber Tamblyn)

Dawn's pal and partner in parental subterfuge, Janice embarks on an outing with Dawn and (unbeknownst to them) some groovy teen vampire dudes while the girls are ostensibly staying over at each other's houses. Janice gets bitten, but survives and goes on to share some traveling pants, write odd poetry, and hook up with David Cross.

Doug Perren (Jack McGee)

Is there a better name for an archeologist than Doug? In the season-two two-part finale, Perren, curator at the Sunnydale Museum of Natural History, seeks Giles's assistance after construction workers uncover an obelisk that turns out to be the remains of Acathla, a vicious demon who turned to stone when his heart was pierced by a knight's sword. Angelus has big plans for Acathla, which don't involve Perren, so he is murdered by Drusilla. For whatever it's worth, the death of a curator ranks among our least favorite storylines.

Rack (Jeff Kober)

Skeezy magic pusher and powerful warlock (and, per Clem, pedophile) who ran a mystically concealed meeting space for magic junkies. Amy introduces Willow to Rack, who creepily calls her "Strawberry," psychically violates her mind, and gets her wasted on potent magic, leading to her and Dawn's near demise. When Dark Willow manifests after Tara's murder, she visits Rack, paying him back (and then some) for his ministrations: she drains him of his magic and kills him.

Ethan Rayne (Robin Sachs)

A colleague of Giles from his Ripper days, the louche, shifty Ethan Rayne is a chaos-worshipping warlock with a sick sense of humor and lousy timing. He periodically pops up in Sunnydale to bedevil Giles, turning him into a demon one day, regressing all of Sunnydale's adult population to mental adolescence another. Ethan's the charming rogue type, with the emphasis on "rogue"; he's more mischief-maker than outright villain, though his disregard for everything save himself inevitably leads to dangerous consequences.

Richard (Ryan Browning)

A friend of Xander's from the construction crew, Richard is among the guests magically prevented from leaving the Summers home by Dawn's wish to Halfrek. A nice-looking, chill dude, Richard was intended as a setup for Buffy but ends up getting stabbed by a demon, which is the "dating Buffy Summers" experience in a nutshell.

Manny Rocha (Brent Hinkley)

Buffy's extremely weird—but ultimately harmless—manager at the Doublemeat Palace. A true corporate drone, Manny seems to live only for his job, and resolutely refuses to discuss the proprietary meat process.

Ronnie (Jack Sundmacher)

Nancy's boyfriend-turned-worm-monster. No prize, per Nancy, but we flinch when Spike impales him through the shoulder mid-transformation back to naked human.

Sheila Rosenberg (Jordan Baker)

Willow's mom, though, from all indications, clearly not a role she has any aptitude for, especially since she attempts to burn her daughter at the stake for being a witch. True, she *was* under the influence of a demon at the time, but this is the same woman who goes six months before recognizing that her daughter got a haircut and can't be bothered to accurately remember the correct name of her daughter's best friend, whom she consistently identifies as Bunny rather than Buffy. Much later on, in season seven, we learn from Willow that her mom was "proud" of her for being gay, like it was some kind of achievement, but didn't even bother to get to know Tara—Lord only knows how she would have messed up her name. Sheila seems to embody the worst traits of academia, with an overdeveloped cerebrum and underdeveloped common sense, and she had recently co-authored a paper on the rise of mysticism among adolescents, so the shoe seems to fit. She is thoroughly incapable of making a meaningful emotional connection to anyone, most of all her teenage daughter, who at one point complains that "the last time we had a conversation over three minutes it was about the patriarchal bias of the *Mister Rogers* show." Not such a beautiful day in the neighborhood, is it?

Lorraine Ross (Kirsten Nelson)

Manny's successor as manager of the Doublemeat Palace. Buffy plays hardball with Lorraine, threatening to expose their "meat process" (it's veggies!) unless Lorraine hires her back after her dismissal for trashing the place. Lorraine predicts a bright future for Buffy at the DP, which suggests she's kind of an idiot.

Rusty (Jack Jozefson)

Museum guard, victim of Trio's freeze ray. A cool customer (sorry).

Ryan (Jordan Belfi) and Simon (Adam Weiner)

A couple of overly aggressive bros who won't take no for an answer from Amy and Willow at The Bronze. The witches strip the boys to their skivvies and set them go-go dancing in suspended cages for the delectation of the crowd.

Mr. Savitsky (Michael Merton)

Buffy could face down the direst supernatural threats to humanity—but up against more quotidian adversaries, such as loan officer Mr. Savitsky, she often fell short. No collateral, no loan. Punch your way out of *that* one, Slayer.

Katrina Silber (Amelinda Embry)

Warren Mears's lovely, bright, creative human girlfriend (as opposed to his android sex toy, April). Katrina dumps the creep after discovering his perv-bot, and suffers further humiliation when Warren attempts to "win her back" with a brain-controlling "Cerebral Dampener" intended to render the girl a pliant sex slave for him and his friends, eventually killing poor Katrina with a blow to the head when she defies him. Yeah . . . Warren sucks.

Detective Paul Stein (James G. MacDonald)

Not much to say about the good detective, except he makes multiple appearances during the high school years and displays no evidence of being "in on the fix," unlike his boss man, SPD honcho Bob Munroe. The Stein way is the right way.

Principal Stevens (Anne Betancourt)

Dawn's middle school principal, who informs Buffy of Dawn's truancy. Seems pretty nice—again, this middle school is surprisingly un-hellish, particularly considering its location.

Hank Summers (Dean Butler)

Summers is not coming: Buffy's estranged dad, merely neglectful at first but eventually a deadbeat who moves to Spain with his secretary, under some arrangement that makes it impossible for his daughter/daughters (depending on how you calculate his relationship to Dawn) to reach him when Joyce Summers passes away. Hank appears in just four episodes, thrice in dreams or hallucinations, though presumably he would have appeared in a fifth if he hadn't bailed on Buffy on her eighteenth birthday, when he was supposed to take her to an ice show, a father-daughter tradition. In a 2003 interview with the *New York Times*, Joss Whedon said, "It's true that Buffy's father started out as just a divorced dad and then turned into this sort of 'evil pariah' figure of not even bothering to show up, and that was simply because we had a father figure in Giles." Whedon added that he was more interested in the "created" family than the biological one, and beyond that there were certain practical implications, meaning that if Hank Summers had been featured more prominently Whedon would have had to invent a subplot for him, and he really didn't feel like it.

Tarantula (Rebecca Jackson)

Spike took this skanky goth chick to Xander and Anya's wedding in a bid to make Buffy jealous. As if.

Gary Tilson (T. Ferguson)

The one sort of normal employee at the Doublemeat Palace, counterman Gary was consumed by the Wig Lady. Fast food is a rough gig.

Tito (John Jabaley)

The world needs the Slayer. It also needs plumbers, like Xander's acquaintance Tito. After the Summers home's basement floods, Tito assesses the damage and makes a grim financial prognosis, providing Buffy with another real-world problem seemingly more insurmountable than averting the apocalypse.

Tony (Paul Gutrecht)

Xander's (and briefly Buffy's) boss at the construction site. Initially dismissive of and belittling toward Buffy on the basis of her gender, he comes around to respect her abilities, but has to fire her anyway after a demon attack causes severe damage. Whaddayagonnado?

Vince (Noel Albert Guglielmi); Marco (Enrique Almeida); Ron (Derrick McMillon)

Buffy's co-workers on her construction crew who resented her superhumanly quick pace while performing physical labor, which made them look bad by comparison. Damn it, Patriarchy!

Doctor Weirick (James Stephens)

Zookeeper, zookeeper, what do you see? I see a pack of hyenas, devouring me. Weirdo Weirick was a primal (animal worshipper), craving the power of the demonic hyenas in "The Pack," and crazy enough to do whatever it takes (like slicing Willow's throat) to get it. Too bad for him then that Buffy tosses him into the pit of hyenas. Who's laughing now?

The White Hats

Alt-reality version of the Scoobies, the White Hats appear in the season-three episode "The Wish," in which Anya grants Cordelia's wish that Buffy Summers never set foot in Sunnydale. This creates a dystopian parallel universe, commonly referenced as the Wishverse, where vamps rule, led by the Master, and Willow and Xander unleash their dark, toothy side. Still fighting the good fight are the White Hats: Giles, Oz, Larry Blaisdell (of all people), and a girl named Nancy (Mariah O'Brien), but without the Slayer they are essentially powerless against the armies of the night.

Dr. Wilkinson (Juanita Jennings)

A by-the-books medicine woman at Sunnydale Memorial (also known as Sunnydale General Hospital), Wilkinson shows up in "Killed by Death," fighting with Dr. Backer over his unorthodox practices and sic'ing security guards on an impaired Buffy as she tries to wander around the hospital in search of der Kindestod. A hard-ass, but not a monster.

Olivia Williams (Phina Oruche)

This strikingly gorgeous compatriot of Giles from his "Ripper" days visits the librarian in Sunnydale for a romantic liaison, to the shock and horror of the Scoobies (we just think it's nice to see the untethered Giles catch a break; she is really something). She is present for the incursion of the Gentlemen, which apparently sours her on Sunnydale, go figure. Olivia is the strongest evidence yet that Giles is secretly devastatingly cool. Very secretly.

Willy the Snitch (Saverio Guerra)

Willy makes an appalling first impression, selling out Angel to Drusilla and Spike and encouraging Buffy and Kendra to pose nude for "art photographs" (Whedon's idea), and it's impossible to dispute Buffy's characterization of him as a "double-dealing snitch," but over time he becomes a likable enough guy, even helping the Scoobies with free information, likely because he's tired of being smacked around. Willy calls it an "experience of the spiritual variety," and to commemorate the conversion he changes the name of his establishment—long a favorite dive of demons—from Willy's Bar to the more upscale-sounding Willy's Place, though still catering to demons, which accounts for the addition of a deep fryer. As he explains to Buffy: "These demons just go crazy for chicken fingers."

Professor Lester Worth (Hal Robinson)

A little information can be a dangerous thing, which is the unfortunate lesson learned by this visiting professor of geology in season three's "Graduation Day, Part 1" when he is stabbed to death by Faith, acting as an emissary for the mayor, who's threatened by Worth's discovery of a huge carcass during the excavation of a lava bed near a dormant volcano in Kauai. Though Worth posits that it belongs to some heretofore unknown breed of dinosaur, Giles and Wesley deduce that it was the same variety of demon into which the mayor is planning to transform. Thus, while the mayor is impervious to harm as a human, he becomes mortal once he ascends—information that Hizzoner clearly feels is worth Worth's life.

1630 Revello Drive

The Summers manse. A cozy suburban Craftsman house, Buffy's home is a key setting in the series and the location of many significant events, including Joyce's tragic death. After the destruction of The Magic Box, the house becomes the Scoobies' tactical HQ, garrisoning the Potentials during the conflict with the First Evil. Bad plumbing.

The Bronze

Every show about teenagers seems to require a hangout spot: on *BTVS*, it's The Bronze, an industrial-chic dance club that hosted innumerable indistinguishable shoegazer acts and served as a locus for romantic shenanigans and vampire attacks. Olaf, the troll, wrecked the interior with his hammer, leading to an uptick in prices when the club reopened, as its insurance didn't cover Act of Troll.

Summers Residence: The Summers sisters (Michelle Trachtenberg, Sarah Michelle Gellar), at home at 1630 Revello Drive.

Where the Action Is: Sunnydale's one hot spot, The Bronze.

The Factory

An abandoned industrial plant outside Sunnydale that the Master used as a base of operations. Unlucky place: Cordelia is impaled there, and Angel is tortured. Giles burns the place down with a flaming baseball bat. Badass.

Kingman's Bluff

Sunnydale landmark where, over the life of the series, two key events happen: In season three's "Amends," Angel, under relentless torment by the First Evil, goes to the bluff on Christmas Eve to await the sunrise, ready to die, though Buffy ultimately talks him out of it. In "Grave," the season-six finale, Dark Willow, seeking to end all life on Earth, heads to the bluff to raise the satanic Temple of Proserpexa, which had been swallowed up by an earthquake six years earlier.

Magic Shops

Do you believe in magic? If you live above the Hellmouth, why wouldn't you? Magic shops are prominent on *Buffy*, including, early on, Dragon's Cove, where Jenny Calendar shops for an Orb of Thesulah, needed to restore Angel's soul in season two. The owner of that shop, never identified by name, is murdered soon after by Drusilla, furious at the prices (kidding; she's punishing him for assisting Jenny). Uncle Bob's Magic Cabinet is another local "boogedy-boogedy store" (Angelus-speak), which eventually becomes The Magic Box, owned and operated first by Giles and then, once he returns to England, Anya, and succeeds the Sunnydale High Library as Scooby HQ ("NORAD, when we're at DEFCON 1," per Xander), until it's decimated by Dark Willow in season six, highlighting just how dangerous a place magic shops can be in Sunnydale.

Shadow Valley Vineyards

Sunnydale-adjacent winery where the scythe was hidden and the First Evil and Caleb hung out.

Spike's Crypt

William the Bloody's crib, conveniently located in the Sunnydale cemetery. Quite austere when Spike establishes residence, the place spruces up considerably during his stay; he eventually manages to get cable TV down there, somehow. When he leaves for Africa, Spike bequeaths his lair to the friendly demon Clem.

Sunset Club

In "Lie to Me," this term refers to both a location—a Goth-themed nightclub in Sunnydale—and a cult of teenagers (or, as Buffy prefers, morons) who worship vampires as exalted beings known as "The Lonely Ones" and are seeking to be "changed" themselves so that they can "ascend to a new level of consciousness," according to Chanterelle, a charter member. Though Billy "Ford" Fordham hangs with the Sunset Clubbers, he is not really one of them, as he himself recognizes when he tells Buffy that his own quest for immortality is motivated by his terminal brain cancer, while the others—whom he is knowingly leading to slaughter—are seeking deliverance from their "lonely, miserable, or bored" existence.

Weatherly Park

Local park popular with the homeless crowd, but also with a vampire known as Claw Guy, who likes to go around shredding them.

8

Lots of Schools Aren't on the Hellmouth

Sunnydale High

Formatia trans sicere educatorum: Enter all ye who seek knowledge.
—*sign posted at entrance of Sunnydale High School*

Season I

Aphrodesia (Amy Chance) + Aura (Persia White)

Cordettes (Cordelia groupies) Aphrodesia and Aura are the unfortunate lassies who, in the series premiere, discover Chris Boal's body in Aura's Sunnydale High gym locker, signifying the beginning of Buffy's realization that she may have fled the City of Angels, but only to land in hell.

Jesse McNally (Eric Balfour)

Xander's buddy appears in just the two-part series premiere, which is probably a blessing, because how much humiliation and suffering can one guy stand? The thing about Jesse is he struts around like a peacock—he even has the courage to ask Cordelia to dance, which, surprise, doesn't end so well. "With *you*?" she says. Joss Whedon calls this the "infamous Jesse asks Cordelia to dance scene," adding, "This is one of the few things that is actually based verbatim on something that happened to me, one of the only times I ever asked a girl to dance in high school, and her reply was, 'With *you*?' I didn't actually say anything after that, the way Jesse does. I just sort of slunk off for four years." Jesse eventually is sired by Darla, and winds up digging the vamp scene: "Jesse was an excruciating loser who couldn't get a date with anyone in the sighted community," he tells Xander, who winds up dusting him. Not a bad point. In real life Eric Balfour was married to actress Moon Bloodgood, which *is* pretty cool. On his DVD commentary, Whedon said he wanted to put Balfour in the opening credits for the premiere, to shake the audience up, but the notion of producing two credit sequences ultimately seemed cost prohibitive and time consuming.

Principal Robert Flutie (Ken Lerner)

As high school functionaries go, Principal Robert ("All the kids here are free to call me Bob . . . but they don't") Flutie isn't a bad guy, unless you count his deplorable taste in sports coats, and even then doesn't exactly deserve the tragic fate that befalls him: being devoured alive by a pack of students possessed by demonic hyenas in the sixth episode of season one ("The Pack"). Flutie *means* well: he offers Buffy a clean slate upon her arrival at Sunnydale,

Study Buddies: Willow (Alyson Hannigan) and Buffy (Sarah Michelle Gellar) take a break from slaying to focus on homework, or maybe their love lives?   *WB/20th Century Fox/Photofest*

and seems sincere, though he has either deep denial issues or no clue at all about modern teens and the supernatural weirdness unfolding around him (he hasn't met a problem that can't be solved by a boost in either school spirit or detention—until those hyenas, that is). In the twenty-minute pilot presentation Whedon made for the WB, Flutie was portrayed by Stephen Tobolowsky, who says he was under contract with ABC and thus unable to continue with the role, whether Whedon wanted him or not.

Cordettes

Sounds like a sixties girl group, but in reality is something far more nefarious: Cordelia's high school sycophants, whom Angel compares (on *Angel*) to the Soviet secret police "if they cared a lot about shoes." Additional card-carrying members include Harmony, Gwen, Aura, and Aphrodesia.

Amy Madison (Elizabeth Anne Allen)

Amy has mommy issues, which, understandable, given that Mommy is a witch (literally), which is bad, but also a faded star cheerleader, which is worse. Catherine Madison (Robin Riker), once anointed Catherine the Great for her superlative rah-rah skills, can't quite accept the reality that her pompom-and-spankies days are kaput, so switches bods with daughter Amy (six years before Jamie Lee Curtis and Lindsay Lohan did likewise in *Freaky Friday*) and endeavors to recapture her glory days, which she sort of does, just not in the way she intended (she winds up trapped in the high school trophy case when Buffy redirects one of her spells right back atcha). Amy pops in and out of *Buffy* over the seasons, though sometimes as a rat, which she transforms herself into during the third-season episode "Gingerbread" to avoid being burned at the stake by a fanatical community group of witch hunters captained by Joyce Summers (under the influence of a demon), which presents two problems: one, she neglects to save Buffy and Willow, also tied to stakes, and two, she has no way to turn herself back, and it is not until the sixth season that Willow is able to figure out how to do it, during which time Amy, the rat, lives in a cage in Willow's room. This is a ramification of the fact that Amy and Willow were once, in junior high, close friends, with Amy frequently seeking refuge at the Rosenbergs (which shows you how bad things were over at the Madisons) when her mom, a former homecoming queen who had been deserted by Amy's dad for a woman identified only as "Ms. Trailer Trash," went on one of her "Nazi" binges, padlocking the fridge and subsisting on nothing but broth if she gained even a pound. Amy is one of those characters who just never seems to go away for good, because she shows up again in season seven, inflicting a "standard penance malediction" (translation: hex) on Willow, so that she looked and sounded like the despicable Warren Mears, just because she was jealous of her. What a rat.

Mr. Pole (Jim Dougan)

Irritable driver's-ed teacher who—surprisingly, given the death rate among his colleagues—appears to survive his years at Sunnydale High. In "The Witch," he has the unfortunate experience of instructing Cordelia, whom he clearly considers a danger to herself and everyone else on the road.

John Lee Walker (Nathan Anderson)

We all have our demons, and John Lee's is he's just been demoted to second string on the Sunnydale High football squad, which for a teen jock is only marginally preferable to being exposed as a virgin. While not thoroughly uninteresting, this would have no relevance to our purposes if not for the fact that John Lee views this embarrassment as sufficient cause for rejecting the advances of Cordelia, who is endeavoring to make Xander jealous post-breakup, since Xander is considered even more pathetic than John Lee. Stand-up punk that he is, however, John Lee is more than willing to duck into a closet or somewhere else private with Cordelia to address certain hormonal needs. So what we have here is this: a high school girl who just caught her boyfriend cheating being rebuffed by a member of the football team who has just been bumped off the first unit but is still willing to have sex with her in private because he doesn't want to be seen as a bigger loser than the boyfriend, who meanwhile is drowning in guilt over his indiscretion. Wow, and we thought slaying vampires was hard.

Natalie French (Jean Speegle Howard)

Kindly old retired Sunnydale High biology teacher whose identity is snatched by the She-Mantis in "Teacher's Pet."

Dr. Stephen Gregory (William Monaghan)

"One of the only teachers that doesn't think Buffy's a felon," according to Willow, Dr. Gregory is the science prof who encourages Buffy to demand more from herself in the classroom, and winds up a headless corpse in the high school fridge (found by Cordelia, of course) for his kindness, courtesy of the buggy Miss French.

Blayne Mall (Price Jackson)

Blayne endures excruciating humiliation in "Teacher's Pet," and by that we mean not that he is kidnapped and assaulted by the She-Mantis Miss French, but rather that he is exposed as a virgin, despite frequent and loud protestations to the contrary. High school is hard.

Owen Thurman (Christopher Wiehl)

Owen has the distinction of being Buffy's first romantic interest in the TV series if you exclude Angel, who at this point is, you know, a little hard to figure. In "Never Kill a Boy on the First Date," Owen—described as "solitary" and "mysterious" and capable of brooding for forty minutes straight (Willow's clocked him)—gets a taste of danger when inadvertently thrust into the Scooby world of vampire slaying, and likes it a little too much for the comfort of Buffy, who doesn't want his death on her hands. Too much risk, too little reward.

The Pack (Heidi Barrie/Kyle DuFours/Tor Hauer/Rhonda Kelley)

In the real world a disastrous field trip is when a child comes down with a stomach bug or momentarily wanders off; on *Buffy* it's when a pack of students is possessed by the spirit of demonic hyenas at the zoo and winds up devouring (literally) both the school's razorback mascot and the principal, which is exactly what happens in season one's "The Pack." The students are Heidi Barrie (Jennifer Sky), Kyle DuFours (Eion Bailey), Tor Hauer (Brian Gross), and Rhonda Kelley (Michael McCraine), four bullies who sneak into a quarantined hyena exhibit and plan to toss a fifth, Lance Lincoln (Jeff Maynard), into the pit, and Xander, who follows them in with the best of intentions, to rescue Lance, but winds up getting ensnared by the magic.

Coach Herrold (Gregory White)

Gym teacher aroused by dodge ball, especially when played by a pack of bullies who have been possessed by hyenas and are tormenting a poor, helpless classmate like Lance Lincoln, as in "The Pack." Probably loves the smell of napalm in the morning.

Jenny Calendar/Janna Kalderash (Robia LaMorte)

Sure, she calls herself Jenny Calendar, computer science teacher at Sunnydale High, but she's still Janna from the block, from Clan Kalderash, Romanian gypsies who cursed Angelus with a soul in 1898 after he tortured, drained, and killed a cherished young member of the tribe. Ninety-nine years later Janna shows up undercover in Sunnydale, dispatched by the Kalderash elders to watch over Angel and do everything in her Romani power to ensure that he continues to suffer for his multitudinous sins as the legendarily cruel Angelus, who roamed the world for over a hundred years inflicting death and destruction everywhere he went. So how's that go? Not great, considering that Jenny winds up dead, her neck snapped—by a resurgent Angelus—late one night in the halls of Sunnydale High. Still, let's be fair: the Kalderash curse included one of the most lopsided loopholes in the history of gypsy-demon bargaining, which was hardly Jenny's fault: if Angel experiences even a moment of true bliss, he loses his soul and resorts to Angelus (so: have sex, don't worry, be happy; seems like a gimme to us). Angelus's resurrection—the driving narrative of the second half of season two—is triggered one dark and stormy night when he and Buffy finally consummate their tortured relationship, and pretty clearly falls into the "no redeeming value whatsoever" category for anyone, though it is especially harsh on Giles, who by this time has become Jenny's beau, and whose torment is magnified by the way in which he learns of her demise: Angel tricks him into believing Jenny is waiting for him at home, in bed, which technically she is, except she's dead.

Jenny's passing wasn't easy on us, either: true, she alienated the Scoobies by keeping her real identity a secret, but she was feisty and unpredictable, a coquettish computer geek who patronized both Burning Man and monster-truck shows, relished ribbing Giles about his Neo-Luddism, and oozed sexual charisma. If it makes you feel any better, writer/producer Marti Noxon didn't suffer Jenny's death at the hands of Angel's gladly either; she told *Cinefantastique* in 1999 that when Whedon broke the news, "I stood up and said, 'No! You can't do that to us!'" Whedon was actually pleased by her response—how can we find a boss like that?—because that was exactly the powerful, emotional reaction he was looking for. On his DVD commentary for the episode, Whedon says, "The death of Jenny Calendar was another very specifically placed pivotal moment in the show. We needed to kill somebody because we needed to tell the audience that not everything is safe, that not everyone is safe, that we are willing to take a character who's interesting and integral and get rid of them, to show that death is final and death is scary." Um, already knew that?

Whedon adds that there was considerable discussion in the writers' room over whether Angel should kill her in his human face or his vamp face, before ultimately deciding on the latter, "because we thought it would just be too disturbing if he had his human face on, and that nobody would ever want to see that face kissing Buffy again." Still, the fact that it was Angelus who killed her—rather than Drusilla, who was sidekicking on the mission to stop Jenny from restoring Angel's soul—was necessary "to show that Angel isn't just pretending to be evil," per Whedon. "He's not just a little bit evil. He's not grouchy. He's, you know, he is now her enemy." Another interesting fact about Jenny (originally named Nicki, changed to avoid on-set confusion with actor Nicholas Brendon, who portrayed Xander) that emerges in conversations with the writers: early on, she wasn't intended to be a gypsy or to have any connection at all to Angel's curse, but as the story developed, the writers began to see exciting opportunities in taking the narrative in this direction. "A lot of time, as with gypsy Jenny, we'd go, 'Ooh, wouldn't this be cool? Let's do it,'" Noxon said. Whedon echoes her in his DVD commentary on "Innocence," explaining the writing team's belief that Jenny's transformation to gypsy "would be neat and interesting and solve a lot of problems." He calls a potent confrontation between Jenny and her uncle Enyos (Vincent Schiavelli) in that episode, in which Enyos (also later killed by Angelus) explains the curse and says, "It is not justice we serve; it is vengeance," one of his prouder moments on the show, "because I had to take a lot of disparate elements that just didn't work." He recalls solving the problem while taking a solitary walk along the Santa Monica Pier, and coming up with a single phrase—"Vengeance is a living thing"—that cracked the conundrum, calling it a "quiet little accomplishment, but an important one." He elaborates, "It was the idea of vengeance as a living thing, the idea that they serve a kind of arbitrary god that was itself irrational, completely justified the idea that nothing we had written before actually connected that way." Jenny was portrayed by Robia LaMorte, once a dancer for the musician Prince, who became a born-again Christian, reportedly after an encounter with a Christian biker gang.

David Kirby + Fritz Siegel (Chad Lindberg and Jamison Ryan)

"Off-the-charts-smart" (per Buffy) Dave is a tragic figure, or would be if anyone cared: under the sway of the demon Moloch the Corrupter, who has morphed into virtual villain Malcolm, he tricks Buffy into visiting the girl's locker room, where fellow computer nerd Fritz flubs a plot to electrocute her. Dave's conscience ultimately prevails, so Moloch/Malcolm orders Fritz to kill him, which he does. Their surnames, presumably, are a hat tip to comic book icons Jerry Siegel (co-creator of Superman) and Jack Kirby (co-creator of Captain America, Thor, and X-Men), given the geek proclivities of Team Whedon.

Principal R. Snyder (Armin Shimerman)

He's got little hands, little eyes, he walks around tellin' great big lies. He is, in short, a short person. Snyder arrives at Sunnydale with his Napoleon complex fully developed in the ninth episode of season one ("The Puppet Show"), following the grisly murder of his immediate predecessor, Principal Flutie, devoured by a pack of demon-hyena-possessed students, and lasts through the end of season three, when consumed by the purebred ginormous snake demon Olvikan, who until minutes earlier had been Mayor Richard Wilkins III, with whom Snyder was conspiring to cover up the many bizarre and sinister events transpiring at Sunnydale High School. While the reasons for this are never made completely clear, we're pretty sure Snyder had no clue what the mayor was really up to, and was just a clucking poltroon intimidated by a powerful politician (years ago, Shimerman told *Buffy Magazine* that, at one point, he asked Joss Whedon what his conspiracy with the mayor and top-level Sunnydale law-enforcement officials was all about, and Whedon told him he didn't know). Viewers eyewitness only one in-person interaction between Snyder and the mayor (not including the time Wilkins eats him, of course), in "Graduation Day, Part 1," which clearly illustrates the mayor's dominance and suggests both the principal's basic cluelessness and the facility with which he is able to lie to himself: "You've done a great job here," Wilkins tells him. "I know things are, um, well, different here in Sunnydale. We've both seen all sorts of things. What's important is that we keep it under control, and that's what you've done."

"I believe in order," Snyder responds.

"Sunnydale owes you a debt," Wilkins says. "It will be repaid."

You betcha.

That Snyder is aware at least of his own pusillanimity is evidenced by the manner in which he takes his self-hatred out on everyone who is powerless against him, especially students. "Kids," he tells Giles soon after arriving, "I don't like them." He especially doesn't like one kid: Buffy Summers, whom he loathes from the day of his arrival until the day he dies, and even expels once, at the end of season two, when she is wanted in connection with Kendra Young's murder and bolts from police custody in order to, you know, save the world. Even after Buffy is cleared of the murder, Snyder resists letting her back in, advising her to apply for a job with Hot Dog on a Stick instead,

Little Little Man: Principal Snyder (Armin Shimerman)—first initial "R," full name never revealed—encouraged students to think of him as their "judge, jury, and executioner." We can think of another word for him.

infuriating both Joyce (she calls him a "nasty, little, horrid, bigoted rodent man") and Giles (who prefers "twisted little homunculus," and threatens to beat Snyder up), though he is finally overruled by the school board. No matter how repellent you find Snyder, it's impossible not to chuckle when he, along with all the other adults chowing down on Ethan Rayne–cursed chocolate bars in season three's "Band Candy," is transformed into the emotional equivalent of a teenager, and we get to see the relentless, dorky, completely unself-aware pariah that he was—which sounds kind of cruel now that we articulate it. On the other hand, it *is* Snyder we're talking about. Shimerman originally auditioned for the part of Principal Flutie, but lost out to Ken Lerner, whom he wound up succeeding anyway. His performance as the twenty-fourth-century Ferengi Quark on *Deep Space Nine* paralleled, for a time, his tenure on *Buffy*.

Emily Djemanowicz (Krissy Carlson)

Tiny dancer Emily Djemanowicz, Sunnydale High student, is scheduled to perform in the Giles-supervised talent contest in "The Puppet Show," but is fatally attacked by the one surviving Brotherhood of the Seven demon, who rips out her tender heart, which he needs to retain his human form as the student Marc.

Marc (Burke Roberts)

Sunnydale High student Marc (no last name given) is the identity assumed by the last surviving member of the Brotherhood of Seven as he searches for a new heart and brain to prolong his life in "The Puppet Show." It is his death that finally frees Sid, the demon hunter, from the body of a ventriloquist's dummy. Don't you wish *you* lived over a Hellmouth?

Morgan Shay (Richard Werner)

The good news? Morgan is the smartest kid at Sunnydale High. The bad news? Everything else. He's a "Grade-A large weirdo" (Buffy's words), is afflicted with brain cancer, and, as we learn in "The Puppet Show," possesses ventriloquism skills that wouldn't even cut it on radio. Morgan's "horny dummy" (Buffy again) is Sid, in reality a cursed demon hunter trapped in the mannequin's body—long story, but bottom line: by episode's end, Morgan is no longer weird, just dead.

Mrs. Jackson (Lenora May)

History teacher who, in "The Puppet Show," gets annoyed with Sid the Dummy for interrupting her class, then shoves him into a cupboard, which, if you ask us, is no way to treat a dummy, especially a live one, expert on the Monroe Doctrine or not.

Laura Egler (J. Robin Miller)

In "Nightmares," Laura takes a licking from Ugly Man while sneaking a smoke in the basement at Sunnydale High, but is still able to report to Buffy that the only words she remembers hearing were "lucky nineteen."

Wendell Sears (Justin Urich)

What's worse: being ambushed by spiders or berated by Cordelia for blocking her sunlight? In season one's "Nightmares" poor, ponytailed Wendell Sears endures both. The former we can blame on the actualization of an anxiety dream: Wendell's prized arachnid collection was destroyed years earlier when he was away at camp and his brother neglected to switch off the heat lamp, killing every last one of them. The latter? Just bad luck.

Ms. Tishler (Terry Cain)

You think inner-city schools are tough? Try teaching over the Hellmouth. Ms. Tishler is the unlucky health and human development educator who freaks out in seasons one's "Nightmares" when Wendell Sears pops open his textbook and a cluster of fidgety spiders jumps out. We know very little about her, except that a) she doesn't like spiders, b) she's got a great set of pipes, and c) she looks fetching in a tight midnight-blue angora sweater—or at least Xander thinks so.

Marcie Ross (Clea DuVall)

Now you see her, now you don't. Sunnydale High introvert Marcie Ross ("Out of Mind, Out of Sight"), long ignored by teachers and fellow students alike, becomes literally invisible, which happens when you live above the Hellmouth (perception becomes reality, explains Giles, not so helpfully). Hell hath no fury like a teen scorned, so Marcie leverages her new power to haunt those who slighted her, especially Cordelia, whose face she intends to mutilate before she is stopped by Buffy. In the end, Marcie is turned over to two men in black, Doyle and Manetti, who haul her off to an FBI academy for invisible people, where the teacher (visible) asks students to turn to page fifty-four of their text, titled "Chapter 11: Assassination and Infiltration." The first case example is "Radical Cult Leader as Intended Victim," and the text that appears underneath comprises mostly lyrics from the Beatles song "Happiness Is a Warm Gun," though "Happiness is a warm gun/(Bang bang, shoot shoot)" becomes "Joy is a hot revolver, and he is afraid of the monkeys who are in possession of digital skeletons of Swiss cheese," which makes absolutely no sense to us, but in a way that evokes the Cheese Man from the season-four dream episode "Restless," who, according to Joss Whedon, was deliberately nonsensical. The original script, incidentally, also has the teacher instructing students to open to page fifty-four of the text, but includes no mention of a chapter title or text. In any event, the larger point seems to be that there is no shortage of people feeling invisible in the world, and that in the eyes of creepy G-men like Doyle and Manetti they are suitable candidates for government-sponsored assassins.

Mitch Fargo (Ryan James Bittle)

Can't be easy being Cordelia's squeeze even under the best of circumstances (which is not to say there aren't obvious advantages). Exhibit one: Mitch Fargo, who takes a beating with a baseball bat in the boy's locker room at Sunnydale High from invisible Marcie Ross in season one's "Out of Mind, Out of Sight" simply because he's Cordy date for the dance and Cordy is numero uno on Marcie's payback list for years of neglect. Cordelia's sympathy extends just so far: she's worried the beating will mar their yearbook photos.

Ms. Miller (Denise Dowse)

Invisible Girl Marcie Ross strikes again: In "Out of Mind, Out of Sight," Ms. Miller is the Sunnydale High English teacher whom Marcie nearly suffocates with a plastic bag, presumably because she a) never called on her in class, and b) was helpful to Cordelia, the real target of Marcie's wrath.

Season 2

Chris Epps + Eric Gittleson + Daryl Epps (Angelo Spizzirri + Michael Bacall + Ingo Neuhaus)

In "Some Assembly Required," Chris and Eric are weird-science geeks who succeed in the Frankensteinian task of resurrecting Chris's brother Daryl, a onetime Sunnydale High football stud who died tragically young in some kind of accident. Now they're out to create a Bride of Frankenstein to keep Daryl company, which involves kidnapping Cordelia so they can attach her head (of all things!) to some assemblage of female body parts. (Hey, nobody ever said the second season of *Buffy* was consistently great.) Chris, at last, is beleaguered by his conscience, so helps Buffy rescue Cordy, but Eric is unrepentant to the end, confirming Buffy's armchair diagnosis that he's in serious need of "industrial-strength therapy." Chris and Daryl's mom (played by Melanie MacQueen) has no idea what her progeny is up to because she's been a complete wreck ever since Daryl's death, never leaving the house and obsessed with watching videotapes of Daryl's football games over and over and over. Eventually she goes on to invent ESPN Classic (not).

Sheila Martini (Alexandra Johnes)

Sometimes a surname is appropriate; sometimes not. There's nothing elegant about Sheila, a ruffian who's been smoking since she was five, gets in frequent trouble for fighting and class-cutting, and once stabbed a horticulture teacher with pruning shears. In other words, a peach, and it's Buffy's bad fortune to be paired with her on the prep team for Parent-Teacher Night in "School Hard" (oh, that Snyder). Of course, she totally blows off the assignment, but does show up at school that night, except as a vampire, having already been kidnapped by Spike and fed to Drusilla. Because bad things happen to those who can't wait to grow up.

Sven (Hendrik Rosvall)

Cordelia's exchange student from Sweden, who pretends to neither speak nor understand English, probably so he doesn't have to engage in conversation with the queen of mean. Does Cordy berate him mercilessly nonetheless? Ya.

Rodney Munson (Joey Crawford)

Why bother crafting an eloquent description of Rodney when Xander has already done it for us: "God's gift to the Bell curve. What he lacks in smarts he makes up in lack of smarts." In season two Rodney tries to purloin the Inca Mummy Girl's sacred seal, thereby reviving her, triggering an avalanche of problems, including his own death. The only positive thing we can say about him is he had a soft spot for Willow, who tutored him in chem, and in our book that counts for something. RIP, Rodney.

Mr. Whitmore (Rick Zieff)

Whitmore really isn't a bad egg; he just traffics in them. Whitmore is a Sunnydale High health teacher who passes out eggs to students to impress upon them the negative functions of having sex ("Are you talking about sex in the car or out of the car?" Cordy wants to know), unaware that they are in reality the spawn of bezoars, pre-prehistoric parasites that attach themselves to a host and take control of their motor functions.

Devon MacLeish (Jason Hall)

Lead singers get the girls, so Devon gets Cordelia, though we could argue all day whether that's a good or bad thing. He has the distinction of being her last boyfriend before her entanglement with Xander Harris, and we all know how that went. Devon's band is Dingoes Ate My Baby, a popular attraction at The Bronze, which you probably also recognize as Oz's band.

Larry Blaisdell (Larry Bagby III)

Master of the single entendre (H/T, Oz), Larry is the Sunnydale High football player who, when first encountered, can't seem to refrain from tormenting girls and making crude sexual jokes, which we discover to be classic symptoms of latent homosexuality when he outs himself to Xander in season two's "Phases." The hilarity of this development is predicated on the fact that Xander is trying to expose him not as gay, but as a werewolf ("The guy's practically got wolf boy stamped on his forehead"), which, of course, he isn't, but handles it so ineptly that in the process he convinces Larry that he too is gay, which of course *he* isn't. The good news is that by season three's "Earshot" Larry is so comfortable with his sexual orientation that "I've got my grandmother fixing me up with guys." In the alt-universe of the third-season episode "The Wish" (the "Wishverse"), Larry surprisingly pops up as a White Hat, one of the good guys. Sadly, Larry is among those killed in the epic battle with the mayor at Sunnydale High graduation.

Theresa Klusmeyer (Megahn Perry)

When you're a seventeen-year-old girl in Sunnydale, you have a lot more to worry about than boys and acne, like werewolves and vampires, both of which play a defining role in Theresa Klusmeyer's life, and death: a werewolf (Oz) chases her, and a vampire (Angelus) sires her. Her final words, delivered to

Buffy just before being staked by Xander: "Angel sends his love." Yeesh, you don't have to be mean about it.

Ms. Beakman (Lorna Scott)

Ms. Beakman's world is the classroom at Sunnydale High. Costantin Stanislavski famously said, "Remember, there are no small parts, only small actors," but Ms. Beakman is here to prove otherwise; her sole relevance is in "Bewitched, Bothered and Bewildered," where she's tricked by witchcraft into believing that Amy Madison has turned in her homework. This gives an observant Xander Harris the idea to blackmail Amy into casting a love spell, which has the unintended effect of making every woman, except Cordelia but including Ms. Beakman, in Sunnydale fall head over heels in love with him.

Benjamin Straley (Ryan Taszreak)

Sunnydale High student Ben Straley (not to be confused with the other Ben Straley, a demon who appears in "Bachelor Party," portrayed by Ted Kairys) breaks the venerable rules of the Sadie Hawkins Dance by asking Buffy to attend with him in "I Only Have Eyes for You," but is re-Buffed and never heard from again. Probably not dark enough.

Grace Newman (Meredith Salenger) + James Stanley (Christopher Gorham)

Forty-three years is a long time to haul around guilt, but that's what happens when you kill your lover and then yourself. Meet James Stanley, who did exactly that, and whose ghost is trying to atone for his sins (hmm, maybe James and Angel should form a support group). In 1955, Jim was a Sunnydale High student carrying on a clandestine affair with teacher Grace Newman, whose conscience finally convinces her to break off the relationship. Distraught, Jim shoots her dead, then turns the gun on himself, on the night of the school's annual Sadie Hawkins Dance, which is again approaching. In "I Only Have Eyes for You," James's poltergeist seeks to undo the deed by reliving the final moments of their lives through the possession of others at the school, but the scenario ends the same exact way every time—until the lovers are finally played by Buffy and Angelus. The twist is the roles are flipped, so that Buffy's the shooter and Angelus the shootee, and since he's a vampire he survives, finally bringing peace to James and Grace. Pretty brilliant, no? When originally aired, "I Only Have Eyes for You" ended with a public-service announcement about teen suicide by Sarah Michelle Gellar.

Ellen Frank (Miriam Flynn) + George (John Hawkes)

Victims of circumstance, Sunnydale High teacher Ellen and janitor George are ensnared in a forty-three-year-old lovers' quarrel involving the ghosts of a student and a teacher. George survives, but shoots Ellen, who doesn't, proving once again that on a per-capita basis, teaching at Sunnydale High is the single-most dangerous job in the universe.

Mr. Miller (James Lurie)

Sunnydale High teacher who pops up every now and then, most infamously in "I Only Have Eyes for You," where, under the influence of James Stanley's spirit, he writes, "DON'T WALK AWAY FROM ME BITCH!" on the chalkboard during a lecture on labor practices before a roomful of tittering students.

Cameron Walker (Jeremy Garrett)

Sunnydale High swim star Cameron Walker is so amped up on fish DNA that he can't seem to shut his motormouth, and feels entitled to whatever he wants, including Buffy's body. This ends up costing him a broken nose, which irritates Principal Snyder, who is desperate to see the swim team win the state championship. On the other hand, a broken nose is nothing compared with his ultimate fate, which is to be transformed into a gill monster, courtesy of Coach Marin's psychotic obsession with steroids as the breakfast, lunch, and dinner of champions.

Sean Dwyer (Shane West)

One of the unfortunate Sunnydale High varsity swimmers transformed into a gill monster—yes, we just said that—due to excessive absorption of steroids, thanks to the harebrained scheme of a Neanderthal coach obsessed with capturing a state championship. Sean's distinction is that it was he who informed an undercover Xander Harris that the drugs were being piped in through the sauna.

Gage Petronzi (Wentworth Miller)

An arrogant, privileged jock—or is that jerk?—Petronzi swims competitively for Sunnydale High, and, like so many of his teammates, winds up a mutated gill monster because of his coach's twisted obsession with winning. It is Gage's chance encounter with Angelus, who finds the swimmer's blood distasteful, that alerts the Scoobies to the fact that athletes are being treated with fish DNA in an attempt to turn them into super swimmers.

Dodd McAlvy (Jake Patellis)

Yet another member of the Sunnydale High boys' swim team transformed into a gill monster, leaving behind only his eviscerated human skin and cartilage, which is pretty gross but leads to a bunch of great jokes, like:

> *Willow:* So we're looking for a beastie.
>
> *Giles:* That eats humans whole, except for the skin.
>
> *Buffy:* This doesn't make any sense.
>
> *Xander:* Yeah, the skin's the best part.

Nurse Ruth Greenliegh (Conchata Ferrell)

Ruthie sleeps with the fishes, her punishment for threatening to blow the lid off Sunnydale High swim team Coach Carl Marin's twisted scheme to win the championship by pumping his athletes full of fish DNA. Not a horrible idea if you want to field a team of mutant fish monsters, but less advisable if you care anything at all about the kids, which Ruth does (although she initially went along with the scheme), which is why Marin tosses her into the sewer tunnel, where she is devoured by the ravenous mutated forms of her onetime patients. It was either that or her refusal to accept most major insurance plans.

Coach Carl Marin (Charles Cyphers)

Those who can't do, teach. Those who can't teach, teach gym. And those who can't teach gym, coach, like this chauvinistic, round-bellied dope who is so desperate to win the championship that he turns his Sunnydale High swimmers into mutant gill monsters by overdosing them with fish DNA, and then feeds them Nurse Ruth Greenliegh when she threatens to blow the whistle, the same fate that eventually befalls Carl himself.

Season 3

Andy Hoelich (Uncredited)

Agile vamp/erstwhile Sunnydale High gymnast who escapes staking once as the Buffyless Scoobies patrol the cemetery in the third-season opener, "Annie," but is not so lucky the second time around, when he is tag-teamed by Cordelia and Xander, which they evidently find hot, since it leads to copious smoochies.

Scott Hope (Fab Filippo)

"Hope" is a four-letter word, like "jerk." Scott makes a play for Buffy early in season three, inviting her to a Buster Keaton festival, gifting her with a friendship ring, yada yada, and while Buffy isn't uninterested—she compares him to that "crunchy, munchy stuff on top of a blueberry muffin"—she's still getting over Angel, and the fact that just a few months earlier she stuck a sword in his heart, dispatching him to a demon dimension, doesn't really help. The situation doesn't get any easier once Angel returns to Earth. Scott eventually becomes so frustrated by Buffy's distractedness that he dumps her, just before the homecoming dance, which he winds up attending with another girl. This doesn't sit well with Faith, who tells him, in front of his date, "Hey, good news, the doctor says that the itching and the swelling and the burning should clear up but we gotta keep using the ointment." Eventually, in season seven, Buffy finds out that Scott floated rumors that she was gay, before coming out himself, though by then she had long since abandoned hope.

Pete Clarner (John Patrick White) + Debbie Foley (Danielle Weeks)

Epically mismatched Sunnydale High couple: She's sweet, gentle, and a member of the jazz band. He's a pathologically jealous and paranoid scientific genius who, forever fearful that Debbie would dump him, concocts a potion to turn himself into a "super *mas macho*" monster, as Willow phrases it. In his Mr. Hyde iteration, Pete racks up quite a roster of corpses, including Jeff Walken, school counselor Mr. Platt, and Debbie, before Angel finally snaps his neck.

Jeff Walken (Uncredited)

Death from mauling by a high school student transformed into a monster by jealous rage is rare even in Sunnydale, but that's exactly what happens to Jeff

Walken. Jeff's crime is that he likes to kibitz around with high school jazz-band mate Debbie Foley, whose boyfriend, Pete Clarner, is a raving lunatic.

Mr. Stephen Platt (Phill Lewis)

It is a long and winding road from Sunnydale High to the Tipton Hotel, but that is the journey actor Phill Lewis took between gigs on *Buffy* and Disney's *The Suite Life of Zack and Cody* (though you could argue that each is hellish in its own way). We will leave Mr. Moseby to future generations of TV deconstructionists and focus here on Mr. Platt, the Sunnydale High counselor who, sadly, is "pureed" to death by high school student Pete Clarner, who literally turns into a jealous monster whenever he suspects someone of coveting his girlfriend, Debbie Foley. Platt clearly is eccentric—he is, after all, a high school counselor—but Buffy finds him endearing, and she's a good three or four sentences into opening up to him about her problems before coming to the disheartening realization that he's not listening—not because he's uninterested, but because he's dead.

Michelle Blake (Tori McPetrie) + Holly Charleston (Uncredited)

Vying for the Iron Throne in the Seven Kingdoms is only slightly more cutthroat than running for homecoming queen at Sunnydale High, a four-way contest involving these two girls plus Buffy and Cordelia. According to Buffy's elaborate chart deconstructing the strengths and weaknesses of her opponents, Holly is a nice, sweet kid and straight-A student, but introverted and with few friends; Michelle is a popular cheerleader and yearbook editor, but has bad skin and dandruff and wears polyester. Cordelia is—surprise—blunter in her assessments: Holly is "brain dead" and "doesn't haven't a prayer," while Michelle is "open to all mankind, especially those with a letterman's jacket and a car." In the final analysis perhaps all that really matters is that they played the Game of Thrones and won, as Michelle and Holly are named co-homecoming queens, while Buffy and Cordelia go home empty-handed.

Ms. Moran (Jennifer Hetrick)

Superheroes often cultivate marginalized public identities, to avoid unwanted attention: hence, Clark Kent, "mild-mannered reporter for a great metropolitan newspaper." During her Sunnydale High years, Buffy experiences a different problem, as she herself articulates in "Homecoming": "I'm like a nonperson." The most immediate provocation for this bout of self-doubt is an encounter with Ms. Moran, Buffy's favorite teacher, whose course on, ironically, Contemporary American Heroes, from Amelia Earhart to Maya Angelou "changed my life," but who can't, for the life of her, remember who Buffy is.

Michael Czajak (Blake Soper)

Boy warlock who hangs with Willow Rosenberg and Amy Madison and gets bullied at school and beaten by an angry mob—including his own dad after a demon turns the bulk of Sunnydale's population into a rabid army of hateful witch hunters, possibly because he had nothing better to do with his time. Cordelia, who is unaffected by the demon, refers to Michael as a "poster child for yuck."

Jack O'Toole (Channon Roe)

According to Cordelia, Jack is a sub-literate psycho who repeated twelfth grade three times, capable of macramé-ing Xander's face if he is ever to make him angry enough, which he does, twice, after Xander drops a football on Jack's lunch and rear-ends a car that Jack was, in all likelihood, in the process of swiping. One other thing worth noting about Jack is that he's dead, the victim of a drive-by shooting, although his magic-savvy grandpa was able to resurrect him in no time at all (sub-ten minutes), which explains why Jack looks nothing at all like the zombie that he is. Jack eventually warms to Xander, after the Scooby refuses to narc on him to the police, and even recruits him as the wheel man as he hops around from grave to grave raising the other dead members of his gang, meaning Big Bob, Dickie, and Parker, though Xander finally bolts when he gets a sniff of their plans, which include killing him, plus "baking a cake"—building a bomb—to blow up Sunnydale High. Xander wins the final stare-down between the two by refusing to budge in a game of chicken as the bomb ticks off its final seconds, and while Jack saves them both by defusing it, he is shortly after that coincidentally consumed by a hungry sheep in wolf's clothing, meaning Oz, and this time he's not merely dead, he's really most sincerely dead.

Percy West (Ethan Erickson)

What Percy West can do exceptionally well is "swish and dish," as Walt "Clyde" Frazier would say, being that he is the star point guard on the Sunnydale High boys' basketball team. He is far less accomplished academically, especially in history, which he is flunking, so Principal Snyder, who recognizes that Percy is "lazy, self-involved, and spoiled," and has already demonstrated his Nixonian devotion to varsity sports in season two's "Go Fish," assigns Willow to tutor him, which Percy interprets to mean that she will research/write his papers for him under his own name ("Oh, and don't type too good. Dead giveaway"). The good news is Percy is not beyond self-help, especially when motivated by fear, as demonstrated after an encounter at The Bronze with Dark Willow, who nearly strangles him to death. In the end he writes, on his own, not one paper on Roosevelt but two (being unsure as to which of the two presidents by that name he had been assigned), and presents Willow with a shiny red apple to boot. Percy survives graduation day and lands a scholarship to the University of Southern California, though, oddly, for football rather than basketball, but his freshman-year girlfriend attends UC Sunnydale, where he runs into Willow at a party and hurts her feeling when she overhears him calling her "captain of the nerd squad."

Mr. Beach (Robert Arce)

Buffy picks up bad, bad, bad, bad vibrations from this Beach man, an avuncular-seeming history teacher whom she bumps into in the hallway in "Earshot," when she can read minds, and his is thinking, "Students—if we could just get rid of all the students." When Willow divvies up suspects among the Scoobies for interrogation, under the guise of soliciting information for the yearbook, it's Cordelia who draws Mr. Beach, and, in her typically tactless way, inquires, "Hi, Mr. Beach, I was just wondering, were you planning on killing a bunch of people tomorrow? It's for the yearbook." The sentiment turns out to be nothing more than a red herring, however, when Xander discovers that it's the lunch lady—and not Mr. Beach—who is scheming to bump off the entire student population, though if you've ever tried to interest high school students in sixteenth-century British history you might sympathize with Mr. Beach's sentiment.

Hogan Martin (Justin Doran)

Xander's fawning relationship with Sunnydale High hoops star Hogan Martin foreshadows his eventual enslavement to Count Dracula, though at least in that case he is under the influence of a vampire's magnetism, which makes his adoration of Hogan even more pathetic. Hogan is a minor character and we learn little of his personality and attributes, though we do know (courtesy of Willow) that he is an exception to the rule that white men can't jump, and (per Oz) that his high school rep—and we all know how important that is—is "the guy who does everything right." Though he good-naturedly ribs his buddy and teammate Percy West about his unintelligence quotient, there are indications that Hogan is no genius either, since, when asked in "Earshot" by Oz, who is investigating a threat to wipe out the student body, how much of a strain upholding his reputation is, answers, "Huh, wow, uh, I guess moderate strain? Is that a good answer? I wanna get this right."

Lunch Lady (Wendy Worthington)

Be nice to your lunch lady, because you never know when she might put rat poison in your food, especially if you live above the Hellmouth.

Nancy Doyle (Lauren Roman)

Prodigiously self-deluded Sunnydale High student who resents Buffy's blossoming, if patently dishonest, relationship with English teacher Ms. Murray over *Othello*, and is convinced she can climb the clock tower just as superhumanly as Buffy, who is trying to prevent a mass shooting. Cannot!

Freddy Iverson (Keram Malicki-Sánchez)

Sunnydale High newspaper editor Freddy Iverson is, in Willow's estimable estimation, "sardonic," but if you ask us it borders on cognitive distortion, so negative is he about everything he comments on (on the other hand, maybe he's just a typical newshound). This includes Oz's band Dingoes Ate My Baby, which, he opined in his review, "played their instruments as if they had plump Polish sausages taped to their fingers" (Oz's response: "Fair"). Freddy's moroseness makes him a prime suspect in the "Who is trying to trying to kill the entire student body" mystery of "Earshot," but it turns out he is acting suspiciously only because he is trying to evade Oz, and he is really just another disgruntled member of the Fourth Estate.

Ms. Murray (Molly Bryant)

Lit teacher whom Xander finds hot, and whom Buffy impresses with her profound insights into Iago and Othello, even if she was stealing them from inside Ms. Murray's head, thanks to her newly acquired mind-reading abilities in "Earshot."

Jack Mayhew (Damien Eckhardt)

We cannot stress how crucial it is to maintain your sense of humor when you live above the Hellmouth, which would seem to make Jack, named Sunnydale High class clown of 1999, an especially valuable member of the community, though, honestly, wearing balloon animals on your head and mugging shamelessly as you approach the podium to accept your award doesn't do much for us. We empathize thoroughly with Xander for feeling slighted by this decision.

Tucker Wells (Brad Kane)

Tucker Wells is a poster child for how *not* to deal with rejection, which, in his case, means sic'ing hell hounds—brain-eating canine demons—on his classmates in attendance at the big dance, though Buffy, of course, picks them off one by one. Tucker is clearly psychotic, though he has at least one friend, a kid named David Metz, whom he e-mails that the "Sunnydale High lemmings have no idea what awaits them. Their big night will be their last

Strategy Session: The Sunnydale High Library doubles as Scooby HQ for the first three seasons, before it is blown to smithereens in the battle with the mayor. *WB/20th Century Fox/Photofest*

night." Interestingly, Tucker was supposed to head up the Trio, season six's "Big Baddies," but actor Brad Kane was unavailable, so the writers created a new character, Tucker's brother Andrew, and installed Warren Mears as leader instead. Kane was the singing voice of Aladdin in the 1992 animated Disney film of that name.

Season Seven

Kit Holburn (Alex Breckenridge)

Dawn's classmate at the new Sunnydale High School. Has a troublemaker rep. Incurred the wrath of some vengeful spirits with a beef against Buffy.

Robin Wood (D. B. Woodside)

The son of Slayer Nikki Wood, who was slain by Spike in the 1970s, comes to Sunnydale as principal of the newly rebuilt Sunnydale High School—and on a mission of revenge against vampkind. Handsome, charming, and remarkably easygoing (he manages to suspend his vendetta against Spike in the interest of fighting the First), he turns Buffy's head, going on a date with the Slayer, before entering a relationship with Faith. Respect the game.

Carlos Trejo (David Zepeda)

Another notorious Sunnydale High student, Carlos was sneaking off for a smoke (wotta rebel) when he ran afoul of the "manifest spirits" of students whom Buffy had failed to save.

Cassie Newton (Azura Skye)

Another classmate of Dawn's, Cassie had a precognitive awareness of her imminent death, which Buffy unsuccessfully tries to prevent—she saves Cassie from a ritual sacrifice, but the precog (no accident she's named Cassandra) passes away at her anointed time due to a congenital heart condition.

Mike Helgenberg (J. Barton)

A goofy, sweet-natured Sunnydale High student with a massive crush on Cassie Newton. Strikes us as a Xander-in-training.

Principal Plus Woman of Interest: Robin Wood takes over as principal of the reconstructed Sunnydale High in season seven, and brings Buffy on board as a student counselor.

Peter Nicols (Zachery Ty Bryan)

Talk about Tool Time: the erstwhile *Home Improvement* star here plays a loath-some frat boy who has the bright idea to sacrifice Cassie Newton in a ritual intended to summon the demon Avilas—who Peter assumes will reward him with great wealth. Dummy. Cassie is spared, but Avilas does show up, and he promptly takes a bloody hunk out of Peter's neck. Buffy contemptuously leaves him to his fate.

Tomas (Rick Gonzalez)

Buffy counsels this Sunnydale High student, who is concerned for his soldier brother's safety.

Josh (Kevin Christy)

A precocious Sunnydale High student who tries the old "maybe I'm gay" gambit to score a date with his counselor, Buffy. Bold, Josh. Bold and dumb.

Martin Wilder (Jarrett Lennon)

A weasely Sunnydale High student who participated in Peter Nicols's ill-fated cult. Bad attitude, worse hair.

R. J. Brooks (Thad Luckinbill)

Sunnydale High student with an enchanted letterman jacket that renders him irresistible to females—including Willow, who finds her reaction very confusing. It's another supernatural high school metaphor: social status mat-ters more than any individual qualities. Anyone in that jacket would reap the same benefits. Xander and Spike, striking for nerds everywhere, put a stop to Brooks's amorous adventures (he nearly sleeps with Buffy), burning the jacket and ending the spell.

O'Donnell (Yan England)

A Sunnydale student and athletic rival of R. J. Brooks whom Dawn, under the influence of Brooks's magic jacket, pushes down the stairs.

Lori (Angela Sarafyan)

Captain of the Sunnydale High cheerleading squad, girlfriend of R. J. Brooks, and kicker of Buffy in the leg (the Slayer was breaking up a catfight between Dawn and the jealousy-maddened spirit leader).

Hoffman (Bobby Brewer)

Another Sunnydale High ne'er-do-well, Hoffman is busted, along with his buddy Grimes, for vandalism.

Grimes (Roberto Santos)

Fellow vandal and associate of the dread Hoffman. Sunnydale High—it ain't for wimps.

Roger (Chris Wiley)

Another troubled Sunnydale High student, Roger has a hard time keeping Counselor Buffy Summers' attention. She's pretty understandably distracted, you know.

9

If the Apocalypse Comes, Beep Me

Season One

"All things are difficult before they become easy," the medieval Persian poet Saadi Shirazi once said, though it took him several tries to get it right. Buffy's first season is generally not considered its greatest, yet contains moments of greatness, and even superlative episodes, including the season finale, "Prophecy Girl." All thirteen episodes of the first season, including a two-hour opener ("Welcome to the Hellmouth" and "Harvest"), were written and shot before even a single one aired.

The series premiered as a midseason replacement on the WB at 9:00 p.m. on Monday, March 10, 1997. The two-hour opener, comprising "Welcome to the Hellmouth" and "Harvest," was the highest-rated episode of the season, with 4.8 million viewers. After the following week's episode, "Witch," the show never hit the 4 million mark again until "Prophecy Girl."

David Greenwalt, fresh off the critically embraced but popularly shunned *Profit*, was brought on board to exec produce along with Whedon, and the first writing staff was hired, including Dana Reston and the teams of Dean Batali and Rob DesHotel, Ashley Gable and Thomas A. Swyden, and Matt Kiene and Joe Reinkemeyer. "It was a weird mix of people," Batali recalls. "There was Rob and I, and we had just come off a comedy, and next door to us were two writers [Kiene and Reinkemeyer] who had just come off of *Law + Order*, there was a brand-new young writing team [Gable and Swyden], and then there was Dana, who had just come off *Mad About You*. So there was this weird, eclectic mix."

Batali further recalls:

> This was not a hot show. I don't think people remember. It was kind of an afterthought. We didn't have the interview until July. Most of the writers are already working, and you kind of get into the next level. . . . We had come off a sitcom which had just been canceled and we got this job because we had written an episode of a show called *The Adventures of Pete and Pete* . . . and Joss read our *Pete and Pete* script and there was like

one line, Joss said I love that line, "Now begins the age of Pete." I didn't think that was a great line, but he quoted that line specifically, and I think that's why we got the job, because we had that kind of quirky, twisty dialogue.

Picking up from where the movie left of (sort-of): sixteen-year-old high school sophomore Buffy Summers and Mom Joyce make the move from fast-and-furious L.A. to the (ostensibly) sleepy Sunnydale, California, a

Scoobies Don't: The original Scooby Gang takes a well-deserved breather to pose for this publicity shot.

one-Starbucks burg so small that the good and bad parts are half a block apart. The goal? A new start, much needed: Joyce is now divorced from Buffy's dad, Hank, who stays behind, and Buffy has been booted from Hemery High, blamed for burning down the gymnasium (in the film, the gym is decimated, but not torched, during the final confrontation, between the Buffy-led students and vampires, but the TV show embraces Whedon's original ending for the film, before director Fran Kuzui asked him to rewrite the script).

An eventful first day at Sunnydale High (Mom's parting advice: "Try not to get kicked out"): Buffy meets super smart but painfully inhibited Willow Rosenberg and super geeky but painfully awkward Xander Harris, soon to become her two best friends and charter members of the Scooby Gang, and Cordelia Chase, snarky girl/coolness arbiter (James Spader, good; John Tesh, bad). Hitting the library in search of a textbook, Buffy is greeted by Rupert Giles, tweedy Brit librarian and, she learns presently, her new Watcher, who dumps the big book of *Vampyr* on her instead. Buffy bolts, wanting no part of it.

Gym is canceled, Cordelia informs the group, because of "extreme dead guy in the locker." Sounds like a job for Buffy; she checks him out, finding bite marks and blood drainage. Next stop: library.

"I was afraid of this," says Giles.

"Well, I wasn't," says Buffy. "It's my first day. I was afraid that I was gonna be behind in all my classes, that I wouldn't make any friends, that I would have last month's hair. I didn't think there'd be vampires on campus. And I don't care."

Here we encounter the central conflict of the series: Buffy versus Buffy, on the one hand, desperate for normalcy, resisting destiny; on the other, embracing it as the only ethical choice.

When Giles reminds her that the Watcher's job is to prepare the Slayer, Buffy responds: "Prepare me for what? For getting kicked out of school? For losing all of my friends? For having to spend all of my time fighting for my life and never getting to tell anyone I might endanger them?" Yet the moment she spies Willow in peril, she takes off in pursuit, ambivalence be damned.

Thank Goddess, because Buffy's arrival in Sunnydale isn't coincidence. The high school sits atop the Hellmouth (Boca del Infierno, the early Spanish settlers called it), a center of mystical energy, a magnet, Giles explains, for "everything you've ever dreaded was under your bed but told yourself couldn't be by the light of day. They're all real."

Note to Giles: forgo parenting.

Foremost among this motley assortment of demons is the Master—the Big Bad of season one—an exceedingly ugly, ancient, and powerful vampire who has spent the past sixty-plus years trapped underground because of an earthquake in 1932, and is undying to bust out (note to self: forgo puns).

Bad news, yes, but about to get worse: everyone keeps hinting at some imminent apocalypse, including Angel, the tall, dark, and handsome mysterioso apparently stalking Buffy: "You're standing at the mouth of hell, and it's

Watch Man: Rupert Giles (Anthony Stewart Head): If only he had known, he would have been a fighter pilot or a grocer.

about to open," he says, tossing her a necklace with a cross (yeah, like that'll keep the apocalypse at bay). Giles nails it: the Harvest! A once-in-a-century opportunity! The master will sap strength from one of his minions (a.k.a. "the vessel") as he feeds on a victim, thus empowering himself to finally bust loose from his underground lair. Once topside, he'll pry open the Hellmouth, and demons will pour forth from another dimension. Or, as Luke (said vessel) so eloquently understates it: "The blood of men will flow as wine when the Master will walk among them once more. The Earth will belong to the old one, and hell itself will come to town."

Or not. Buffy winds up dusting Luke (though not before disobeying Mom, who forbids her from leaving the house because of truancy issues at school), the Harvest comes and goes . . . and the Master? Still stuck like glue, whutoo whutoo. Still, it's hard keep a good vamp down, and before you know it the Master has moved on to Plan B, a convoluted affair involving the Anointed One and an ancient text named the Pergamum Codex, which prophesies that Buffy will encounter the Master one night hence, the Vampire King will finally rise from his sunken prison, and the Slayer will die—all of which indeed comes to pass, though not necessarily in the way that certain nefarious forces had imagined.

Prognostication notwithstanding, Buffy insists on dueling with the Master—someone has to save the world—who munches on her neck, then leaves her to drown in a shallow pool of water, though Xander, Everyman hero, does one of his patented awesome Everyman heroic things by performing mouth-to-mouth resuscitation. The Master is not pleased by this turn of events, but on the plus side, we get to ear-witness vintage Buffy snark, including this, our personal favorite:

The Master: Where are your gibes now? Will you laugh when my hell is on Earth?

Buffy: You're that amped about hell? Go there.

This, immediately before impaling him on a piece of furniture in the Sunnydale High library, dispatching him permanently (we think) to hell, leaving behind only his skeleton. Thus closes the book on season one. But wait: What's high school drama without romance? During the season, Buffy runs into "dark, gorgeous-in-an-annoying-sort-of-way" Angel at The Bronze—local nightery—where, thinking she looks cold, he donates his black-leather jacket, and a new Halloween costume is born. Eventually they kiss, she finds out he's a vampire, born 240-plus years earlier, once one of the most vicious creatures on the face of the Earth, who had killed his family, used to hang with another of the Master's minions (name: Darla), cursed with a conscience after ravaging a gypsy, now one of the good guys, yada yada. So yawny. Willow has a crush on Xander, who has a crush on Buffy, who has a crush on Angel, who used to have a crush on Darla, who is beholden to the Master . . . suddenly we're in Carson McCullers's country. (Cordelia's the only one with a requited crush, and that's because it's on herself.) "We saved the world," Buffy says, post-Master-dusting. "I say we party."

Amen.

Season Highlights

"Welcome to the Hellmouth"/"The Harvest"

> Watching Joss break a story was like watching Mozart play the piano.
> —*David Greenwalt*

Premiere episodes, originally running together in a two-hour slot on the WB on March 10, 1997, but subsequently split into two for the DVD release, both scripted by Whedon. Of course we meet all the major players here—Buffy, Joyce, Giles, Willow, Xander, Cordelia, Angel, etc.—and are introduced

Hack: Willow (Alyson Hannigan) invades cyberspace as Xander (Nicholas Brendon) and Buffy (Sarah Michelle Gellar) look on.   *WB/20th Century Fox/Photofest*

to the central mythology of the show, including the Hellmouth and the inverted–Garden of Eden concept that the Earth was originally populated not by humans but by demons, who in time "lost their purchase on this reality, and the way was made for mortal animals, for man" (Giles, as if you didn't know).

"Welcome to the Hellmouth" opens with the same teaser used in the presentation, which has drawn so much acclaim over the years: a young man and young woman (Darla) sneak into Sunnydale High at night for a little hanky-panky, followed by one of the great genre subversions (Whedon specialty) of all time, in which the vampire turns out to be the girl rather than the guy. Opines Dean Batali: "I continue to feel that the entire DNA of the series is in that teaser, you know, the girl and the guy and the girl's all scared in the dark high school and then she turns to him and eats him, and I just thought right there's a rug pull that established the show."

"Angel"

Much ado about Angel, including, newsflash, he's a vampire, cursed by the Romani after feasting on a young gypsy woman. Much ado too about Darla, his sire, staked here by Angel, infuriating the Master: "She was my favorite, for four hundred years!" Not bad, but not as good as this:

> *Darla*: Do you know what the saddest thing in the world is?
>
> *Buffy*: Bad hair on top of that outfit?

"The Puppet Show"

One of the lowest-rated episodes in the show's seven-season history, but what do they know? The revelation that Sid the dummy turns out not to be the demon, but the demon hunter, was a welcome twist, unlike Cordelia's tone-deaf rendition of "The Greatest Love of All," probably dedicated to herself, which is twisty but hardly welcome. Stick around to the very end and you're rewarded with a hilarious performance by Buffy, Willow, and Xander of a scene from *Oedipus Rex*, split-screened with the closing credits included when the episode originally ran on the WB, the only time the series ever included a closing tag.

"Prophecy Girl"

Two words: Buffy dies. Okay, more than two words—a lot more. We love the mom-daughter chat between Buffy and Joyce, who encourages her to attend the school dance even without a date, remembering a similar experience from her own high school years, which was responsible for her meeting Buffy's dad (and hence, for Buffy herself). All that Bark (Buffy snark—we coined it!) in the final showdown between the Master ("You were destined to die. It was written!") and the Buffster ("What can I say? I flunked the written") is extremely satisfying, as is the heroism of the two least-empowered Scoobies: Xander, who brings Buffy back to life, and Cordelia, who rescues Willow and Jenny from an army of vamps in her car, which she proceeds to drive through the high school library, not because she's a bad driver, which she is, but because she's kick-ass. Xander's invite to the school dance, though re-Buffed kindly, is still excruciating, and we couldn't help noticing, in light of season-four developments, his comment to Buffy that "Willow's not looking to date you, or if she is she's playing it pretty close to the vest." Note the similarities between this episode and the *Buffy* film: in both, Buffy temporarily walks away from slaying, has to choose between fighting vampires and going to a dance (eventually getting to do both), and confronts the vamp kingpin (the Master here, Lothos in the flick) in a formal dress and black leather jacket. This episode is Whedon's directorial debut on the series, excluding the unaired presentation (the first episode, although including many scenes that adhere to the presentation, was directed by Charles Martin Smith rather than Whedon; Smith is perhaps better known as an actor, specifically for his performance as Terry "The Toad" Fields in George Lucas's 1973 film *American Graffiti*).

10

When You Kiss Me, I Want to Die

Season Two

Buffy's sophomore season premiered at 9:00 p.m. on Monday, September 15, 1997, and ran for twenty-two episodes, ending with a two-parter tracing Angel's evolution from Irish wastrel to—in Master parlance—"the most vicious creature I ever met" to, finally, vampire with a conscience. In "Surprise," the heavily touted thirteenth episode, Buffy celebrates her seventeenth birthday by sleeping with Angel, a good-news/bad-news scenario. Good: Well, bliss. Bad: Also bliss, since the gypsy curse leveled at Angel dictates that he revert to Angelus should he experience even a single moment of true happiness.

By the start of the following episode, "Innocence," *Buffy* had a new day (Tuesday), a new time (8:00 p.m.), and a new Big Bad. "Innocence" was the highest-rated episode of the season, with about 8 million viewers, but ratings were generally up during the season, with the finale drawing two and a half million more viewers than the final episode of season one. *Buffy* ranked 142nd among all prime-time shows for the season, making it the third-highest-rated WB show, after *Dawson's Creek* (132nd) and *7th Heaven* (141st).

"By the second season we knew that we had something special," says producer-director David Solomon. "The first season we were paying garage bands $500 to be on the show . . . and we had no money, and nobody really knew what was gonna happen, and by the time the second season rolled around stuff was starting to come together. We hired a music supervisor. We started to get calls from the music companies, like, 'Hey, can you put our music in the show?' and we realized it was, like, happening."

Dean Batali and writing partner Rob DesHotel, story editors on season one, were bumped up to executive story editors, which may have been just process of elimination, says Batali: "Between the first and second season, all the other writers were fired, and a lot of the subtext here is this kind of volatility that *Buffy* was [at that point in time]. . . . I'm the youngest of four boys, and if you asked any of us what kind of father we had, all four of us would give you a different answer, because we had different experiences with him at different times in his life. I think it's the same for working with Joss on *Buffy*." (According to Batali, Whedon did not renew his and DesHotel's contracts for season three, though he says he was ready to leave anyway.) Carl Ellsworth was brought on board in season two, but he was credited with just one episode, "Halloween," before being let go, and Howard Gordon—later exec producer of such shows as *24* and *Homeland*—came and went, Batali said, convinced he couldn't grasp the demands of writing for *Buffy*. But one hugely valuable addition to the staff in season two was Marti Noxon, who went on to pen many of the most important episodes, and developed such a strong relationship with Whedon that he turned the reins of the show over to her in season six.

Creatively, too, the show evidenced profound changes, with fewer one-shot monster-of-the-week yarns and a sharper focus on relationships among the characters—especially of the smoochy variety, and not just Buffy and Angel. Willow hits it off with Daniel "Oz" Osbourne, a Sunnydale High

Party Downer: In "Reptile Boy," Buffy (Sarah Michelle Gellar) and Cordelia (Charisma Carpenter) attend the worst frat party ever, and nearly wind up as sacrificial lambs.

WB/20th Century Fox/Photofest

senior/lead guitarist for Bronze faves Dingoes Ate My Baby (also a werewolf, but only three nights a month). Giles digs Jenny Calendar, but Angelus crimps that romance by snapping Jenny's neck. Spike and Drusilla, the Sid and Nancy of the bloodsucker set, arrive in town madly (literally, in Dru's case) in love, though Angelus mucks that up too. Most shockingly, Xander and Cordelia connect hormonally, resulting in much kissing but more bickering, which devastates Willow, his co-founding member of the I Hate Cordelia Club. (In the March 1999 issue of *Cinefantastique*, Whedon says the Xander-Cordelia romance "came more or less out of thin air" as the writers prepped for season two: "I looked at the episodes we had already done, and the way they were fighting was growing in intensity so much, it was like they were telling me, 'We must kiss!' That's where the 'I hate you but I'm wild about your hormones' relationship between these two kids sprang from.")

Key plot developments in season two

Buffy returns to Sunnydale post-summering in L.A. with Pops, presumably accounting for her foul mood. Ever spend a summer in L.A.? With Buffy's dad? Just kidding. She's testy because she died at the end of season one, remember? Though inexperienced ourselves, we presume death to be a life-altering experience. Still, her intentions are cruel: she cruelly teases Xander on the dance floor at The Bronze, fully aware that Willow and Angel are watching, and swaps invectives with Cordelia, who claws back:

"You're really campaigning for bitch of the year, aren't you?"

"As defending champion, you nervous?" Buffy responds. Meow.

Meanwhile, some vamp named Absalom won't shut up about the ascension—enough already with ascensions!—of a "new hope," which isn't even as good as *The Empire Strikes Back*. Buffy can't stop dreaming about the Master. The Anointed One is marshaling troops, hoping to resurrect the vampire lord. Buffy puts a fast end to that game, mashing the Master's bones to smithereens with a sledgehammer, seriously annoying the Anointed One, who announces to an empty room: "I hate that girl."

The horror! The horror! No, not the Master's near resurrection, but Parent-Teacher Night. Rushing room to room, awkward chats, finding out all those things your kids "forgot" to tell you. Plus, this being Sunnydale, you can add this to the mix: crazy-as-a-bat vampires Spike and Drusilla, newly arrived in town, just in time for the Night of St. Vigeous, when, according to Giles, "The unholy ones scourge themselves into a fury, culminating in a savage attack (not unlike a Republican National Convention)." Spike, who's already killed two Slayers, can't wait to add a third (looks way better on LinkedIn), so crashes Parent-Teacher Night with an army of vampires—classic *Buffy*

Yowsers: Buffy the vampire Slayer (Sarah Michelle Gellar).

mashup of real and supernatural trauma. First up, an emotional reunion with Angel: "You were my sire, man, you were my Yoda! (this contradicts later episodes, which firmly established that it was Drusilla who sired Spike— whoops!). Next, a duel with the Buffster, broken up when Joyce bops Spike on his bleached-blonde head, scaring him off with, "Nobody lays a hand on my little girl!" You go, big girl! In the aftermath of this debacle, Principal Snyder pow-wows conspiratorially with Sunnydale copper Bob, establishing that both know more about the Hellmouth than they are publicly acknowl-edging. Meanwhile, back at the factory they call home, Spike, fresh from the Mommy whipping, tosses the Anointed One into a cage and hoists him up into the sunlight. Bye-bye, little guy. "From now on," Spike says, "we're gonna have a little less ritual around here and a little more fun." Ooh, can't wait.

Buffy swaps dreams of the Master for disturbing visions of Angel and Drusilla, hardly an upgrade. Angel shares: pre-curse (when known as Angelus) he was obsessed with Dru. "She was pure and sweet and chaste."

"And you made her a vampire," Buffy says.

"First I made her insane," he replies.

Buffy sure can pick 'em.

Spike summons three assassins from the Order of Taraka—a Taraka troika, if you will—to terminate Buffy with extreme prejudice. All three fail, of course, but in the process this happens: a new Slayer, Kendra Young, activated when Buffy momentarily died in the season-one finale, arrives; Cordelia and Xander are mugged by worms, literally; and Angel is betrayed by a worm, figuratively, meaning Willy, the snitch, who turns him over to Spike, who needs the blood of Dru's sire to perform a ritual, restoring her to full health. Jonathan (designated here as "hostage kid"), is briefly grabbed by one of the assassins, which has no deeper consequences for the time being, but just wait until season six. Buffy saves Angel. Oz likes Willow's sweet, sweet smile. Xander and Cordy make out. Kendra leaves town. Dru's super-strength returns, but the battle with Buffy weakens Spike, who starts showing up in a wheelchair.

Remember Jenny Calendar? Turns out she's really Janna of the Kalderash, dispatched to Sunnydale by her gypsy tribe to keep an eye Angel, who, you hopefully recall from season one, was cursed by this very same tribe with a soul/conscience for killing its "favorite daughter," meaning he is burdened with the agonizing memory of every single vicious murder he ever committed, and trust us, that's a lot. "Vengeance demands that his pain be as eternal as ours," says Jenny's uncle Enyos, who wants her to split Angel and Buffy up, to deny Angel happiness, which triggers a loophole in the curse and converts Angel back into Angelus. Takeaway? If happiness is indeed two kinds of ice cream, Angel can have only one.

True, it's tough to take Enyos seriously with that hat and that accent, but who are we to judge? This is a gratuitous comment, yet transitions neatly into our next section, which is about the Judge, a demon brought forth eons earlier to separate the righteous from the wicked and to burn the righteous down. What an ego on this guy! "No weapon forged can kill me!" Blah, blah, blah. Not helping: his huge powder-blue head, the reason Buffy dubs him "Smurf." Ages ago an army of good guys dismembered him, scattering his body parts across the Earth. Now, crazy Dru is reassembling the package, intending to spark an Armageddon—yes, another one of those. The Scoobies are in possession of the final missing piece—one of the Judge's arms—and Angel is nominated (by Jenny) to bury it somewhere in Nepal, but he and Buffy (there to see him off) are ambushed at the docks by Dru's gang, which escapes with the limb. Buffy and Angel retreat to Angel's pad, where Buffy, on the night of her seventeenth birthday, makes possibly the worst decision of her life: she feeds Angel that second scoop of ice cream. Not literally, of course. Literally they have sex, which, you know *could* be a great thing, but here, not. That's because making love to Buffy grants Angel the "one true moment of happiness, of contentment, one moment where the soul that we restored no longer plagues his thought, and that soul is taken from him," as Enyos warns Jenny. Translation: goodbye Angel, hello Angelus. (In his DVD commentary for the episode "Innocence," Whedon says one of the reasons the writers turned Angel into a villain was to avoid the "Sam and Diane problem. . . . We knew Angel and Buffy were going to get together, and we knew the moment they did people would become bored with it, much as in *Cheers*.")

Those wacky gypsies! What were they thinking? If happiness *relieves* Angel of torment, why not welcome it? Maybe even seek it out? Ironically (though not coincidentally), just as Angel is freed from relentless torment, Buffy, Willow, and Xander are all consumed by it: Buffy devastated by the consequences of her lovemaking, Willow walloped by the Xander-Cordelia smoochies, Xander shamed by Willow's discovery. Angelus, on the other hand? Having the time of his life—never felt this way before—popping in at Sunnydale High one minute to threaten Buffy's friends, slaughtering old Uncle Enyos the next, leaving behind a message for Buffy, written on the wall in blood: "Was it good for you too?"

More bad news for Jenny: Buffy discovers her true identity, and that she's been keeping secrets from the Scoobies. Not cool. Restore the spell, Buffy demands. Not possible, responds Jenny: the magicks used to curse Angel all those years ago are "long lost, even to my people." More on this soon.

So where do vamps go for fun in Sunnydale? Depends. If you're looking to burn human souls you might try the mall, especially on Tuesdays, when you get 10 percent off with a GAP card. Angelus, Dru, and the Judge hit the shops, and are having a pleasant enough night out incinerating people until Buffy and the gang show up with a rocket launcher, which the Slayer uses to turn the Judge into a giant fireball, his hilarious last words being, "What's that do?" (Curious about that "No weapon forged . . . " nonsense? "That was then; this is now," says Buffy.) Mayhem ensues: Buffy chases a fleeing Angelus around the mall, finally cornering him and delivering a swift kick to what Whedon calls the "goolies."

"You can't kill me," Angel taunts.

Cheese!: Season-two Scooby gang poses for PR shot.

"Give me time," Buffy counters.

As the sun sets on Buffy's birthday, she shares one tender moment with surrogate-dad Giles, who refuses to blame her for sleeping with Angel ("All you will get from me is my support. And my respect."), and another with real-Mom Joyce, who asks what she did for her birthday.

"I got older," daughter says.

Joyce looks her over: "You look the same to me."

Have we mentioned just how awesome this show is?

Now, back to Jenny: working late at the high school, she finally succeeds in translating the restoration spell into English, saving it to a floppy disk. Yup, Jenny rocks. Not for long, though. Angelus gets wind of this endeavor, tracks her down, snaps her neck. Coincidentally, the disk drops between two desks in her classroom, out of sight.

Season two ends with a two-parter flipping back and forth between Angel's past and events unfolding in current-day Sunnydale.

The past: A pre-vampiric, rakish Angel, known then as Liam, is tossed from a pub, turned by Darla, cursed by gypsies. The guy's a wreck, sifting through garbage in search of rats to feast on when he encounters a strange dude by the name of Whistler, technically speaking a friendly demon but functionally more like Clarence, the guardian angel from *It's a Wonderful Life.* "You could become an even more useless rodent than you already are, or you can become someone, a person, someone to be counted," Whistler says. He and Angel sojourn to the City of Angels, specifically Hemery High, the main setting of the movie version of *BTVS*, where the two of them observe from a distance as Buffy is first approached by Merrick, her Watcher, who informs her of her destiny. The Slayer's a kid, Whistler says; she'll need help. Angel, smitten, has found his purpose in life. "I want to help her," he says.

The present: construction workers inadvertently uncover a giant slab of concrete with hieroglyphics on it, eventually determined to be the embodiment of the demon Acathla, whose primary purpose in life was to swallow the world, thereby creating a vortex that would suck every living creature on the planet straight to hell, where they would suffer eternal torment. (Hey, we all have to have goals.) Thankfully, a virtuous knight pierced the demon's heart with his sword before any of this could transpire; Acathla turned to stone and was buried deep beneath the Earth. There is, however, a way to resuscitate the fiend: a worthy supplicant must extract the sword from the obelisk (look for Disney's animated musical version, *The Sword in the Demon,* coming soon to your neighborhood Cineplex, with Nathan Lane voicing the role of Acathla). Angelus, no shrinking violet he, is sure he's the worthy supplicant, but dammit, can't budge the sword. Let's ask Giles; he knows everything!

Meanwhile. the Scoobies cram for junior-year finals, because, well, what high school teacher on Earth is going to cancel finals just because the apocalypse looms? Kendra returns, warned by her Watcher that something bad is going down. Buffy drops a pencil in the computer room and, bending down to retrieve it, discovers Jenny's floppy disk, which Willow deciphers; all she needs to do now is to cast the spell (no easy task, mind you). Angel challenges Buffy to a duel; Kendra gifts her with her lucky stake, the famous Mr. Pointy. Too late, Buffy recognizes the scheme for the scam it is: as she battles Angel, Drusilla and minions storm the library, kidnapping Giles and killing Kendra (Dru, slicing her throat with a fingernail). Xander tells Willow he loves her, but Willow doesn't respond, as she's unconscious after a bookcase falls on her during the mayhem. Angelus tortures Giles, who finally gives up the goose—Angel's own blood is the key to the sword-in-the-stone thingy—but only because Dru tricks him into believing she's Jenny.

Notice anyone missing? That would be Spike, peeved at Angel's relentless taunting, plus all that hitting on Drusilla. The enemy of your enemy blah, blah, blah: Spike proposes a temporary truce with Buffy, promising to skip town stat with Drusilla if together they are able to take Angelus down. Buffy bites.

One complication, however: Joyce, who finally witnesses Buffy dusting a vamp.

"Mom, I'm a vampire Slayer," Buffy confesses.

Mom's response: "Well, I just don't accept that."

Yeesh. Who hasn't had *that* talk?

Joyce absolutely forbids Buffy from leaving; Buffy absolutely disobeys her. "You walk out of this house, don't even think about coming back," Joyce says. Not *really* an option, Mom; gotta save the world. Willow, having woken up, cracks the restoration spell, urging Xander to relay the news to Buffy lickety-split. Xander, no fan of Angel's, doesn't. Buffy rescues Giles, confronts Angelus.

"Angel's the key," Whistler had told her during their one meeting. "His blood will open the door to hell. Acathla opens his big mouth, creates vortex, then only Angel's blood will close it. One blow will send them both back to hell."

Just as Buffy's about to smite Angel with a sword, Willow's spell clicks; Angelus is Angel once again. Bad, bad timing. They embrace, but, of course, Acathla has to go and open his big fat mouth. Vortex created? Yup. Buffy, left with no choice, strikes Angel dead, sending them both to hell.

Final scene: Buffy on a bus, heading out of town.

Besties: Xander (Nicholas Brendon) and Willow (Alyson Hannigan): it's complicated.

WB/20th Century Fox/Photofest

Season Highlights

"School Hard"

Parent-Teacher Night at Sunnydale High., and the arrival of Spike and Dru, a whole different breed of villain from the Master: younger and funkier. Neat little fact: Willow is wearing a Scooby-Doo T-shirt, though the term Scooby Gang had yet to be coined in *Buffy*.

"Halloween"

Chaos worshipper Ethan Rayne creates mayhem, magically imbuing the customers of his costume shop with the personalities of their outfits, which, thanks to a brilliant twist in the script (credited to Carl Ellsworth), reflects their individual repressed insecurities as established earlier in the episode. Cordelia, who may or may not know the meaning of the word "repressed," is unaffected (having bought her costume elsewhere). Buffy is hilarious as a delicate eighteenth-century noblewoman (Willow: "She couldn't have dressed up like Xena?"), but really, the whole troupe shines. This is also the first reference to Giles's dubious past, as the Ripper. Memorable quote, from Buffy to Willow: "Look, Halloween is the night that not you is you, but not you, you know?"

"What's My Line" Parts 1–2

Xander's allusion to the Scooby Gang, in conversation with Cordelia ("You wanna be a member of the Scooby Gang, you gotta be willing to be inconvenienced every now and then"), is the first such overt reference in the series. Part one is credited to Howard Gordon, years later exec producer of *24* and *Homeland*, and eventual *Buffy* showrunner Marti Noxon, here netting her first screenplay credit for the series. In her DVD commentary, Noxon takes credit for introducing a perverse sexuality to the show (seconded in DVD commentary by Whedon: "[T]he idea of torture and pain and power and bondage and all of these things working together in the minds of these people—Marti really brought a lot of cool, twisted sexuality to the characters that fit really well"), evidenced here in the scenes of a bound, shirtless Angel held prisoner by Spike and Drusilla. More firsts: the first (and only) time Buffy ever kisses Angel with his vampire face on, the onset of The Xander-Cordy "romance," and the debut of Kendra Young, the Slayer who activates when Buffy is momentarily drowned by the Master in the season-one finale. And a near-last: Spike was originally supposed to be killed in this two-parter, but Whedon liked the character so much he decided to merely paralyze him instead.

Joss Speak: Whedon directs Spike (James Marsters).

Noxon mentions on the DVD that the "animal crackers scene" between Willow and Oz is partially improvised by the actors, extremely rare for *Buffy*, where the scripted word was gospel.

"Surprise"

Final Monday night episode. Buffy and Angel sleep together; Angel becomes Angelus. The WB touts this episode as "the television event you've been waiting for. Everything you know about Buffy and Angel is about to change." Jenny Calendar is exposed as a gypsy, dispatched to Sunnydale by her tribe to ensure that Angel is deprived of the happiness that would transform him back into Angelus. Angel gifts Buffy with a Claddagh ring, representing friendship, loyalty, and love; *Entertainment Weekly* reported in March 1998 that the Claddagh ring was a real deal, designed by a sixteenth-century Irishman from the ancient town of—get this—Claddagh, as a symbol of love for his bride-to-be. Following the airing of "Surprise," the ring became a chic Hollywood symbol, with Jennifer Aniston, Julia Roberts, and *General Hospital* actress Kimberly McCullough among the wearers. Ironically, McCullough was reportedly given the ring by then-boyfriend Freddie Prinze Jr. who later married Sarah Michelle Gellar.

"Innocence"

One of the most important episodes of *Buffy* ever made, if not *the* most important, according to Whedon, for both practical and artistic reasons. First, "Innocence" aired at a new time, 8:00 p.m. on a new night, Tuesdays, arousing jitters among the studio, network, and creative team, unsure if viewers would follow (they did). More profoundly, it was "important to me and the other writers creatively because it fulfilled the mission statement that we first came up with: the idea of the emotional resonance of horror, the idea of the high school experience, and it also showed how much the show had evolved in the season and a half that we had done." Now convinced the actors were up for profound emotional material, and that viewers were hungry for it, the writers were encouraged to pursue more ambitious storytelling. "Innocence," like "Surprise," functions on dual levels: mythic (the hero's journey, as Buffy grapples with betrayal, and emerges stronger than ever) and personal (girl sleeps with boy; boy humiliates her). Whedon explains on his DVD commentary for the episode: "What we basically wanted to show was a horror movie version of 'I slept with my boyfriend and now he doesn't call me and also he's killing hookers in alleys.'"

In his illuminating DVD commentary for "Innocence," Whedon reveals that the scene in Buffy's bedroom, where she's coolly rebuffed by Angel, still hiding his transformation into Angelus, was originally filmed outdoors, with each of the characters wearing overcoats. However, the scene wasn't working, and Gellar in particular was getting frustrated with herself, so Whedon sent everyone home. Finally, he came to the realization that it needed the intimacy of the bedroom. Whedon says he felt like an "ugly person" writing Angel's dialogue: "I didn't know how I was able to write this so easily. It felt icky that I could make him say these things."

The following scene, involving Jenny and Uncle Enyos, is even more of a creative achievement, per Whedon, "because I had to take a lot of disparate elements that just didn't work. The fact is Jenny had been sent there as a gypsy but had never done anything, had never accomplished anything. The gypsy curse didn't make any sense. [Angel would] become a monster and kill more people if he was happy—that's not a good plan—and we introduced the idea of Jenny being a gypsy really late, so I had a lot of disparate ends to take care of, a lot of things that didn't make sense." Whedon solved the problem while taking a therapeutic walk along the Santa Monica Pier, finally realizing that "it was the idea of vengeance as a living thing, the idea that they serve a kind of arbitrary god that was itself irrational that completely justified the idea that nothing we had written before actually connected that way." That single phrase—"Vengeance is a living thing"—convinced him the viewers would accept the logic of it.

The final scene, in which Buffy shares a quiet moment on the living room couch with her mom, is another artistic triumph.

"The title of the episode actually means something," Whedon says. "It means not just the loss of innocence, but the fact that the innocence isn't lost, that Buffy is, in this sense, an innocent, that she hasn't lost anything of herself even though she's gone through a painful maturing process, . . . she's still the same good person that she was." He praises both actors—Gellar and Kristine Sutherland—effusively, adding, "They leave me with exactly the feeling I wanted to have at the end of this: with regret, of loss, of love."

Trivial fact: in the flashback scenes of Buffy and Angel having sex, it is not actually Sarah Michelle Gellar and David Boreanaz breathing, but rather supervising sound editor Cindy Rabideau and Whedon, who says he was too embarrassed to ask the actors to do the voiceover.

"Passion"

The death of Jenny Calendar, described by Noxon in the March 1999 issue of *Cinefantastique* as "one of those surprises that we keep coming up with to keep our viewers on their toes." Further, the writers wanted to establish beyond any doubt that Angel has turned rotten, and it wasn't some gimmick to mislead the audience. Whedon gives huge props to the WB for allowing him to taint the hero in so radical a fashion.

"Becoming Parts 1–2"

Flashbacks fill in the missing pieces in Angel's evolution from Liam to Angelus to Angel over the previous 240-plus years, with appearances by Darla, Drusilla, and the enigmatic Whistler, plus Merrick, Buffy's first Watcher, played in the film by Donald Sutherland but here by Richard Riehle. Interesting to see Gellar interpret pre-Sunnydale Buffy, portrayed in the film by Kristy Swanson. Kendra dies, Giles is tortured, Xander withholds key info from Buffy, Buffy and Spike form a pact, Joyce learns that Buffy is the vampire Slayer, and, finally, Buffy sends Angel to hell—all of which transpires as the Scoobies are studying for junior-year finals. Can you possibly imagine a better metaphor for junior-year anxiety?

Priceless quote, by Cordy, who calls Principal Snyder "a tiny, impotent Nazi with a bug up his butt the size of an emu."

Did I Mention That I'm Having a Very Strange Night?

Season Three

Season three is transformative for *Buffy* (and Buffy), ending with high school graduation and the departures of two core characters, Angel and Cordelia, both off to L.A. to star in the spinoff series *Angel*. To emblematize, Sunnydale High is itself demolished in the climactic battle of the season finale, a metamorphic moment that effectively bifurcates the series into two eras: early *Buffy* (seasons one through three) and later *Buffy* (four through seven), the first excavating adolescent anxieties and the latter navigating the passage to young adulthood. Monster-of-the-week yarns pop up with less frequency, as the season focuses on longer, deeper arcs with powerful emotional resonance, especially the torturous breakup of Angel and Buffy.

Key characters introduced include Slayer Faith Lehane, called to action following the second-season death of Kendra; Watcher Wesley Wyndam-Pryce, arriving in Sunnydale after Giles is axed by the council for interfering in Buffy's training; vengeance demon Anyanka Jenkins, wreaking havoc with her spells before finally being stripped of power; and Mayor Richard Wilkins III, the Big Bad, whose planned ascension to full-fledged demon drives the season's omphalic storyline. Behind the camera, Jane Espenson and Douglas Petrie joined the writing team.

On the vamp front, Angel returns from hell, though Buffy initially keeps the news secret, driving a wedge between her and the other Scoobies once they find out. Spike is back (sans Drusilla, who left him for a chaos demon in Brazil), just for a single episode, "The Lovers Walk," but it's enough to persuade Joss Whedon to promote him to series regular in season four.

Xander and Willow both stray from their respective significant others (Cordelia and Oz) when they suddenly find themselves irresistibly attracted

Oz (Seth Green): "Guys. Take a moment to deal with this. We survived." Buffy (Sarah Michelle Gellar): "It was a hell of a battle." Oz: "Not the battle. High school."

WB/20th Century Fox/Photofest

to each other, leading to the breakup of Xander and Cordelia, though Oz ultimately forgives Willow and their relationship survives the indiscretions.

The First Evil, which would emerge as the Big Bad of season seven, appears briefly here, in the Christmas episode "Amends," which seems to establish that the First (absolute evil, older than either man or demon) was responsible for returning Angel from the demon dimension, scheming to convert him back into Angelus so he would kill Buffy.

Two episodes—"Earshot" and "Graduation Day, Part 2"—made news when the WB delayed their airing because of subject matter that evoked the Columbine High School massacre in Colorado on April 20, 1999, in which Eric Harris and Dylan Klebold murdered one teacher and twelve of their fellow students before committing suicide. The "Graduation Day, Part 2" decision in particular wasn't controversy free, especially since an entire month had passed since the Columbine shootings. The decision to delay was made the day before the scheduled airdate of May 25, but the episode aired as scheduled in Canada two days earlier, so that resourceful U.S. viewers could watch bootlegged copies over the Internet. Publicly, Joss Whedon agreed with the decision to postpone, but also encouraged viewers to "bootleg the puppy," and Seth Green (Oz), appearing on ABC's *Politically Incorrect,* also supported the network's decision, even while opining that a scenario involving high school students going to war against a human being who turns into a humongous serpentine demon was so farfetched that it was ludicrous to believe anyone would commit violence because of it. Brad Turell, the WB's senior vice president of publicity, had this to say: "If anything [violent] had happened at graduation anywhere, every news organization would have run *Buffy* clips."

Season three launched on September 29, 1998, running for twenty-two episodes, again in the regular time slot of 8:00 p.m. Tuesdays. "Graduation Day, Part 2" officially closed out the season on July 13, 1999, seven weeks after its originally scheduled airdate. However, "Earshot," originally slated for April 27, 1999, exactly one week after Columbine, wound up airing on September 21, two weeks before the start of season four.

According to A. C. Nielsen, *Buffy* ranked 124th among all prime-time shows during the 1998–1999 season (up from 142nd the previous season), finishing fourth among WB shows, after *7th Heaven* (110), *Dawson's Creek* (120), and *Charmed* (123), with a rating a 3.6, or about 3.5 million households (versus a 3.3 rating in 1997–1998).

Key developments over the season

Having furtively skipped town at the close of season two—after defying her mom, who told her, "You walk out of this house right now, don't even think about coming back" on her way to confronting Angelus, whom she wound up stabbing and thus sending to hell just as he reverted to Angel—Buffy opens season three living in a whole City of Angels, meaning Los Angeles, slinging hash at Helen's Kitchen, using her middle name (Anne), and trying to keep as low-pro as possible. Not happening, B. She's spotted by runaway Lily Houston, who looks familiar, and should, because we've seen her before, in season two's "Lie to Me," though then she was known as Chantarelle, the vamp worshipper rescued by Buffy from Spike and gang at the Sunset Club. Lily's main squeeze, fellow runaway Rickie, has vanished, so Lily wants Buffy to find him. "That's who you are and stuff, right? I mean, you help people. . . . You know how to do stuff." Yup, that's Buffy. She does indeed locate Rickie, though dead and, from appearances, about sixty years older than he was just days earlier. This leads to a showdown at an underground slave-labor camp overlorded by demons, where Buffy leads an Exodus-like flight to freedom. No time to explain, but main takeaway: Buffy recognizes that she can't escape her destiny as the chosen one, so returns to Sunnydale.

New in town: Kakistos, ancient, hoofed vampire looking for a bite to eat, not a Happy Burger, though he and sidekick Mr. Trick do stop by the fast-food dive for a soda and a window man, but the Slayer's heart, which he plans to devour after ripping her spine from her body, followed by sucking the marrow from her bones. Mmmm, yummy. (Sounds like the menu at a French bistro.) Naturally, we assume the Slayer is Buffy, but we assume wrong.

New in town: bad-girl Slayer Faith, who had a run-in with Kakistos before, back in hometown Beantown, resulting in the brutal murder of Faith's Watcher, to which Faith was an eyewitness, and the disfigurement of the hoofer, who now seeks vengeance—all of which Faith lies about to the Scoobies, the first of multiple untruths told by the five-by-fiver (Faith's shorthand for A-OK: five by five). Buffy and Faith kill that dream when they tag-team to dust the demon, bonding in the process, with Buffy referring to Faith as "my bestest new little sister," five little words setting in motion one of the more fun riddles of the series.

The Foreshadow Knows

Who knows what foreshadow lurks in the mind of Joss Whedon?

Buffy's sister Dawn first appears in the final moments of "Buffy vs. Dracula," the season-five opener. At first, only viewers are surprised; every character she encounters seems to know exactly who she is, and acts as if she has been there all along. Dawn herself has no suspicions that anything is amiss, and has fully formed memories of being a fourteen-year-old girl, Buffy's sister and Joyce's daughter.

Four episodes later, in "No Place Like Home," Buffy learns the truth: Dawn is the human embodiment of "the Key," a collection of mystical energy that unlocks the gates between every dimension in existence, most of which you don't want to be caught in after dark (or any time, for that matter).

In 2000, the three surviving monks from the Order of Dagon, charged with protecting the key, converted it to human form—i.e., Dawn—to prevent rampaging hell goddess Glorificus from getting her paws on it so that she could return to her native dimension, which would mean unlocking the gates and allowing dimensions to flood into each other. In short: demon soirée. The monks placed Dawn in the Summers home so Buffy could protect her, retconning everyone's memories, including Buffy's, to conform to this false reality.

According to writer/producer Douglas Petrie, the writers knew as early as season three that Dawn was coming, and started planting clues along the way suggesting as much, which only become apparent in retrospect. These clues apparently start dropping in season three:

In "Faith, Hope + Trick" (written by David Greenwalt), Buffy, while conversing with Giles, sarcastically refers to Faith as "my bestest new little sister."

Later in season three, "Graduation Day, Part I" (written by Whedon), Faith shoots Angel with a poison arrow; the only known cure is a Slayer's blood, so Buffy pays Faith a visit at her apartment, determined to extract some, even if it means killing her. During their confrontation, Faith says to Buffy, "Look at you. All dressed up in big sister's clothes." (Worth noting? "Big Sister's Clothes" is the title of an Elvis Costello song, though released over fifteen years earlier, in 1981.)

In part two of "Graduation Day" (Whedon again) Buffy and Faith are both hospitalized: Faith comatose after Buffy stabs her, Buffy weakened after Angel—at her insistence—gulps her blood to survive the arrow attack. Buffy dreams she's in Faith's apartment, with boxes stacked everywhere, when a cat jumps up onto the bed. During the course of their conversation, Buffy says to Faith: "There's something I'm supposed to be doing."

"Oh, yeah," Faith says. "Miles to go. Little Miss Muffet counting down from 7-3-0."

At this point the cat disappears for a split second—you have to freeze the image on your screen just to see it—and an image of a girl in a white hospital gown (pretty clearly Faith) quickly flashes on and off screen.

This dream is significant for a number of reasons. First, it is the same dream in which Faith cryptically alerts Buffy to the mayor's Achilles' heel ("Human weakness—never goes away, not even his"), which proves to be the key to his defeat. But more to our point here: as numerous deconstructionists have pointed out, if "7-3-0" is interpreted as 730, it is the equivalent of two years (365 days times two). The fifth-season finale of Buffy, titled "The Gift" (more Whedon), aired on May 22, 2001—728 days from when "Graduation Day, Part 2" was originally scheduled to air, before it was delayed by WB because of the Columbine shooting. In that episode, Buffy dives to her death in order to save Dawn's life, and avoid an apocalypse. "Miles to go before I sleep" is a line from the Robert Frost poem *Stopping by Woods on a Snowy Evening*, in which "sleep" is a metaphor for death. Further, in the fifth-season episode "Real Me," Dawn encounters a crazy man on the streets of

Faith (Eliza Dushku): Rogue Slayer, Buffy Summers's dark reflection.

UPN/20th Century Fox/Photofest

Sunnydale who appears to recognize her for what she really is, and says, "I know you. Curds and whey. I know what you are. You . . . don't . . . belong . . . here"—"curds and whey" being a line, of course from the nursery rhyme "Little Miss Muffet."

The number 730 pops up again in "Restless," the fourth-season finale (guess who scripted—starts with a "J" and ends in an "n"), an oneiric episode comprising four dreams—one each by Willow, Xander, Giles, and Buffy. But before we get to that, there's a crucially relevant scene in an earlier season-four episode, "This Year's Girl," scripted by Petrie. Here, Faith, still comatose, dreams that she and Buffy are again in a bedroom, but this time Buffy's room, at 1630 Revello Drive (so, Faith's dream, Buffy's bedroom—the inverse of Buffy's dream in "Graduation Day, Part 2'). Faith and Buffy are making the bed, acting like old buddies. At one point Buffy glances at the clock, though viewers don't see what time it is. Buffy tells Faith she wishes that she could stay, but has to go. "Little sis coming, I know," Faith says. "So much to do before she gets here." From here the dream deteriorates into conflict, with Buffy eventually stabbing Faith in the abdomen. Now, back to "Restless": Once again we're in Buffy's room at home, watching as Buffy looks at the bed. Tara is also in the room. She and Faith just made the bed, Buffy says; when Tara asks for whom, Buffy replies, "I thought you were here to tell me." Now the clock says 7:30; Buffy comments that "It's so late," but Tara tells her the clock is "completely wrong." ("The Gift," and hence Buffy's death, is now almost one year to the day away, not two.) Tara holds out a Tarot card with the word "Manus," with a picture of two hands crossed, one open, the other balled into a fist. As some fans have observed, this is "Sun AM" spelled backward. "You think you know . . . what's to come . . . what you are. You haven't even begun," Tara tells her. When Buffy says she has to leave, to go find "the others," Tara replies: "Be back before Dawn."

One last possible clue, from the same episode: In his dream, Xander is handing out ice cream from inside a truck; four youths are on line waiting. On the left side of the screen, standing apart from the other three children, is a young girl in a tie-dyed shirt with long brown hair, who, glimpsed by the back, seems to very closely resemble Michelle Trachtenberg, the actress who will play Dawn.

Interestingly, on his DVD commentary for "Restless," Whedon says that Trachtenberg visited the set while filming that episode, even before she was cast for the role (she was a *Buffy* fan and had worked before with Sarah Michelle Gellar, who later recommended her for the part of Dawn). "And so I think there's some fate going on there," Whedon says, "the fact that she showed up the first time the character was ever mentioned, and then went on to play her."

But is that girl by the ice cream truck really Trachtenberg?

Only the foreshadow knows.

Buffy finally fesses up to Giles and Willow about what happened in the moments before Angel's death, revealing that Willow's soul-restoration spell worked. Now she's hoping for a "normal" relationship, preferably one excluding the undead. Sunnydale High senior Scott Hope asks her out, but it's complicated, especially once Angel returns from hell, and Scott's a dork anyway, so, no Hope for Buffy. Mindful that Angel, as Angelus, murdered Jenny, tortured Giles, and tormented every single one of her friends, Buffy chooses to keep his return quiet, which, as we write it, sounds reasonable, though it gets her into a whole lot of trouble once the Scoobies find out, which they do when Xander spies Buffy "sucking face with [her] demon lover" (Cordy's words, and why not?). Intervention time. How's that go? Not well, unless you appreciate accusations of jealousy and spying and harboring a vicious killer.

Anyway, life-and-death matters await: Buffy challenges Cordelia for homecoming queen, but the two are compelled to ally for self-preservation when Mr. Trick stages SlayerFest '98, in which a truly despicable assortment of humans and demons vies for the privilege of killing the two Slayers. (Why Cordelia instead of Faith? Mistaken identity.)

Back in town: morally depraved sorcerer/unrepentant coward Ethan Rayne, this time cooking up "band candy," chocolate bars that magically convince adults they're "sweet sixteen" again, a scheme directed by Mr. Trick, now working for the mayor, who is seeking to distract the Sunnydale population so that he can fulfill his promise to sacrifice newborns to sewer demon Lurconis. Seems excessive, though infants *can* be a handful. Over a hundred years old, the mayor somehow retains his relatively youthful looks. Grecian Formula? Perhaps, but also an absence of conscience, freeing him to bargain with the devil (not literally, but close enough), like establishing, in exchange for certain favors, the town of Sunnydale over the Hellmouth so that demons would always have a place to feed—kind of like mom and pop saying you can come home for dinner anytime you want, even after moving out.

Band candy sounds crazy, but it works, at least until Buffy sniffs it out. Wild and wacky things happen. Snyder admires "foxy ladies" and Oz's hair. Dads gun their engines at stoplights, ready to drag race. Elderly Ms. Barton, a teacher at Sunnydale High, calls Willow "little tree" as she wanders around The Bronze looking for nachos. Joyce and Giles have sex. Twice. On the hood of a police car (mercifully unwitnessed by viewers, but confirmed later, in "Earshot," when a horrified Buffy temporarily acquires mind-reading capabilities).

Still, at least the grownups have an excuse. Not so for Xander and Willow, unless you count teen hormones. Smoochies? Footsies? In study hall? Get a room, guys. On second thought, don't. *Le pied veut ce que le pied veut.*

Harry Groener as Sunnydale's warm, avuncular, spider-gobbling demon-snake mayor. That old cliché.

This just in from the Watchers Council: Faith is to hang out in Sunnydale for now, with Giles assigned to watch over both Slayers.

New in town: Gwendolyn Post, axed by the council for dabbling in the dark arts, claiming (falsely) to be Faith's new Watcher, when what she's really after is the powerful Glove of Myneghon, which she eventually gets her hand in, though probably not worth it, since she winds up dead.

Back in town: Spike, seeking a spell so that Drusilla will come to her senses (also not happening) and fall in love with him again. Not Amy, please. He abducts Willow and Xander, threatening to kill both if Willow doesn't deliver. Willow and Xander evidently find this hot, because they start again with the smoochies, but this time they're discovered by Cordelia and Oz, who burst in to rescue them. Storming out, Cordelia falls through a wooden plank, speared in the abdomen by a protruding piece of wood. She recovers, but tells Xander in no uncertain terms that their relationship is over, and blames Buffy for all of her problems, wishing the Slayer had never come to Sunnydale. Man-hating vengeance demon Anya happily obliges, creating an alternate universe ("Wishverse") in which the Master still lives, Xander and Willow are vampires, Cordelia dies, and Buffy is off slaying demons elsewhere until the final act, when her neck is snapped by the Master, all of which is reversed when Giles demolishes Anya's necklace, the source of her power.

Snow falls in Sunnydale on Christmas morning, just the miracle Angel and Buffy need to rebuff the First Evil, at least for now.

Amy transmogrifies into a rat to escape being burned at the stake along with Willow and Buffy by a group of frenzied witch-hunting adults led by Joyce, under the influence of a demon. So Amy. "She couldn't do us first?" Buffy wonders. On the plus side, she has a nice new home, living in a cage in Willow's bedroom. We finally get to meet Willow's mom, who won't be winning any mother of the year awards, unless they are handed out by the Princess of Ukok.

On Buffy's eighteenth birthday, the Watchers Council dispatches another thoroughly clueless "grownup," Quentin Travers, to Sunnydale to direct her Cruciamentum, a ridiculously mean and stupid rite of passage in which the Slayer is furtively drained of her powers and locked up in a room with a ferocious vampire, whom she must defeat by outwitting, or die. (We especially like the part where they sing "Sunrise, Sunset.") Giles goes along at first, but eventually his conscience overtakes him, so he confesses everything to Buffy, rupturing his relationship with her (briefly) and with the council (permanently, as he is fired).

New in town: Wesley Wyndam-Pryce, Giles's equally Brit, far more officious and buffoonish successor, whom nobody listens to and nobody likes except Cordelia, and even that doesn't last for long—no chemistry, they deduce after kissing. Twice.

An apocalyptic demon cult known as the Sisterhood of Jhe—fourth-wave feminists?—opens the Hellmouth, unleashing an even bigger and uglier iteration of the Hellmouth Spawn, which just goes to show you anything is possible, but the Scoobies are getting pretty good at this and manage to slam the portal shut once more.

Faith sleeps with Xander.

We repeat: Faith sleeps with Xander.

In the heat of battle, Faith inadvertently stakes a human—Deputy Mayor Allan Finch, who possibly was seeking the Slayers out to narc on his boss, the mayor—creating a schism between her and Buffy, who has a policy against killing humans, especially if they're trying to help. Buffy's idea: let's tell Giles. Faith's idea: let's not. Faith's other idea: let's tell Giles, but say it was Buffy who killed him. Giles is no sap, and isn't buying, but Faith's instability is increasingly vexing, and about to get even worse: after staking Mr. Trick (who was wringing Buffy's neck at the time), she applies for a job with the mayor, who not only hires her, but practically adopts her, showering her with gifts, including a fully furnished pad, a video game console, a dress, and a shiny new knife she can use whenever she has the urge to gut someone.

Faith makes a play for Angel, hoping to resurrect Angelus, but Angel, Buffy, and Giles suss the plot out and, with a little help from a friend, the mysterious Shrouded Man, trick Faith into believing Angel has turned, so they can learn more about the mayor's plans. Something about an ascension? At high school graduation? In the middle of his commencement address? Sounds scary, but still better than a speech by Rudolph Giuliani.

To prep for ascension, the mayor must chow down on a platter of spidery-looking creatures that arrive from Central America in something called the Box of Gavrok. In a daring, Ethan Hunt–like caper, with Buffy suspended by cable from a floor above, the Scoobies swipe the box, but have to surrender it in exchange for Willow, who's captured by Faith. Good news? Crafty Willow, during her time in captivity, rips three pages from the Books of Ascension, providing Team Buffy with additional insights into the mayor's grand plan. Huge library fine for that, but still.

G-Day fast approaches, so everyone reflects. Willow and Oz have sex.

We repeat: Willow and Oz have sex (Willow losing her virginity). You never know: it could be the end of the world as we know it; why not feel fine?

Joyce pays a visit to Angel, sternly encouraging him to break up with Buffy. Angel tells Buffy he's skipping town after graduation. Buffy tells Joyce to leave town, for safety. The Scoobies all mull life after high school, if there is one. Rather than attend Northwestern or any of the other schools that accepted her, Buffy will stay in Sunnydale and fight the good fight. Willow, despite being accepted at every tier-one school in the universe, will stay and fight alongside her, continuing her Wiccan studies. Xander plans a road trip, following in the footsteps of his new muse, Jack Kerouac. Cordelia, faced with financial ruin because Daddy has been defrauding the IRS for the past twelve years, is in a dark, uncertain place (though we eventually learn, in the premiere episode of *Angel*, that she leaves Sunnydale for L.A., hoping to 1) become an actress and 2) live in close proximity to so many shoes, only one of which winds up happening).

Faith, not so big on self-reflection, goes back on the attack, piercing Angel with an arrow poisoned with a toxin fatal to vampires. Wesley reaches out to the council for assistance, but it refuses to help a vampire; in protest, Buffy quits, saying from now on she's working on spec. Willow discovers there's a cure, but you're not going to like it: the blood of a Slayer. By our reckoning that leaves two options: A) Buffy, and B) Faith. Buffy chooses B, but Faith has something to say about it: specifically no, even though it comes with two cookies and a cup of juice. They fight. Buffy stabs Faith (with the knife the mayor gifted her). Faith congratulates Buffy, then leaps off the roof onto a moving truck below, and into a coma. Buffy, no blood for you.

So, one option left, though you're still not going to like it. Angel refuses to drink from Buffy. Buffy refuses to let Angel die. Is it just us or can these two not agree on anything anymore? Don't worry, Buffy has a backup plan: she punches Angel in the face, repeatedly. (We didn't say it was a polite plan.) Still, it works: Angel turns, Buffy yanks his head to her neck, he drinks. Kind of sexy, in a twisted sort of way. Who ever thought vampires could be erotic?

Unfortunately, Angel has a little difficulty shutting off the spigot, so Buffy winds up in a hospital bed, not far from the comatose Faith. In a strange dream involving a cat, a nursery rhyme, and a Robert Frost poem, Faith tells Buffy, "You wanna know the deal? Human weakness. It never goes away. Even his." Important? You betcha. Buffy wakes up, kisses Faith on the forehead, and tells the Scoobies to prepare for war.

Graduation day is a day like all other days in Sunnydale, except that the mayor transforms into the titanic snake demon Olvikan, who eats Principal Snyder (poor little guy, barely more than a snack); battles the entire senior class, finally banding together after three seasons of infighting and self-absorption (killing sexually liberated gay football player Larry Blaisdell, among others); and is blown to smithereens after chasing Buffy into the Sunnydale High Library, wired with explosives that are detonated remotely by bad-ass librarian Rupert "Ripper" Giles.

Like we said, a day like all other days.

Whither Faith, as the season comes to a close? Still comatose, back in the hospital, but it was her cryptic comment—"You wanna know the deal? Human weakness. It never goes away. Even his"—that inspired victory, thanks to Angel's deduction: Wilkins's human weakness was Faith, so Buffy lured him to the library by taunting him with the knife and explaining, in graphic detail, how she stabbed Faith.

"We survived," says Oz, as the Scoobies (sans Angel, who's already disappeared into the night) gather around to survey the remains of Sunnydale High.

"It was a hell of a battle," says Buffy.

"Not the battle," Oz says. "High school."

How much harder can college be?

Season Highlights

This is a particularly tough season to highlight the best episodes, because there are so many of them, including:

"Band Candy"

Discussed in some detail above; a real tour de force for Armin Shimerman's Snyder, who, as a teenager, turns out to be every bit the "filthy little ponce" (Giles's words) expected. In her DVD commentary for "Earshot" (see below), Espenson points out that that episode and this one share a message: "Be careful what you wish for"; here Buffy learns that adult supervision isn't such a bad thing after all.

"The Lovers Walk"

Spike's lone appearance this season, but a great one, if for no other reason than his hot-chocolate scene with Joyce, who apparently still thinks lovelorn Spike is a singer in a rock band, as he was introduced to her by Buffy in season two's "Becoming, Part 2." When Angel intervenes to warn her that Spike is a murderous low-life vampire, Joyce—thinking he is still Angelus—refuses to let him in, which Spike finds hilarious (it is). Spike's encounter at the magic shop with Willow, wearing a pink sweater, will be remembered in a remarkable scene from season four's "The Initiative," in which Spike's inability to bite Willow because of the chip in his head is treated as a metaphor for impotence. Spike's trenchant lecture on Buffy and Angel's relationship—"You're not friends. You'll never be friends. You'll be in love till it kills you both"—is another highlight, as is the devastating discovery by Cordelia and Oz that Xander and Willow are cheating.

"The Wish"

Ms. Jenkins comes to town: the debut episode for Anyanka, vengeance demon/mayhem maker who, in response to Cordelia's wish that Buffy had never come to Sunnydale, creates an apocalyptic alternate reality in which Sunnydale is ruled by the Master and his minions, including Vamp Willow ("Bored Now") and Vamp Xander.

"Amends"

First appearance of the First Evil (plus his high priests, the Harbingers/ Bringers), who afflicts Angel with such anguish and shame that he climbs to the top of Kingman's Bluff on Christmas Eve to await sunrise, and thus welcome his own death. According to Whedon, the ensuing confrontation between Angel, who has lost all faith in his own goodness, and Buffy, who refuses to stop believing in him, rates among his finest work on the series, and is interrupted by a gentle snowfall that seems to come out of nowhere on a balmy Southern California night, finally shaking Angel from his despair.

"Doppelgangland"

Vamp Willow redux, thanks to another round of mischief-making by Anya, but this time she comes to Willow's world, leading to much wackiness, including a face-to-face meeting between the two Willows. Real Willow's assessment of her vamp counterpart: "I'm so evil, and skanky. And I think I'm kind of gay."

"Helpless"

Buffy turns eighteen and, thanks to Quentin Travers and the Watchers Council, upholds her "special birthday tradition of gut-wrenching misery and horror," in this case due to the Cruciamentum, a rite of passage in which Slayers are stripped of their physical prowess and forced to confront a ferocious demon using their wits only. The crux of this episode is the relationship between Buffy and surrogate dad Giles (her real father is supposed to take her to the ice show for her birthday, an annual daughter-daddy ritual, but bails, claiming he is too busy at work). Giles initially goes along with what he himself calls "an archaic exercise in cruelty" out of obligation to the council, secretly draining Buffy of her powers, but eventually breaks with protocol and alerts her to what is going on. This act of conscience costs him his job—he's fired by the council—but salvages his relationship with the one person he cares most about in the world.

"Zeppo"

Stranger things have happened, but Xander has an exceptionally weird night, picking up a buxom blonde with an automobile fetish, cruising around town with a quartet of dead *Walker, Texas Ranger* fans, having sex with Faith, and, finally, foiling a scheme to blow up Sunnydale High, all the while completely unaware that the rest of the Scoobies are engaged in a cosmic war with an apocalyptic cult called the Sisterhood of Jhe, which has succeeded in opening the Hellmouth and releasing the Hellmouth Spawn. Likewise, the other Scoobies have no clue as to, and hence no appreciation of, Xander's heroism, which seems pretty par for the course. Did any of this *really* happen?

"Earshot"

Notable as Jonathan Levinson's first big role (he would emerge in season six as one-third of the big-bad Trio), in addition to premiering five months after its originally scheduled airdate because of what the WB deemed uncomfortable similarities to the tragic events at Columbine. Buffy, having acquired mind-reading capabilities after touching a demon's skin, overhears an unidentified voice say, "This time tomorrow, I'll kill you all!" giving the Scoobies twenty-four hours to prevent a school massacre. Writer Jane Espenson reveals on her DVD commentary that this episode emerged from a pitch session with Whedon and David Greenwalt at which they rebuffed all of her suggestions until she came up with a "scratch of an idea" about a student who used psychic powers to cheat on a test.

"The Prom"

Buffy singlehandedly takes on maladjusted Tucker Wells and his trio of Hell Hounds so her friends can enjoy senior prom, but is rewarded in the end with a glittering miniature umbrella and plaque ("Buffy Summers, Class Protector") from her fellow seniors (nice speech, Jonathan), and a surprise slow dance with Angel, looking pretty spiffy in a tux. Brings tears to our eyes every time. Plus, the Angel-Buffy breakup scene in the sewer tunnel, directed by David Solomon:

That scene particularly was one where I went to them and said, "This is a huge scene in the series and we've designed the set just for this to happen and you've got a ton of stuff and we're gonna take as much time as we . . . need. We went through an emotional hell, because it was really hard for them both to play this, and it took me all day to shoot that scene, twelve-plus hours, and I loved every second of it."

"Graduation Day, Parts 1–2"

Also discussed in detail above, this two-parter not only features the final appearances of Angel and Cordelia as regular cast members, but also closes the book on the early, high school era of the series.

12

We've Got Heady Discourse

Season Four

Buffy's fourth season stakes (sorry) out completely new territory for the characters and the series as a whole; the show's central metaphor, high school, has quite literally been exploded, and as Buffy and her coterie struggle to redefine themselves in the new context of independent college life, so *Buffy* the series makes some regrettable decisions, stumbles a bit in confusion, and tries out some looks that don't quite work. Still, Buffy's freshman year at University of California, Sunnydale, features the virtuosic, largely dialogue-free "Hush" episode, inarguably a series highlight, and the character development of our major players, while at times tortuous to experience, pays massive dividends down the line.

Season four generally ranks low on lists of fan-favorite arcs, as the shadowy secret government-sponsored demon-hunting Initiative proved to be a bit of a non-starter (in spite of a nifty Marvel Comics-like premise and the presence of David Mamet muse Lindsay Crouse), and Adam, the Frankensteinian Big Bad with a weakness for labored badinage, was more of an annoyance than a terrifying threat. Perhaps the least compelling—and, confoundingly, longest-lived—product of the Initiative storyline was Riley Finn, super soldier and Intro Psych T.A., an all-American beefcake Dudley Do-Right as dynamic and charismatic as a bowl of vanilla pudding. He and Buffy flirt, fight, and madly fornicate episode after episode to approximately zero dramatic effect; so egregiously bland and robotic is Riley that the show hangs a lampshade on his lameness by having Spike repeatedly mock the overgrown Boy Scout's stiffness.

More engaging is the romantic journey of Willow, who experiences devastating heartbreak when her first love, Oz, sleeps with a fellow lycanthrope and abruptly leaves town to seek a remedy for his werewolfin' ways. But the departure of Oz gives Willow the opportunity to explore other possibilities . . . such as a sweetly romantic connection with fellow Wiccan Tara Maclay. The sensitive depiction of their credible, slow-burn attraction and its attendant complications was groundbreaking for the era, a milestone in the history of gay representation on television, and it's a significant entry in season four's "Pros" column.

Less happily, the "Cons" list includes a ham-fisted mea culpa for the Native American genocide in the eye-rolling Thanksgiving episode "Pangs," a gratingly unfunny exercise in drunken *Animal House* hijinks titled "Beer Bad," and the unsettling spectacle of an erotically possessed Buffy and Riley all but devouring each other in the unpleasantly sweaty "Where the Wild Things Are."

But these are quibbles, forgivable missteps in a twenty-two episode season of television. What makes season four a challenge to love unreservedly is the (understandable) sense of dislocation, unfamiliarity, and fraying bonds between the Scoobies. As the season progresses, Giles, now unemployed both as a Watcher and librarian, battles feelings of abandonment and irrelevancy; Xander spirals into self-doubt and resentment over his apparent lack of a viable future; and Willow grows distant from Buffy after her best friend reacts awkwardly to Willow's relationship with Tara.

The unique alchemy of *BTVS* depends on our deep investment in the characters and their relationships, so the fracturing of those relationships and the resulting isolating pain it confers upon those characters is particularly painful to experience. While this narrative development is thematically sound, as the transition from adolescence into young adulthood is a fraught and isolating (and necessary) experience, with the fierce attachment, loyalty, and grounding enjoyed by the Scoobies now badly compromised, viewers accustomed to the affectionate, quippy, hang-out vibe of the high school era will find themselves adrift. As is surely Whedon's intention.

The fourth season of *Buffy the Vampire Slayer* ranked 129 on the Nielsen ratings, with an average viewership of about five million. This season garnered the series three Primetime Emmy nominations: for Writing and Cinematography ("Hush"), and, er, Hairstyling—way to go, "Beer Bad". Beginning with this season, and continuing until the finale, *BTVS* was filmed in 16:9 widescreen format.

The Story

Buffy and Willow have matriculated at UC Sunnydale, and we observe an interesting inversion as the two settle in: Willow thrives, imbued with a new self-confidence and feeling of belonging, while Buffy, the former high school cheerleader dream girl, has trouble fitting in. Not helping matters is her new roommate, Kathy, whose true secret status as a soul-stealing demon is only the twelfth most aggravating thing about her. Roommate from hell: another metaphor wittily embodied.

Buffy quickly dispatches this nuisance, only to attract a worse one: fellow student Parker Abrams, a wet-eyed sociopath horn dog in sensitive-guy drag who seduces Buffy with faux-soulfulness before coldly discarding her. Unlike

The College Years: Welcome to the fold, Spike (James Marsters). Uh, and, yeah, Riley (Marc Blucas). Fine.

her previous lover, Angel, Parker doesn't literally turn into a monster the morning after; he was a sleaze all along, and falling for his act shakes Buffy's faith in her own judgment (and we can't really argue, insomuch as it applies to selecting romantic partners). Parker tries the same routine on Willow, who instantly sees through him and hilariously shuts him down in a triumphant scene for the erstwhile naïve and accommodating wallflower.

Sultry rock singer Veruca arrives on the scene, and Oz, catching her performance, is more than smitten—he is positively pheromonally addled, as the sloe-eyed vocalist is secretly a fellow werewolf (we have no confirmation that Veruca was based on Courtney Love). Nature takes its course, Oz couples with the canine songstress, and Willow shatters at the betrayal. After Veruca nearly kills Willow and exacerbates Oz's animal tendencies, Oz departs Sunnydale to seek a lycanthropy cure . . . and, aside from a visit later in the season, this is where we bid goodbye to the most stoic and level-headed of the Scoobies (excluding a couple of dream sequences later on).

One door closes, another opens: Oz leaves, Spike returns, which is bad news for our heroes but very good news for the audience. The peroxided predator is after the Gem of Amara, a power-boosting MacGuffin located on the Hellmouth. Accompanying Spike on this mission is former mean girl, current vampire, eternal nitwit Harmony Kendall, now Spike's girlfriend. In further strange-bedfellows news, vengeance demon Anyanka drops in on Xander to declare her amatory intent, and Giles enjoys a liaison with Olivia Williams, a gorgeous former flame from his shady "Ripper" past.

The Hellmouth-adjacent UC Sunnydale endures more than its share of weird goings-on: Buffy must contend with such headaches as Sunday the snotty vampire and her crew, bewitched beer, university housing issues like sex-hauntings and fear curses, and vengeful Native American spirits crashing Thanksgiving.

But the real story is happening below the surface. Under the Sunnydale campus, a gleaming, high-tech secret laboratory seethes with white-coated scientists and special-forces soldiers, under the administration of Buffy's icy psychology professor, Maggie Walsh. This is the Initiative, a modern, militarized response to the demonic threat that stands in marked contrast to Buffy's mystical mandate as a Slayer. Among the Initiative's innovations is a behavior-modifying computer chip that, when surgically implanted in a demon's brain, prevents it from harming humans. One of the captured "hostiles" to have undergone this treatment turns out to be none other than Spike, who really has lousy luck in Sunnydale.

Spike quickly escapes and fails in his attempt to bite and drain Willow in her dorm room, which plunges him into self-recrimination as Willow tries to reassure him about his potency in a very funny, if questionably appropriate, satire of sexual impotence. This neutered Spike, all bilious resentment and nasty comments, spends much of the season crashing at Giles's or Xander's place, irritating everybody amusingly.

Elegant Emma Caulfield, who played the conflicted ex-demon Anya, was perhaps the series' nimblest comic performer.

A despondent, post-break-up Willow throws herself into her spellwork, assisted by new friend Tara; she inadvertently blinds Giles, turns Xander into a literal demon magnet, and charms Buffy and Spike into sickly sweet couplehood (and briefly, hilariously, restores Amy to human form and back to rat again without even noticing) before getting a handle on things and seriously weighing an offer from Anya's old boss, D'Hoffryn, to become a vengeance demon. Tempting, but no.

The Gentlemen, a group of floating, grinning ghouls, arrive in Sunnydale and steal the voices of every soul in town, as their only weakness is a human scream. Unable to communicate conventionally, the Scoobies nonetheless make personal breakthroughs as Buffy and her crush, the T. A. Riley, discover that they have demon fighting in common, and Tara and Willow draw closer after discovering their strength increases exponentially when joined together.

Spike's spirits improve when he discovers that, despite the chip, he can wreak mayhem on demons with no trouble at all, while Giles's downward spiral includes a terribly misjudged boys' night out with degenerate spell-caster Ethan Rayne, temporarily transforming into a demon for his troubles.

Back at the Initiative, Maggie Walsh, uncomfortable with the Slayer's supernatural orientation and refusal to play by "the rules," sets an unsuccessful deathtrap for Buffy and reveals her passion project: Adam, a cyborg zombie composed equally of human parts, robotics, and demon anatomy, rendering him a formidable combatant and insufferable pontificator on the nature of existence and identity. Created to be a "super soldier," Adam shows surprising "initiative" by killing (sort of) his creators and embarking on the construction of cybernetic demonoid spare-parts monsters for his own personal army. Spike signs on to help, as Adam promises to remove that troublesome chip as payment for some Scooby sabotage. Spike's plan: further erode the fraying bonds between the friends with well-placed comments targeting their various insecurities. It works.

When it rains . . . Faith wakes from her coma determined to pay Buffy back for the near-fatal knife wound Buffy dealt her, getting right to work by terrorizing Joyce at home and later switching bodies with Buffy, leading to some pretty funny opportunities for Gellar and Dushku to lampoon each other's personae. Faith-as-Buffy infiltrates the Scoobies intent on mischief, but, ensconced in Buffy's world of emotional connection, the rogue Slayer begins to take on some of the actual Buffy's heroic characteristics.

For her part, Buffy, now looking like Faith, is tracked and captured by the entirely unpleasant Watchers Council Special Operations Team, a squad of brutally efficient killers charged with discretely cleaning up the council's messes—kidnappings, executions, that sort of thing. Pip pip, cheerio.

Buffy prevails and the Slayers return to their respective original bodies . . . but not before Faith uses Buffy's original body to sleep with Riley. Faith, sweetheart, stop punishing yourself. This leads to strife between the young lovers when everyone is back where they started, which is as irritating as every other stage in this stultifying relationship.

In a delightfully unexpected turn, Jonathan Levinson—the diminutive troubled nerd from Sunnydale High—arrives on the scene, now impossibly brilliant, suave, and capable, adored by all and universally considered the absolute paragon of every human virtue. Duh, it's a spell, dire unexpected consequences included, and Buffy must join forces with the once and future Poindexter to avert catastrophe, AGAIN.

Oz returns as well, having mastered his lupine urges, to pick up where he and Willow left off; unfortunately, Willow has moved on, realizing that she now loves Tara when Oz attempts to rekindle their romance. He ultimately takes it well—much better than Buffy, whose surprisingly uncomfortable reaction to Willow's news furthers the growing distance between the girls.

Everything comes to a head in a savage final battle in the Initiative, as Adam unleashes the caged demons in the midst of the gathered Initiative soldiers, instigating a bloodbath (bonus: he can use the resulting dead body parts to build more zombie soldiers). We learn that Maggie Walsh has been zombified to assist her monstrous creation, and that Riley himself was engineered, complete with a chip of his own, as part of Walsh's super soldier program. Controlled now by Adam, Riley responds robotically to stated commands, blank-faced and inert. We read this as a meta-commentary on Blucas being directed by Whedon (we kid, we kid).

As it had to, the conflict comes down to a standoff between Buffy and Adam. The Slayer is badly overmatched: Adam is stronger, faster, and smarter than Buffy; alone she doesn't stand a chance.

But Buffy is not alone: Despite a truly upsetting argument in which Buffy angrily cuts herself off from her friends, Giles, Willow, and Xander—the core Scoobies—cast a spell joining their essences with Buffy's to form one perfect entity. Giles represents the brain, Willow the spirit, Xander the heart, and Buffy the hand, set into motion to work the will of the gestalt.

After a season of the show's central characters separated and alienated from one another, it is hugely cathartic to see their bond reaffirmed and literalized by this spell; Buffy's unique effectiveness as a Slayer derives from the strength of her emotional connections, and, with the band back together, so to speak, she easily destroys Adam.

The Denouement

An embarrassed U.S. government shuts down the Initiative and fills it in with concrete. Finn is discharged and, having summoned the will to dig out his chip with his bare hands (*ew*), returns to normal (emphasis on normal).

The Big Bad defeated, the Scoobies convene at Chez Joyce for a restorative evening of vegging out in front of the VCR. Instead, the exhausted group falls deeply asleep and dreams disquieting dreams, which both crystallize the deepest fears of the dreamers and suggest the even grimmer challenges to come.

Season Highlights

"Hush"

The Overhead Projector: Giles's wordless presentation to the Scoobies outlining the threat of the Gentlemen is, arguably, the comic highpoint of the entire series: from Giles's disturbingly bloody childlike drawings to Buffy's misunderstood hand gesture (the dirtiest joke ever to sneak into an ostensibly youth-oriented series?), this scene perfectly encapsulates the sharp wit, tonal fluidity, and deft characterization cherished by *Buffy* fans. The fact that the scene accomplishes all of this completely without dialogue—Whedon's universally acknowledged strong suit—makes it all the more remarkable.

"Pangs"

Buffy and Spike Get Engaged: Willow's errant wish spell's funniest consequence was the sick-making puppy love that instantly blossomed between Buffy and Spike, mortal enemies disgusted by the mere mention of each other under normal circumstances. Marsters and Gellar enact the absurd situation beautifully, as the natural chemistry between the actors and the opportunity to play completely against type bring out the best in the game performers; they're so obviously having fun. Of course, Buffy and Spike would later embark on a romantic relationship sans witchy interference, to much ado indeed. Their pairing in "Pangs," then, works as a sort of proof of concept, and it succeeds brilliantly.

Hey, let's literalize a metaphor! Spike (James Marsters) and Buffy (Sarah Michelle Gellar) work out some issues (yeah, right).

Tara and Willow: A Love Story

The gradual, relatable, and sensitively handled evolution of Willow and Tara's friendship into a passionate love affair unquestionably ranks among season four's best efforts; seldom has any adolescent romance been depicted so thoughtfully and touchingly on network television, much less one between two young women. Willow matures tremendously in her first year at college, gaining self-knowledge and self-confidence in equal measure as she redefines her relationships and steps out of the wallflower sidekick role and cultivates her magical talent with Tara, another shy girl with hidden depths. Hannigan and Benson, actresses particularly gifted at engaging audience empathy, never put a foot wrong. Their relationship is touching without being idealized (jealousy, uncertainty, and fear are honestly acknowledged), sexy but not titillating (there is heat between them, but it's never there for our delectation), and, frankly, a relief to viewers weary of the tortured heartbreak that is the usual fare for our Scoobies. Also, they adopt a cat named Miss Kitty Fantastico. Flawless.

I can read you like a book: Dream Tara in a reverie, from an erotically charged scene reminiscent of a sequence from Peter Greenaway's *The Pillow Book* (1996).

"Restless"

The Cheese Man: He wears the cheese. The cheese does not wear him.

Deconstructing "Restless"

For many *Buffy* fans and scholars, "Restless," the season-four finale, belongs in the holy quintet of episodes, along with *Hush*, *The Body*, *Normal Again*, and *Once More with Feeling*. "Restless" is perfect for the Internet age; people can spend endless hours deciphering it, and do. (Maybe not people you want to be friends with, but still.) The main body of the episode comprises four dreams, one by each of the core Scoobies: Willow, Xander, Giles, and Buffy (in that order). All four are symbol-drenched expressions of the identity crises the characters are undergoing. Two threads cut across all of the narratives: each character is (1) menaced by the spirit of the First Slayer (the Primitive, or Sineya), and (2) harassed by an irritating bald man with cheese—in Giles's dream he is actually wearing the cheese on his head and shoulders ("I wear the cheese. It does not wear me").

We are here to tell you that the Primitive means everything, and the bald man nothing at all (if we can take Joss Whedon at his word). More on this presently, but first, background:

This is the only time in the entire run of *Buffy* that the season doesn't conclude with a decisive battle between the forces of light (the Scoobies) and dark (usu-ally the Big Bad, but not always). Think about it: the Master (season one), Angel (two), the mayor (three), Glory (five), Dark Willow (six), and the First (seven). In season four, the ultimate confrontation between the Scoobies and Adam occurs in "Primeval," the twenty-first and penultimate episode, scripted by David Fury, also marking the first time said battle episode wasn't authored by Whedon, who does, however, write (and direct) "Restless." In his DVD commentary on the episode, Whedon explains that "we really felt like it would be nice to do something very, very different. And I thought a nice coda to this season, which had been a very anarchic and upheavaly season [yes, 'upheavaly'] . . . for all the characters, would be just to do a piece that commented on all of the forming characters that we've grown to know and love, and where they were in their lives, and what they felt about things and each other."

Season four had been a whirligig for the Scoobies—true, every season is turbu-lent when you're fending off apocalypses, but in the past at least they could count on each other. This time, Buffy and Willow are off at college, leaving behind Giles, jobless since Sunnydale High was blown up at the end of season three, plus officially no longer Buffy's Watcher, having been fired by the council, and Xander, adrift and insecure after choosing to skip college, and floundering around for purpose in life. As the season progresses, Buffy's attention is more and more consumed by Riley and the Initiative, leaving Willow to fend largely for herself as she wrestles with the consequences of Oz's departure and her emerging bisexuality. Fury's "Primeval" addresses this estrangement both literally and metaphorically: through one of Willow's spells, the four essentially merge into one super being to vanquish Adam, with each Scooby contributing his/her most defining attribute (so, *spiritus*, or spirit, for Willow; *animus*, or heart, for Xander; *sophus*, or mind, for Giles, and *manus*, or hand, for Buffy, the warrior). Through this spell, they invoke the power of all Slayers, from the Primitive on.

"Restless" rather brilliantly advances these themes, by positioning Sineya as the predator in each of the dreams, and having her attack them not through their weaknesses, but through the very strengths they contribute to the group. Giles eventually surmises that Sineya was offended when the Scoobies tapped into the power of the Slayer in "Primeval," but what she resents even more specifically is their presence in Buffy's life, since the only community the Slayer is supposed to be part of is the sisterhood of Slayers—those who were, those who are, and those who will be.

As "Restless" opens, the Scoobies plan a quiet evening at the Summers home in front of the TV, recovering from their exhausting battle with Adam. However, moments after Xander pops *Apocalypse Now* (how appropriate) into the VCR (how quaint), they enter dreamland.

Willow

Up first: Willow, whose dream opens with a tender, though off-kilter, scene between her and Tara, which Whedon says is "largely about their intimacy and trust, and the safe place in her life, which is her relationship with Tara." The poem Willow inscribes on Tara's back in Greek is Sappho's "Aphrodite Ode," in which the author, a spurned lover, pleads for divine intervention. Reluctantly, Will leaves the nest for school, where she discovers, much to her horror, that she's about to appear in a play she knows absolutely nothing about (Willow's stage fright had been firmly established by this point in the series). "Your costume is perfect," Buffy tells her, except that she isn't wearing one. "Nobody's gonna know the truth, you know, about you." Naturally, we suspect Willow is anxious about her sexual identity, but we're wrong: despite having blossomed into a (relatively) confident, powerful witch, Willow is fearful of being exposed as the same timid, insecure geek she was in high school (though if you ask us, she was pretty awesome back in the day). This same insecurity surfaces again in season six's "Two to Go," when Dark Willow dismisses her lighter iteration as "a loser, and she always has been. People picked on Willow in junior high school, high school, up until college, with her stupid, mousy ways." Whedon admits there's even more here than doesn't meet the eye, in that he was having a bit of fun at the WB's expense: near the end of the dream, Buffy rips off Willow's "costume," exposing the same type of nerd-fit she wore in the first episode ("Willow Episode One," Whedon calls it), before the WB complained that she was "too square," demanding that they "change her clothes!" Willow's dream ends when she is attacked by Sineya, who sucks the life/spirit out of her (remember, in "Primeval," Willow was identified as the "spirit" of the Scoobies).

Xander

Xander's dream involves all sorts of weirdness, like a come-on by Buffy's mom, a failed attempt to pee before a contingent of Initiative lab rats, and a parody of the Kurtz scene from *Apocalypse Now*, with Principal Snyder in the Marlon Brando role, but it all comes down to this: Xander's anxiety over the direction—or directionlessness—of his life, his fear of winding up like his father, and his insecurity over being left behind by his two closest friends, both pursuing college sheepskin ("The others have all gone on ahead," Giles tells him at one point)—all of which explains why he keeps winding up back in the basement of his parents' home. "The journey for Xander always seems to end up in the same place, and it's the place he doesn't want to be, partially because of a sense of failure and partially because there's something in there that frightens him," Whedon says. In the end, Xander's heart is ripped from his chest by the First Slayer—in his basement, of course.

Giles

Giles endures a profound identity crisis of his own in season four, jobless since the Sunnydale High library blew up and officially fired as Buffy's Watcher in season three. Still, he's a Watcher emeritus of sorts, as committed as ever to protecting Buffy to whatever degree possible—or at least to whatever extent she allows, as she yields to the twin pull of Riley and the Initiative. All of this explains the early part of Giles's dream, in which he attends a carnival with Olivia, his girlfriend, who's pushing a stroller, and Buffy, his "little girl," in overall and pigtails. Is this "normal" lifestyle one Giles secretly craves? Is it even possible, knowing what he does about the darkness in the world? Giles's musical performance at The Bronze—which Whedon calls the precursor to "Once More with Feeling," since he enjoyed writing it so much—similarly speaks to Giles's longing, in this case to enjoy the relatively carefree life of a musician, whose accomplishments are celebrated rather than performed in anonymity. He "can't decide who he wants to be," Whedon says. "'Should I raise a family? Should I be a rock star? Or should I give the boring exposition in every episode of 'Buffy'? And of course we combine the two by having him get up and sing the exposition" (according to Whedon, Alyson Hannigan couldn't stop cracking up during the scene where Willow and Xander are holding up lighters). The pocket watch, despite its evocation of the White Rabbit in *Alice in Wonderland*, is—rather starkly—a literal reminder to Giles of his responsibilities as a Watcher, though it comes too late, as he too is killed by the First Slayer, who scalps him (attacking him through his head, or mind).

Buffy

Lots going on here; just par for the course for Buffy. For more on the cryptic references to the coming of Dawn and the events of season five, ending in Buffy's sacrificial death, see page 194. In his DVD commentary, Whedon does acknowledge these signposts, but doesn't have much more to say about them. On the other hand, he denies that Buffy's encounter with her mom, living inside a wall, intentionally foreshadowed Joyce's season-five death, even though he knew at that point it was happening. "The idea that Mom lives behind the wall . . . just seemed correct," Whedon says.

Buffy has always struggled with the conflict between her individual identity and the demands of slaying, the essence of what transpires here. Buffy is a superior Slayer specifically because she answers to her own conscience, and refuses to abide by dictates that contradict a personal code of behavior. She won't be identified as a killer. She won't work with the Watchers Council. She refuses to turn her back on the other Scoobies. Here, Sineya is the symbolic representation of all the traditions Buffy rejects (it is not hard to interpret this storyline as a rejection of organized religion, especially since Whedon is an atheist). Sineya resents Buffy's maverick bent, understandably, because she herself had been forced to sacrifice so much, including her humanity, to become a weapon in the fight against evil.

"The Slayer does not walk in this world," Sineya tells Buffy, but Buffy replies: "I walk. I talk. I shop. I sneeze. I'm gonna be a fireman when the floods roll back. There's trees in the desert since you moved out, and I don't sleep on a bed of bones. Now give me back my friends."

In the end, Buffy vanquishes Sineya not by *slaying* her (remember, Buffy refuses to be defined as a killer) but by *rejecting* her: "You're *not* the source of me," she says, walking away.

The Cheese Man

In his DVD commentary on "Restless," Whedon says, bemused, that many people consider the bald man with the cheese to be "the crux of the entire show." Whedon states declaratively that the Cheese Man "is meaningless. Why? Because I needed something in the show that was meaningless, because there is always something in the dream that doesn't make any sense at all. In this case it was the Cheese Man. He confounds everybody because of that, and people ascribe him meaning." As usual, Whedon is correct; fans have theorized that the bald man who wears the cheese (Whedon has described this line as an homage to the 1998 film version of

The Man in the Iron Mask, in which Leonardo DiCaprio says, "I wear the mask. It does not wear me.") as all sorts of things, even as Whedon himself, embracing the cheesiness of *Buffy* (a theory we dismiss as being full of holes). The Cheese Man actually returns briefly in the seventh-season episode "Storyteller," when Willow is extracting memories of the First Evil from Andrew.

13

Lord, Spare Me College Boys in Love

UC Sunnydale + The Initiative

Professor Maggie Walsh (Lindsay Crouse)

David Mamet mainstay Lindsay Crouse brought her signature icy authority to the role of Maggie Walsh: intro psych professor, director of the secret paramilitary demon-hunting Initiative, and self-proclaimed "Evil Bitch-Monster of Death." That last was ostensibly a joke, but as Walsh's storyline progresses it seems an increasingly accurate assessment. Initially a supportive and affirming mentor figure for Buffy, Walsh quickly becomes disenchanted with the Slayer's unpredictability and laissez-faire approach to demon hunting (and increasingly jealous of Buffy's relationship with Riley) and contrives to kill the Slayer with an all-but-certainly fatal mission assignment. Underestimating Buffy isn't Walsh's only mistake—she also miscalculates with the super-soldier 314 Project, as evidenced when her Frankenstein's monster–like creation Adam impales her as his first waking act. Maggie can be read as a toxic mirror image of Joyce Summers: the bad mom, controlling and rigid, in contrast with Joyce's flexibility and support. Walsh grooms Riley as a surrogate son, lavishing him with approval even as she secretly chemically alters his mind and body and installs in him the same behavioral control chip used on the Initiative's demon prisoners. Buffy flourishes under Walsh's attention and rigor until Walsh perceives her as a threat, and, coldly, as a loose end to be cut. Adam's gutting and subsequent zombifying of his "mother" stands as a grimly satisfying end for the character; for the sin of hubris, she is hoisted upon her own petard (actually, a Polgara demon arm spike, which is worse).

Marc Blucas as Riley Finn, genetically enhanced super-commando/secret demon-hunter. Sounds pretty cool, right? (*Sigh*).

Parker Abrams (Adam Kaufman)

Of all Buffy's monstrous foes, few are so hateful as her human classmate Parker Abrams, a dreamily handsome young man with a line of "sensitive guy" BS sufficiently convincing to trick the emotionally vulnerable Slayer into a night of "carpe diem" passion. It's not the soul connection Buffy believed; after figuratively carving a notch into his bedpost, he cruelly disposes of Buffy to move on to a new target. He tries the same routine with Willow, who hilariously calls him on his crap. Even better: when Riley overhears Parker bragging about the conquest, he punches him square in the face, which actually made us appreciate Riley for five seconds or so.

Dr. Francis Angleman (Jack Stehlin)

Maggie Walsh's assistant on the 314 Project. Like his boss, killed and zombified by their creation Adam. One wonders if the Initiative offered a really amazing benefits package.

Major Ellis (Nick Chinlund)

A no-nonsense soldier sickened by red tape and obfuscation, craggy Major Ellis recruits ex-Initiative commandos for a non-ideological, non-scientific team of international demon hunters, extending an invitation to Riley. (Take it Riley, take it!!!)

Forrest Gates (Leonard Roberts)

An Initiative soldier close to Riley and Graham, Forrest was the most gung-ho and unreflective of the trio, displaying blind obedience to the Initiative's mission. Forrest resented and disliked Buffy for reasons similar to Professor Walsh's (her inquisitiveness, irreverence, and influence on Riley), and, after being killed by Adam and reanimated as a techno-zombie, he attacks the Slayer with gusto. Zombie Forrest is a real threat, massively strong and durable (Spike jabs his eye with a lit cigarette, causing only minor annoyance), but he takes himself out of the game by failing to observe electrical safety protocols, which is kind of ironic since he was all about protocol while fully alive.

Professor Gerhardt (Margaret Easley)

A well-meaning anthropologist, Professor Gerhardt was killed by the Native American vengeance spirit Hus. Happy Thanksgiving!

Colonel George Haviland (John Saint Ryan)

Maggie Walsh's successor as head of the Initiative, Colonel Haviland mostly just sycophantically deferred to the magically augmented Jonathan Levinson. Great mustache, though.

Professor Hawkins (Joyce Guy)

A rare example of a pleasant UC Sunnydale instructor. She advises Willow on re-entering school.

Professor Lillian (Leland Crooke)

Buffy's poetry professor, who, unlike most of the Sunnydale U faculty, treats the Slayer with respect (but wait . . . does he remind anyone a little of Archduke Sebassis?).

Mike (Jonathan Goldstein)

Buffy's sociology professor at UC Sunnydale. Utterly incomprehensible.

Graham Miller (Bailey Chase)

Riley's fellow Initiative commando and close friend, Graham Miller (named for *BTVS* writer/producer Doug Petrie's college friend) exhibited level-headed competence and loyalty to Riley. Happily, he survived the meltdown of the Initiative, joining Major Ellis's team of demon hunters.

Colonel McNamara (Conor O'Farrell)

Colonel Haviland's replacement as Initiative top dog. The disciplined, silver-haired McNamara was arrogant and officious, disdainful of Buffy's supernatural status and the efforts of her "unqualified" Scoobies. A true military man, the salty old soldier maintains his belief in proper procedure and the supremacy of the U.S. military right up until the moment he is brutally killed by an escaped demon. The paths of glory lead but to the grave.

Rachel (Jennifer Shon)

A UC Sunnydale student who, after being humiliated in a fraternity prank, gets revenge via vengeance demon Anya, who sets a spider monster on the

Cheer up, guys, it's not the end of the world or anything.

louts, which kills them horribly. Rachel is traumatized, but we found it hard to work up much sympathy for the murdered bros. Maybe *we* should be vengeance demons?

Vaughne (Megalyn Echikunwoke)

UC Sunnydale student and member of the unimpressive Wiccan group "Daughters of Gaea." More bake sales than dark rites, is what we're saying.

Mr. Ward (Bob Fimiani)

A distinguished-looking, unspecified government official who gives the order to shut down the catastrophic Initiative: "Burn it down and salt the earth."

14

Do You Think We're Dancing?

Season Five

> Death is your gift.
>
> —*Sineya, the First Slayer, to Buffy Summers*

S eason five of *Buffy the Vampire Slayer* is haunted by death. It may sound odd to single out this run of episodes as specifically thanatotic; after all, *BTVS*'s entire premise is explicitly predicated on violent death (and the implications of un-death). "Slayer" is right there in the title. But where the earlier seasons used the threat of death as a plot engine, thematic ballast, and source of action-genre stakes, season five brings the concept home, literally and figuratively, as Buffy copes with the tragic passing of her mother, Joyce; wrestles with the death wish that is part and parcel of Slayerhood; and, ultimately, sacrifices her own life to save her sister (and the world). A mature reckoning with the true meaning of death is an essential component of growing up, and, in important ways, season five marks the end of Buffy's childhood and sentimental education.

It also heralds the arrival of Dawn Summers, Buffy's annoying little sister, as a major character. We briefly met Dawn in the closing moments of the season five premiere, in an all-time WTF reveal—the audience had never heard any mention of a second Summers girl, but Buffy and Joyce (and, for that matter, everyone else) act as if Dawn had always been there. Whedon slyly refuses to explain, and the audience is forced to accept Dawn's presence as the new status quo. It's a canny narrative ploy: the increasing uneasiness and confusion the characters experience in regard to Dawn is shared by the viewer, though for all intents and purposes, Dawn is a perfectly normal, average tweener, resentful of big sister's bossiness and freedom but basically well-intentioned and good-humored.

Life goes on: the reaffirmation of group ties ended season four on a heartening note, but season five opens with Giles continuing to question his

Sister Act: It's always darkest before the Dawn (Michelle Trachtenberg).

usefulness as an unemployed Watcher, mulling a move back to England. He's persuaded to stay by Buffy, who asks him to help her better understand her nature and potential as a Slayer. He also buys a sweet little convertible sports car, because he is middle-aged. When Harmony and the Gang That Couldn't Bite Straight attack The Magic Box and kill the owner in a failed attempt on Buffy's life, Giles makes another major life decision and buys the place, which provides him with a new vocation, the Scoobies with a new headquarters, and the writers with a handy new exposition-delivery venue.

Xander runs afoul of a demon called Toth, who splits the hapless lad into two separate entities: a passive, sensitive loser and a confident, aggressive go-getter. Toth intended to split Buffy's Slayer and human natures, making her easier to kill, but how funny would that be? Instead we get Type-A Xander breaking hearts and making dollars while Type-B Xander mopes around ineffectively, giving Nicholas Brendon room to be hilarious (always a solid strategy on *BTVS*).

A heartsick Spike crafts a Buffy mannequin and romances it. Hey, Spike: welcome to rock bottom.

Riley is also suffering, confessing to Xander that he knows Buffy doesn't truly love him. You know, lots of people like Nilla Wafers, but does anyone

I wish I could quit you: A typically fraught exchange between Spike (James Marsters) and Buffy (Sarah Michelle Gellar).   *WB/20th Century Fox/Photofest*

actually LOVE them? Riley overcompensates by pushing his Initiative enhancements to the max, demonstrating impressive strength, resistance to pain, and stupidity. On the verge of burning himself out and expiring, Riley is finally convinced to have his super-parts removed, and he survives. Yay?

Troubling: Joyce seems to have a moment of confusion (or clarity) about Dawn, and immediately collapses. More troubling: Spike has Buffy sex dreams. We suppose cold showers aren't very effective for vampires, but come on, buddy. Get a grip.

A new Big Bad arrives in Sunnydale: The Beast, also known as Glorificus (but her friends just call her Glory). Wearing the form of an attractive young woman, Glory is, in fact, an exiled god, late of a hell dimension, searching for the Key that will take her home. The fact that using said Key will open a demonic portal that spells doom for all life on Earth troubles her not one whit. Glory is immensely powerful—she repeatedly cleans Buffy's clock without breaking a sweat—but, despite the best efforts of her scabby minions, she can't find that damned Key. In fact, she doesn't even know what form the Key takes. *Hmm.*

Speaking of Dawn (*heh*), when Buffy uses magic to examine her mother for supernatural causes of her recent collapse and chronic headaches, all signs of Summers the Younger disappear. *Hmm*, again. Buffy and Giles confer and figure it out: Dawn is the Key, a being of mystical energy given the form of a young girl; all memories of life with Dawn before her arrival in Sunnydale are magical fakes. Trouble is, the emotions are real, and they remain. Buffy and Giles agree to keep Dawn's nature a secret between them.

The Maclays, Tara's hillbilly family, visit, and they are terrible, but the ordeal results in the timid Wiccan feeling more fully integrated into the Scoobies.

On a routine patrol, Buffy, despite her recent intensive training, is nearly bested by a run-of-the-mill vampire. Shaken, she interrogates Spike about his two Slayer kills, desperate to understand the flaw that almost brought her down. Spike's story is a series highlight: we meet young William the Bloody—bloody awful poet, that is. William is a simpering weakling, scorned by his beloved muse and taunted by his peers until a meeting with a certain Drusilla gives him a whole new outlook.

Spike recounts killing a dragon-like Chinese Slayer during the Boxer Rebellion and a Pam Grieresque Slayer in '70s New York City. His explanation for his success: Slayers, so intimate with death and burdened by their mission, harbor a death wish. All it takes for a vampire to prevail is for a Slayer to have one bad day and succumb. Buffy's intense connection to life—in other words, her relationships—has so far countered this urge toward self-destruction, but the epiphany is sobering.

Joyce is diagnosed with a mundane, non-supernatural brain tumor, which is somehow more terrifying than any demon threat. Spike, driven to madness by his frustration over his unreciprocated feeling for Buffy, arrives on the scene to bring his Slayer count up to three—but when he sees her distraught and sobbing over her mother's condition, he instead comforts her.

Which is a lot cooler than Riley's move: the gloomy lug has taken up quasi-erotic voluntary vampire victimhood, allowing Sandy (remember her? Pretty girl Vamp Willow sired?) to very suggestively "drain" him in a creepy sexual metaphor. It's a perversely cruel betrayal of his relationship with Buffy, and Riley comes into clearer focus as an early example of the toxic "friend-zoned" "nice guy."

Say, who's this orderly Ben at the Sunnydale hospital? He seems quite nice, aside from summoning a "queller demon" from outer space to help him get a handle on the sudden influx of mentally ill patients whose brains have been scrambled by Glory's invasive psychic Key hunting. What's up with that?

Joyce, temporarily non compos mentis due to the tumor, is attacked by the queller demon. She survives, but learns the truth about her younger "daughter." She still loves and wants to protect Dawn, because Joyce is the best.

Spike, flagrantly flouting the Guy Code, lets Buffy in on Riley's bloody little secret, and Buffy confronts him as he is being serviced in a vampire brothel. It doesn't go well. Riley hits the road with a cadre of former Initiative soldiers to hunt vamps in South America. We'll give co-executive producer Doug Petrie the last word: "He wasn't dark; he wasn't mysterious; he was not very interesting. And the fans were not very interested. So we kind of messed him up, and that's when he did get interesting—he got darker toward the end, when he's sucking on vampires (sic) for fun. That's when he got interesting. But that's also when we knew that this guy's got to go . . . by the time we got to season five, when he went down his dark road, we knew he was going to be out of there."

Smell ya later, oh bland and rigid one.

Giles briefs the Watchers Council on Glory, and the Council, true to form, immediately starts interfering, sending a detachment (including head honcho Quentin Travers) to Sunnydale to test Buffy's fitness for the coming confrontation. Buffy proves her worth by refusing to kowtow to the Council, defiantly claiming her power as the Slayer, and demanding Giles's reinstatement (with retroactive remuneration) as full Watcher. Good news: the Council agrees. Bad news: the Council informs Buffy that Glory is, in fact, a god. *Ulp.*

Spike, now a full-time Nosey Parker, helps a frightened and confused Dawn—she's twigged to the fact that her loved ones have started regarding her very strangely—discover the truth of her identity; understandably, she's upset. Oh, by the way: Glory and Ben are two entities sharing the same body, sort of . . . when Ben is manifested, he is aware of Glory's existence but has no knowledge of her activities, and vice-versa. Better than being a sentient-energy-fake-teenager-thing? Debatable.

Drusilla returns! The mad vampiress quickly assesses her erstwhile boyfriend Spike's sorry, chip-implanted state and exhorts him to overcome the inhibitor through sheer ferocious demon will. He does, killing a woman, and the Spike and Dru Show is back in full flower. The duo kidnaps Buffy and are about to kill her when Spike reveals he's been faking, releases Buffy, and offers to stake Dru. (Harsh.) Dru gets away, and Buffy again coldly rejects Spike, who, whatever he professes, has not been making a good case for himself as boyfriend material.

Another lousy boyfriend, genius engineering student Warren Mears, is bedeviled by April, the sex robot he created and tired of, abandoning her in his dorm room. April commits an impressive amount of lovelorn mayhem before being brought to heel by Buffy, but Spike likes what he sees and sets Warren to work on a sexbot for himself . . . a Buffy sexbot. Guys. The sexbots. Not cool.

Later, the gang spies Spike out with Warren's doting Buffybot and, believing it to be the real McCoy, are appropriately horrified. Sarah Michelle Gellar clearly has a ball playing the cloying automaton.

Joyce, after a successful surgery, shockingly dies from a lingering complication. The profound impact of Joyce's death on Buffy and the rest of the Scoobies cannot be overstated; Whedon's direction of "The Body," the episode portraying Joyce's death, received high praise for its formally rigorous and emotionally devastating acuity, and the event established a new sense of stakes and seriousness for the entire series. Death had been previously played for suspense, comedy, shock value, and even tragedy, but the loss of Joyce hurt in a way that no previous reversal had. Buffy had known horror, and sadness, and terror, and despair, but never the world-nullifying totality of grief; Buffy post-Joyce is not just older and sadly wiser, but a new person altogether.

Spike thoughtfully sends anonymous flowers, and less thoughtfully helps Dawn resurrect Joyce as a zombie creature, with the aid of the mysterious Doc, who looks like a nice old professor if you can overlook the reptilian tail. Fortunately, this plan never comes to full fruition, but it does allow Buffy to fully face the reality of her loss.

Remember Glory? Well, she tortures a monk (love their spheres!) for information pertaining to the Key; he reveals it is a person, but resists giving the person's identity. She and her scabby minions kidnap Spike (this is a really kidnap-y season) and torture him horribly for the name of the Key, but, utterly devoted to Buffy, Spike resists and is left for dead. Yes, he's already dead, but they really go to town on the poor guy.

Glory also makes a mess of poor Tara, psychically enfeebling the witch in another effort to find the Key. Willow, whose exponentially increasing magical abilities have been a source of concern, goes full Dark Willow and vengefully attacks Glory with a spectacular display of eldritch might. Still, god > witch, and Willow goes down.

Buffy, impersonating her robot double, visits the mangled Spike to get the lowdown on his interrogation. Learning he bore untellable pain to keep Dawn safe, she is moved and drops the subterfuge, expressing her appreciation.

As the inevitable confrontation with Glory approaches, the incoherently babbling Tara lets slip that Dawn is the Key, and the Scoobies attempt to get the hell out of Dodge to save her. Sensible, but they are stopped by the Knights of Byzantium, a cosplaying band of cultists opposed to Glory and intent upon killing Dawn, thus thwarting Glory's plan to open the portal to her hell dimension. Every teenager thinks the whole world is against them. Dawn is the only one to be correct.

Giles is seriously injured by the Knights, and is saved by Ben, delighting fans of ironic foreshadowing. (By the way, none of our heroes yet realizes the Ben/Glory connection, due to a spell that makes them forget it.) Less happily, Glory succeeds in acquiring Dawn, plunging the already grieving Buffy into a state of catatonia, requiring an astral rescue mission/encounter session, compliments of Willow, to retrieve her.

Glory can't fully enjoy her success, because the divide between her Ben and Glory personas begins to weaken, and she/he flips back and forth with disorienting frequency. But that's okay, because Ben gets on board with Glory's agenda in the interest of self-preservation. Girl's got a blood ritual to complete, so it's off to a tall, dubiously stable construction tower they go.

Buffy asks Spike to protect Dawn—this is how dire things have become. The vampire is filled with noble resolve by Buffy's trust and, mid-rescue attempt, heroically gets thrown off the tower by Doc. Remember Doc, Professor Creepy Tail? Turns out he's a big Glory supporter, which is bad news because the man (?) has serious magical mojo.

But Buffy has a few tricks of her own ready to go: the Buffybot is put to good use (for once) as a decoy, putting Glory in place for a walloping by Buffy with Olaf the Troll's (an ex of Anya's who dropped in for a visit earlier in the season) magic hammer. Xander delivers the coup de grace—a direct hit with a wrecking ball—temporarily disabling Glory as she helplessly transforms into Ben.

BTVS goes full X-Men: Behold, Dark Willow (Alyson Hannigan).

Glory's down, but Doc proves to be a more than capable stand-in, beginning the blood ritual (poor Dawnie) and opening the demon portal.

As Buffy goes after Doc, Giles, now aware Ben and Glory are one, very chillingly and cold-bloodedly kills the helpless Ben, remarking that he's able to employ ignoble means in the interest of expediency because, unlike Buffy, he is not a hero. It's a great character moment for the usually stuffy and flustered Watcher (Ripper alert), and neatly underscores the season's mandate to more fully define the exact nature and qualities of Buffy as the Slayer.

Buffy manages to rescue Dawn from Doc, and Glory is no longer a threat, but the damage has been done: the portal is open and flooding Sunnydale with murderous demons, and will not shut until the blood of the Key is spilled. Buffy realizes that Dawn's essence was drawn from her own, and that they share the same blood, and we tragically see what Giles was talking about a minute ago.

"Death is your gift," the first Slayer told Buffy, and now she understands: her death is her gift to Dawn (and the world). Sacrificing her life will save her sister and seal the portal. Without hesitation, she does just that. Because she's a hero.

Season five of *BTVS* averaged around 4.5 million viewers and marked the end of the series' network-defining tenure on the WB. Sarah Michelle Gellar was nominated for a Golden Globe for her performance, and the AFI listed *Buffy* among the year's best dramas.

Season Highlights

"Buffy Vs. Dracula"

Xander "Renfield" Harris: When the real-life-no-kidding Count Dracula shows up in Sunnydale, his dark charisma sets the distaff Scoobies' hearts aflutter—but no one falls for the Dark Prince as hard as Xander, who quickly finds himself head over heels in thrall to the übervamp. Xander's feeble attempts to conceal his new allegiance (responding to Buffy's strategy: "Like any of that is enough to fight the dark master . . . bater") are as funny as his slavering devotion to Drac. The guy's just a born sidekick. The special relationship between Xander and Dracula endures past the series, as the two reconnect in the comics, much to our delight and Xander's chagrin. At least he doesn't have to eat any flies.

David Solomon, the director of "Buffy vs. Dracula," states:

> I had seen many different versions of *Dracula*. I actually love the character. If I'm being perfectly honest I did not love the person we cast for it, I just didn't. But that's neither here nor there, and we worked together

fine. It was a little bit of a strain if I remember correctly, like there were some things in it that I didn't really like. But when you're given a classic character it's a little bit more pressure, because you really want to get it right . . . . It wakes you up because you realize it's a big responsibility to carry the baton, even if it's just for a forty-two-minute episode, and I felt that way about Dracula. I didn't want to let anything slip through the cracks in terms of what Dracula needed to be. We had all very different ideas of what Dracula was. I saw him as a great seducer, not solely of women but just a seducer in general, and I wanted to lean into that because his power came from his ability to get people to do what he wanted them to do.

"Fool for Love"

A Remembrance of Spike Past: Spike's origin story stands as a series highlight, as we learn that pre-siring, William was a hopeless dork, reciting bad poetry to his scornful crush. High comedy, but Vampire Spike has some juicier stories: we see his two Slayer kills, in China during the Boxer Rebellion and on a New York City subway in the punk-rock seventies. The sequences are thrillingly cinematic and offer tantalizing glimpses of Buffy's predecessors, and the lesson Buffy takes from the story is profound. Funny, thrilling, unexpected, suspenseful, thought-provoking, and surprisingly affecting: the Spike flashbacks are everything great about *BTVS* condensed into a few indelible sequences. Bravo.

"The Body": Loss and Grief

Whedon directed this keystone episode, in which Buffy experiences the death of her mother, with a wounding, disorienting approach (no music, off-center framing) that conveys Buffy's trauma and confusion to the audience with startling directness; death had never quite looked like this on TV before, as the mundanity of the situation somehow makes the horror and pain almost unbearable to endure. "The Body" is a formal masterpiece, and its emotional impact is unequaled in the series.

"Tough Love": Dark Willow

When Glory psychically brutalizes Tara in an interrogation, leaving the witch mentally shattered, Willow decides she owes the hell god some reciprocal pain, and attacks. Season five saw Willow's abilities grow exponentially (to the concern of Tara), but this new Willow, a vengeful fury with jet-black eyes, levitating in a crackling field of magical energy, is something new. The raging witch actually manages to hurt Glory—the first time we've seen the hell god staggered—but alas, rock beats scissors and god beats witch. Happily, Willow is able to later use her burgeoning powers to repair Tara's mind. Dark Willow will return, again because of Tara, but that's too sad to go into here.

"The Gift"

Buffy's Gift: "Dawn, listen to me. Listen. I love you. I will always love you. But this is the work I have to do. Tell Giles . . . tell Giles I figured it out. And, and I'm okay. And give my love to my friends. You have to take care of them now. You have to take care of each other. You have to be strong. Dawn . . . the hardest thing in this world is to live in it. Be brave. Live. For me."

BUFFY ANNE SUMMERS
1981–2001
BELOVED SISTER
DEVOTED FRIEND
SHE SAVED THE WORLD
A LOT

He Is Dracula?

> We men are determined, nay, are we not pledged, to destroy this monster? But it is no part for a woman. Even if she be not harmed, her heart may fail her in so much and so many horrors and hereafter she may suffer, both in waking, from her nerves, and in sleep, from her dreams. And besides, she is young woman and not so long married, there may be other things to think of some time, if not now. You tell me she has wrote all, then she must consult with us, but tomorrow she say goodbye to this work, and we go alone."
>
> —*Professor Abraham Van Helsing,* Dracula

Chauvinistic much?

As *Dracula* fans know, Van Helsing is the esteemed vampire hunter, summoned by Dr. John Seward to examine the afflicted Lucy Westenra, in Bram Stoker's 1897 Gothic novel, which, though certainly not the first vampire story ever told, did more than any other to popularize certain widely accepted tropes about these undead creatures of the night. What many of these fans *think* they know, but don't, is that Van Helsing drove a wooden stake through the count's heart, converting him to dust, when in fact it was two men—neither named Van Helsing, but rather Jonathan Harker and Quincey Morris—who did the deed, using not a wooden stake but knives: Harker's kukri, slicing across Dracula's throat, and Morris's

Bowie, plunged deep inside his heart (true, it is Van Helsing, portrayed by Edward Van Sloane, who vanquishes Dracula with a wooden stake to the heart in Tod Browning's bastardized 1931 film version, starring Bela Lugosi, but we are purists, so don't even try that argument on us).

The more we delved into this Dracula bloke (who, of course, appears in "Buffy vs. Dracula," the season-five opener of *Buffy*) the more we discovered how widely misunderstood he is. Elizabeth Miller, professor emeritus at Memorial University of Newfoundland, Canada, and the Transylvanian Society of Dracula's honorary Baroness of the House of Dracula, has carved out a nice little career debunking these myths, most notably in her superb 2000 book *Dracula: Sense + Nonsense*.

The greatest fallacy of all, according to Miller: that Dracula was modeled on Vlad Tepes, a.k.a. Vlad the Impaler, the fifteenth-century Wallachian ruler ("Wallachia" being an archaic term for a region of Romania). This is tricky business, because there's no disputing that Dracula, originally named Count Vampyr, was *renamed* after Vlad, who was, in fact, known by that sobriquet, even if Stoker didn't know it. Explanation: Stoker came across the name Dracula in William Wilkinson's *An Account of Wallachia and Moldavia* (1820), which included the following footnote: "Dracula in the Wallachian language means Devil. The Wallachians were, at that time, as they are at present, used to give this as a surname to any person who rendered himself conspicuous either by courage, cruel actions, or cunning." While Wilkinson does identify Dracula as a Wallachian ruler who battled the Turks in the fifteenth century, there is no mention of Vlad Tepes or Vlad the Impaler or any Vlad at all, and no reference to alleged vampirism or even to Vlad/Dracula's now-legendary cruelty (including his nasty little habit of impaling foes on wooden stakes).

Another popular misconception about Stoker's Dracula: that sunlight is fatal (in *Buffy* and *Angel*, it is specifically *direct* exposure to sunlight that sets the night creature ablaze. "Vampires don't sleep in coffins," Angel says. "It's a misconception made popular by hack writers and ignorant media. In fact, we can and do move around during the day, as long as we avoid direct sunlight. Got it?"). In the novel *Dracula*, Van Helsing specifically advises the others that Dracula's "power ceases, as does that of all evil things, at the coming of the day," but clearly Dracula is not in mortal danger from the sun. Even then, the vampire does, on two separate occasions, exhibit what appears to be supernatural agility or strength in the daytime. (As Miller points out, destruction by sunlight was introduced in the 1922 silent German film *Nosferatu*, loosely based on *Dracula* and appropriating as its title a term first presented as synonymous with "vampire" in Emily Gerard's 1885 magazine article "Transylvanian Superstitions," another of Stoker's known sources.)

Interesting conceptual conflicts also arise between Dracula and the Buffyverse vamps. For instance, in *Buffy*, vampires are hybrids, descendants of both pure-breed demons and human beings, birthed by mutual blood sucking between undead perpetrator and human victim—in "Welcome to the Hellmouth," Buffy calls it "a

Tod Browning's *Dracula* (1931) elevated Stoker's vampire to mythic status in the popular imagination.

whole big sucking thing." In *Dracula*, vampires are simply dead bodies that continue to live in a grave, which they depart at night in search of the blood of the living, which invigorates them, fending off decay. Victims are turned regardless of whether they engage in mutual blood sucking or not.

As to Dracula's vampiric genesis: some scholars argue that Stoker never adequately addresses the question, but he certainly offers a strong suggestion, having Van Helsing report back to the group on the findings of his friend Arminius: "The Draculas were, says Arminius, a great and noble race, though now and again were scions who were held by their coevals to have had dealings with the Evil One. They learned his secrets in the Scholomance [a school of black magic run by the Devil, as superstition has it], amongst the mountains over Lake Hermanstadt, where the devil claims the tenth scholar as his due. In the records are such words as 'stregoica,' witch, 'ordog' and 'pokol,' Satan and hell, and in one manuscript this very Dracula is spoken of as 'wampyr' . . . "

Yup, the Devil made him do it.

Nevertheless, we risk overstating the anomalous: Stoker's *Dracula* did indeed spread certain vampiric conventions that pop culture in general—and the Buffyverse in particular—have embraced, including the inability to cast shadows or reflect mirror images (no soul, no reflection), plus the notion that vampires must be invited into the home before entering for the first time, though not after that: "He may not enter anywhere at the first, unless there be some one of the household who bid him to come, though afterwards he can come as he please," Van Helsing says.

In "Buffy vs. Dracula," the count is depicted as an übervamp of sorts, capable of enslaving victims (like, hilariously, Xander) or transforming into a bat or mist, powers that more conventional vampires lack, all of which can be traced back to Stoker. Still, no match for the Buffster, who stakes him once, then hangs around for his inevitable return:

"You don't think I watch your movies?" she says. "You always come back."

Note to self: Say nothing of this to Miller.

Dacre Stoker (Bram's great-grandnephew and co-editor with Miller of *The Lost Journal of Bram Stoker: The Dublin Years*)

FAQ: You've got basically two main characters who are females in Lucy Westenra and Mina Harker. We're writing a book about *Buffy*, which is about vampires but also about this feminist hero. And we have the quote that we started this section with from Van Helsing, which seems to treat women as these dainty people who need to be protected by men. How do you perceive your great-grand-uncle's book in terms of its depiction of women in these Victorian times?

Dacre Stoker: Mina is really the star, if you can believe it. Van Helsing is the old-school guy, he knows medicine and the supernatural. He's got this knowledge, but without Mina, who's depicted as the New Woman [a term believed to have first appeared in a periodical in Britain in 1893, in an article titled "The Social Standing of the New Woman," from the feminist journal *Woman's Herald*, and that Mina herself uses on three occasions]. She's got her act together, she doesn't lose her head like some of the men do at certain times and flop all over the place when things happen, she has this interaction with Dracula where there's the blood exchange, and she still is the glue. She's also the one, just like Buffy, who pulls all the information together of this whole band of heroes. Mina is, to me and many others, the star, the so-called New Woman.

FAQ: Why do you think he wrote it that way?

DS: Bram had a mother who was a social activist, very strong, she raised seven kids, she championed all kinds of social causes in Dublin, where working conditions

were terrible, she wrote essays and presented them on women's rights, on education of the handicapped, she spoke at society meetings about how you can judge
somebody as criminally insane or not, so I personally believe that Bram's mother is
partially the role model for Mina, a very, very strong woman. His two sisters were
no slouches, either. They were very well educated in the arts. And I'm sure his
wife, Florence, was a lot like that. She was a tough cookie and wanted to originally
be in the theatrical world, and she was very close to my great-grandfather. I really
believe that he felt strongly about new social issues, and his depiction of Mina as the
New Woman was a statement, and that Bram placed her there to prove that even
though you've got Dr. Seward being a medical man, you've got the lawyer Jonathan
Harker, you've got the aristocracy in Arthur Holmwood, you've got the American in
Quincey Morris, all those different facets of society are still sort of needing a strong
woman to make everything work and come together. Now short of her stabbing
Dracula, like [screenwriter] Jim Hart did in the [Francis Ford] Coppola movie [*Bram
Stoker's Dracula*, 1992], she was the one responsible for keeping the band of heroes
on track and figuring everything out. Because of the weird way that *Dracula* is written, in this epistolary style, she's the glue that says, "Hey, guys, don't you realize
what's going on? I've taken all your notes, all your information, there's a freaking
vampire here, get with it, and this is how we've got to deal with it." Now Van
Helsing is old school, so Bram is using him to sort of say, "Wait a second, she's too
weak and feeble." Well, she has been affected at that stage by the blood exchange
with Dracula, so she is in a weakened state, but she's still the glue, and when it
comes to the end she's the one who's now raising a child, the next generation. She's
tougher than nails.

One of the most interesting and exciting of recent novels is Mr. Bram
Stoker's 'Dracula.' It deals with the ancient mediaeval vampire legend, and
in no English work of fiction has this legend been so brilliantly treated. The
scene is laid partly in Transylvania and partly in England. The first fifty-four
pages, which give the journal of Jonathan Harker after leaving Vienna until
he makes up his mind to escape from Castle Dracula, are in their weird
power altogether unrivalled in recent fiction.

—*Jane Stoddard,* British Weekly, *July 1, 1897*

15

We Will Walk Through the Fire

Season Six

Where Do We Go from Here?

Buffy and crew pull up stakes (sorry, we can't stop doing that) at the WB, ending their network-defining tenure there to move to UPN, maintaining their "Tuesdays at 8" timeslot. Ratings rose a bit, averaging around 4.6 million viewers, and the show was nominated for Emmy Awards in various technical categories. Executive producer Marti Noxon steps in as showrunner.

Buffy's heroic death at the climax of season five feels like an appropriate ending point for the saga of the Slayer; Buffy had grown from child to adult and fulfilled her destiny by sacrificing herself to save the world. But the problem with stories is that, after their tidy conclusions, life goes on, usually messily and full of inconvenient contradictions and compromises. Whedon is wise enough to recognize that this is where things get *really* interesting, and so: Willow, high on her own (magical) supply, hubristically rips Buffy out of heaven and thrusts her back into her life of loss, duty, and pain. We have moved beyond the coming-of-age narrative and plunged headlong into the terrors of existentialism, resulting in the bleakest, saddest, most disturbing era of *BTVS* thus far . . . as well as some of the series' most transcendent, unforgettable moments.

We open with the semi-functional Scoobies, aided by the Buffybot, continuing the fight against demon-kind. They do a decent job of it until a vampire discovers the deception and excitedly reports the death of the Slayer to the Hellions, a demon biker gang. They promptly kill the "Shempy" bloodsucker and make for Sunnydale, where they wreak bloody havoc on the under-defended Hellmouth.

Willow, who, with Tara, has been acting as de facto guardian of Dawn, has continued to advance by leaps and bounds in her magical abilities, and commences a plan to resurrect Buffy, whom Willow fears has been banished to a hell dimension. Her logic is questionable—who's to say where Buffy wound up?—but the grief-stricken gang gets on board. The process is bloody and exceedingly dangerous (Willow keeps the more unpleasant aspects of the operation to herself), and seemingly fails when the Hellions' arrival disrupts the casting, but it works. Unfortunately, this means a near-catatonically disoriented Buffy awakes buried in her coffin, unaided by her friends, who still think her dead. Not a great start to a new life.

See you in October: *BTVS* stakes out new territory on UPN.

UPN/20th Century Fox/Photofest

Buffy being Buffy, the shell-shocked Slayer punches her way out of the grave and takes out the Hellions, but all is not well: Buffy's come back "wrong," distant, disconnected, and adrift, a veritable zombie unable to reconnect with her former existence. We learn the devastating truth: Buffy was not in hell, but heaven, relieved of her burdens and at peace. Willow has not saved Buffy, but damned her. How bad is it? Buffy can find a kind of solace only with Spike. That's how bad it is.

Giles, who had no Slayer to Watch, had left for England shortly before Buffy's revival; he returns immediately upon her reemergence and immediately upbraids Willow for her recklessness, calling her a "rank, arrogant amateur." Stung—she had been pridefully eager to relate the skillful spell-casting that brought Buffy back—Willow shockingly *threatens* her mentor, underlining how far down the road to addiction the powerful witch has traveled. The metaphor isn't subtle, but it works: Willow's a magic junkie, and the consequences will be profound.

MEANWHILE: remember that little turd Warren Mears, the one with the creepy robot sex doll? And remember Jonathan Levinson, briefly the coolest dude in the universe? They have formed a trio, along with newcomer Andrew Wells, with the objective of becoming supervillains and taking over Sunnydale. Stereotypical fanboy nerds, the trio members obsessively quote and reference sci-fi classics and moon over collectable figurines in between criminal activities, and in the early going they are largely played for laughs. This will change.

In addition to her existential crisis, Buffy is broke, and the mundane responsibilities of home ownership and childcare become more anxiety-provoking than any previous apocalypse. Giles pitches in, but things don't go smoothly; Dawn sneaks out of the house and is attacked by her vampire date, for instance. Also, the basement's flooded. Adding insult to injury, the Trio begins to harass the Slayer by various technological and magical means.

Couple drama: Xander, despite misgivings, announces his engagement to Anya, while Tara and Willow begin to fight over Willow's over-reliance on magic. Willow, shockingly, magically erases the conflict from Tara's mind, an unforgivable violation that Willow commits without a second thought. Is this the bottom of the spiral? Nope.

The demon Sweet comes to Sunnydale and magically transforms reality into a Broadway-style musical, in which all of the characters helplessly express their hidden thoughts and feelings through song. Turns out Giles feels like an enabling hindrance to Buffy's full personhood; Xander and Anya have doubts about holy matrimony; Dawn feels neglected and ignored; Spike is very agitated about his love for the Slayer; and Tara is (heartbreakingly) over the moon in love with Willow. Buffy reveals to her friends the truth of her

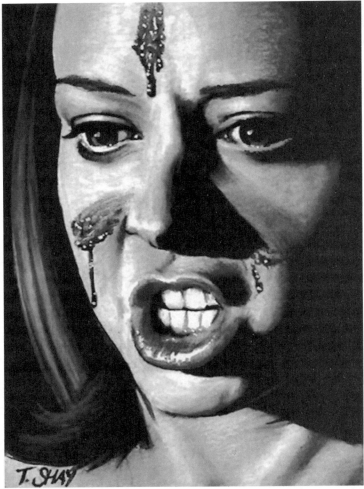

"Rank, arrogant amateur" Willow Rosenberg recklessly invokes powerful
dark magic to raise Buffy from the dead.   *Art by Tim Shay*

afterlife experience—she was finally happy—leaving her friends reeling with
guilt. That's entertainment!

After this tuneful airing of grievances (and enough praise cannot be
lavished on the brilliant artistic success of "Once More With Feeling"—the
episode actually inspired a brief vogue for special musical episodes of non-
musical programs), Giles returns to England AGAIN (he must have insane
frequent flier miles) and Buffy lip locks with the besotted Spike; not great.
Worse: Willow promises to give up magic cold turkey after Tara discovers
her mind-meddling, but the witch immediately casts a memory-erasing spell

AGAIN, accidentally giving everyone in the group total amnesia. It's amusing (Giles and Anya assume they're a couple; Spike believes himself to be a noble, Angel-like vampire named Randy) until Teeth, a shark-like demon loan... er...shark (groan) arrives at The Magic Box to collect a debt from Spike, putting everyone's lives in danger, AGAIN. Jeez, Willow.

Tara understandably (and terribly sadly) breaks up with Willow, who, now lacking a magical playmate, uses her rapidly growing magical facility to de-rat Amy, who had been contentedly nibbling cheese in a cage in Willow's room since season three. After a crash course in recent Sunnydale history, Amy is ready to par-tay, and she and Willow embark on a magic-fueled rager that leaves Willow badly spent; no problem, says Amy, she knows a guy. The guy is Rack, a supremely seedy and loathsome warlock who deals in black market spells. Rack's place is a dump, and, with its twitchy tweakers eagerly awaiting their fixes on Rack's shabby couch, the resemblance to a drug den is pretty unmistakable. Despite all of this, Willow's reaction to Rack's wares is euphoric. Uh oh.

Speaking of uh oh: Buffy and Spike have violent, house-wrecking sex. We'll leave that there for a moment.

Willow continues her Magical Jerkface World Tour by taking Dawn along to Rack's while babysitting. Completely wasted on contraband hoodoo, Willow wrecks her car, breaking Dawn's arm, and nearly gets them both killed by a demon (yeah, it's Sunnydale). Is this bottom yet? Yes, yes it is, and Willow goes on the wagon, vowing to magic no more. Uh huh.

Back to more quotidian concerns: Social Services threatens to remove Dawn from Buffy's care after a disastrous home visit (Spike was there), but Buffy makes use of some temporary invisibility (courtesy of a Trio plot gone awry) to put matters right. Newly recommitted to responsible parenting, she cuts her hair short and gets a job, at fast food nightmare Doublemeat Palace. She also continues her self-destructive, self-punishing sexual affair with Spike. Yay, adulthood!

The Trio graduates from amusingly irksome dorks to contemptible sexual predators when Warren designs a mind-controlling device the little scamps plan to use to recruit sex slaves. Warren's first target: Katrina, his ex . . . so wrong on so many levels. It's a quick leap from sexual assault to murder when Warren accidentally kills Katrina with a bottle after she balks at his commands and calls him on his pathetic rapist fantasy. Warren sees the murder as a convenient opportunity to frame Buffy. Andrew seems to go along, but crossing the line into murder clearly rattles Jonathan, who is an immature doofus, as opposed to Warren, who is a psychopathic serial killer in the making.

Riley (remember him? No? Big lad, real dull?) returns to Sunnydale with his demon-slaying wife, Sam, in tow. Everyone gets along okay, but Buffy is super-embarrassed when Riley catches her in bed with Spike. So embarrassed and disgusted, in fact, that she breaks things off with the platinum-headed predator. Riley leaves, and we never see him again, THANK GOD.

On that happy note, back to the misery: Xander, fearing he will grow into an abusive alcoholic like his father, leaves Anya at the altar, prompting her return to vengeance-demoning. Xander and Anya's breakup still makes us upset; they were the perfect weirdos for each other, and Anya's devastation is palpable. It's enough to drive her into the arms of the similarly dumped Spike, which prompts Xander to attack and nearly kill the vampire with an axe. After recovering, Spike attempts (and nearly succeeds) to rape Buffy, then leaves town in horror over his actions. Bad times all around.

Did we say bad? How's this?

Buffy Summers might just be a normal, human girl, suffering delusions of demons and Slayer-hood in a psychiatric facility. In fact, textual evidence strongly supports this position. Doug Petrie on the conundrum (a topic of fervent debate among the Buffy faithful): "You know . . . we left it entirely up to the audience. Is the show a figment of an insane person's imagination? Maybe. If a fan says that's what the show means, then they're right. If someone says no, no, that's impossible, the hospital was the fake stuff, then they're right. We left that one up to the viewers. Almost no one wants to think it's an insane girl's imagination, by the way."

Moving on.

Tara reconciles with the recovering addict Willow. Everyone finds out about Spike and Buffy's fling. The Trio escalate their plans, but are foiled during a robbery attempt by Buffy, and here's where it all really goes to hell: furious, Warren sets aside all of his wondrous techno-gadgetry and walks into Buffy's yard with an ordinary, and tragically effective, handgun. He shoots Buffy in the chest, mortally wounding her . . . and accidentally shoots and kills Tara, who dies in Willow's arms.

That wagon Willow was on goes up in flames as Dark Willow returns, all vengeance, fury, and power. After healing Buffy's wounds, she captures and sadistically tortures Warren (hey, we get it) before flaying him alive ("Bored now"). So this is like, Willow Extra-Dark. But we like her taste in victims: next is slimeball Rack, whom Willow drains of magic and, consequently, life. After dispensing with Warren, the grieving witch goes after Andrew and Jonathan, who receive the reluctant protection of Buffy and Anya. Willow makes short work of them (and The Magic Box—so long, Exposition Hut), only to be confronted by Giles, teleported in from England and wielding the magic (on loan) of a powerful coven.

"I am trying to break your heart": Anya (Emma Caulfield) on her ill-fated wedding day.

Giles's expertise and borrowed power are enough to briefly check Willow, but the witch has grown too strong; she drains Giles of the coven's magic (and it's interesting to note that Dark Willow's attacks—which drain the victim's essence—are somewhat vampiric in nature). Now positively thrumming with dark magical power, Willow uses her heightened perceptions to take in the pain of the entire world (how much gother can you get?), which prompts her to initiate a magical apocalypse in an act of radical euthanasia.

But Xander is still standing: self-confessed coward and weakling Xander Harris, a man of no supernatural might or particular skills, whose crippling self-doubt has cost him his true love and left him directionless and defeated. Xander never understood his true value to the Scoobies; he became a fair physical combatant through sheer necessity, but he was never one of the big guns. His research skills were comically inept (mistaking a Dungeons + Dragons reference for a legitimate grimoire, for instance), but no one on *BTVS* consistently displays more loyalty, courage (Xander's lack of special prowess makes his dedication to fighting demons incredibly brave), or moral certainty. When Giles, Willow, and Xander joined their essences with Buffy's in her showdown with Adam, Xander's contribution represented the heart of the metaphorical body. This was not an accident.

Unarmed, un-magicked, unexceptionally human, Xander confronts Willow, his oldest and closest friend, with simple love and acceptance. With every proclamation of his love, Willow cuts gashes into Xander's face, but he refuses to relent, making the case for embracing life in the face of loss and pain—season six's unifying theme. Willow collapses into Xander's arms, sobbing, her human appearance restored, disaster averted.

The aftermath: Giles returns to England (drink) with Willow in tow for recuperation and rehabilitation. Buffy emerges from this latest apocalypse with a renewed commitment to living, the imminent destruction of the entire world having brought her personal existential crisis into perspective.

And Spike? He travels to Africa, where he endures a series of demonic trials and wins back his soul.

So that happened.

Season Highlights

Randy and Joan

Buffy and Spike, suffering the effects of Willow's amnesia spell, try to work out who they are. Spike's stolen jacket has "Randy" stitched in it, and he glumly accepts it as his name. Buffy, oddly unfazed by their predicament, christens herself "Joan," which is somehow just as comically inappropriate as

Randy. Upon discovering his vampiric nature, Randy fantasizes that he must be an ensouled, noble vampire seeking redemption (sound familiar?). Joan, for her part, is thrilled to find she's a "superhero." *BTVS* is so much a show about identity, and it's a hoot watching these richly developed characters improvising new ones on the fly.

Mustard Man (portrayed by writer/producer David Fury)

When Sunnydale is demonically transformed into a musical, every player has his part—including this resident, ecstatic over his dry cleaner's successful removal of a mustard stain. Everyone is the star of their own movie, at least in their heads; some days you save the world, other days, you struggle with condiments. It's a rich tapestry.

Is That a Worm Demon Sprouting From Your Head or Are You Just Happy to See Me?

The wig lady, devoted customer of the Doublemeat Palace, has a surprise: a grotesque, fanged, man-eating phallus coiled beneath her coif. Sometimes the monster effects on *BTVS* charmed with their low-budget cheesiness—this thing straight up freaked us right out. No no no no no no no.

16

Here Endenth the Lesson

Season Seven

Full Circle

We open the final season of *BTVS*, appropriately enough, in the graveyard, with Buffy instructing Dawn on the finer points of staking vamps, neatly foreshadowing how these last episodes will cement Buffy's role as mentor. The student has become the teacher, and, narratively, the circle is complete.

Buffy's final season saw ratings decline, as the show averaged around 4 million viewers. *BTVS* again earned several Emmy nominations in technical categories.

Everything old is new again: Sunnydale High School reopens just in time for Dawn to begin her freshman year. The new campus is sleekly attractive, as is the new principal, Robin Wood, who takes an instant interest in the Summers girls when Buffy drops Dawn off on her first day. Unfortunately, the town zoning commission still doesn't have its head around this "Hellmouth" idea, and Dawn begins her high school career pursued by vengeful ghosts.

Meanwhile, back in England, Giles is overseeing Willow's rehabilitation with the Devon Coven; our girl is fragile and grieving, but recognizably good ol' Willow again. The good ol' insecurity is back again too, as Willow balks at returning home to face her friends. Giles, sticking to his tough love guns (you can tell by that imposing duster coat he means business), insists she learn to stand on her own and face the consequences of her actions. Honestly, the country estate where all this takes place looks so beautiful we wouldn't want to go back to America either.

How's Anya? According to Halfrek, earning a reputation as a "soft serve" vengeance demon . . . after her time as a human, Anya's heart just doesn't seem to be in the bloody revenge game anymore. She turns a guy into a worm monster for a while, but the worst that happens is a dog gets swallowed. Still, she's doing better than Spike, who, driven to the brink of madness after the reinstatement of his soul, is apparently trying to finish the job by skulking around under the school, soaking up crazy Hellmouth vibes.

Buffy takes a guidance counselor position at the new school at the behest of Principal Wood, despite a total lack of credentials. Willow returns home but unconsciously renders herself invisible to her friends, fearing rejection, and winds up getting paralyzed and snacked upon by the absolutely repulsive

Sarah Michelle Gellar gives a master class in Slayer-tude.

demon Gnarl, whose recent spate of flayings has prompted the Scoobies to wonder whether the witch has returned to her victim-skinning ways. It all comes out in the wash eventually and she is warmly welcomed back into the fold.

Anya, eager to prove herself as a vengeful monster, unleashes horrifying spider demons on a frat house after the brothers humiliate a girl with a practical joke; the creatures tear the boys' hearts out, and Anya is clearly shaken by the brutality of the scene. As is Buffy, who decides that Anya has just moved to the top of the Scoobies' Most Wanted Demons list. Xander defends Anya, but she entreats her boss, D'Hoffryn, to undo the deaths, knowing that the sacrifice of a vengeance demon (presumably her) is necessary to work the magic. Instead, the demon master cruelly takes the life of Halfrek, more or less Anya's only remaining friend, to teach the recalcitrant Anya a lesson. A harsh lesson indeed, in a season all about harsh lessons.

A series of seeming hauntings—Joyce appearing to Dawn, Warren appearing to Andrew, and student Cassie Newton, dead of heart failure, appearing to Willow—actually represents the opening salvo of Season Seven's Big Bad, the First Evil. This impossibly ancient entity, the personification of the concept of evil itself, had previously attempted to manipulate Angel into killing Buffy; now it's back with plans to end the entire Slayer line, permanently, and its strategy from the outset is to insidiously undermine possible obstacles and manipulate catspaws to do its bidding. Dawn and Willow are emotionally battered by their visitations (Cassie Newton claims to be able to communicate with Tara), while Andrew is compelled by "Warren" to kill Jonathan, thus opening the Seal of Danzalthar, which will spell very bad news for all involved (Jonathan's anemic blood isn't up to the job, but they get it opened eventually).

The First really gets cooking when he sets poor, brain-scrambled Spike on a killing spree, using a folk song favored by Spike's mother as a trigger. Now a sort of undead Manchurian Candidate, Spike quickly loses all credibility as a changed man as his victim count mounts—except with Buffy, who now believes in him. She ties him up to keep him and everyone else safe while they try to figure out a solution, also taking Andrew into custody for interrogation.

Here's a fun new crew: The Harbingers of Death, mutilated demon servants of the First Evil, colloquially known as Bringers. Giles, having barely escaped an attack by the Bringers while in England, arrives with three girls classified as "Potentials," which means they are possible alternates for the current Slayer upon that Slayer's death. The First Evil intends to kill them all, thus ending the Slayer line permanently and leaving the Earth an undefended human smorgasbord for demonkind.

The First, not yet through with Spike, captures and tortures him relentlessly, but he hasn't read the brief on this guy: after Glory and the Demon Trials, Spike has proven that withstanding torture to protect a loved one is right at the top of his list of special skills. The pain, psychic and physical, is unrelenting, but Buffy's belief in his goodness is enough to sustain him. It looks like a Pyrrhic victory when the First reveals his ace: the Turok-Han, or "übervamp," an especially tough, powerful, and vicious breed of vampire light years more lethal than the standard bloodsuckers Buffy is used to. Her first encounter with the thing goes badly, but instead of breaking Buffy's spirit, the threat inspires her to stop passively waiting for the First Evil's strikes and actively take the fight to him (her? them? it?).

Potential Slayers from around the world begin to congregate at the Summers house as they become aware of their hunted status. Buffy gives them a crash course in Slaying and survival, but an alarming number of them are killed by Bringers along the way. Buffy manages to rescue Spike, and he joins her in training the bewildered Potentials. One of them, a vivacious girl named Kennedy, begins making advances on a flummoxed Willow.

When Spike's chip begins malfunctioning, effectively crippling the vampire, Buffy arranges for what's left of the Initiative to remove it, despite her colleagues' concern that this means letting Spike fully off the leash. She goes to dinner with that handsome Principal Wood—and she should really know better by now not to date people at work—learning his history as a "freelance" demon hunter and son of Slayer Nikki Wood, killed decades earlier by Spike. Awkward.

A now-repentant Andrew, eager to help, goes undercover wearing a wire to meet with the First Evil, which is a pretty funny idea. That doesn't go so great. Wood joins the team, as he has demon fighting experience (in Sunnydale, who doesn't?), which is cool, but Buffy is visited by Sineya, the First Slayer, in a dream and informed that they don't have "enough" to defeat the First Evil. Again we shake our fists at the frustratingly gnomic proclamations of spirit guides.

Spike frees himself completely from the First Evil's influence when he recalls the song used to trigger his attacks as one sung by his mother. Sentimental bastard, right? But Wood, who has learned that Spike is his mother's killer, and Giles, who never liked Spike sniffing around Buffy, conspire to kill him anyway. This earns Wood a severe beating from Spike (who consciously spares the man's life) and Giles an icy distance from Buffy, who claims that he has nothing left to teach her. She's right.

Faith's back! Yay! A Slayer, she is also a target of the First Evil, and she joins Buffy's Potentials Commando Unit as a sort of senior adviser. This should all go smoothly, right? Nope. After the Potentials question Buffy's leadership following a brutal defeat by Caleb that costs some Potentials their lives and Xander his eye (we'll get to Caleb in a second), the panicked girls gravitate toward Faith, who gives many fewer angry speeches than Buffy and generally seems like the coolest girl alive. Buffy is consoled by Spike, who reminds her of her worth.

So, Caleb: defrocked priest, psychosexual serial killer, and demonically empowered first lieutenant of the First Evil, Caleb cuts a dashingly (he's played by Nathan Fillion) terrifying figure. He repeatedly thrashes Buffy and kills a fair number of Potentials, all while spewing hateful sexist rhetoric; he's like toxic masculinity made flesh. When Buffy discovers a powerful object located in Caleb's base of operations, the Potentials refuse to back her plan to retrieve it, instead electing to follow Faith on a raid on the Bringers' stronghold. Big mistake: Faith leads them instead into a lethal trap, and she herself barely survives. Buffy finds the object Caleb was hiding, a mystical scythe, and uses the devastating weapon to rescue the survivors. Buffy resumes command.

The population of Sunnydale, no longer able to pretend there isn't something very wrong with its town, begins evacuating en masse. Xander reluctantly chloroforms Dawn to drive her away to safety, but she just tases him upon awakening and drives back. Buffy meets the Guardian, sole survivor of an order tasked with aiding the Shadow Men and Slayers, who explains that the scythe contains the essence of the Slayer. Okay. Then Caleb crashes in and kills her.

More than a match for Buffy, Caleb is checked only by the surprise arrival of Angel, who fights him off a bit but allows Buffy to strike with the scythe, apparently killing the creep. He pops back up like Jason Voorhees, but Buffy ends him for good by splitting him vertically from the groin with the scythe. Somewhere Freud is nervously playing with his cigar.

Angel came to Sunnydale to deliver a powerful magical amulet to Buffy, intended to be wielded by someone ensouled but more than human . . . someone like Angel. Or, now, Spike. Buffy sends Angel back to Los Angeles to prepare a contingency lest she not prevail against the First Evil—she chooses Spike as her Champion, the ultimate display of faith. She and Spike, no longer using the act of love to punish or escape, spend the night in each other's arms, now able to love each other purely.

Full Circle. Buffy, once the reluctant novice, now takes full ownership of her power and her destiny: she instructs Willow to use the scythe to fully activate all of the Potentials in the world simultaneously, thus breaking the Shadow Men's protocols and sharing her power with all girls who can wield it. This is what Sineya meant when she told Buffy she wouldn't be enough; she needed an army, and now she has one.

One scythe fits all: The usually charming Nathan Fillion terrifies as woman-hating serial killer Caleb.

New romance blossoms between Willow (Alyson Hannigan) and Potential Slayer Kennedy (Iyari Limon).

Even still, the final confrontation with the First Evil will cost them dearly: Anya is killed in the battle, as is (apparently) Spike, who activates the amulet to destroy the legion of attacking Turok-Han, forever close the Hellmouth, and level Sunnydale to the ground. He sacrifices himself to the consuming luminescence, a poetic affirmation of his path to the light, and what it cost him.

As the survivors regard the smoking ruin of Sunnydale, Dawn asks where they will go from here. Her only answer is the Slayer's enigmatic smile.

Season Highlights

Run Potential Slayer Run

A German girl with shocking pink hair careens through crowded streets to pulsing techno music—we loved Tom Tykwer's 1998 film *Run Lola Run*. Apparently, the writing staff over at *BTVS* felt the same, as the above description also applies to the opening scene of "Beneath You." The stylish homage has a different ending, though: the girl here is a Potential Slayer, brought down by Bringers' daggers. The entire sequence is exhilarating, unexpected, and a sly nod to Buffy's influence on popular culture; Lola was one of a host of post-Buffy action-oriented young female characters suddenly popping up all over TV and film.

Aud and Olaf

Anya's pre-demon life in ninth-century Sweden sounded pretty dull, but seeing it in flashbacks proved an absolute delight. Shot to resemble a grainy old kinescope, the scenes of neurotic Aud and her oafish husband, Olaf, inspire daydreams of a sitcom spinoff, subtitles and all. The sequences speak to the special appeal of Anya: they are funny, off-kilter, and pack a surprising emotional punch.

Aimee Mann at The Bronze

The Bronze hosted any number of interchangeable shoegazer acts, but on one memorable occasion, singer/songwriter Aimee Mann performed there, doing a couple of numbers from her album *Lost in Space*. Aimee is in the loop re: vampires—she witnesses the dusting of Charlotte mid-song and barely bats an eye, remarking later, "Man, I hate playing vampire towns." Could we love Aimee Mann more? (P.S. Her striped suit is faaaaabulous.)

17

Don't Taunt the Fear Demon

Monsters of the Week

Season One

Natalie French/She-Mantis (Musetta Vander)

Sleeping with your teacher—not a great idea under any circumstances (plus, illegal maybe?), but especially if she's secretly a giant sentient insect who seduces young virgin men to procreate and then bites off their heads. In "Teacher's Pet," just the fourth episode of the series, a praying mantis disguises herself as a fetching substitute biology teacher named Miss French and targets the hormonally charged Xander, who doesn't exactly resist and nearly winds up the headless patriarch of a mantis litter, except that Buffy barges in at the last minute and hacks the bugger to death.

Moloch the Corruptor (Michael Deak/Mark Deakins)

All he needs is love, but plenty of it, and he has a wacky way of reciprocating, which sometimes involves snapping the devoted one's neck. When first encountered, Moloch is a horned demon with huge, clawed hands, living in Cortona, Italy, in the year of our Lord 1418, mesmerizing and murdering town residents, including a young man named Carlo, who has just professed his love for the demon (imagine what would have happened if he told Moloch his mother wore combat boots). A brotherhood of monks devises an ingenious way to stop Moloch, throwing the book at him, literally, conjuring up a spell that traps him inside a huge medieval tome, hoping it will never be opened again. That might work at most high schools, but not at Sunnydale, where the book is cracked almost six hundred years later by Willow, who is scanning texts into a computer, thus unknowingly releasing Moloch onto the Internet. Moloch now assumes the virtual identity of Malcolm Black, wooing a boyfriend-hungry Willow and other computer nerds who apparently never heard the expression "Don't trust anything you read on the Internet," including a posse of scientists he has persuaded to build him a robotic body. We can confidently state that this is the only episode of *Buffy* in which the Slayer vanquishes her enemy by tricking it into punching a high-voltage fuse box, causing it to overload its circuits and explode.

The Brotherhood of Seven

The unmagnificent seven are demons capable of maintaining human form for seven-year stretches by harvesting human brains and hearts. Gross, right? By the time we are introduced to them in "The Puppet Show," only one of these bad boys still survives, in the guise of a Sunnydale High student named Marc (Burke Roberts), who is performing as a magician in the talent show—the same talent show featuring a cursed demon hunter as a ventriloquist's dummy, Cordelia's painfully tone-deaf rendering of "The Greatest Love of All," and a "Springtime for Hitler"-esque performance of *Oedipus Rex* by Buffy, Willow, and Xander. All in all, a must-miss. On Marc's trail is Sid, the demon hunter, his soul trapped inside the dummy by a brotherhood curse. For Sid, there's just one way out: slay the organ bandito, which he does, but, sadly for the little guy, Marc's death means his as well, since his body had moved on to the afterworld decades earlier. Did Sid know? Well, he *was* a dummy.

Kiddy League Coach (Brian Pietro)/Ugly Man (Uncredited)

In "Nightmares," this unnamed cretin, known only as Kiddy League Coach, beats little Billy Palmer into a coma after the boy's miscue on the baseball diamond costs their team the game, making him *Buffy*'s first human monster of the week, though the incident does have supernatural repercussions when Billy's astral projection inadvertently turns the Scoobies' nightmares into reality. The comatose boy's fear of his coach manifests itself as the so-called Ugly Man, a grotesque malevolence who goes around clubbing people with his deformed hand. The ordeal finally concludes when Buffy, having been buried alive by the Master in her own nightmare, arises as a vampire and so is able to vanquish the Ugly Man, thus conquering Billy's fear and freeing the boy to wake from his coma.

Season Two

Inca Mummy (Ara Celi)

Like Buffy, the titular character of "Inca Mummy Girl" was the chosen one, but sometimes it's better to be overlooked. Named princess at the age of sixteen, she was entombed alive as an offering to the mountain god Sebancaya, to protect her Peruvian people from the netherworld. The tomb was magically sealed so that no one would ever wake her—and no one did, for five hundred or so years, until some Sunnydale High clown named Rodney Munson tries to swipe the seal on a school field trip to the Sunnydale Museum, breaking it in the process. This is bad not just for Rodney, who winds up strangled by the princess, but for Sunnydale at large, since the girl goes around sucking the life out of people so that she can retain her youth and prevent her body from decomposing. Naturally, because she is dangerous and unattainable, Xander falls in love with her, and she with him, but like so many high school romances it doesn't last, not the least of it because her dried-up corpse shatters when she just can't bring herself to drain Xander. Now that's love.

Richard Anderson (Greg Vaughn) + Tom Warner (Todd Babock)

Reptilian "Reptile Boy" villains, one of whom (Anderson) Cordelia is all aflutter over and the other of whom pursues Buffy, yet all they really want to do is sacrifice them, to the giant snake demon Machida. Upper-crust Crestwood College students/ Delta Zeta Kappa frat boys, Anderson and Warner owe their wealth to these sacrifices, so what you have here, literally, is a case of selling your soul to a demon in exchange for privilege, though, of course, it's the proletariat who pays.

Machida (Robin Atkin Downes)

Half-man, half-snake, and the patron deity of the privileged, upper-crust Delta Zeta Kappa frat boys at Crestwood College. In exchange for extreme prosperity and protection, the DZK crew (including Tom Warner and Richard Anderson) feed the famished reptile on the tenth day of the tenth month of every year, which wouldn't be so bad if we were talking about earthworms, but Machida is a finicky eater who insists on comely high school coeds, which explains how Buffy and Cordelia wind up drugged and chained to the wall in the dungeon-like basement of the frat house, awaiting sacrifice. In the aired version of the episode, Buffy breaks free and slices the creature in two, thereby killing it, but in the original script (by David Greenwalt, who also directed) Machida survives the showdown ("A squooshy sound of flesh and protoplasm meeting and the two halves re-join!"), grabs Tom, and quips: "Lil' somethin' for the road," before slithering back into his pit. On his DVD commentary, Greenwalt says he ran out of time, so wasn't able to shoot the sequence.

Ted Buchanan (John Ritter)

Danger, Will Robinson! Ted Buchanan was a covert robot who had nearly everyone eating out of his hand—Joyce was totally smitten with him—thanks to an Ecstasy-like tranquilizer with which he laced cookies and probably other food he was cooking and serving, making its consumers mellow and compliant. The only one who wasn't rolling over for Ted was Buffy, who was convinced there was something malevolent about him, especially after he threatened to "slap that smart-ass mouth" of hers during a round of miniature golf. Things escalate when Ted, sneaking around in her room, discovers her diary, which includes accounts of her exploits as a Slayer; he threatens to share this information with Joyce, at this point still unaware of Buffy's secret life, and to have her committed as delusional, a foreshadowing of the events in season six's "Normal Again." When Ted refuses to surrender the diary, he and Buffy get into a brawl, during which Ted tumbles down the stairs and appears dead, prompting enormous guilt in Buffy. Sounds like a job for the Scoobies, who dig around, discovering that Ted was a robot built some forty years earlier by the real Ted, a mad, sickly inventor whose wife had bolted.

Three's a crowd when Ted (John Ritter) comes between Buffy and Joyce.

The robot kidnapped Ted's wife and held her captive until she died, then sought out other women who resembled her, eventually leading him to Joyce. Ted was portrayed by John Ritter, who rose to fame in the seventies/ eighties as Jack Tripper in the ABC "jiggle TV" sitcom *Three's Company* and was clearly the biggest star ever to guest on *Buffy*. The episode is another renowned example of the Whedon metaphor-for-life paradigm, in this case the reluctance of children to accept their parents' divorce, and the introduction of a new boyfriend.

Kristine Sutherland, the actress who played Joyce, had this to say about the "Ted" episode:

> This is another general thing about *Buffy* that I loved: my mother was a divorced mother. My parents were divorced in the sixties, when there were very few divorced families. It wasn't the norm, so nobody knew what to make of you, so you felt like this very strange family. In the same way Buffy wrestles with that, being a vampire Slayer. How do you fit yourself into the world? But my mother, she would date sometimes, when I was in junior high school, and I would run off every boyfriend she had. I was having none of it. The "Ted" episode was so fascinating for me, because I totally understood Joyce and her exhilaration at finding this guy she thinks is so great, and then I thought it was so amazing because—and again, it's that thing that Joss is writing about. It isn't really that he's a creepy robot; it's what you think when your parents are divorced and they start dating someone else—the intruder, crazy person, threatens everything. "We have to get rid of them."

Bezoar (None)

Goo goo g'joob. Bezoar is the egg monster, appearing in the appropriately titled "Bad Eggs," in which Sunnydale High students are assigned eggs to nurture by their health teacher, to help them fully grasp the potential consequences of unprotected sex. This being Sunnydale, those consequences turn out to be a lot worse than expected, since the eggs have been hatched by the queen Bezoar, a gross, slimy, prehistoric parasite that's stuck in a cave beneath the floor in the high school boiler room, egging to get out (sorry, but hard to resist). On top of all its other sins, the queen mother is a grossly negligent parent, insouciantly dispatching her hatchlings into an inhospitable world so they can attach themselves to the spines of the school population, thus draining them of energy and usurping their bodies and minds, all with the intent of helping Mommy bust free of her restraints (demon-world Ibsen?). Nearly works, too, except that buckaroo vampire Lyle Gorch tosses Buffy into the Bezoar's pit, where it is slain by the Slayer, who emerges unscathed, though badly in need of shampoo.

Gib Cain (Jack Conley)

Gib Cain (first name acknowledged only in the shooting script, available on the awesome website BuffyWorld) is a Campbell's Chunky soup kind of guy, a werewolf hunter who wears a tooth from every one of his prey around his neck to prove it. Cain prefers his werewolves dead—he peddles their pelts for a "pretty penny" in Sri Lanka—which explains the friction between him and Buffy, who, knowing that the lycanthrope in question is Oz, prefers at least this one alive. Cain is—surprise!—a blunt speaker, so when he first meets Buffy and Giles he mistakes them for lovers and gets a good laugh out of that, but an even bigger kick at the notion that they are hunting a werewolf: "This guy [Giles] looks like he's auditioning to be a librarian," he tells Buffy, "and you, well, you're a girl." Sexist though he is, Cain is impossible to uncategorically despise, simply because he is so adept with one-liners. Asked if it bothers him that a werewolf is a person twenty-eight days of the month, he replies, "That's why I only hunt them the other three." Apparently Buffy feels differently, as her parting words to him are: "How about you let the door hit you in the ass on your way out of town?"

The Judge (Brian Thompson)

Nobody likes a sanctimonious demon (to be fair, very few people like a humble one). This gasbag was summoned ages ago to weed out the righteous by burning them to death. Who died and made him king of the universe? In his favor is that no weapon ever forged could kill him, which effectively gave him allowance to do whatever he wanted without having to pay the consequences. At least that's what *he* thought. Eventually an army of humans rises up against him, and while most are killed, the few survivors discovered a loophole: true, they couldn't kill him, but they could disassemble him and spread his body parts across the globe (excised line by Xander: "Do you think they left his heart in San Francisco?"). The story might have ended there, except that Drusilla and Spike insist on reassembling him, and actually succeed in doing so, and decide, along with new pal Angelus, to test their blue-headed toy (Buffy calls him the Smurf) out by visiting a local mall and sic'ing him on shoppers. Unfortunately for Smurf guy, the Scoobies get their hands on a rocket launcher, and there goes the Judge. No weapon forged? "That was then," says Buffy. "This is now." Case closed.

Acathla (None)

The demon who swallowed the world, almost. Acathla figures prominently in the late stages of season two, primarily because Angelus is obsessed with liberating him from his rock-hard existence, which we mean literally, since he was transformed into a stone obelisk ages ago by a virtuous knight who pierced the demon's heart with his sword. Lest you feel sorry for Acathla, know that he was on the verge of triggering a vortex that would have sucked every living creature on earth into hell, meaning eternal torment, including weekly Chaucer lectures. Good, knight. How do you wake up a sleeping slab of demon rock? By pulling the sword from his stone, but only if you are worthy, which, as Hellmouth luck would have it, Angelus is (college degree not required). Thankfully Buffy arrives in the nick of time, or maybe just past the nick of time, since she is too tardy to stop Acathla from opening his big mouth but just early enough to thwart another potential apocalypse, this time by smiting Angel (having just re-emerged from deep within Angelus, thanks to Willow's spell) and punching him what is supposed to be, but ultimately isn't, a one-way ticket to hell.

Der Kindestod (James Jude Courtney)

What's in a name? For a rose, maybe, nothing, but "Child Death" (English translation of the German *der kindestod*), not so much. Buffy likens the physical appearance of this hideous demon, who preys exclusively on youngins, to a nineteenth-century undertaker, but with a skeletal face, bulging solid-white eyes, a beak-like nose, and tusk-like lower teeth. So, probably not a babe magnet. In season two's "Death by Kill," Der Kindestod sucks the life out of infirmed youths in the children's ward at Sunnydale General, which the "Homerically insensitive" (Giles's words) Cordelia describes as "basically an all-you-can-eat kind of thing" for the gluttonous fiend, by pinning them down and draining their life force with his eyeballs. Yes, his eyeballs suck (according to co-scripter Dean Batali, this episode, as originally conceived, was supposed to feature the Scoobies performing community service work at a retirement home that doubled as a daycare center, and while it initially appeared as if the old people were killing the children, it was actually the other way around—the youths were doing away with the oldies, feeding on their souls in search of immortality; the concept was nixed by the WB). Der Kindestod is invisible to all but feverishly ill youths, so Buffy injects herself with a super-duper dose of virus, yet still manages to snap the sucker's pasty-white neck because, well, she's just that awesome. In the process of confronting this demon, Buffy learns that Der Kindestod was responsible some ten years earlier for the mysterious death of her cousin Celia (Denise Johnson), which occurred in a hospital in Buffy's presence and still accounts for her visceral hatred of such institutions. Personally, we blame *Grey's Anatomy*.

Season Three

Ken (Carlos Jacott)

Ken masquerades as the gentle-souled head of a Covenant House–like shelter for runaways in Los Angeles, when, in fact, he is the hideous lord and master of an underground demon labor camp where youths have the life sucked out of them as time advances at an accelerated pace, so that they age decades in just days. All of this unfolds in the third-season opener "Anne," in which Buffy has fled Sunnydale after killing Angel and is looking to carve out a quiet, low-key existence in L.A., but is roped back in once she uncovers Ken's nefarious scheme, eventually emulating Moses as she leads the runaways out of bondage, though it is Gandhi she evokes while bludgeoning Ken to death.

"Gandhi?" asks a confused runaway.

"Well, you know, if he was really pissed off," Buffy says.

Ovu Mobani (None)

A demon who takes up residence in a primitive Nigerian mask that Joyce brings home from the art gallery in season three's "Dead Man's Party" (what, she couldn't have been satisfied with a couple of pens and a roll of Scotch Tape?), Ovu Mobani (translation: Evil Eye) awakens the dead and summons their zombified corpses to him, which, as you can imagine, raises quite a ruckus at Buffy's welcome-home-from-L.A. shindig. Whoever dons the mask has the truly auspicious honor of transforming into Ovu Mobani incarnate, and can be subdued only by an attack to the eyes. We don't mean to sound snide, but it couldn't have happened to a nicer person than Joyce's oppressively peppy book-buddy Pat.

Gruenshtahler Twins (Frederick + Hans) (Jeryn Daube + Joseph Daube) + Old Man (Ian Abercrombie)

Formidable three-person SlayerFest '98 team, with the Bobbsey Twins deployed in the field and the sullen, craggy Old Man directing their movements from his wheelchair inside Mr. Trick's mansion. Going into the contest the twins were already a dynamic duo, wanted in Germany for capital murder, terrorism, and the bombing of a commercial jetliner; by the end they were just a couple of blundering idiots tricked into killing each other by a resource-ful high school teenager named Buffy Summers. Ironically, it is the Old Man who represents the future, embracing technology and the computer in a way we're pretty sure Charles Babbage never intended.

Kulak (Chad Stahelski)

A yellow-skinned demon of the Miquot clan who may have come up with an ingenious way of outsmarting the Transportation Security Administration at airports (no jokes, please), since his weapons of choice are bones eject-ing from his own body. In "Homecoming," Kulak vies for the top prize in SlayerFest '98, attacking Buffy and Cordelia in a cabin in the woods, where things don't go exactly as planned—unless his plan involved dying when the cabin is blown to bits by two of the other contestants.

Frawley (Billy Maddox)

A SlayerFest '98 contestant aroused by hunting down Slayers, reaffirming the notion that in the Buffyverse humans can be just as odious as demons. When last encountered, "Jungle Bob" (Buffy's nickname for him) was snagged in one of his own bear traps, after having been frightened by two high school girls into surrendering the names of the other contestants. Hey, hey, macho man.

Lurconis (None)

If it's Tuesday there must be another snake demon in town, this one going by the handle Lurconis, whose distinguishing characteristic is his fondness for newborns. That may sound sweet, but when you consider that what he likes to do with them is eat them, not so much. Lurconis (meaning "glutton"), who appears in the hilarious "Band Candy," is among the demons Mayor Wilkins made certain promises to in exchange for his privileged existence, including his eventual ascendancy to full-fledged demon himself. Snake boy is mighty ugly and mighty fierce and, by the time Buffy is done with him, mighty crisp, since she incinerates him with a broken gas pipe.

Lagos (Gary Kasper)

Formidable speckle-faced/fanged warrior demon who visits Sunnydale in "Revelations" in search of the mystical Glove of Myhnegon (or, as Buffy calls it, the "magic mitten thingy") and winds up getting his head handed to him—more or less literally—by Buffy Summers.

Sisterhood of the Jhe

Never were there such devoted sisters. This cult of cannibalistic femme demons exists for one reason and one reason only: to bring about the end of the world. You got a problem with that? Still, this business about opening the Hellmouth is getting to be exhausting. Hello? Krazy Glue? In "Zeppo," the *sestras* nearly hit the jackpot: the portal opens all right, triggering an encore performance by the Hellmouth spawn (yet he *still* won't play "Incident on 57th Street"), who's even bigger and badder than before, but eventually the Scoobies prevail, staving off the apocalypse once again.

Balthazar (Christian Clemenson)

Evidently magnetism isn't a must-have for cult leaders in the demon world, because Balthazar is slightly less physically appealing than Jabba the Hut and has the temperament of a rabid dog, yet somehow persuaded a fifteenth-century cult of dueling vampires called El Eliminati to worship him, which includes ladling scoops of water onto his bleached, bloated body (he needs to be moistened constantly) as he sits in a commodious tub yelling, "Unacceptable!" and excoriating them as incompetent and unmanly. Vanquished by mortal enemy Mayor Wilkins a century earlier, Balthazar had been believed dead ever since, but Angel gets a tip that while crippled, he is still very much alive and, even worse, back in town. Balthazar, immobile himself after spending decades on the lam in the sewers, dispatches his minions on assorted assignments—kill the Slayers, assassinate the mayor, kidnap the Watchers, yada yada—most of which they fail at spectacularly (though they do get to wear cool El Eliminati vests), but his ultimate aim is to recapture his source of power, a magical amulet, which upon his death was usurped by a wealthy landowner named Gleaves, with whom it now rests in the family crypt. Of course, they fail spectacularly at that, too. Ultimately Balthazar is electrocuted by the quick-thinking Buffy, but just before vanishing from this Earth once and for all (we think, though one can never be certain in the Buffyverse) warns her, "Slayer! You think you've won. When he rises, you'll wish I killed you all," a reference we understand immediately to be about the mayor, though the Scoobies have no clue of whom he is speaking.

Hell Hounds

No friends of ours, these ferocious devil dogs are, according to Giles, "sort of a demon foot soldier," bred during the Mahkash Wars (no clue) to kill their foes, and then devour their brains. (Brain food? Teriyaki salmon for us.) In "The Prom," supremely twisted malcontent Tucker Wells (Andrews's bro) trains the hounds to raid the Sunnydale High titular formal dance, where they can feast on the cerebra of those in attendance, by forcing them to watch prom movies, including *Carrie*, though not the remake because that would have been cruel and unusual punishment even for brain-eating demon dogs.

Gretta Strauss + Hans Strauss (Lindsay Taylor + Shawn Pyfrom)

In "Gingerbread," Gretta, six, and Hans, eight, are the illusory human iterations of the demon determined to provoke Sunnydale into destroying itself by planting seeds of fear and hatred among the community. The Scoobies deduce as much by combing through old newspapers and discovering that these same two youths had been turning up dead every fifty years since 1649, when the first account was recorded by a German cleric who found the bodies himself in the Black Forest. (Who says newspapers are dying?) Giles speculates that the eighteenth-century German fairy tale *Hansel and Gretel* was based on these two young ones.

Hellmouth Spawn (None)

Tough to imagine an uglier creature than this, a ginormous, slimy, multitentacled glob of something with a V-Shaped head, which rises from the depths of Hellmouth in the season-one finale, thrashing about in the Sunnydale High Library as Buffy battles the Master, then retreating once the Master is destroyed. The creature is apparently always first out of the gate when the Hellmouth opens; he returns even bigger and badder in the season-three episode "Zeppo." Though the name Hellmouth Spawn is unofficial, fans seem to dig it, and we don't blame them. According to *Buffy the Vampire Slayer: The Watcher's Guide*, the episode's budget precluded computer-generated effects, so the FX team at Optic Nerve wound up crafting tentacle "costumes," so that each tentacle you see flailing about actually has a human being inside, manipulating it from within. Imagine having *that* on your résumé.

Season Four

Kathy Newman (Dagney Kerr)

One of the most common anxieties facing incoming college freshmen concerns the potential for disaster in a randomly selected roommate: "What if she's some kind of psycho monster?" Buffy being Buffy, this metaphor is made terrifyingly literal in the form of Kathy Newman, a diabolically perky go-getter devoted to power diva Celine Dion and relentlessly intrusive and dictatorial regarding dorm room etiquette. Worse yet, she makes weird noises in her sleep and blares the grating late-era Cher hit "Believe" on a maddening loop. It's enough to drive a girl insane, really, so it just seems like overkill when it is revealed that Kathy, actually a Mok'tagar demon in disguise, has also been undermining Buffy's mental stability by nightly stealing portions of the Slayer's soul in a bid to fool her other-dimensional parents into letting her remain in school. (Those college kids and their wacky pranks!) Kathy is ultimately found out and dragged home by Taparrich, her angry father. Kathy's departure frees up a bed for Willow, who proves a much more congenial cohabitant.

Gachnar (Adam Bitterman)

Don't underestimate the importance of party prep: when the occult "Mark of Gachnar" symbol is inadvertently included in Alpha Delta house's Halloween shindig décor and subsequently bled upon by an injured Oz, the eponymous demon is summoned (though remains unseen) and immediately begins animating the hidden fears of the partygoers, to disastrous and ultimately fatal effect. Gachnar's machinations reveal deep-seated insecurities in the Scooby Gang, effectively demoralizing them to the point of defeat . . . until Buffy accidentally brings the fear demon fully into physical reality, revealing the terrifying creature to stand about two inches tall. In a classic *BTVS* reversal, the formerly intimidating Gachnar is humiliated by Xander and Willow cooing over his "cuteness" before Buffy casually crushes him with her foot. It transpires that while researching Gachnar, Giles missed some fine print under an illustration of the demon: "Actual size." A second Gachnar demon would appear on *Angel* as part of a witches' coven's fear-mongering plot, leading to the emergence of the goddess Illyria.

Beer

Most college students are intimately familiar with the two-edged sword that is the beer blast: a lowering of inhibitions leading to dumb, destructive fun, followed by intense pain and regret. Perhaps the series' most heavy-handed metaphor, the cursed beer (a revenge scheme perpetrated by a long-abused pub owner fed up with the boorish behavior of his collegiate clientele) turns imbibers into dumb, violent cave people—much like regular old uncursed beer! It's a pretty obvious joke, and Gellar's drunk act is Jerry Lewis–like in its cartoony broadness. "Beer Bad" is frequently cited as one of the show's least-loved episodes.

Hus (Tod Thawley)

Thanksgiving dinner was served with a heaping side dish of White Guilt in the holiday episode "Pangs," as Buffy and company confront Hus, a spirit warrior of the indigenous Chumash tribe that was devastated by white Sunnydale residents of generations past. Hus manages to kill a museum curator and a priest (and give Xander syphilis) before being bested by Buffy with his own knife. Everyone feels lousy about it, particularly Willow, as they sympathize with Hus's outrage . . . but murdering people and cutting off their ears just isn't cool.

Serparvo Demon (None)

Xander so often gets the sticky end of the lollipop: after being inadvertently turned into a "demon magnet" by an accidentally spell-casting Willow, our Mr. Harris attracts all sorts of new friends, including the Serparvo Demon, a fearsomely fanged marauder invulnerable to all harm, save drowning. Luckily, ex-demon Anya remembers this little piece of demon trivia, and helps Xander dispatch the beast in a sink.

The Gentlemen

"Can't even shout/can't even cry/the Gentlemen/are coming by." This eerie children's rhyme heralds the arrival of the Gentlemen, a cadre of hovering ghouls intent on collecting seven human hearts (sort of a Hellmouth spin on Pokémon Go). As their sole weakness is the sound of a human scream, the exaggeratedly courteous vivisectionists prepare their way by magically stealing the voices of every soul in town.

Instant icon: The primary Gentleman (Doug Jones), along with his courtly cohorts, stands as *BTVS*'s most unforgettable avatar of pure horror.

They are assisted by feral, demonic, strait-jacketed Footmen, who preserve their master's dignity by handling the rough stuff, leaving the scalpel-wielding Gentlemen to preen, nod, and gesture floridly to one another before slicing up their victims like fresh-caught trout.

The brilliantly conceived and executed Gentlemen are a triumph, both visually—they are the series' most iconic non-recurring figures, lent surreal grace by the performances of actors Camden Toy and Doug Jones—and narratively, as their presence precludes reliance on the show's signature dialogue to express character, theme, humor, etc.

Behemoth

Behemoth and two of his Vahrall Demon colleagues attempt an apocalyptic ritual ("The Sacrifice of Three") in Sunnydale; despite the monsters' prodigious strength and razor-sharp claws, they are summarily rebuffed by Buffy and friends. Smell ya later, Behemoth.

Rupert Giles, Fyarl Demon (Anthony Stewart Head)

On a night out together on the town, Ethan Rayne, that sorcerous scamp, contrives to transform Giles into a Fyarl Demon, a species of subservient, inarticulate monster. Hilarity (for Rayne) ensues, as Buffy nearly mistakenly kills her helplessly grunting, slime-spewing mentor. Ah, life on the Hellmouth.

Polgara Demon

Adam, the Initiative's Frankensteinian demon/human/cyborg creation, picked up a cool spare part from a captured Polgara Demon: the creature's switchblade-action arm spike. *Snikt!*

Thaumogenesis Demon

When Jonathan Levinson casts a spell rendering himself a paragon of humanity, he inadvertently creates this disagreeable fellow as a side effect; essentially, an equally evil/repellant/malicious entity appears to balance the sorcerous scales, in some sort of Newtonian "equal and opposite reaction" law of magical physics. "Thaumogenesis" means "created by magic," for you amateur etymologists out there. Jonathan and Buffy shove the thing in a pit, killing it and ending Jonathan's spell.

Genevieve Holt (Kathryn Joosten)

The Initiative was secreted on the Sunnydale UC campus under a frat house that, in a previous era, served as the Lowell Home for Children, a refuge for disadvantaged kids. Well, ostensibly: the Lowell Home was run by Genevieve Holt, an abusive harridan hell-bent on punishing her "sinful" charges for their sexual urges. The resultant repressed sexual energy bubbles over during an eventful fraternity party decades later, attended by Buffy and Riley, who succumb to erotomania, as do the other guests, before Xander and Anya are able to break the spell. To tell the truth, the couple seem pretty unfazed by their "ordeal."

Season Five

Toth (Michael Bailey Smith)

Toth was a slightly more sophisticated-than-usual demon opponent: he used tools (see: Ferula Gemini) and had a plan. Unfortunately for Toth, the plan—which involved splitting Buffy into her Slayer and human components, the better to weaken and kill her—went awry when he tagged Xander instead. Buffy kills him with a sword. Nice try Toth, but no cigar.

Lei-Ach Demons

Lei-Ach demons have seen better days: once a proud warrior race, they have been reduced to skulking around hospitals feeding off the sick and weak when Glory captures one and directs it to kill the Slayer. It might have worked, too . . . Tara had cast a spell rendering demons invisible to her friends (it makes sense in context), and the functionally transparent beasties make a mess of The Magic Box before things are set right. By which we mean Buffy kills them.

Spawn of Sobek

Remember the terrifying snake-man centaur thing from the eighties movie *Dreamscape*? Like that.

One of Buffy's more unsettling demon opponents, the Spawn of Sobek was a humanoid serpent (or serpentine human) of incredible speed, strength, and murderousness. Glory transmogrified a cobra to create him, calling on magicks dating back to ancient Egypt (Sobek is an Egyptian reptile god). Life in Glory's employ is pretty simple: find Key, kill Key. Spawnie tries, and dies (Buffy chokes him with a chain—HARDCORE), but he freaks us out quite a bit before that.

Queller Demon

Sort of a slime-spitting fang-faced homunculus half-emerging from an insect chrysalis situation (*shudder*).

Season five burdens us with another real nightmare generator in the form of the queller demon, a semi-humanoid/insect chrysalis hybrid that scoots along the ceiling, spits goo, and gives us no end of fits, creeps, heebie-jeebies, and general NOPE. One is summoned to Earth by Ben Wilkinson, in an effort to deal with the increasing number of Glory-fied mental patients piling up at the hospital (they like to eat the mentally ill). One targets Joyce Summers when her mental faculties are compromised by her brain tumor, but Buffy takes care of it. Seriously, these things are gross.

Olaf (Abraham Benrubi)

Anya's ex! A Swedish human cursed by witches into trollhood centuries ago, Olaf appears when a spell of Willow's goes sideways (drink) and prepares to sack Sunnydale for fun. Fantastically strong and durable, wielding an enchanted hammer, the jocular giant proves a formidable opponent, but Willow is able in the end to dimensionally banish him. Buffy keeps the hammer and later flattens Glory with it.

April (Shonda Farr)

A sex-slave robot made, used, and abandoned by Warren Mears, April shows up in Sunnydale looking for her master and prettily wreaks havoc before being taken out by Buffy, who comforts the forlorn automaton as it shuts down.

Ghora Demon (None)

A nasty three-headed beastie whose eggs are harvested by Spike and Dawn for use in a spell to resurrect Joyce Summers.

Season Six

Hellions

A demon biker gang (redundant?), led by Razor, who tore a swath through Sunnydale after learning of the Slayer's death. The Hellions had a strict no-vampire policy (just ask Shempy) and evidently enjoyed sexually assaulting their victims, "tearing up little girls" with their "anatomical incompatibilities." (*Ugh ugh ugh.*) Yeah, it's a treat to see Buffy tear through these scumbags.

Child of Words/White Woman Demon (Lisa Hoyle)

A ghostly demon created by the magical energies released during Buffy's resurrection, the body-possessing Child of Words stymies Buffy with her incorporeal form . . . until Tara and Willow magically render her solid, enabling Buffy to dispatch her with an axe.

M'Fashnik Demons

Mercenary demons who perpetrate mayhem for fun and profit, contracted by the Trio to take out Buffy. Strong, ugly, and, let's face it, doomed. Buffy ain't going out like that.

Bro'os (Raymond O'Connor)

A humanoid, sharklike demon loan shark (groan), to whom Spike owed a considerable number of kittens. Bro'os, nicknamed "Teeth," inconveniently shows up to collect while Spike and the Scoobies are under the influence of an amnesia spell. After that little misunderstanding, Bro'os heads to post-apocalyptic Los Angeles, where he sets himself up as King of Santa Monica. Makes sense that he'd want to live on the ocean.

Mandraz (Fleming Brooks)

A bloodthirsty demon inadvertently summoned by Willow while magically tripping at Rack's place, Mandraz nearly kills Willow and Dawn, whom Willow was supposed to be watching. It slashes Dawn's face and precipitates the car crash that breaks her arm. Willow, your membership in The Babysitters Club is hereby revoked.

Wig Lady (Pat Crawford Brown)

A demon Doublemeat Palace patron who resembles a little old lady—with a huge, horrible, phallic-snake thing under her wig that likes to eat fast food employees (and cherry pie). It nearly gets Buffy after spitting paralyzing goo on the Slayer (so much yuck), but Willow intervenes and kills it.

Rwasundi Demons

Time-muddling creatures summoned by Andrew Wells to help frame Buffy for the murder of Katrina Silber. Sweet cloaks.

Sword-Wielding Demon Warrior

Buffy spars with this horned fellow in the graveyard. After winning the fight—so she thinks—she nabs the demon's very cool sword to take home as a souvenir. Turns out the demon is merely dormant, hiding in the blade, and is accidentally released later in the Summers home by Tara. When the sword breaks (pity), he's gone for good.

Suvolte Demons

Vicious, mindless, and be-snouted, Ann Coulters—er, Suvolte Demons—are an endangered species (yay?) that Spike attempts to make a buck off by selling their eggs on the black market.

Glarghk Guhl Kashmas'nik Demon

A bald, shiny fellow who injected Buffy with a hallucinogen via its arm-stinger, prompting her psychiatric hospital hallucination. It was a hallucination, right guys? Guys?

Nezzla Demons

Craggy, thick-skinned demons tasked with guarding the Orbs of Nezzla'khan, which granted the possessor superhuman strength. The Trio procures the orbs by sending in a Nezzla skin-wrapped Jonathan to breach their defenses. We imagine that smelled just awful.

Earth Golems

Dark Willow forms these mud men to keep Buffy busy during DW's magical apocalypse prep. After the spell ends, they crumble back into the earth.

Season Seven

Harbingers of Death

Formerly human, these demon henchmen of the First Evil are into self-mutilation (they all blind themselves, for instance) and emit a toxic aura. They also fight, psychically linked, as a collective organism, which makes them formidable foes. Their primary task in Sunnydale is the elimination of Potential Slayers, which they perform with total dedication and frightening efficiency.

Sluggoth Demon

A revolting, fireplug-sized worm creature with a ring of sucking fangs. Anya transforms a young woman's boyfriend into one, which then eats her dog. So win-lose.

Gnarl (Camden Toy)

A truly grotesque humanoid demon who paralyzes his victims before feeding on strips of their flesh, Gnarl holds Willow captive upon her return to Sunnydale from England and proceeds to slowly, teasingly eat her alive before she is rescued by Buffy. The. Worst.

Avilas (Troy Brenna)

Tall, horned, incredibly strong demon summoned by UC Sunnydale student Peter Nicols. Buffy burns him up with a torch.

Grimslaw Demon

Absolutely hideous giant spider-like creatures that tear the hearts from their victims. Anya sets them upon a group of frat boys as an act of vengeance on behalf of a humiliated girl, and is horrified by the resultant slaughter.

Turok-Han

Called "übervamps" by the Scoobies, Turok-Han are a race of vampires resembling the creature from *Nosferatu* (the title character played by German

Übervamp: The dreaded Turok-Han: vamps on steroids.

actor Max Schreck): bald, pale, and twisted. Much stronger and more savage than ordinary vampires, Turok-Han are used as foot soldiers by the First Evil. Horribly effective, they kill many of the Potentials before being wiped out by Spike, who uses the amulet to blast them into atoms with magical light.

Torg (Josh Braaten)

Demon restaurant owner who has a brief thing with Anya. She's done better.

Lissa (Ashanti)

A demon associate of the First Evil disguised as a spectacularly beautiful woman (played by pop princess Ashanti), Lissa seduces Xander in an attempt to use him as a sacrifice to open the Seal of Danzalthar. It must be said that her "spectacularly beautiful woman" disguise is very, very good.

18

Gee, Can You Vague That Up for Me?

Magic + Mythology

S unnydale's defining "mystical whoosit" (Buffy's term), the Hellmouth, is what the town's Spanish settlers called "Boca del Infierno," a portal between the human and demon dimensions that, if ever opened, would unleash an unrelenting flood of demons, creating a severe shortage of parking spaces, if nothing else. As time evolves, we discover that the Hellmouth is located directly beneath the Sunnydale High Library, which just so happens to be the Watcher's office—great for the commute, though not for life insurance premiums. Giles refers to it as a "center of mystical energy," like a black hole sucking in "everything you ever dreaded was under your bed and told yourself couldn't be by the light of day. They're all *real*." While the Sunnydale Chamber of Commerce understandably may wish to play down such sentiments, the burg's Hellmouth status renders it a locus for all manner of magical activity, extending far beyond matters vampiric; Whedon and crew gleefully raided the nerd canon, pillaging tropes from comic books, monster movies, Tolkien fantasy, ancient mythology, and Grimm's fairy tales to populate their world. The magic and mythology of the Buffyverse is not as rigorously delineated as in some other immersive fantastic narratives—inconsistencies and contradictions abound re: the "rules" governing the supernatural elements of the show. That's fine. *BTVS* largely uses these familiar, iconic fan ideas for color, humor, story devices, and, most importantly, metaphor. Watchers Council applicants should be familiar with the following material. It will be on the test.

Artifacts: Stranger Things

Mystical MacGuffins, necromantic knick-knacks, and other assorted sorcerous swag.

The Amulet

Did the writers run out of mystical names? The amulet was a magical purifying totem used by Spike in the battle with the First Evil to disintegrate hordes of Turok-Han with beams of magical light. Unfortunately, it burned Spike to a crisp; fortunately, he got better.

Box of Gavrok

In season three's "Choices," the mayor, expecting delivery from Central America of a mysterious package "crucial" to his impending ascension, dispatches Faith to the airport to meet the courier, whom she apparently takes it upon herself to kill instead. Buffy, meanwhile, persuades one of the mayor's henchvamps, physically, to cough up whatever he knows about the box, which, she discovers, "houses some great demonic energy or something which Hizzoner needs to chow down on come A-Day." (The girl does have a way with words.) While the Scoobies pull off a daring raid at City Hall and escape with the box, they are forced to return it in exchange for Willow, who was taken

Giles (Anthony Stewart Head), either plumbing ancient magical texts of eldritch lore or torturing ants (he's doing the first thing).

prisoner by Faith. The swap, which takes place at night at Sunnydale High, is interrupted by Principal Snyder, convinced a drug deal is going down (he's initially unaware of the mayor's presence, but cowers once Wilkins steps forth). Despite Wilkins's warning, one of the two dim-bulb coppers hauled along by Snyder insists on opening the box. Bad move. Several spider-like creatures emerge, and the events that ensue evoke some of the great "face-hugger" moments in the Ridley Scott's *Alien*. According to the mayor, there are fifty billion of the creatures crawling around inside that box, just itching to get out (bigger on the inside?). Eventually, the mayor devours several of the spiders as part of the Ritual of Gavrok, to prepare for his ascendance into the pure-bred demon Olvikan (actually squished up Tootsie Rolls, according to Harry Groener, who portrayed the mayor).

Bringers' Knife

Curved, bejeweled daggers favored by the Bringers on their Potential Slayer-killing missions.

Dagon Sphere

A small, yellow, glowing sphere created to repel evil. Buffy uses one, along with Olaf's hammer, to subdue Glory in their final battle at the tower.

D'Hoffryn's Talisman

Sensibly enough, a talisman used to summon vengeance demon honcho D'Hoffryn. Anya receives it at her wedding, and uses it to get her old job back.

Doll's Eye Crystal

A Maclay family heirloom, this rare object aided in the casting of spells in some unspecified way. Willow was impressed.

Draconian Katra

A handheld body-switching device that looks like something Beyoncé would wear. Faith used one of these—a parting gift from Mayor Wilkins—to exchange forms with Buffy.

Ferula Gemini

A short magical staff used by the demon Toth to split Xander into two identical entities, one possessing dominant traits, the other passive. Toth meant to zap Buffy, but missed. Poor Xander. Better than magical syphilis, anyway.

Gem of Amara

A pretty emerald stone that renders vampires immune to staking, fire, and sunlight, making them virtually indestructible. Spike gets hold of one (taking it from his on-again, off-again girlfriend Harmony Kendall) and attacks Buffy in daylight, but she manages to retrieve the gem and defeat him. She sends it to Angel in L.A., and he eventually destroys it.

The Gentlemen's Box

Used by the Gentlemen to contain the voices of their victims, which are the spectral surgeons' sole vulnerability. Willow evidently keeps it after the Gentlemen are defeated; it is pretty.

Ghora's Egg

A key magical ingredient for raising the dead. Fair warning: tough to acquire, and it's a bad idea anyway.

Glove of Myneghon

My goodness, there hasn't been this much fuss about a glove in Southern California since the O. J. trial. "The world's ugliest fashion accessory," as Buffy calls it, the Glove of Myneghon is known to possess extraordinary powers, though their full extent has never been documented (at the very least it can summon and shoot lightning). Still, that doesn't seem to diminish demand for it, as evidenced by the fact that both the warrior demon Lagos and rogue Watcher Gwendolyn Post have added it to their bucket lists, at number one with a bullet, which brings them to Sunnydale, where the glove is hidden in the Von Hauptman family crypt at Restfield Cemetery (one of twelve in town, by the way). Lagos is dispensed with easily enough (sort of), but the duplicitous Post is a bitch, finally managing to get her hands on it (or, more accurately, her hand in it). The glove can be destroyed, by immolation, but the problem is that once donned it can never be removed from the wearer's arm, so Buffy does the next best thing and severs the arm itself, killing Gwendolyn in the process. That's our girl, always thinking.

The Key

A formless entity of magical energy, the Key could open doorways between dimensions and is coveted by exiled hell goddess Glory, who wants to use it to get back home (destroying our world in the process). The Order of Dagon disguised it as a sullen teenager, which was pretty brilliant.

Lethe's Bramble

A magical plant used in "forgetting" spells, abused by Willow in her attempts to placate Tara; one disastrous application led to amnesia for the entire gang, and Willow's violation of Tara's mind led to their temporary breakup. The name comes from Greek mythology: Lethe is a river in Hades that washes away memories.

Mummy's Living Hand

Buffy has a devil of a time trying to sell this obstreperous, skittering horror at the Magic Box.

Olaf's Hammer

Olaf the Troll God's power was contained in this mystical cudgel, a devastating weapon that Buffy employed to batter Glory, who had pretty much effortlessly shrugged off all previous attacks—into unconsciousness. Preternaturally heavy, so that only Buffy is able to wield it effectively; it's an interesting foreshadowing of Whedon's Avengers movies, in which much is made of Thor's powerful war hammer and its resistance to being lifted by the unworthy. Basically, we're saying it's Mjolnir, which is awesome.

Orb of Thesulah

A gypsy-crafted crystal ball that shines in your hands (but not in your mouth), the Orb of Thesulah is, according to Dragon Cove's owner, a "spirit vault for the rituals of the undead," and a key component of Jenny Calendar's plan to restore Angel's soul following his romp beneath the sheets with Buffy. According to Angel, the orb summons a soul from the ether, storing it until it can be transferred. This isn't even as easy as it doesn't sound, since the transliteration annals for the ritual of the undead are lost, so the surviving text is pure gibberish and the spell impossible to cast. Jenny, desperate to make peace with Giles and Buffy after lying to them about who she really is, develops a computer program that translates the Romanian liturgy to English, thus enabling her to use the orb to summon and store Angel's soul. One problem: why would Angelus want his soul back when he no longer has a conscience? We're going to go out on a limb and say this has something to do with his subsequent decisions to shatter the orb and snap Jenny's neck. Fortunately for the good guys, Willow later is able to get her own hands on an Orb of Thesulah, and restores Angel's soul herself (using Jenny's notes).

Orbs of Nezzla'khan

Magical spheres imbuing the possessor with superhuman strength and invulnerability. The Trio steals them, and an orb-enhanced Warren Mears cleans Buffy's clock until she (with an assist from Jonathan) is able to smash the spheres.

Prokaryote Stone

A magical stone used to free repressed memories. Giles and Willow use one to uncover the fact that Spike is under the mystical command of the First Evil.

The Scythe

An ancient Slayer weapon forged by the Guardians that embodied the mystical essence of Slayerhood. Devastating in combat—Buffy wielded it to finally end Caleb—it is also used to activate all of the world's Potential Slayers, thus tipping the battle against the First Evil. (For more on the scythe, see page 330.)

Seal of Danzalthar

A goat-themed rune that, when sufficiently bled upon (anemic Jonathan Levinson couldn't swing it) opened a cavern allowing legions of Turok-Han to run amok. A central component of the First Evil's plan.

Shadow Casters

Metal shapes used to tell stories through the shadows they cast, Shadow Casters are also capable of opening portals to other times and places.

Slayer Emergency Kit

Given to Buffy by Robin Wood, the kit contains: a boomerang-like weapon; a small urn; a Sumerian spell book; and a box of Shadow Casters. We would have included a holy water super-soaker, but what do we know?

Sphere of the Future

Stewart Burns uses this unimaginatively named crystal ball to show Xander false visions of his future, thereby prompting him to call off his wedding to Anya. Burns should have invited Xander to invest in some Florida real estate while he was on a roll.

Urn of Osiris

A small clay pot of great magical power necessary for the resurrection of Buffy Summers. Anya finds one on eBay.

Word of Valios

A scarab-shaped charm instrumental in performing the Sacrifice of Three.

Grimoires: Reading is Fundamental(ly Dangerous)

The written word has a lot to answer for.

Books of Ascension

O brave new world that has such books in 't! These "very powerful" tomes are precious enough to cost one squirrelly demon (identified as Skyler in the script, though his name is never spoken) his life, and the bloodshed might not have ended there if rogue Faith hadn't snatched them on behalf of the mayor before the Scoobies could get their hands on them: "The mayor would hate it if somebody got a hold of them before, you know . . ." Skyler tells the Slayers, from whom he is seeking five thousand dollars in exchange for the vade mecums. *Hmm*, very mysterioso. The books are, at first, a complete puzzle to Watchers Giles and Wesley, though Willow remembers a reference to ascension in the genocide section of the Merenshtadt Text (film adaptation pending), and Giles eventually locates a brief reference to it in the journal of Desmond Kane, pastor of a small town named Sharpsville, dated May 26, 1723: "Tomorrow is the ascension, God help us all." That, Giles adds, is the last anyone heard of Sharpsville: "The town more or less disappeared." While the Scoobies lose out on the books, they do uncover valuable information, specifically that Faith has turned to the dark side and the mayor is planning something very huge and scary on graduation day. Later on in season three, Willow gets her hands on all five volumes of the books while being held prisoner at City Hall, and even manages to surreptitiously rip out several pages, which she eventually delivers to Giles for study.

Books of Pherion + Hebron's Almanac

When the apocalyptic cult known as the Sisterhood of Jhe threatens to open the Hellmouth, Gilles, Willow, and Buffy hit the books, specifically these books, in an attempt to stop them.

Bynum's History of Witchcraft

A beginner's primer Dawn consults for information on resurrection spells. Very Hogwarts.

The Diary of Lucius Temple

Another of Giles's demonology tomes, *The Diary of Lucius Temple* is consulted in season three's "Amends" as the Scoobies attempt to ascertain why Angel was sent back to Earth from the demon dimension. The author was not only an acolyte of the demon Acathla, but also an accomplished gardener, specializing in beets.

Pergamum Codex

The codex, a crucial book of Slayer lore, is believed to have been lost since the fifteenth century, but Angel tracks it down in season one and delivers it to Giles, who probably wishes he never heard of the Pergamum Codex. The book, which contains the most complete prophecies of the Slayer's role in the end of days, augurs the death of Buffy at the hands of the Master the following night, which does indeed come to pass, though only temporarily (sure, leave out the most important part). Giles is so unnerved by this prophecy that he insists on fighting the Master himself, but Buffy puts a stop to that crazy idea by knocking him out.

Tiberius Manifestor

Very little is known about it, except that Giles references it in season one's "Out of Mind, Out of Sight" as one of two particularly "salient" lost books of Slayer prophecy, along with the Pergamum Codex, which goes on to play a much bigger role.

Magical Entities: Demons and Demi-Gods, Sinners and Saints

You're not from around here, are you?

Aradia

Known as "Goddess of the Lost," she is invoked for guiding spells.

Beljoxa's Eye

A blobby extra-dimensional being that could reveal the truth about past and present events. Covered with eyeballs, floating eerily, this little nugget is *très* gross.

Brother Thelonius (Pierrino Mascarino)

If you're named Brother Thelonius you're either a bebop pianist or a monk, but this is *Buffy*, so there's really only one option, and that is that you are the monk who imprisons the scaly green demon known as Moloch the Corruptor inside a book that, as Hellmouth luck would have it, turns up hundreds of years later in the Sunnydale High Library, in season one's "I Robot, You Jane." There, it is unknowingly opened and scanned into a computer by Willow Rosenberg, thus unleashing Moloch, though this time as a virtual demon. This won't be the first or last time we say this: only in Sunnydale.

Stewart Burns (George D. Wallace)

The once human, now demon former victim of Anyanka, Stewart took the form of Xander's "future self" to discourage Xander from marrying Anya (and thus breaking her heart). It works, damn it.

Clem (James C. Leary)

A friendly, peaceful demon covered in droopy folds of loose skin, Clem is a poker buddy of Spike's who befriends the Scooby gang after crashing Buffy's twenty-first birthday party. Clem is fond of Dawn, whom he babysat, and he eventually became the personal assistant to vampire Harmony Kendall, who, in the canonical comics, becomes a reality-television star. Again, nice guy, but don't leave your kittens with him.

Doc (Joel Grey)

Slight, courtly, unassuming, Doc has the air of a beloved old professor or small-town physician, provided one doesn't happen to notice his reptilian tail. Doc, a dark magic expert known to Spike, assists Dawn in her attempt to resurrect Joyce Summers. The results are horrific, but Doc isn't finished with the Summerses: secretly a powerful demon in the thrall of Glory, Doc assaults Dawn (and Spike), completing the blood ritual Glory had set in motion. Despite his formidable powers, Buffy disposes of him quickly, tossing him off of Glory's sacrificial tower. Academy Award winner Joel Grey makes Doc an indelible character, infusing his sinister monster with a disarming avuncular charm and playful wit that make his maliciousness all the more disturbing.

D'Hoffryn (Andy Umberger)

An extremely powerful demon, ruler of the hell dimension Arashmaharr, D'Hoffryn recruits Anya for service as a vengeance demon, and also tries to get Willow to sign on. Hurt and angered by his favorite employee's (Anya) desire to reverse the damage she's done, D'Hoffryn immolates her friend Halfrek to fulfill her request. So, more of a stick, not so much the carrot, style of motivator.

Dramius

While Dramius's identity is never clear, we know from a conversation between Giles and Kendra that he produced several volumes of writings, the sixth of which referenced the Order of Taraka, the deadly assassins summoned by Spike to kill Buffy in season two.

Eryishon the Endless

In season three's "Doppelgangland," Anya, having lost her demonic powers earlier in the season and being rebuffed by D'Hoffryn when she sought to have them restored, decides to take matters into her own twelve-hundred-year-old hands, misleading Willow into casting a spell that, in effect, is like ordering in, except in this case it is the source of her power, a necklace, rather than moo goo gai pan that is on the menu. The spell is supposed to create a temporal fold, which it does, enabling an entity known as Eryishon the Endless to bring forth the necklace from the time and place it was destroyed—meaning 1) the past and 2) the so-called Wishverse—which it doesn't. Instead, Vamp Willow crosses over from the Wishverse into the "real"-verse, raising quite a rumpus, especially since human Willow is there, too: much peril, but much wackiness, too. Bored now.

Eyghon the Sleepwalker/The Mark of Eyghon

Remember that special episode of *Diff'rent Strokes* when Nancy Reagan urges students to just say no to Eyghon? Of course you don't, because it never happened. Perhaps if we as a people worried more about demons and less about drugs Eyghon never would have terrorized Sunnydale in the second season of *Buffy*. Explanation: Back when he was in his twenties, Giles was matriculating at Oxford during the day and attending to his studies in the occult at night, plus navigating familial pressure to fulfill his destiny as a Watcher (he would have preferred becoming a fighter pilot or grocer). Major pressure, which eventually overcame him, so he dropped out of school and moved to London, falling in with a rogue gang of sorcerers. Yes, his famous "Ripper" stage. Others in this group included odious chaos worshipper Ethan Rayne, plus Thomas Sutcliffe, Philip Henry, Deirdre (sometimes spelled Dierdre) Page, and Randall (last name unknown). Eyghon? We're getting to it. He wasn't a cohort, but rather a possession demon they discovered during one of their exercises in depravity. We all know the demons in *Buffy* are metaphors; Eyghon is pretty clearly a surrogate for addiction (hence, the Nancy Reagan opening). Summoning him produced an "extraordinary high." His initiates got so into it they tattooed themselves with the Mark of Eyghon, establishing a psychic connection between the demon and his followers, enabling Eyghon to track them. The way it worked was this: one member of the group enters a deep sleep; the others summon Eyghon, who takes possession of the slumberer. On one such occasion, Randall, the possessee, lost control, and couldn't shake free of the demon. The others tried to exorcise him, but wound up killing Randall instead. That should have been the end of that, but Eyghon returns in "The Dark Age," killing off the other members of the group one by one, until Giles and Ethan are the only two left. Eventually, Eyghon possesses Angel, triggering a *mano-a-mano* demon fight, which Angel wins, seemingly dispensing with Eyghon once and for all, though the noodge does pop up again in the canonical comics. Nope, not going there.

Halfrek (Kali Rocha)

Anya's snarky old vengeance demon pal, Halfrek poses as Dawn's guidance counselor, goading the girl into making a wish that turns out to greatly resemble the plot of Luis Buñuel's *The Exterminating Angel*. Halfrek was also apparently Spike's pre-vampire inamorata Cecily Addams, disguised as a human—she and Spike seem to recognize each other upon meeting in Sunnydale, and she calls him "William." Halfrek dies when Anya implores D'Hoffryn to undo her legacy of vengeance; D'Hoffryn disintegrates Halfrek to power the spell and hurt Anya. It's a bummer: Halfrek was a hoot and had a particular penchant for working on behalf of wronged children. You suck, D'Hoffryn.

Josephus du Lac

You rogue, you. Du Lac was a theologian/mathematician who belonged to a religious sect excommunicated by the Vatican around the turn of the twentieth century for reasons never fully explicated, though presumably having something to do with the fact that his greatest legacy is a manuscript compiling rituals and spells "that reap unspeakable evil" (Giles). Du Lac was so crafty that he recorded them in archaic Latin, so only fellow members of his psycho cult could understand what he was saying, and invented something called the du Lac Cross, a.k.a., in Slayer Slang, a decoder ring, to decipher. What does any of this have to do with us? The du Lac Manuscript was held at the Sunnydale High Library, until, that is, it was lifted by a vampire under the command of Spike, whose sole interest was in a spell to restore Drusilla to full potency.

Lloyd (Steven W. Bailey)

An Africa-based Asphyx Demon who puts Spike through torturous trials before restoring his soul. Friend of D'Hoffryn. Unsentimental regarding the tender feelings of love.

Local Boy, a.k.a. Muscles (Tanoai Reed)

Lloyd's first trial pits Spike against this 'roided-up, flaming fisted demon warrior. He's formidable, but Spike manages to snap his neck.

Olvikan/Olukai

Olvikan, or Olukai to his friends, of which he had none, is the titanic pure-bred serpentine demon that the mayor ascends into while delivering the commencement speech at the Sunnydale High 1999 graduation in the finale of the third season. As evil as he is, we applaud him for making one of his first acts the devouring of the diminutive Principal Snyder. Giles and Wesley come across an earlier reference to Olvikan while researching the death of Professor Lester Worth (stabbed by Faith), who had discovered a giant carcass near a dormant volcano in Kauai, where the locals had made references to the legend of Olukai, a bastardized form of Olvikan. The Watchers correctly deduce from this that the previous embodiment of Olvikan had been killed during the volcano's eruption, meaning that the mayor—who, in his final days as a human, had become impervious to harm—would become vulnerable again once he ascended. This leads Buffy to concoct a battle plan for graduation day that ends with Olvikan lured to the school library, where he is blown to smithereens in an explosion donated by none other than the librarian himself, Rupert Giles, who couldn't have enjoyed decimating all those books.

Old Ones

Never trust anyone over thirty . . . thousand years old. We can't really say with specificity when these pure-breed demons ruled the earth, but we know from Giles that it lasted for "untold eons" before they "lost their purchase on this reality" (reasons: unknown, at least from the TV series), making way for man. If this sounds like an inversion of the Garden of Eden mythology, that's because it is; in *Buffy*, the world began not as paradise, but as hell (*Angel* suggests a slightly altered version, involving a struggle between higher, beneficent beings and the demonic Old Ones, but the source is a higher being who adopts the name of Jasmine and is an inveterate liar, so who knows?). All that remains of these pure-breeds, according to Giles, are "vestiges, certain magicks, certain creatures," including vampires, which the Old Ones created. Again, from Giles: "The books tell us that the last [pure-breed] demon to leave this reality fed off a human, mixed their blood. He was a human form possessed, infected—by the demon's soul. He bit another, and another, and so they walk the earth, feeding, killing some, mixing their blood with others to make more of their kind, waiting for the animals to die out, and the Old Ones to return." In season one, the Master and his Order of Aurelius minions are particularly eager for this happy day. In season three, Mayor Wilkins assumes the form of Olvikan, also known as Olukai, also an Old One. As Anya, the only living eyewitness to an ascension, explains, pure-breed demons are "different" from those the Scoobies are accustomed to vanquishing. Different, how? "Well, for one thing, they're bigger," Anya says, a ginormous understatement. *Angel* and the season-nine comics are more expansive on the Old Ones, but our focus is on *Buffy* the TV series, so we'll keep it brief. The essences of the most powerful of the Old Ones—those who couldn't be killed—are entombed in sarcophagi (crystals embedded in stone) in the Deeper Well, a crypt deep beneath the earth stretching from one end of the planet to the other, with two access points: one in England and one in New Zealand, both heavily guarded. In this account, it is explained that the Old Ones were vanquished when mortal creatures (i.e., humans) rose up and banished them. Illyria, a character from *Angel*, is herself an Old One, though she eventually possesses the human form of Winifred "Fred" Burkle (played by supercool Amy Acker). In the season ten comics, Giles refers to Old Ones as "the mightiest of all demonkind . . . primordial forces that cannot truly die," which confuses us, because earlier explanations seem to contend that only those who couldn't be killed were buried in the Deeper Well, which would seem to suggest that some *could* die. Not as brief as we intended, but this mythology stuff is pretty addictive.

Lovecraft Actually

Buffy's Old Ones—fearsome pure-breed demons that roamed the earth for "untold eons" (per Giles) before finally giving way to humankind and human-demon hybrids like vampires—have antecedents in the short stories of Howard Phillips (H. P.) Lovecraft, an early-twentieth-century pulp writer who specialized in a niche genre known as weird fiction, combining elements of horror, fantasy, science fiction, supernatural, and the occult. Lovecraft was criminally undervalued both critically and commercially in his own time ("bad taste and bad art," Edmund Wilson wrote of him in *The New Yorker* in 1945); his death, of complications from intestinal cancer, on March 15, 1937, at age the age of forty-six merited just a one-paragraph obit on page five of the next day's *New York Times*, which virtually ignored his literary output, focusing instead on how he had charted the progression of his disease to benefit science.

However, Lovecraft (the name sounds too good to be real, but it is) generated fierce devotion within a circle of contemporaneous like-minded writers, including August Derleth, who coined the term Cthulhu Mythos to identify the fictional folklore prevalent in his work, which evolved into a shared universe comprising not just short stories, poems, sonnets, and novels, but television, film, pop music, video-games, and comic books as well (including *Batman*, whose Elizabeth Arkham Asylum for the Criminally Insane, created by Dennis O'Neil, is named after a fictional New England town in Lovecraft's stories). Lovecraft's popularity surged most recently in 2014, thanks to the critically adored first season of HBO's *True Detective* ("a crime story told through a Lovecraft lens," according to the Nerdist's Benjamin Bailey), which sprinkled allusions to the Cthulhu Mythos into its Byzantine plot, along with Robert W. Chambers's *The King in Yellow* (1895), which Lovecraft read and pointed to in his own work, including "The Whisper in Darkness," a short story, and the sonnet *Fungi from Yuggoth*.

The mythos is named after the frightful, grotesque title character in Lovecraft's most famous story, "The Call of Cthulhu," first published in the pulp magazine *Weird Tales* in 1928, which, along with the novella "At the Mountains of Madness" (written in 1931, but published five years later), provides the most detailed description of the Old Ones, sometimes referred to as the Great Old Ones and sometimes as Elder Things (confusing, we know). In "Cthulhu," New Orleans police, investigating the serial disappearance of women and children, venture deep into the swamps, where they discover nearly a hundred naked men "braying, bellowing, and writhing about a monstrous ring-shaped bonfire"—worshippers of the Great Old Ones, "who lived ages before there were any men, and who came to the young world out of the sky. Those Old Ones were gone now, inside the earth and under the sea, but their dead bodies had told their secrets in dreams to the first men, who formed a cult, which had never died."

The visionary horror writer H. P. Lovecraft created a mythos of angry elder gods and unspeakable evil that heavily informed the Buffyverse.

When the stars were rightly aligned in the cycle of eternity, Cthulhu, great priest of the Old Ones—described as a "gigantic thing, miles high," with "an octopus-like head whose face was a mass of feelers, a scaly, rubbery-looking body, prodigious claws on hind and fore feet, and long, narrow wings behind"—would alert his acolytes from his tomb in the city of R'lyeh, submerged beneath the sea, to liberate him through the use of dark arts so that he "should rise and bring the earth again beneath his sway." Turns out the Old Ones aren't exactly "dead," but rather hibernating, due to an inhospitable realignment of the stars, in stone houses in R'lyeh, preserved by the spells of Cthulhu, awaiting their glorious resurrection, which they are incapable of effecting themselves in their slumbering state. (In "Harvest," part one of the two-part *Buffy* premiere, Giles makes a similar point about vampires seeking to open the Hellmouth to allow the pure-bred demons to return to Earth: "And so they walk the Earth, feeding, killing some, mixing their blood with others to make more of their kind, waiting for the animals to die out and the old ones to return.")

How exactly will their acolytes know the time is right to liberate Cthulhu? Kind of a no-brainer: "Mankind would have become as the Great Old Ones, free and wild and beyond good and evil, with laws and morals thrown aside and all men shouting and killing and reveling in joy. Then the liberated Old Ones would teach them new ways to shout and kill and revel and enjoy themselves, and all the Earth would flame with a holocaust of ecstasy and freedom."

In other words: when the apocalypse comes, beep him. Fans of Whedon's 2012 horror film, *The Cabin in the Woods* (co-scripted with Drew Goddard, who also directed), will recognize the Lovecraftian presence of the "Ancient Ones," belligerent gods that once ruled Earth, but now slumber peacefully beneath it, where they'll stay as long as they are appeased by human sacrifice. Failure to do so, as a character known as the Director explains, will result in the "agonizing death of every soul on the planet."

David Greenwalt had this to say about Whedon's views on religion:

> You know, Joss is a pretty stern atheist, but what he does is so connected to the universe. One time—I wish I could think of the episode, this great *Buffy* episode that had me in tears—I said, "There's no way you're an atheist." And he says, 'Oh, I'm an atheist, but I know the myths.'

Lovecraft, another avowed atheist (not to mention racist and anti-Semite, but not going there), is credited with developing a literary philosophy known as cosmicism, or cosmic indifference, positing a fraught, purposeless universe in which humankind is as insignificant as insects in the face of such vast horror. The less we know about it the better, for the sake of our sanity. Whedon embraces a similarly bleak outlook personally ("I can't believe anybody thinks we're actually going to make it before we destroy the planet," he told *Entertainment Weekly* in 2013), but, in *Buffy* at least, clings to a certain faith in humankind (he named a character after it, didn't he? And we have to believe the fact that she was so troubled a character means something)."Faith is something we have to embrace," he said in accepting the Outstanding Lifetime Achievement Award in Cultural Humanism at Harvard University's Memorial Church in 2009. "Faith in God means believing absolutely in something with no proof whatsoever; Faith in humanity means believing absolutely in something with a huge amount of proof to the contrary. We are the true believers."

Osiris

Egyptian god of the dead Osiris—depicted in *BTVS* as a giant, ghostly head—is in charge of authorizing resurrections, and he rejects Willow's appeal for Tara, as Tara has perished by non-supernatural means. Osiris seems like he'd be right at home working at the DMV.

Proserpexa

A demoness worshipped by an apocalypse cult, Proserpexa, a.k.a. Sister of the Dark, was burned in effigy as part of Dark Willow's world-ending ritual. Medusa vibe.

Saint Vigeous

Boy, the things you have to do to have a night named after you. Once upon a time, Vigeous led a band of vampires on the warpath through Edessa, Harran, and points East (we looked these up for you; they're ancient Turkish cities. You're welcome.), massacring legions, which for vampires is a joyous occasion, so they named the Night of Saint Vigeous after him, to commemorate a time when their power peaks (Jenny Calendar was supposed to call it a "Holy Night of Attack," though the line was eventually cut, for length). In the early episodes of season two, the Order of Aurelius is planning a huge attack to celebrate, but Spike gets impatient and ruins their plans by attacking Sunnydale High on Parent-Teacher Night, which is kind of similar, if you think about it, two days early, getting his head thumped by Joyce Summers in the process.

Shrouded Man (Gary Bullock)

Season three's "Enemies" is like a supernatural version of *The Sting*—stay with us here—with the Shrouded Man analogous to "Black Gloved Gunman"

(Joe Tornatore), whom we suspect all along is out to execute Johnny Hooker (Robert Redford) but is really there to protect him. Here, the Shrouded Man, so named because his entire body is, well, shrouded, with the exception of his orange eyes, is hired by the mayor to extract Angel's soul, so that Angelus can emerge again and join his crusade against Buffy, but, in fact, is scheming with Angel, Buffy, and Giles to dupe the mayor and Faith into revealing crucial information about their imminent ritual of ascension, which works perfectly. As to why a nasty-looking shaman would cast his lot with the Scoobies: seems he owed Giles a favor, for introducing him to his wife. That's what we call a match made in hell.

Sid the Dummy

Lascivious demon hunter trapped in the body of a ventriloquist's dummy, and one of the great rug pulls of season one, occurring in "The Puppet Show." The Scoobies initially believe Sid has possessed Sunnydale High student Morgan Shay, and is manipulating him to murder schoolmates so that Sid can harvest their organs, but eventually discover the truth, from the dummy's mouth: "I hunt demons. . . . Let's just say there was me, there was a really mean demon, there was a curse, and the next thing I know I'm not me anymore. I'm sitting on some guy's knee with his hand up my shirt." Sid's actual age is unknown, but if you can take him at his word he was sexually involved with a Korean Slayer in the 1930s, before his transformation. There's one way to break the curse, though not ideal, since it means Sid's death as well: wipe out the entire Brotherhood of Seven, demons capable of assuming human form for seven years at a time by harvesting human brains and hearts, which is exactly what happens. *Annyeong-gaseyo*, Sid. As Dean Batali recalls:

> We went to Joss with an idea of doing a show about the talent show, that our guys would do the talent show, and how out of place they are and how awkward it feels, and I think we pitched a couple of different ideas. There's this guy with a ventriloquist's dummy who's convincing him to kill people, so the ventriloquist's dummy is possessed, and possessing the boy, and Joss goes, "You know, I've always wanted to do a story where the dummy is good." And right there is the story. As soon as he says that, then the episode becomes what the episode becomes.

Sweet (Hinton Battle)

A remarkably suave demon who, when summoned by Xander, turns Sunnydale into a musical—the inhabitants, including the Scoobies, are compelled to break into song and dance to express their feelings. He almost marries Dawn, which is odd, and performs some transporting numbers himself. No wonder: Sweet was portrayed by Tony Award–winning Broadway superstar Hinton Battle.

Thespia

Invoking the nymph-goddess Thespia could aid in locating and identifying demons—sort of a Wiccan Google Maps.

Uurthu the Restless

Some sort of supernatural entity invoked by the grave-hopping Jack O'Toole as he summons the zombified corpses of his "boys" (Big Bob, Dickie, and Parker) for a night out on the town. The ritual involves reciting a prayer, spilling human blood over the grave, and waving a chicken's foot. Wish we could have been in the writers' room for that.

Veruca (Paige Moss)

The sultry (and insufferably pretentious, in a "Burning Man" sort of way) lead singer of shoegazer outfit Shy, Veruca enchants fellow musician Oz—not so much with her soporific crooning, but rather her werewolf pheromones, which send our diminutive Lycan Scooby into something like heat, much to his girlfriend Willow's dismay. Oz's animal passion drives him to break out of his cage during his transformation to copulate with Veruca, who, in a strange take on pillow talk, encourages Oz to embrace his primal nature as a killer. Willow is devastated when she learns of Oz's indiscretion, and further insulted when Veruca attacks and attempts to kill her. Oz tears Veruca's throat out instead and leaves town immediately after, unable to face the trauma he has caused and unwilling to risk more should he stay. In short, Veruca is a deeply unpleasant jerk who ruins everything (and probably smells like dog).

Werewolves

There are two key lycanthropes in *Buffy*: Oz and Veruca, presenting two opposing approaches to coping with the beast (insert metaphor here) in them: Oz wants to tame it; Veruca, to embrace it. Unfortunately, what we have is not two opposing forces working together in harmony, but two opposing forces colliding, with disastrous consequences, for many, including Veruca, who dies; Oz, who kills her; and Willow, who loses her boyfriend over it.

Werewolves are old hat, of course, dating back at least to medieval European folklore. Emily Gerard, in her 1885 article "Transylvanian Superstitions," writes that transformation occurs either "voluntarily or as penance for [a man's] sins"—no full moons or werewolf bites here. In Transylvania and other parts of Romania the term for werewolf was *prikolitsch*. Gerard attributes the tenacity of the legend to the abundance of real wolves living in the area at the time, and the threats they posed, attacking flocks and farms "with a skill which would do honour to a human intellect. Sometimes a whole village is kept in trepidation for weeks together by some particularly audacious leader of a [pack] of wolves, to whom the peasants not unnaturally attribute a more than animal nature, and one may safely prophesy that so long as the real wolf continues to haunt the Transylvanian forests, so long will his spectre brother survive in the minds of the inhabitants."Gerard may be a big deal with scholars and authors (like Bram Stoker, who drew from her article while penning *Dracula*), but with popular imagination she's no match for Hollywood, especially the 1941 Universal film *The Wolf Man*, from writer Curt Siodmak and director George Waggner. The film stars Lon Chaney Jr. as Larry Talbot, afflicted after being bitten on the chest by a werewolf while trying to save a young woman's life. Contrary to popular belief, this film makes no reference to the transformation occurring under a full moon, but rather "when the wolfbane blooms and the autumn moon is bright" (although this is changed by the first of four sequels, *Frankenstein Meets the Wolfman*, released in 1943, when it is suggested that the transformation is triggered by the light of the full moon).In *Buffy*, Giles explains in "Phases," the second-season episode that reveals Oz's lycanthropy, that "while there's absolutely no scientific explanation for lunar effect on the human psyche, the phases of the moon do seem to exert a great deal of psychological influence. And the full moon seems to bring out our darkest qualities." The werewolf, Giles adds, is "such a potent, extreme representation of our inborn animalistic traits that it emerges for three full consecutive nights"—the full moon and the two nights immediately surrounding it. The beast acts on pure instinct, Giles says: "predatory and aggressive." Like the vampire, whom Gerard called "the first cousin" of the werewolf, the lycanthrope is conscienceless and feeds on humans, but the evening spree for werewolves is like a hangover from hell, in that the following morning, recollections of it are hazy, and the perpetrator is once again human, both physically and emotionally. On the subject of lycanthropy-themed *Buffy* episodes, Dean Batali opines:

> When I teach writing at colleges, "Phases" is the episode I teach. I talk about how we broke that story the inside out because we knew we wanted to reveal to the audience that Oz was a werewolf, and we also knew that we wanted Oz to turn into a werewolf in front of Willow. And

once you start putting those ideas together you realize—there's a way to tell the story, you can wait until the very end and show that Oz is a werewolf or you can show it at the very beginning, but we thought, "Let's show that Oz is a werewolf in the middle of the episode and then deal with that and then have him change into a werewolf in front of Willow at the end of act three," which is a great act break. And then we realized, "Well, okay, we're obviously changing the mythology, aren't we? Because we need him to change into a werewolf more than once, so then he's not just a werewolf one night a month."

Oz leaves Sunnydale early in season four, after ripping apart Veruca's throat (literally) and Willow's heart (figuratively), though he and Veruca are both in wolf form at the time and she's trying, understandably, to kill Willow. He returns briefly at the end of the season, hoping to win Willow back, after furloughing in Tibet, where, he believes, he has finally tamed his inner beast, through herbs, charms, chanting, and meditation. Wrong! Sniffing out Willow's budding relationship with Tara, the typically laconic Oz goes ballistic, chasing after Tara. Once a werewolf always a werewolf? The Buffyverse can be an unforgiving place. This being Whedon, of course, a werewolf is never just a werewolf, as Batali, who co-scripted "Phases" with Rob DesHotel, confirms: "When we were given the story, we started talk about it as adolescents, we started talking about the relatable adolescent thing. So we looked at 'Phases' as, 'Here I am, I'm an adolescent, there's all these weird hairs growing all over my body, what's going on?' That's how we addressed the story, and that's still sort of in there just a little bit, but that's how we were looking at it, as the person who feels so out of place because their body is all gangly as an adolescent."

Whistler (Max Perlich)

You know how to Whistler, don't you? You just put two episodes together and blow everything up, sending Angel to hell, Buffy to Los Angeles, and Spike and Drusilla to Barcelona. As best we understand it, Whistler—quoting Buffy here, and even *she's* guessing—is "just some immortal demon sent down to even the score between good and evil," and while appearing in just two episodes (parts one and two of the second-season-ending "Becoming"), he is hugely influential, in that it is Whistler who 1) persuades Angel, in 1996, to become an agent for good in the world, whisking him from New York, where he is roaming the streets filthy and unkempt, to Los Angeles, where they observe the new Slayer, Buffy Summers, with Whistler encouraging Angel to "become someone . . . someone to be counted," and 2) counsels Buffy, two years later, on how to thwart another apocalypse, by sending Angelus to hell and so preventing him from liberating the demon Acathla. Beyond this we don't know much about Whistler, except that he is humanoid looking, at least in this iteration (portrayed by the puckish Max Perlich, whose first wail out of his mother's womb was sardonic) and—despite seeming to know a good deal about the future—was as surprised as anyone that Angel had reverted into Angelus, thus necessitating Whistler's return to this earthly dimension, having been under the impression that Angel was intended not to unleash Acathla but to kill him. Oh, this too: he has a wicked sense of humor, even if he doesn't use it judiciously. With time winding down, Buffy presses for clues on how to stop Angelus, but Whistler is preoccupied with finding something to eat or drink at Giles's apartment: "You know," he says, "raiding an Englishman's fridge is like dating a nun. You're never gonna get the good stuff." Whistler reportedly was supposed to appear as Angel's sidekick in the spinoff series, but it never happened, for reasons that have never been settled to everyone's satisfaction, although Perlich has been quoted as saying that he "never got the call."

Rituals: There Will Be Blood. And Chanting, Probably.

The rite stuff.

Ascension

We all aspire to greatness, but only a select few ascend, and only a select fewer would even want to. Basically we're talking two types of folk: psychopaths and politicians (or maybe just one?). In any event, Mayor Richard Wilkins III is eminently qualified. In the Buffyverse, ascension is the act of transforming from human (in the clinical sense) to pure demon, typically accompanied by mass murder involving everyone in the general vicinity. Mercifully, ascensions are extremely rare: prior to Wilkins's in the season-three finale, Anya was believed to be the only living person ever to witness one, and that was eight hundred years prior, in the Koskov Valleys above the Ural Mountains, when a sorcerer transmuted into the four-winged demon Lohesh (Anya was a vengeance demon at the time, cursing an unfaithful shepherd). We understand that tickets are not hard to come by.

Circle of Kayless

Formed during the ritual to bind demons, as when Brother Thelonius imprisons Moloch the Corrupter inside a book in season one's "I Robot, You Jane."

Cruciamentum

You pronounce it; we'll explain it: The Cruciamentum, known formally as the Tento di Cruciamentum, is kind of like a bat mitzvah for Slayers (we didn't promise to take it seriously). Translated from the Latin it means "torment," which only reaffirms the analogy for us. This rite of passage, occurring on the Slayer's eighteenth birthday, involves secretly weakening her physically and locking her in a room, where she is then required to battle a particularly nasty vampire selected especially for the occasion, as a test of her ability to outwit her opponents. Buffy herself is unknowingly scheduled to undergo this ordeal in the third-season episode "Helpless," pitted against a psychotic vampire named Zachary Kralik, a serial killer and cannibal *before* becoming a creature of the night, but things go awry, leading to a more improvisational Cruciamentum, in which she emerges victorious by tricking Kralik into taking his pills with holy water. Despite this happy outcome, the Cruciamentum ripples with consequences, none pleasant. First, Buffy rages at Giles, who, in the run-up to the event, adhered to his Watcherly duty by hypnotizing Buffy and injecting her with an organic compound of muscle relaxants and adrenal suppressors to zap her powers, even though he himself believed the Cruciamentum to be an "archaic exercise in cruelty." Buffy is so infuriated by this betrayal that she threatens to kill Giles if he touches her. Second, Giles, who eventually defied authorities and alerted Buffy to the test, is booted off the council by Quentin Travers, who tells him, "Your affection for your charge has rendered you incapable of clear and impartial judgment. You have a father's love for the child, and that is useless to the cause." Travers then congratulates Buffy, who responds "Bite me." But let's not lose sight of the true significance of these events, as Buffy herself points out: "The important thing is that I kept up my special birthday tradition of gut-wrenching misery and horror."

Formatia Trans Sicere Educatorum

Latin for "Enter all ye who seek knowledge," it's the sign outside Sunnydale High School, which is all the invite Angelus needs to enter late one night and snap Jenny Calendar's neck as she is working on the spell to restore his soul.

The Harvest

Dream up, dream up, it's Harvest time. We paraphrase, but that's essentially what Angel cryptically (default Angel mode back in those early days) tells Buffy in "Welcome to the Hellmouth," our first encounter with the word. We have no idea what it means then either, but it sounds ominous, and guess what? It is: a once-in-a-century event (more than enough, thank you), the Harvest is when the Master absorbs power from a minion (a.k.a. the vessel, identified by the three-pointed star carved into his forehead) as he/she/it feeds. Sufficiently juiced, the Master can bust free from the underground prison in which he is trapped and open the portal between dimensions, paving the way for a demon infestation and yes, another apocalypse (actually, the first such threat the Scoobies face). Luke, said vessel, phrases it more colorfully: "The blood of men will flow as wine . . . and hell itself will come to town." Ooh! A must-miss.

Key Embodiment Ritual

The Order of Dagon employed this rite to transform the Key—an opener of interdimensional gateways—into a young girl. Specifically, Dawn Summers, younger sister of Buffy, who, along with everyone else in the Scooby orbit, is magically implanted with false lifelong memories of the newly created girl.

Mark of Gachnar

An occult symbol used to summon the wee demon Gachnar. Oz activates it by accidentally bleeding on it after cutting his hand while moving musical equipment into the Alpha Delta house.

Ritual of Mok'tagar

Not fun: a demon crouches on your body and force-feeds you animal blood while you sleep, thereby stealing a part of your soul. We've all had those nights, eh? Buffy's freshman roommate Kathy Newman subjects the Slayer to this unpleasantness in a bid to conceal her identity and hide from her dad. Which, when we meet Taparrich, is understandable.

Ritual of Restoration

Say you know a vampire and he's killing people left and right without remorse, so you think it might be a good idea to restore his soul. This is when you haul out the dusty old Ritual of Restoration. This, of course, is what happened to Angel back in the nineteenth century, after draining and killing a "favorite daughter" of the Kalderash clan of Romanian gypsies. We know that it requires an Orb of Thesulah, because Jenny Calendar shops for one when she is determined to restore Angelus's soul in season two. We also know that the ritual wasn't performed for a century because the transliteration annals were lost, so the surviving text is gibberish and the spell impossible to cast. But Jenny does succeed in creating a computer program that translates the Romanian liturgy to English, thus enabling the spell to be cast again, which Willow does, to restore Angel's soul. What we don't quite get is why Willow and others aren't doing a dozen or so of these a day, to at least make a dent in Sunnydale's demon-infestation problem.

Ritual of Revivication

This ritual to revive a vampire was attempted by the Anointed One to resurrect the Master in the early episodes of season two, but the Order of Aurelius is thwarted once again by Buffy. The ceremony involves mixing the blood of those humans in closest proximity to the deceased vampire at the time of his death with the remains of said vampire, typically accomplished by hanging the humans by their ankles over the remains and then cutting their throats. (Man, sounds worse than a bris.) The curious thing about this ritual is that so far as we understand, most vampires don't leave any remains. Do they?

Sacrifice of Three

A Hellmouth-opening, world-ending ritual performed by some Vahrall demons. It's a one-time proposition, as it requires the deaths of the participants (and also baby bones—*gross*).

SlayerFest '98

Sounds like an annual thrash-metal festival with copious amounts of illegal mind-altering substances, but is, in reality, something else entirely: a competition to see who can be the first to exterminate Buffy and Faith, hosted by Mr. Trick, since Jeff Probst either wasn't available or wouldn't sell his soul to the devil (and let's not pretend we don't know which). SlayerFest '98, transpiring on homecoming night in the appropriately titled third-season episode "Homecoming," featured seven contestants, four human—and we use the term loosely—(Frawley, the Gruenshtahler Twins, and the Old Man) and the rest demon (Kulak and Lyle and Candy Gorch). Due to a last-minute change in plans among the Scoobies, it turns out to be Buffy and Cordelia they hunt, rather than Faith, but you'll get no complaints from us, because chances are Faith wouldn't have had the absence of mind to try to subdue a demon assassin by smacking him over the head with a spatula.

Spells: You Can Do Magic

Charms, hexes, curses, and other thaumaturgical phenomena.

Aspect of the Demon

A phenomenon in which a person absorbs some characteristic—physiological
or otherwise—of a demon's identity by coming in contact with the creature's
blood, which is precisely what happens to Buffy in season three's "Earshot"
when she develops mind-reading abilities after slaying a mouthless, telepathic
demon (could have been worse, given that the demon is covered in scabs).
Giles and Angel both have come across earlier references to the condition,
and there is reputed to be a previous case, involving a man in Ecuador.
Good news: there's a cure. Bad news: it involves Buffy drinking a potion that
includes the heart of a second scabby demon. Better news: because of this
infection, Buffy discovers the lunch lady's plot to wipe out Sunnydale High's
student population (at least those who don't brown-bag it or go off-campus
for lunch) by lacing their food with rat poison. Worst possible news: by reading Joyce's mind, Buffy learns that her mom and Giles had sex during the
episode "Band Candy" . . . on the hood of a police car . . . twice. Worth it?
You decide.

Augmentation Spell

Jonathan Levinson cast this spell to briefly turn himself into a human paragon of unparalleled success and esteem—and considering actor Danny
Strong's post-*Buffy* meteoric rise as a screenwriter and show creator, we
wonder if that fairy dust might have rubbed off a little?

Barricade Spell

Self-explanatory. Employed in the Giles/Dark Willow sorcerous showdown.

Breath of the Entropics

In season three's "Choices," the Scoobies plan to use this "down and dirty
black magic" (Willow's words) to destroy the mayor's Box of Gavrok, but never
get the chance once Willow is abducted by Faith, forcing them to swap the box
for the Wicca, plus two players to be named later. We are aware of at least two
ingredients involved: essence of toad and twice-blessed sage.

Communication with the Dying Spell

An interrogatory charm used by Willow to question a dying Bringer. They could really use these on *Law + Order*.

Energy Blast Spell

What it says on the tin. Giles uses it to slam Dark Willow through a wall.

Enjoining Spell

Giles, Willow, and Xander join their essences with Buffy to create a gestalt superbeing capable of defeating Initiative cyborg Adam. In the spell, Giles represents the mind; Willow, the spirit; Xander, the heart; and Buffy, the hand—literalizing the Scoobies' metaphorical roles within the group.

Field Binding Spell

Combat spell used by Giles to ensnare and subdue Dark Willow. She immediately negates it.

Killer of the Dead

Nothing subtle about the name of this mystical compound, a doozy of a poison used to terminate vampires, which pops up in season three's "Graduation Day, Part 1" when Faith Lehane shoots Angel with an arrow laced with it. The good news is there's a cure; the less good news is it's not like you can order it from your local CVS pharmacy, since it involves draining the blood of a Slayer. That's fine with Buffy, who's planning on killing Faith anyway, but when the bad girl from Beantown winds up escaping, Buffy is compelled to force Angel to drain her own blood instead. From all indications this is an incredibly erotic experience, though it doesn't sit well with Buffy's friends, who wind up having to rush her to the hospital for recovery. In *Buffy*, every dark cloud has a silver lining, so here it is: it is during a dream at the hospital that she discovers, from Faith, the key to defeating Mayor Wilkins—"human weakness."

Penance Malediction

A self-punishing hex. Amy cast one on Willow, which had the unfortunate effect of transforming Willow, guilty about betraying Tara's memory, into the image of Warren Mears after she kisses Potential Slayer Kennedy. Would also make an excellent death metal album title.

Slayer Activation Spell

Willow uses the scythe to power this massively powerful spell, which grants, simultaneously, all the Potential Slayers in the world their full Slayer powers.

Time Loop Spell

Jonathan Levinson trapped Buffy in a temporal Mobius strip with this nifty charm, forcing her to futilely attempt to make, over and over again, a sale (she's newly a clerk at the Magic Box). *BTVS* loves a metaphor, and this one's pretty amusing, as anyone with retail experience can tell you that time absolutely refuses to progress while working a shift.

Tirer La Couverture

Per Anya, "A spell to see spells." Sort of a magical version of that blue light CSI types use to detect otherwise invisible bloodstains and whatnot. Buffy's use of the spell reveals Dawn's magical nature.

Team Players: We Got Spirits

Mystical cults, clans, orders, and other Fortean fraternities.

Clan Kalderash

The Romanian gypsy clan that curses Angelus with a soul, transforming him into Angel, after he drains and kills a teenage Kalderash girl (played by Ginger Williams) who is gifted to him by Darla in 1898. Darla's attempt to compel the girl's father (Zitto Kazann) to reverse the spell fails, so she snaps his neck. Darla never could take no for an answer. Uncle Enyos (Vincent Schiavelli) and Jenny Calendar (a.k.a. Janna Kalderash) are likewise members of the tribe, with Jenny dispatched to Sunnydale to keep an eye on Angel, so that the curse is never broken. Epic fail, Jenny.

The Devon Coven

A British coven of witches who temporarily loan Giles their magical power for use in his confrontation with Dark Willow.

Glory's Minions

Servile, cringing, dementedly devoted servants of the other-dimensional hell goddess Glorificus.

- Dreg (Kevin Wiseman)A wormy, sycophantic minion of Glory. He's taken out, unmourned, by a Knight of Byzantium.
- Gronx (Lily Knight)A rare female Glory minion, Gronx answers the question: Are lady minions as gross and irritating as the males? (Yes)
- Jinx (Troy Blendel)The alpha minion of Glory's coterie, Jinx was often singled out for important tasks . . . and abuse. Scabby, black-eyed, hunched, and pathetically ingratiating, he should have been a talent agent (*ba-dump-bump*).
- Murk (Todd Duffey)Another of Glory's obsequious minions, albeit one of no particular distinction.

The Guardians

A powerful, ancient order of women who are tasked with aiding the Slayer in her battle against evil. The Guardians forged the scythe, which came in *very* handy in Buffy's showdown with the First Evil.

- Guardian (Christine Healy)The last remaining member of the powerful female order pledged to aid the Slayer, this aged woman instructs Buffy on the nature of the scythe before being killed by Caleb.

The Hellions

Demonic motorcycle gang (literal Hell's angels) who terrorized Sunnydale following Buffy's (second) death.

- Klyed (Mike Grief): Hellion demon biker, mentioned here mostly because the actor portraying him is awesomely named "Mike Grief." They should have just called the character that!
- Mag (Geoff Meed): The one with the facial piercings/leather straps arrangement. Actor Geoff Meed also played Andrew Borba, the murderer-turned-vampire (kind of a lateral move) who killed Buffy's high school crush Owen Thurman.
- Razor (Franc Ross): Leader of the Hellions. Big, strong, and mean, Razor sported nifty retractable steel claws (Joss does love those merry mutant X-Men, huh?) and was killed by Tara, with an axe—her one slaying in the series.

Knights of Byzantium

A brotherhood of medieval-style knights of unknown provenance pledged to destroy the Key and thereby prevent Glory from destroying the earth. Religiously devout and, unlike the Order of Dagon, uninterested in protecting the Key (no matter that it's now an innocent child), the Knights brutally attack the Scoobies and nearly kill Giles before being wiped out by Glory.

- Dante Chevalier (Karim Prince)
- Stoic Knight of Byzantium who leads the group after Gregor's capture and mercy kills Orlando after Glory scrambles his brains. Great name, right?
- General Gregor (Wade Andrew Williams)
- Leader of the Knights of Byzantium. Focused, competent, and determined, he is nonetheless taken captive by Buffy, who pressures him to reveal critical information about Glory. He does, and pays later when Glory nearly halves him with a tire rim. For a guy intent on killing a fourteen-year-old girl, he's a decent enough chap. Impressive resolve.
- Orlando (Justin Gorence)
- A Knight of Byzantium pledged to destroy the Key, Orlando gets his brains scrambled by Glory and recognizes Dawn's true nature. Little good it does him: babbling madly, he is euthanized by his brother in arms, Dante Chevalier.

Order of Aurelius

Venerated vampire sect founded ages ago by some dude named—get this—Aurelius, who has since passed on, leaving the Master in charge. Aurelius's twelfth-century writings hypothesized that, in the words of the Master, a gifted hyperbolist, that there "will be a time of crisis, of worlds hanging in the balance, and in this time shall come the Anointed, the Master's great warrior. And the Slayer will not know him, will not stop him. And he will lead her into hell." Having been sired by the Master, Darla too belongs to this sect, as do Angel (sired by Darla), Drusilla (sired by Angel), and Spike (sired by Dru). These wild and crazy vamps worshipped the Old Ones, waiting for "that promised day when we will arise! Arise and lay waste to the world above!" (yep, the Master again). Their symbol was the sun and three stars, which Giles finds on a ring in a cemetery, and their rituals included the Harvest and the Night of Saint Vigeous.

Order of Dagon

An order of monks dating back to the Middle Ages that was tasked with protecting the Key. Decimated by Glory. These are the guys who disguised the Key as Dawn Summers, so if you hate that storyline, blame them.

Order of Taraka

A society of deadly (are there any other kind?) assassins—some human, some not—dating back to the time of King Solomon, the Order of Taraka is summoned to Sunnydale about mid-second season by Spike, who's had just about all he can take of Buffy Summers. Three bounty hunters show up: Octarus, who attacks Buffy at an ice-skating rink, but is dispatched when she slits his throat with the blade of her skate (awesome Buffy move); Patrice, who disguises herself as a cop on career day at Sunnydale High, and likely dies in the fire at the Church of du Lac; and Norman Pfister, a.k.a. the bug man, not for any metaphorically interesting reason but rather because in his true visage he is a swarm of maggots, who is eventually stomped to death by Cordelia and Xander.

Shadow Men

Three African shamans who, in the prehistoric era, imbued a young girl with demonic powers, creating the First Slayer. In effect they were the First Watchers, and their affiliation would eventually evolve into the Watchers Council.

Spirit Guides

Oracles whose wisdom is solicited by Giles as a last-gasp attempt to thwart the Sisterhood of Jhe, an apocalyptic cult of demon warriors scheming to open the Hellmouth in season three's "Zeppo." According to Giles, the Spirit Guides "exist out of time but have knowledge of the future." Cool, right? Sadly, not good at sharing. "These secrets belong to time and the dark regions," the spirits tell Giles. "To reveal them would bring chaos down upon the living Earth." What they don't seem to get is that chaos is about to rain down upon the earth whether they share or not. Good thing the spirits seem to reside at Restfield Cemetery, since they are dead to us anyway.

19

No One Ever Dies, and Everybody Lives Happily Ever After

> There were certain things we couldn't do, and many things we couldn't afford to do [in the TV show]. . . . So now we can do pretty much whatever we want, within the bounds of common decency. Well, *near* the bounds of decency.
>
> —*Joss Whedon, on the* Buffy the Vampire Slayer Season Eight *comics, mtv.com, January 31, 2007*

S o, like what, exactly? Transform Dawn into a centaur (or "centaurette," as she prefers)? Resurrect Warren Mears, still without skin? Or how about this: gay sex for Buffy?

Yup, yup, and yup.

Buffy the Vampire Slayer Season Eight, a forty-issue run published by Dark Horse Comics from 2007 to 2011, was *huge* news, marking Joss Whedon's full-fledged return to the Buffyverse four years after the conclusion of the TV series ("You cannot abandon the universe you created," Buffy is counseled at one point in the story). Dark Horse had published *Buffy* comics before, from 1998 to 2004, but Whedon had little to no involvement in most of them, and the events that unfolded within their pages are largely considered noncanonical, or not part of the official *Buffy* story (exceptions worth noting: *Tales of the Slayers*, published in 2002, and *Tales of the Vampires*, published from 2003 to 2004, both of which Whedon oversaw and contributed to, and *Fray*, an eight-issue series written solely by Whedon—his first comic books—about a Slayer living two hundred years in the future).

That's not to say these other comics are uninteresting, however; they include, for instance, the three-issue *Buffy: The Origin* (1999), a more faithful adaptation of Whedon's original script for the 1992 feature film than director Fran Kuzui's regrettably jocular version. And while Whedon himself did not pen any of these, other TV-series alum did, including actors James Marsters (Spike) and Amber Benson (Tara).

Season Eight, however, was Whedon's progeny; he scripted or co-scripted seventeen of the issues and was billed as executive producer throughout. TV-show writers Jane Espenson, Drew Goddard, Drew Z. Greenberg, Doug Petrie, and Steven S. DeKnight all contributed scripts, as did Brian K. Vaughan (*Y: The Last Man*, a highly regarded comic series), Jeph Loeb (TV's *Lost* and *Marvel's Agents of S.H.I.E.L.D.*, plus such comics as *Batman: The Long Halloween*, *Batman: Hush*, and *Age of Apocalypse*), Brad Meltzer (novelist and creator of DC's *Identity Crisis* series), and Scott Allie, who edited the Buffy books for Dark Horse. Georges Jeanty was lead penciler. "We looked at gritty options, we looked at cartoony options, but we kept coming back to a balance of realism, superhero dynamics, expressiveness, and an interesting way of handling characters," Allie wrote in his introduction to *Buffy the Vampire Slayer: Panel to Panel*, a look at the artwork from seasons eight and nine.

Season Eight is considered strictly canonical. If you don't believe us, take it from Allie: "I cannot say it enough: *Season Eight* is canon. That's why it's *Season Eight*."

The series is set at some indeterminate point following the conclusion of the TV series, as about eighteen hundred Slayers are spread across the globe, five hundred of them in Scotland, where Xander and Buffy call the shots. Following the devastation at Sunnydale, the Slayers are designated domestic terrorists by certain forces within the U.S. military, who are in cahoots with the season's Big Bad: a masked supervillain known as Twilight. (So meta! "My God, is that really the name you picked? Twilight?" Buffy says at one point, obviously alluding to Stephenie Meyer's *Twilight* books, also about a young woman in love with a vamp. "Y'know I lived that idea first, right? And my vampire was so much better.")

Season Eight is wild: funny, clever, stirring, provocative, and remarkably fantastical. Most of the old gang is back, including Oz, now nesting in the mountains of Tibet with a partner and baby, having successfully suppressed his lycanthropian tendencies (but really, this time); Riley, ostensibly soldiering for the bad guys but really playing for Team Buffy; and Harmony, still vamping, but now the star of an MTV reality show (*Harmony Bites*) so popular that demons are rad, and Slayers pariahs. Melaka Fray shows up in a Whedon-scripted yarn ("Time of Your Life") in which a time rift catapults Buffy two hundred years into the future; also featured is the return of Dark Willow, whom Buffy fatally stabs. Dawn, having bedded the roommate of a jealous thricewise demon, is transmogrified into a giant, a centaur, and a porcelain doll, in that order (oh, those puckish thricewises), and, finally, herself again. At that point Xander becomes her cuddle-monkey, much to Buffy's initial mortification, though she comes around. Drac is back, and by that we mean Dracula, though a shell of his former self, having gambled away his powers to a gang of Japanese vampires whose motorcycle he had coveted.

We could go on, but why bother? Anyone who knows anything about *Season Eight* knows that four story threads stole the thunder:

1. In Goddard's "Wolves at the Gate" (March 5, 2008), Buffy sleeps with Satsu, another Slayer (and therefore, of course, a member of the female persuasion), a development that, in the rumpus that followed, Allie referred to as causing "a bit of a stir," which we refer to as "a bit of an understatement." Some readers flat-out didn't love the notion of Buffy having gay sex, but others fired salvos at Dark Horse for buzz-baiting. DH had encouraged retailers to order additional copies of the issue without explaining why, and arranged a single interview, with the *New York Times*, to run on release day. "We're not going to make her gay, nor are we going to take the next fifty issues explaining that she's not," Whedon told the *Times*, in an article headlined "Experimenting in Bed When Not After Vampires." "She's young and experimenting, and did I mention open-minded?" Whedon further commented that the episode was dramatically useful, provoking complicated emotions within Buffy's circle of friends (which turned out to be a hoot), adding, "It's always fun to give Buffy something to be awkward about besides 'I'm lonely' and 'I don't have a boyfriend.'" Allie defended the article, saying it was "not set up to drive sales, although we assumed it would have that effect. It was done because we expected a reaction to the comic, and we wanted you all to have it straight from the horse's mouth. . . . Everything Dark Horse did—setting up the *New York Times* article, advising retailers to order extra copies— was more our way of anticipating the reaction rather than cashing in." Whedon also took flak from gender-studies scholars disappointed in the thinness of Satsu as a character, and also in Buffy's subsequent dismissal of the encounter. Of course, legions of readers supported Whedon, and GLAAD (formerly the Gay + Lesbian Alliance Against Defamation) honored the arc as Outstanding Comic Book in 2009.

2. Twilight's "Clark Kent" (secret identity) is revealed in Meltzer's "Twilight, Part II," and it was a shocker—or was supposed to be. In December 2009, three months before the book was scheduled to hit the streets, Dark Horse jokingly released a Georges Jeanty mockup depicting President Obama as Twilight—whip-smart marketing that tickled the press. *Not* whip-smart marketing: flash-forward a month and DH erroneously delivers full—rather than cropped—cover solicitations by Jeanty and Jo Chen to the website Comic Book Resources, which covers the industry

(solicitations are comic-book equivalents of publisher blurbs, appearing in trade publications to encourage sales), clearly revealing that Twilight was, in fact, Angel. Whedon learned of the foul-up via phone from Allie ("the terror in his voice was both palpable and hilarious," Whedon has said). Fans—many enraged that the customarily heroic Angel (though we all know he had his moments) had been outed as the malignant Twilight—flooded Twitter with the news, employing the hashtag #twilightisangel. Dark Horse counterstruck, though lamely: "Readers, we mean not to offend you. Knowing what you do will not spoil the great ending of Joss's *Season 8*. Trust us." Also riled up was Bill Willingham, a writer on the *Angel* comics at IDW Publishing, who called Allie's suggestion that Dark Horse was coordinating storylines with IDW "grossly misleading, at best." Whedon wound up publicly explaining that canonically, *Season Eight* succeeded the resolution of the then-current IDW *Angel* story; hence, no conflict.

3. Think Angel fans were rabid already? Wait till you hear this: Possessed by the spirit of Twilight, the tortured one winds up executing one of the most popular figures in all of *Buffy*dom: Rupert Giles, snapping his neck in order to prevent the destruction of the "Seed of Wonder," which protects all of the magic in the world: no seed, no magic, no invading demons, no Twilight. In an interview afterward with *Entertainment Weekly*, Whedon explained that he was dissatisfied with Giles's role in the comic, and that he "wanted to make all this matter and have something that would send emotional ripples through all the characters. Also, I'm a prick." Anthony Stewart Head, who portrayed Giles on the TV show, was initially worried when hearing the news, Whedon said. "Then I said, 'Angel's gonna kill you.' He said, all excited, 'Oooh! That's great!'" Jeanty toyed at first with the notion of illustrating Giles's murder in extreme close-up, but Whedon asked him to parallel the death of the Watcher's girlfriend, Jenny Calendar, in the second season of the TV show, "right down to the curved arch with Giles and the curved window with her." Jeanty was especially careful with the next panel, depicting a lifeless Giles on the ground, knowing "we were going to be running this image again in the issue and in the future. I thought of it as that one image that sticks in your mind when you see a horrible scene."

4. Angel/Twilight and Buffy, both now extra-superpowered, engage in a cosmic, multipage, rather graphic sex scene, dubbed "space frak" by fans. Obviously, this was unlike anything Whedon ever could have presented on television. However, in typical Buffy-Angel fashion, it winds up having earth-shattering negative consequences, and huge guilt for both.

Buffy's final line in *Season Eight*—"Let's go to work"—exactly echoes the last words spoken in the television series *Angel*, delivered by the titular character.

Season Nine

Season Nine launched in August 2011, seven months after *Season Eight* wrapped, and ran through September 2013, covering twenty-five issues (plus the supplemental e-comic *Magical Mystery Tour Featuring the Beetles*, the first title released under the *Season Nine* banner, and *In Space No One Can Hear You Slay*, distributed as part of Free Comic Book Day in April 2012). Also included under this banner were four spinoffs: *Angel + Faith*, also twenty-five issues (having retreated to London, Faith counsels a post-Twilight Angel, who seeks redemption—so what else is new?—by resurrecting Giles, never mind that it is in the body of a twelve-year-old boy, with guest appearances by TV characters Whistler, Gunn, and Angel-Darla offspring Connor—so Pete Campbell before he was Pete Campbell); the miniseries *Willow: Wonderland* and *Spike: A Dark Place* (five issues each); and *Love vs. Life*, a Jane Espenson–scripted three-parter about Billy Lane, a gay teen/Buffy ally introduced in the core *Season Nine* books, and his fight against zompires—a Xanderism for zombie vampires, the new breed of vamp now that they have lost their connection to the hell dimension in the post-magic world.

> *Buffy:* Everyone who's turned since the Seed was destroyed is a zombievampire.
>
> *Xander:* Zompires! I've named them. My work is done here.

With Whedon now off prepping the first Avengers movie, the bulk of the writing for the core of *Season Nine* was handled by Andrew Chambliss, who had worked with the master on the TV series *Dollhouse* and its subsequent comics, though Espenson, Scott Allie, and Drew Z. Greenberg also contributed scripts. Jeanty again served as primary interior illustrator.

According to Allie: Whedon summited with Dark Horse editors and *Buffy* writers at his house in early 2011 to plot out both *Season Nine* and *Angel + Faith* (the *Angel* books, which had been the property of IDW during *Season Eight*, reverted to Dark Horse in 2010), with three crucial objectives: "to bring the core cast back together, to explore the life of Buffy as a twenty-something woman living in the big city [San Francisco] with a minimum-wage job and superpowers, and finally, to embark on a journey to restore magic." Though commercially successful, *Season Eight* had alienated some critics, who complained that it was too fantastical, and thus a radical departure from the character-driven TV series. Whedon called *Season Nine* a "reset," telling *Entertainment Weekly*: "With [*Season Eight*], we just sort of said, 'Wheee!' Ultimately, 'Wheee!' caught up with us in a cavalcade of mythology. It became clear, as it did with the show, that people really liked when Buffy's adventures reflect what she's going through in her life [and] what we're going through in our lives at that age. That was the thing in *Season Eight* that we didn't tap into as much as I think we ultimately should have."

Several newcomers (in addition to Billy Lane) are on hand, including good guys Robert Dowling, a Frisco copper, and Anaheed, Buffy's roommate, secretly a Slayer tasked with protecting her, plus on-again-off-again-ally Eldre Koh, a Worf-lookalike Nitobe warrior demon falsely imprisoned millennia ago for murdering his own family, now in debt to Buffy for destroying the seed, finally enabling him to break free (though he sometimes has a funny way of showing it). Illyria, once known as "the Merciless" but now a friendly demon, who had been portrayed in the television series *Angel* by Amy Acker, also figures, as does Wolfram + Hart, the demonic law firm so central to the *Angel* narrative. Severin ("the Siphon," a being who rips mystical energy from any demon or Slayer he touches) is the Avis to rogue Slayer Simone Doffler's Hertz in the ranking of season-nine Big Bads; the former seeks to reverse time, thus preventing his girlfriend from becoming a vampire; the latter's ambitions are far grander: she hopes to free Maloker, the last of the Old Ones (the first demons to walk the Earth) to have gone down to defeat and the sire of the first vampire, in a scheme to become the most powerful "slaypire" (a Slayer who becomes a vampire, *duh*) in the world, and finally eliminate Buffy Summers once and forever. Both seek entrance to the heavily guarded (by the Mystic Council, headed by D'Hoffryn) Deeper Well, where the Old Ones are entombed, and which contains "untold amounts of magic," as Willow explains it.

So, what else? Dawn, created from the mystical "key" in season five of the television series, is fading, incapable of surviving in a world without magic. Xander betrays Buffy, blaming her for Dawn's predicament, but later repents. Willow embarks on a sojourn to retrieve her powers and returns triumphant, eventually restoring magic to the world (thus sparing Dawnie).

Oh yeah, we almost forgot: Buffy decides to have an abortion.

Yes, another *Buffy* comics controversy, this one unfolding over three Chambliss-scripted issues ("Slayer, Interrupted" and the two-part "On Your Own," which includes flashbacks to Robin Wood's Slayer mom, Nikki, and her Watcher, Crowley, in seventies New York City) in which Buffy first believes herself to be pregnant, then discovers that she can't be, because, well, she's a robot (long story, natch, but the work of Andrew, who was trying to protect her from unknown enemies, so created the Buffybot and brain-wiped the real thing, shipping the Betty Crocker version off to a top-secret hideaway). Hence, no pregnancy, and no need to abort.

Critical reaction was largely positive. ("The people in charge of this book . . . deserve huge credit for tackling the sensitive and controversial subject of abortion with unflinching honesty and realism," wrote *Comic Book Resource*'s Kelly Thompson), though some critics bristled at the outcome, accusing the creative team of copping out with, as one phrased it, an "'It's all just a dream' level trope." Fans were largely supportive, though some were rankled by the suggestion that Buffy could have been pregnant from a one-night stand at a party, holding her to higher standards of responsibility. In response, Whedon told *Entertainment Weekly* that Buffy was still in her twenties, "about the time in your life when you do things that are irresponsible, or that you *want* to hold yourself to account for. She's a person living her life, she's not running for president. . . . And she's going to make some wrong decisions." In the same interview, Whedon was crystal clear about his own stand on abortion rights, telling *EW:* "A woman's right to choose is under attack as much as it's ever been, and that's a terrible and dangerous thing for this country. I don't usually get soap box-y with this, but the thing about Buffy is, all she's going through is what women go through, and what nobody making a speech, holding up a placard, or making a movie is willing to say." Never a dull moment in the Buffyverse.

Season Ten

Season Ten launched in 2014, with Christos Gage as lead writer (he scripted or co-scripted every issue) and Rebeka Isaacs as primary illustrator. New to the creative team this season was actor Nicholas Brendon (Xander), who co-scripted eight issues with Gage. Also included under the *Season Ten* banner is the sophomore run of *Angel + Faith*.

Giles, having been resurrected by Angel and Faith in *Season Nine*, arrives in San Francisco, though as a twelve-year-old boy (some details from the juvenile-Giles storyline were reportedly appropriated from *Ripper*, a now apparently defunct ghost-story-themed TV project that would have focused on Giles, who went by the nickname Ripper during his rebellious youth). A new-and-improved breed of vampire has risen, shapeshifters who can withstand direct exposure to sunlight (or, in Andrew-speak, "There's been a paradigm shift in the mythos"). That's the bad news. Meanwhile, Xander is haunted by what appears to be the ghost of Anya, who specializes in snarky relationship advice, mostly about Xander and Dawn, who are estranged. Also bad news. The rules of magic need to be recodified, so who wants to be the boss? Everyone. Buffy and Willow negotiate the new rules with a succession of otherworldly creatures, including the nouveau vamps, represented by—God help us all—Harmony Kendall, who tries to steal the book of magic so that "everyone realizes I'm, like, the awesomest and smartest and prettiest one there is, and worships me," which might have been even more bad news except that she is thwarted by Spike. Good news? Well, this being *Buffy, someone* has to find out they're gay, and in this case it's Andrew. (Who knew? Everybody). Buffy—definitely *not* gay, though open to having gay sex at least twice in her lifetime—finally confesses her feelings to Spike, which leads either to passionate sex or sandwich making (*Three's Company* joke), as Dawn and Xander listen in from just outside the bedroom door. Also back for another go: the Slayer Satsu, one-time (literally) Buffy lover (see "Buffy . . . open to having gay sex," above); Hank Summers, Buffy's wanker dad, who could probably turn any self-respecting woman gay; Jonathan (though just digitally), once Andrew's best friend, though only until Andrew killed him (seems fair); and Angel—ooh, lots of awkward there. The Baddies include Archaeus (an ancient vampire whose descendants include not just the Master, but Darla, Angel, Spike, and Drusilla as well), plus the Soul Glutton, Mistress, and the Sculptor. How come demons are never named Tom or Jerry?

The big reveal? The Big Bad: D'Hoffryn, lord of vengeance demons and councilor of magic, whom the Scoobies had counted among their allies until discovering his nefarious plot to bump off the rest of the council, swipe the *Vampyr* book, and rewrite the rules of magic so that he is no longer bound by the wishes of mortals ("If only you'd known I was a soulless demon whose reason for being is revenge . . . Oh, wait, you did.").

The comics are still going strong as of this writing, with *Season Eleven* having premiered in late 2016.

Georges Jeanty

FAQ: One thing that makes you such a great fit with Joss is your facility with expressing emotion, and having the drawn characters really act what the story and emotion are, just complementing his style of storytelling perfectly, because it's really about the people and what they're feeling and saying.

Georges Jeanty: If anything, I took that from the TV show. Joss is very big on saying, "Just let it be the comic. Let the comic be the comic and the TV show be the TV show." There's such emotional content here, I think people reading this, in all honesty they're not reading if for the art. Joss, his greatest strength is his scripts and the dialogue and how he conveys characters together, and in watching *Buffy* and going through all the seasons and all the nuances I really did look for those subtleties that all the characters had and tried to interject that as much as I could into a very static medium. . . . With comics you have to pick and choose the very particular shots and angles and expressions that'll convey whatever the dialogue is saying, because you don't have a lot of time with it, so it was very much a challenge to make that emotion come through in a very Joss Whedon way.

FAQ: You have a knack for capturing likenesses while avoiding that kind of stiffness that some licensed projects can get where it looks very kind of photo-referenced dependent. These characters really don't feel like you're drawing the actors, but the characters feel like themselves from the show. They don't feel like Sarah Michelle Gellar and Alyson Hannigan, they feel like Buffy and Willow.

GJ: Again, that was Joss Whedon. I basically told him when he hired me, "Hey, I'm not very big on likenesses, my whole career I've never had to do anything with likeness; I think you might want somebody else for that." And he said, "Honestly, I'm not interested in likeness." He really did put it succinctly to me when he said, "I'm not interested in Buffy looking like

Ace Buffy comics artist Georges Jeanty

Sarah Michelle Gellar; I'm interested in Buffy looking like Buffy." So, if you capture the nuances I think the rest of it will come through, and as you just said that sort of thing does show through if you're doing it right.

FAQ: It really does. You can just go through and look at the faces of the characters and see, like, "Yeah, that's Xander; that's the reaction he'd have."

GJ: That was the best thing Joss could have told me because it alleviated any anxiety I might have had about saying "Ooh, does this look enough like him? Is it a good likeness?" So, I was already put at ease because I didn't have to do any of that stuff. But me personally, I did feel, if it wasn't so much the likeness then it had to be the nuance of a character, and you're right, with the example of Xander, you know Xander, the character, is very expressive, and he talks with his hands a lot. I mean he gets agitated or anything like that, so you'll notice a lot of me, in my art, drawing Xander with his hands moving whenever he's really getting into his dialogue. So, little, subtle things like that I tried to interject into the comic book.

FAQ: Can we throw some names of characters at you and you talk to us about these nuances?

GJ: If I can remember them, sure.

FAQ: How about Buffy?

GJ: Well, she's so expressive, and I give it to Sarah Michelle Gellar. She brought her game to every episode. I've rewatched the show quite a few times just to get the subtleties and I was so amazed at how much she brought her game all the time, because, if you notice, Buffy is either laughing, crying, mad—she runs the gamut of emotion—and for an actor to do that twenty-two episodes for seven years, that's very impressive.

FAQ: She just seemed to have total commitment, no condescension to the character, no "this is a silly idea." Just in it.

GJ: Yeah, she sold it, even when it *was* a silly idea, she really, really sold it, and with her, with Buffy, it was really the eyes. Whatever she was feeling it's always coming through her eyes, so I really focused on her eyes, and if she was sad it was very much sad eyes and if she was angry it was the angry eyes. So, the subtleties about Sarah Michelle—funny enough, when you really watch something over and over you do pick up little things, and the way she runs is really the only particular thing I could say that really set her apart. I know at some point it becomes the stunt person, but you can tell when she's running. There's a subtlety there as to how Sarah Michelle runs, and how she dresses as well, so I tried to incorporate that into that character.

FAQ: How about Willow?

GJ: Funny, this is something I discovered, I didn't even realize it, having watched the seasons over and over, that, obviously, Willow, her powers are of the Wicca, she's a witch, and witches are very earthy. It's an earth power, and you'll notice, I thought, it was because Alyson Hannigan was a redhead, but it seems that a lot of her garments and the way she acted pertained to the earth, so a lot of her color scheme was basically earth tones. You see a lot of greens, you see a lot of browns, you see a lot of earthy tones within her, so within that character I was always aware—not all the time, but I tried to incorporate a lot of flowers and flora and something that denoted the earth. She has such a subtle humbleness to her that makes you fall in love with Willow every time you see her, and that was probably the hardest thing for me, that subtle raising of the eyebrow and those big sleepy eyes that she has and the way her mouth curves. Whenever I was trying to draw her in an emotional state I was very conscious of where the muscle parts on her face were going.

FAQ: And as an actor she's just so transparent, every feeling and reaction is so clearly legible.

GJ: Yeah, she is. Joss said it himself: "If you ever want in *Buffy* to make anybody feel anything all we had to do was make Willow cry."

FAQ: So, when you're watching are you pausing and rewinding a lot?

GJ: Not so much pausing and rewinding. I would probably watch something and digest whatever it is because, again, I wasn't going on the exact expression. I was going on tone. So, I would watch a scene for the tone of it all and how those characters are. Like, if it was something where Willow—let's say Oz is leaving Willow and he's breaking up with her and she's obviously falling to pieces. A lot of this is just my armchair psychology of the characters, but because of her shyness, you know, she's a wallflower, she was very much in the corner, so in the biggest points of her life she looks like she's very much at ease, like she wouldn't raise her hands or stomp her feet or jump around. She would just kind of stand there and hunch her shoulders, maybe, and try to look as small as possible when something is hurting her. Of course, when she was Dark Willow that was the opposite. Her hands were always out, she had this smirk, and it was a very big character. But a lot of what I did was just Willow the girl, not necessarily Willow the witch, and I focused more on that with her.

FAQ: Last two characters: Giles and Spike.

GJ: Giles, of course, has his own nuances, so much so they would joke about it on the show every now and again. Giles was easy; he would clean his glasses whenever he needed something to do or he would stammer a little bit. You never really saw Giles angry. Giles was always the lovable uncle or something like that, so I was always very conscious not to draw Giles menacingly or anything like that. Of course, he could get mad, but he was very much the pacifist, again in my armchair psychology here, and he was the guy who—he was more like Captain Picard than he was Captain Kirk. He was very much a diplomat. Giles was just very cool and lovable and the Hugh Grant of the character set, for sure. Spike, then, is totally the opposite. Spike is very much the Captain Kirk and not the Captain Picard. He would go in and do whatever he did and consequences be damned, and as a result I always had Spike drawn at the ready, like he was—not necessarily that he was always ready for a fight, but yeah, he was always ready, verbal or physical or otherwise—he was always ready for whatever it was you could throw at him, and in drawing Spike it was very much that concept that he was not necessarily standing at attention all the time but you could tell he was ready. He was never in a passive stance, unless of course he is professing his love for Buffy, and I think that's where a good, subtle nuance is, that around Buffy, because, of course, he loves her so much, you could see him more vulnerable, but around other people, whoever, Spike is more of the dominant, and with Buffy at least Spike was very much a submissive when it comes to that sort of thing.

FAQ: Different writers work with different artists in different ways on these kinds of projects. Like Alan Moore is kind of infamous for outlining every single detail in the background of the panel that he needs to see. What is it like with Joss Whedon in that regard? Is he sort of saying, "I want this room to have a door on the left and these things are on the table" or is he more open than that?

GJ: Like with any writer, there is a getting-to-know-you process, and, of course, Joss and I didn't know each other, we had never worked together, so I think the first few issues scripts were very much, "Here, this is this and that is that," and then I think after Joss started seeing the artwork coming in, because the script is written and then the artist is given more or less a month to do the whole thing, once he got on to issue three or four I think he was very much aware of, "Okay, I see what you can do and I see that you get it, you get who these characters are. I don't have to be so explanatory," and a lot of his script became sparse in description, and it was primarily just the dialogue. It really did come down to at one point just reading the script and it was the dialogue that was carrying me through, very much like, I can assume, a teleplay where there's a little bit of description for what the action is and then, of course, what the characters are saying. I was very conscious as to where the dialogue balloons were going to be placed, because, of course, so much of Joss Whedon is his dialogue, and I was trying to make sure that the word balloons were placed in such a way that they would convey what has been called the Joss-isms, or Joss-speak.

So, I tried to really make those angles and spaces and positives and negatives and all of that conform to the dialogue, because again, I wasn't deluding myself thinking people were really getting into this for the artwork. They were at the end of the day coming in here because this was a Joss Whedon script, and then after that it was a Jane Espenson script, a Doug Petrie or Steven DeKnight, or anybody who was writing, I knew they really appreciated what those writers had done in the TV series, so I was just trying to accentuate that. I certainly was not trying to be the star.

FAQ: What was your reaction when you saw the script about Buffy having gay sex with Satsu? Did you have long discussions with Joss about it?

GJ: Yeah, and oh yeah, and even when Joss wasn't writing, like if it was Jane or Doug or whomever, Joss was always reading the script, so he had to approve the script in order for me to start drawing it, so there were, yeah, a couple of times. I was very big when she was gonna sleep with a woman, because that was early on in the series, and I said—and I don't know where this ego of mine would come out from, but I told him, "No, I'm not drawing this, Joss, unless you could explain to me why Buffy would sleep with a girl I'm not doing this," and he really did. He wasn't like, "Well, this is my thing and if you're not gonna do it then you're fired and we'll just find somebody else." He was very honest about saying, "You know what? If I can convince you then I know I've convinced at least half of the people out there, who will also be bitching and moaning about Buffy sleeping with a girl or something else," and while he did explain it to me and he was very cordial about it, I don't know that I necessarily agree, but with any ensemble there's always a captain and you can voice your opinions and differences with the captain but at the end of the day when the captain says, "This is it, this is how we do it," then that's what you do, and I was very happy that he listened to what I said because, yeah, he could just say, "You know, this is my character and who are you to tell me she wouldn't do this?" There's that, and I remember very distinctly Giles being killed. I was told, the editor told me later on, he was like, "You know what, you got that script very late, not because it was done late but because everybody knew you were gonna object to Giles being killed," and I was like, "Yeah," and again Joss had to be very patient with me and explain how he could do this. How could you kill Giles? Just send him away or let him go on a sabbatical or something. Don't kill him. And, of course, it's not the Whedonverse unless someone gets killed, so at the end of the day that's kind of how I reasoned it, that all of the best characters have some of the best death scenes.

FAQ: We've read that you put a lot of thought into that panel where Giles is killed. Can you talk about that?

GJ: Joss had said, with Giles being killed and, of course, being killed by Angel, he wanted to mirror Angel killing Jenny [Calendar, in season two of the TV show], and he wanted that depth, because, if you notice, Angel kills Giles in the same way, he just twists his neck. He wanted to mirror that and I was like, "I don't know. She got killed on a high school stairway—this is a dungeon down a few hundred feet below earth. I don't know how I'm supposed to do that." So, I just sort of took the images, like in the high school, where Calendar gets killed, there's like an oval arch of windows, so I sort of put an oval arch of pillar behind Giles when he was getting killed. I tried to make the act that Angel does, the actual killing, that pose, I tried to incorporate it as much as I could into the comic because, again, I'm only dealing with one image. Obviously, that death scene might have taken three, four, five seconds. Here I just have one panel to show what took about four or five seconds to do, so I had to accentuate that as best I could with as little as I could. So yeah, that was the thought there, because it really was Joss saying he wanted to mirror the death because of the irony, of course, that Angel was doing it.

FAQ: Just two questions about Angel. One is, I've got to ask you about the season-eight sex scene and what that was like to draw, because that's obviously a crazy, crazy scene, and then the whole controversy over everything that went on with the reveal that Angel was Twilight.

GJ: Well, with the sex, and don't get me wrong, everybody loves sex and, of course, a thing that the fans have been picturing in their minds for years and years and years about how Buffy and Angel were together when they had sex—funny enough, if you remember, they really only had sex once, technically, in *Buffy*, but in the *Angel* series, with that one episode where she went to L.A., they technically had sex again, so you kind of assume the sex if they were doing it, and there were no consequences, would have been a lot like Buffy and Spike having sex in season six. Brad Meltzer, who wasn't one of the writers on the TV show but is a novelist and was very popular writing novels, and he had written some stuff for DC as well, he was coming in because he was a big *Buffy* fan, and he just happened to be pegged with that particular arc where they are going to be having sex, and, of course, at this point Buffy has adopted some superpowers—more than the Slayer—and, of course, Angel is a little more powerful because he was Twilight, so it wasn't just going to be regular sex. Everybody was saying, "Yeah, this is gonna be supersex," and they're like, "I don't know what that looks like, but go and draw supersex," and none of us had an idea of what that was. Obviously, it was going to be more intense than, say, you going home to your wife and having a very nice night. I would think it would have to be earth-shattering, is what was said, so from there—and I think a lot of us were not sure just how much we could show, because while the comics code wasn't on this particular book, and none of the *Buffy* books, there was a certain amount of authority we had to observe—obviously, this isn't porn, we couldn't go all out, but I started to do some drawings about them having sex and what positions we could get away with. Joss was very cool with some and he was very *not* cool with other positions. I think at the end of the day, funny enough, it came very, very subtly, where it was more the effect of their sex—not necessarily seeing them do it, per se. I think it was a lot more graphic when Buffy slept with a woman, if you want my opinion, but with Angel and Buffy it was more about things being affected around them. So, that's why I had the idea that when they were doing it and they're flying over someplace that's probably populated with a bunch of animals, these animals are reacting to what that energy is, you know, as animals do, like, some animals will sense a hurricane or cancer or things like that, they're just freaking out, because these two people are copulating in such a way that nobody's ever copulated before. And then, of course, it just gets to the point where then they're doing it, they're out in space at some point, so the outrageousness of it just took hold and made it a lot easier to do than just saying, "Okay, how do you draw supersex?" I was really just trying to be conscious of everything being authentic, because I remember drawing Angel on top of Buffy and after I drew it I realized, "Oh, my God, I forgot Angel's tattoo!" Because you never see his tattoo, but he's got a big tattoo on his back and of course he's naked, so I had to talk to the editor and say, "Hey, can we get that page back and put a tattoo on his back?" because I totally forgot about it. So, little subtleties like that, but essentially the idea of supersex wasn't so much them, but everybody or everything being affected around them.

FAQ: I never was really clear in *Season Eight* where the line of demarcation was. Was Angel possessed by Twilight from the first time that we saw him?

GJ: If I'm being honest, I think *Season Eight* got away from us a little bit, and as it got bigger and bigger you have to rope it in for the climax, or the ending of it all, and I think we were going to a point where nobody really thought about ending. Nobody at the beginning had any idea where *Season Eight* actually ended. When I actually got the gig, I thought it was only gonna be four issues, like there were just gonna be those four issues that Joss wrote, you know, "Thank you very much" and I'll move on. From there it became twelve issues and then from there it became twenty issues and from there it was twenty-five and then it was thirty-eight and then, finally, forty. So, I think *Season Eight* is more of a learning curve for how a television season can be acclimated into a comic book and what an actual season looks like. *Season Eight* actually took about four years to do, and I think in that time some of the setup from way back in the beginning, like how Angel became all of this and where all that was going, kind of got lost in the mix and we had to bring it in really quick and sort of end it all. I think Joss has said this, that *Season Eight* was more of a learning curve, because, in all honesty, as I understand it this had never really been done before. There had been movies and TV series done in comic book form, but there had never been a season that carried on *after* the TV show had ended.

FAQ: That's why you were such a great choice, because for fans of the show, suddenly you're in a completely different medium, a completely different setting and situation but having that through line of Joss's dialogue and your art evoking the characters. It really eased you into this new *Buffy* world very effectively. You really knew where you were, at least with the characters, even if everything else had changed.

GJ: Well, modesty prevents me from agreeing with you, but I will say I was glad that it was me because I would much rather have somebody do this project who was a fan, and while I didn't start out a fan I became very quickly a fan, and, in being a fan, I really did stay true to the characters. . . . I was very conscious of the details. I even asked Joss at some point, obviously, Buffy doesn't have a costume, like Spider-Man, so I said, "Well, I don't want to draw her in the same thing because as a girl she's now in her twenties; she'd wear different clothes, as girls do." So, I said, "Well, where would she shop, hypothetically, if she were around here?" and Joss was delighted. He's like, "Oh, my God, she would shop at Anthropologie if she was gonna go anywhere," so from then that was pretty much Buffy's outfit. I just kept getting catalogues from Anthropologie and dressing Buffy the way I saw fit. I became very savvy about women's clothing when I was doing *Buffy*.

FAQ: We also wanted to ask you about the Angel-Twilight reveal and what that was like from your perspective as you saw it unfold.

GJ: A friend of mine e-mailed me one night the cover of that particular issue and it had—that particular issue, I believe, was supposed to either have one with Angel with the mask on and the other with the mask off, and I'm assuming, and this is how I got the story later: somebody at Dark Horse didn't realize there were two separate covers, basically the same, just the only difference is you'll have a different head attached to it. So, they let that go for solicitation and, of course, once that happened solicitations just posted it, and, thankfully, my friend, who was an avid *Buffy* fan, e-mailed me saying, "Hey, I thought this was supposed to be a secret," and then I looked and e-mailed my editor, Scott Allie, and I said, "Hey,

I thought this was supposed to be a secret." You know Scott freaked out. They, of course, had no idea, and there was a lot of "Who did this? Who did this? Who did this?" and it came down to somebody at Dark Horse just was not aware. I hope nobody lost their job, but that was a very long and very tense night, because I was told that Joss was not happy at all, and Joss is the most pacifist guy, you know, and for him to get angry you really gotta push the button there.

FAQ: Do you have a favorite character to draw, and is there a character who's the most difficult to draw?

GJ: I usually stay with the girl I came with to the dance, and Buffy is, of course, the star and she was the most central character and probably the character I drew the most, so I would say if I had a favorite it would be Buffy. But you know, I'm an able-bodied, red-blooded American boy, and Faith really did a lot for me, so she was very much a favorite when I was doing it, although I didn't draw her a whole lot. The toughest characters were the ones who had so much expression to them, and nobody was more expressive than Andrew. If you go back and look at those episodes he was in, so much of what he does is subtle, and that is almost impossible to get when you're just doing one image at a time. Jane [Espenson] came in and wrote a story like what she had written in season seven of the TV show about Andrew doing *Masterpiece Theatre* and telling about the Slayers and how they are, and I had to re-create that. Even when I was doing figures and likenesses that were very much like the TV show I found it very difficult, because Tom Lenk is so good at what he does, and we talked about that. We met a few times and talked. He was so good at what he does that it was more the subtlety of it, and it was never the stated thing.

Fray

I'm pissed like this rutting beast can't conceive—I'm a lifetime of pissed, of strong, of muscle built over bruise, I'm slick with power and I feel the fight as it changes . . . as it flows . . . everything into place, perfect, and I finally do what I was born to do. I slay.

—Melaka Fray

We have seen the future, and it is Fray. Specifically Melaka Fray, a nineteen-year-old orphan/"grabber" (thief), sassy as a jaybird as she goes about slaying vampires some two hundred years into the future in a dystopian iteration of Manhattan ruled by deviant mobsters mutated by the sun's radiation, thanks to industrial pollution and the destruction of the ozone ("radies," in Whedon-speak, of which there are beaucoup new entries here). Known to friend and foe alike as Mel, she is the titular

character in an eight-book comic series written by Joss Whedon—his first published comics, the fulfilment of a childhood dream—and published between 2001
and 2003 (beginning as season five of *Buffy* was airing and ending two-plus months
after the series' conclusion, with a thirteen-month delay between issues six and
seven).

In his foreword to the 2003 graphic novel compiling the complete series,
Whedon writes: "I didn't think anybody would be interested in a book from me
unless it was somehow Buffy related, and I was too busy writing *Buffy* to think
about writing *Buffy*." He "toyed" with creating a comics series for Faith, but opted
otherwise because the bad-girl Slayer had transitioned to *Angel*, and he was wary
of disrupting continuity; hence, he not only imagined a new character, but set the
story far enough in the future that he wouldn't have to worry about interfering with
storylines from the two television series. Whedon calls *Fray* a "simple story about
a really cool girl. A girl who might share some personal issues with Buffy and Faith,
but who was very much her own person." What kind of person? "Hard, defensive,
vulnerable, goofy, and yes, wicked sexy." Sample Mel dialogue: "I haven't met an ass
I couldn't kick."

The series was published by Dark Horse Comics (same as the *Buffy* and *Angel*
books), with kinetic, *Blade Runner/The Fifth Element*–inspired "urban-gone-mad"
(Whedon's words) artwork by Andy Owens (ink) and Karl Moline (pencil), who
reveals in his "Sketchbook" appendix to the graphic novel that early designs of
the title character were inspired by a comment Whedon had made about Natalie
Portman's portrayal of Mathilda in *Léon: The Professional*, Luc Besson's 1994 crime
thriller, in which a twelve-year-old girl bonds with a professional hitman after her
family is murdered. Whedon had one stipulation: "No cheesecake. No giant silicone
hooters, no standing with her butt out in that bizarrely uncomfortable soft-core
pose that so many artists favor. None of those outfits that casually—and constantly—reveal portions of a thong. I wanted a real girl, with real posture, a slight
figure (that's my classy way of saying 'little boobs'), and most of all, a distinctive
face."

Mel cat-burgles for Gunther, a purple talking fish—yes, "talking fish"—("Sushi-
Boy," she hails him), but her routine is disrupted when a giant, ram-horned, rust-
colored demon named Urkonn of D'avvrus—yes, "giant, ram-horned, rust-colored
demon"—flashes the news that Mel is the chosen one. Urkonn functions in a Giles-
like capacity, but his motives are murky, and he's not Mel's Watcher—it's complicated, but long story short: vampires, known here as "lurks," were banished from
the Earthly dimension following their defeat in a cosmic battle with an unidentified
twenty-first-century Slayer. *Hmm*, might this be Buffy Summers? In a 2004 interview with Mike Jozic, *Buffy* writer/producer David Fury reported that he had asked
Whedon that question as he was writing Fray, "and I think that he always had the
sense that it was Buffy . . . that she was the last Slayer before Fray was called. I think

it gave Buffy a greater stake in the mythology to know that she was the last one before Fray was called." However, Fury acknowledged, the fact that this is never specifically stated in the comic leaves it open to interpretation.

Meanwhile, the Watchers Council has fallen into disrepair in the intervening years, "held together only by fanatics and fools: those that believed the demons would return," per Urkonn (which maybe explains why Mel's actual Watcher immolates himself in the first book).

The thing is, you see, those crazy Watchers? Not so crazy after all. The lurks are indeed staging a return engagement, with grand plans to uncork the gateway to alternative dimensions in anticipation of one great big awesome bloodsucker reunion. The big reveal is the identity of the Big Bad, and we ain't talking.

While the line of Slayers continued to exist in the years following the war with the vamps, none were called, because, well, what would be the point, without suckers to slay? But now it's up to Fray to save the world—teen drama!—armed with not only her inherent superpowers, but also a mystical scythe gifted to her by Urkonn: "a weapon forged eons ago, for the Slayer alone. Lost for centuries. Carry it, for it is your sword and your scepter. Let it proclaim you the hero—and the monster—that you will need to be." (Buffy fans will recognize the weapon from the final season of the TV show, in which Spike alerts Buffy to its existence; she eventually locates the scythe embedded in a rock in Sunnydale and uses it to channel power into the Potentials, but the weapon had already appeared first in Book Six of Fray.)

Fray is a little bit Buffy and a little bit rock 'n' roll (meaning Faith)—more of a lone wolf than the former (no Scoobies here), but equally defined by her combo of fiery devotion to justice and her soft heart, most pronounced in her relationship with the young mutant girl Loo, a tragic figure. There are whiffs of Faith in her recklessness and defiance (Mel is, after all, a cat burglar, with purple-and-blue hair, and she and older sister Erin—a cop—are forever knocking heads), plus that upper-left-arm tat. She pops up again in the Whedon-scripted volume four ("Time of Your Life") of Buffy the Vampire Slayer Season Eight, thanks to a temporal anomaly, a hoot of a story in which the thoughtful Buffy and the impetuous Mel team up Butch-and-Sundance style and drive each other batty with their conflicting approaches to slaying.

"You really wanna stop this from spreading?" Buffy asks. "Then you gotta look at the big picture."

"You look," Mel responds. "I'm gonna do our job."

Through a twist of fate, Mel is "special" among Slayers, as she herself defines it in the Whedon-authored "Tales," her entry in Tales of the Slayers, a 2002 anthology about Slayers throughout history; she has no awareness of those who preceded her, since those memories were inherited by her twin brother, Harth, instead.

Though high-school drama-less—high school-less even—*Fray* is, like *Buffy*, a Bildungsroman, about a young woman who transcends her devastating past and finds new purpose in life. But *Fray* totes a social conscience too, which Whedon himself has remarked on: "For the rich people, for the normal people, for the people who actually live inside the law . . . everyone is young and beautiful, and it's a whole new world and there's all sorts of ramifications. But if you're poor, nothing has really changed." Except that they have a champion in Melaka Fray.

20

Rather Poetic . . .

In a Maudlin Sort of Way

Angel

An Overview

*A*ngel ran for 110 episodes over five seasons on the WB, from October 5, 1999, through May 19, 2004. Seasons one and two aired from 9:00 to 10:00 p.m. on Tuesdays, as the lead-out to *Buffy*. In season three—the first following *Buffy*'s move to UPN—*Angel* shifted to Mondays at 9:00 p.m., following *7th Heaven*, a strange bedfellow, as the WB had discovered when it tried to pair the show with *Buffy* ("WB has moved 'Angel' and its dark vampire mojo into a fascinatingly inappropriate new time slot—Mondays at 9, immediately following '7th Heaven,' the goody-goody drama about a preacher and his ever-expanding family," Joyce Millman wrote in the *New York Times*). *Angel* shifted days and times again in each of its last two seasons, airing from 9:00 to 10:00 p.m. on Sundays in the fall of season four, after *Gilmore Girls Beginnings* and *Charmed*, before moving the following January to Wednesdays, where it finished out its run the following season, airing immediately after *Smallville*. According to Nielsen, *Angel*'s ratings ranged from a high of 4.8 million viewers on average per episode (123rd best among prime-time shows) in its first season to a low of 3.65 million (138th) in season four; in its final season *Angel* averaged 3.97 viewers per episode, ranking 162nd.

No pilot was shot, though Whedon and David Greenwalt (Whedon's exec producer partner on *Buffy*) did film a five-plus-minute presentation (viewable on YouTube), which was screened at the WB upfront on May 18, 1999. In the run-up to the show's premiere, press coverage focused on how *Angel* would have a darker, more adult sensibility than *Buffy*. "Look, high school's over, boy," one character tells Angel in "City Of," the premiere episode (meta-fun!). "It's time to make with the grownup talk." Not *too* dark, though, as the creative team soon discovered, when the WB pulled the plug on what was supposed to be the second episode, a script titled "Corrupt," penned by David Fury. As Greenwalt, who ran the first three seasons, remembers, the teleplay called for

Joss Whedon directs David Boreanaz: Sit! Good boy! *WB/20th Century Fox/Photofest*

LAPD Detective Kate Lockley (Elizabeth Röhm), working deep undercover, to become a cocaine-addicted prostitute, and also included a scene in which Angel "not only failed to save the girl he was supposed to, but he gets down on the floor and starts licking up her blood." The network saw the script and "starting freaking out," Greenwalt says, "and they were right, because you have to earn it—if you're going to go really far with a character you have to earn it. I think we wanted to have something so different from *Buffy*. We shut down for three or four weeks, as I remember, but life went on after that."

Although the *Times*' Millman, a fan of the series, wrote that Angel's status as a "laconic, celibate loner" seemed to render him "the least promising spinoff candidate on 'Buffy,'" Whedon told *USA Today* in 1999 that the writers were fascinated "by the idea of the character as this person in need of redemption, this person who's had a torturous past and wants to atone for it." According to Whedon, the idea to spin the character off came to him during the second-season *Buffy* episode "I Only Have Eyes for You," about the spirit of a Sunnydale High student who fatally shoots his teacher back in the 1950s when she breaks off their affair; in the climactic scene, David Boreanaz and Sarah Michelle Gellar flip gender roles, so that the spirit of the boy inhabits Buffy, and Angel (or, more accurately, Angelus at this point in the season-two arc) is possessed by the teacher. Boreanaz's performance was so strong that Whedon was convinced he could carry his own series.

On the decision to set the show in Los Angeles, Greenwalt commented that "the place is just alive and well with demons."

Team Angel

At the outset, Greenwalt wanted *Angel* to be a self-containing anthology, rather than a serialized drama with complex mythology and interlinking, season-long plots, like *Buffy*. However, this idea—a throwback to the days of three-network television—was soon abandoned because, as Greenwalt told *USA Today* in 2001, "It just didn't pop. It didn't have resonance. Frankly, it wasn't the kind of thing we do." What *did* pop—at least initially—was the relationship between Angel and fellow Sunnydale alum Cordelia Chase, who accompanies Angel to the new series, even though their connection in *Buffy* was relatively minor (though Cordelia did love flirting with him, especially to irritate Buffy). Greenwalt, who advised the press to "Think Mary Tyler Moore with a good-looking Boris Karloff"—lobbied for the pairing, insisting that Cordelia come along "because Angel is dark, broody guy and Cordelia is bright, sunny, gigantic-smile girl, and they are honey together," as he put it on his DVD commentary for the *Buffy* episode "Reptile Boy."

According to David Greenwalt: "When Joss said, 'What do you think about spinning off Angel and doing it together?' I said, 'I may be old, but I'm not dumb.' I said we should bring Charisma, because she'll bring us great comedy relief and she'll play terrific off of Angel."

Whistler, the demonic cosmic emissary who plays such a crucial role in Angel's meeting Buffy and dedicating himself to the fight against evil, as recounted in the second-season-ending *Buffy* episodes "Becoming, Parts 1-2," was at some point in the process supposed to reprise his role in *Angel*—he reportedly appears in the original script of "City Of"—but it never happened. Max Perlich, who portrayed the character in *Buffy*, says he was never asked; when asked why, Greenwalt responded, "Who's Whistler?"

Rather, Angel teams with a new character, Allen Francis Doyle (Glenn Quinn), a half-demon dispatched by the Powers That Be to re-engage Angel emotionally with the people he is supposed to be championing. "It's not all about fighting and gadgets and stuff," Doyle tells him. "It's about reaching out to people, showing them that there's love and hope still left in the world. . . . It's about letting them into your heart. It's not about saving lives; it's about saving souls. Hey, possibly your own in the process." Unfortunately for Doyle, the PTB aren't big on cell phones, so they communicate via visions, which sounds cool but really isn't, since skull-splitting migraines accompany the pictures. In "Hero," the ninth episode of the first season, Doyle dies a heroic death, a function of personal problems Quinn was having, causing long production delays, according to Greenwalt, who calls Quinn's dismissal "a long, sad story"; the actor died three years later, on December 3, 2002, at the age of thirty-two, the result of what was judged an accidental heroin overdose.

"Glen Quinn was terrific, and that character was great . . . but he would come to work not knowing his lines, he'd be laughing on the set, he wasn't professional," Greenwalt recalls. Steven Bochco, creator of iconic shows like *Hill Street Blues* and *L.A. Law*, who had a reputation for skillfully handling problematic actors, once shared his secret with Greenwalt, telling him, "'I sit down with them and I say, 'Look me in the eye. I'm a serial killer, you are going to die, and if you don't behave, and come prepared, and do what you're supposed to do, I will kill you,'" meaning the character, of course. Greenwalt tried just that approach with Quinn, repeating Bochco's warning verbatim, and the actor started crying. "It was very sad, and he was so great in that role," Greenwalt says. "But he didn't change, or couldn't change. I didn't really know then about the drug addiction. . . . And we did something I'd never seen done on a show, and I was willing to risk the whole show: in episode nine we killed a regular. There were three regulars, and we killed one of them, and Joss went along with it. He supported me on that, and we got the network to go along, and we gave him a beautiful, heroic death, but I got a whole lot of nasty letters. My favorite was 'Dear Mr. Greenwalt, if in fact that is your name.' They reamed me out for killing him, because, rightly so, they loved Glenn's character, but I would rather have a show fail and work with decent, wonderful people than a very talented but very unpredictable and uncontrollable person, because life is too short. So it's a very sad thing, and, of course, he did die of an overdose, and I've buried a lot of people with that disease in my life and it's very ugly and very rapacious, but I did the right thing, and, if anything, the firing of Glenn Quinn could have helped; certainly the coddling of him would only have hastened that death."

Quinn was succeeded by Alexis Denisof, reprising his role as Wesley Wyndham-Pryce, "Rogue Demon Hunter" (having been fired for incompetence by the Watchers Council), initially the same bumbling prig he was on *Buffy,* but a character who, like Cordelia, undergoes a radical transformation over the course of the series, becoming darker, more competent, and, when necessary, ruthless.

According to David Fury:

> When I pitched the [*Buffy*] story that would become "Helpless," in my original version Giles gets fired by the council at the midway point and then gets rehired at the end. It didn't occur to me how I suddenly affected the mythology of the series. I was thinking when I pitched it, "Well, Giles has to get his job back, because Buffy needs her Watcher," and one of the things Joss loved about the pitch was Giles gets fired. "Great! This'll give us a chance to bring in somebody else." And I was feeling upset because I'm going, "I don't want to get Giles fired," but I did. . . . I was never sure about Wesley. He seemed a little arch and buffoonish, and then, in *Angel*, when we had to let Glenn Quinn go and there was talk about who we were going to get to replace him, it was decided to bring Wesley in, but that he has changed, he has become in his own way a rogue demon hunter. He was presented initially as still a little buffoonish, a little bit trying too hard, so you could still have fun with him. He was very proud of calling himself a rogue demon hunter, but then he grew into a much richer character; we let go of that sort of caricature of what Wesley was in *Buffy* and allowed Alexis to become more real and more grounded, and when he went to the dark place he was just great. I mean, look, whenever you give actors a chance to go to the dark place, generally, it's a dream for them because they suddenly get to play the elements that they never got to play before, and he just became a great character, a terrific character.

Carpenter remained with the series through four seasons, returning for one episode in the fifth, when Cordelia dies; Wesley lasted all the way through to the end, though meets a similar fate in the series finale. Team Angel expanded late in season one with the addition of L.A. street brawler Charles Gunn (J. August Richards), and again, in season two, with Winifred "Fred"

Burkle (Amy Acker), a waifish physicist who spends five years enslaved in an alternate dimension before being rescued by the team; and Lorne (known initially as the Host, portrayed by Andy Hallett), a gentle empath demon who runs a karaoke bar and can suss out emotions by listening to humans or demons sing. The first season also introduces the overarching villain of the series, the satanic law firm Wolfram + Hart, whose lawyers include Lindsey McDonald (Christian Kane) and Lilah Morgan (Stephanie Romanov).

Numerous *Buffy* characters dropped in for guest appearances, including Oz, Faith, Willow, Andrew, Drusilla, and Buffy herself. Spike joined the series as a regular character in season five, once *Buffy* had shuttered. Darla played a crucial role in *Angel*, making multiple guest appearances in seasons two and three.

Should I Stay or Should I Go?

In the fall of 2001, *Buffy* switched networks, to UPN, when the WB refused to meet 20th Century Fox's asking price, triggering speculation that *Angel* would follow; UPN already had a deal in place to pick the show up if the WB pulled the plug. UPN agreed to shell out $2.2 million per episode of *Buffy*—more than twice what FOX was getting from the WB—and was prepared to pay about $1.1 million for each episode of *Angel* over the next two seasons (some WB insiders groused that the real reason for the switch was that News Corp., a parent company of UPN, was on the verge of acquiring numerous UPN affiliates in key markets, so that acquiring *Buffy*, with its 4.4 million viewers per episode, third best on the WB, would boost their performance; *Angel*, by contrast, averaged 4.1 million viewers, making it the sixth-highest-rated WB program). In the end this turned out to be much ado about nothing, as the WB held on to *Angel*, and Greenwalt told *USA Today*, "I feel better this year than I have about any year, because I think we've finally found what the show is about: growing up and coming into your own. And coincidentally, that's what the show has to do" (ironically, it was Greenwalt's last season with the show, since he left after season three in a contract dispute when the studio tried to cut his salary—a departure that he called "heartbreaking, like a divorce"). In the end, ratings held more or less steady in the third season, but dropped significantly the following year, which led to machinations on both sides: for the first time, the writers ended one season with a setup for the following: Lilah Morgan offering Team Angel the chance to battle evil from the inside out, by taking over Wolfram + Hart, and the WB initially gave *Angel* a commitment for only thirteen episodes, rather than a full season of twenty-two, although the back-order for the additional episodes eventually came through.

Joss Whedon and the *Angel* cast mark a milestone.   *WB/20th Century Fox/Photofest*

Sarah Michelle Gellar declined an invitation to return for season five's "You're Welcome," the one hundredth episode of the series, by which time *Buffy* had already been off the air for close to a full season. In an interview with Mike Jozic in 2005, David Fury said Gellar "politely declined, which, I will say, she had her reasons. I think there might have been a death of an aunt or something that she was dealing with." According to Fury, Whedon "kind of felt a little bit put off about the way it was done. There was a perceived notion, on both sides, I can say, between Sarah and Joss, of ingratitude for both parties. Joss doesn't feel like Sarah's ever shown the proper amount of gratitude for what he's done for her and her career, and I think she feels the same way, that she feels she was never afforded the credit for Buffy's success and the gratitude from Joss." Reports on whether Gellar offered to appear on the series finale instead are inconsistent, but according to Fury, Whedon felt the last episode should focus on the core cast.

The WB announced *Angel*'s cancellation on February 14, 2004, with a one-paragraph statement (the news had already been leaked via the Internet). That same day, Whedon responded on The Bronze, the popular Internet fan forum, named after the nightclub in *Buffy*, calling the news "hilarious" and saying the cast and creative team "had no idea this was coming."

"Yes, my heart is breaking," he wrote. " . . . we really were starting to feel like we were on top, hitting our stride—and then we strode right into the Pit of Snakes 'n' Lava. I'm so into these characters, these actors, the situations we're building . . . you wanna know how I feel? Watch the first act of 'The Body,'" a reference to the *Buffy* episode in which Joyce Summers dies.

The final episode, "Not Fade Away," aired on May 19, 2004, ending with a fade to black, just as Angel and his crew—or what was left of it—prepared to wage war against a legion of monsters unleashed by the senior partners of Wolfram + Hart. However, from 2007–2009, IDW Publishing released a seventeen-issue comic book series titled *After the Fall*; plotted by writer Brian Lynch and Whedon, it picks up in the apocalyptic aftermath of the television series. At Comic-Con International: San Diego, Whedon stated that the comic was inspired by narrative plans for season six, "but it's not exactly season six."

Angel: Vampire Noir

> Los Angeles. You see it at night, and it shines. A beacon. People are drawn to it. People, and other things. They come for all sorts of reasons. My reason? No surprise there. It started with a girl.
>
> *—Angel*

Early *Angel* is a virtuosic fusion of hard-boiled noir with multiple other genres: horror, superhero, and Byronic romance among them. After leaving Sunnydale at the end of season three in *Buffy*, Angel moves to L.A. and sets up shop as a private eye, battling both inner and outer demons in his never-ending search for redemption. The series was created by Joss Whedon and his fellow *Buffy* executive producer David Greenwalt as a darker, more brooding and morally confused counterpart to the original. Whereas *Buffy* is set in an inverted suburban paradise sitting atop a portal to hell, *Angel* unfolds in the birthplace of noir, a city Raymond Chandler once described as "lost and beaten and full of emptiness." Whereas *Buffy* ingeniously exploited the creepshow genre as a metaphor for coming-of-age anxiety, *Angel* allegorically navigates the emotional pitfalls of adulthood. Whereas *Buffy* ends in victory and hope, *Angel* ends with a fade to black, and almost certainly the apocalypse. As Whedon has said: "We wanted a much darker show."

Early on, Whedon and Greenwalt envisioned wrapping *Angel* in hard-boiled iconography: "The idea with *Angel* was to do a modern noir, was to do a little office with the blinds and the fast patter and the sort of nihilistic toughness and the dark world and the strange turns and all of the things that you find in the great forties and fifties noirs," Whedon said. (While a vampire detective may have seemed like a natural to Whedon, it had been tried just once before on North American series TV, in the Canadian-produced *Forever Knight*, which originated as an 1989 TV movie titled *Nick Knight* before evolving into a series, although shows like *Moonlight* and Canada's *Blood Ties* followed in *Angel*'s wake.) With help from fellow *Buffy* alumnus Cordelia Chase (Charisma Carpenter) and a humanoid half-demon (on his dad's side) named Doyle (Glenn Quinn), an emissary from the oracular Powers That Be, Angel sets up a P. I. firm (Angel Investigations) whose mission is to "help the helpless" by fighting supernatural powers of darkness, particularly a vast and ominous law firm called Wolfram + Hart. On the one hand, Angel is a knight errant in the vaunted tradition of hard-boiled shamuses, navigating his way through a treacherous underworld with ironic detachment, a sharp wit, his two fists, and unwavering integrity, not unlike the generic detective Raymond Chandler described in *The Simple Art of Murder*: "He is the hero; he is everything. He must be a complete man and a common man and yet an unusual man. He must be, to use a rather weathered phrase, a man of honor—by instinct, by inevitability, without thought of it, and certainly without saying it. He must be the best man in his world and a good enough man for any world." Yet on the other hand, Angel isn't a man at all, but rather a demon over two hundred years old who chugs pigs' blood (nifty metaphor for the archetypal booze-guzzling private eye), and harbors within himself a monster of legendary cruelty.

I Won't Be Your Mirror

This theme of doubleness, or the divided self, suggesting confusion of identity, is itself a noir trope, frequently illustrated with reflections in mirrors or windows. The irony here is that, as a vampire, Angel has no reflection, yet the battle between his dark and light sides recurs often—and not just explicitly, as in episodes like the fourth-season arc in which Angel's soul is deliberately extracted so that Angelus can provide the 9-1-1 on the Beast, a ferocious horned monster terrorizing the city. In "The Shroud of Rhamon," a second-season flashback episode with strong narrative ties to canonical noir, Angel pretends to drink the blood of Detective Kate Lockley (Elisabeth Röhm) to protect her from another demon, an experience he sensually enjoys, despite himself. In "Reunion," as Darla (Julie Benz) and her cohort Drusilla (Juliet Landau) prepare to feast on a roomful of Wolfram + Hart employees,

Angel—disgusted with the lot of them—prepares to bolt the door from the out-side and walk away.

"People are going to die," W+H nabob Holland Manners (Sam Anderson) says, pleading for Angel's help.

"And yet somehow, I just can't seem to care," he replies, echoing Manners's earlier response to him, when Angel protested that innocent people were dying because of the law firm. In "A New World," Angel and Darla's human son, Connor (Vincent Kartheiser), demands that his father show him his "face for killing," and when Angel reluctantly obliges, Connor spits at him: "That's what you are."

"It's part of what I am," Angel replies. Yet it is an essential part—it is the demon in him that, because of the curse, inspires him to fight evil, and also the source of his power, which enables him, typically, to prevail.

In the second-season flashback episode "Are You Now or Have You Ever Been," we glimpse Angel inchoate, cold and distant, still grappling with the rami-fications of having a soul. Set in 1952, during the height of the communist witch hunts—the McCarthy hearings unfold on TV sets in the background—the episode recounts an early attempt by Angel to engage with humans, with tragic results. As a paranoia demon (Tony Amendola) haunts the rambling deco Hyperion Hotel, preying on guests' fears, Angel reluctantly comes to the aid of Judy Kovacs (Melissa Marsala), who has recently been fired by a bank, after it discovers that she was of mixed race. The woman exacts her revenge by absconding with a heaping help-ing of the bank's loot, and is now being hounded by a private eye engaged by her former employer. To save herself, Kovacs eventually turns on Angel, and helps whip the guests into such a frenzy that they wind up lynching him (though, of course, he can't die again).

The paranoia demon, drooling at the prospect of tormenting a collection of such spineless humans, taunts Angel: "There's an entire hotel here just full of tor-tured souls who could really use your help. Whaddaya say?"

"Take them all," Angel replies.

This "otherness," which dissipates over time but never disappears—Angel is, after all, aligned with humans but not himself human—is another integral noir motif, a key to the anguish and alienation so common to the noir protagonist: Bradford Galt's famous utterance from the 1946 noir *The Dark Corner*—"I feel all dead inside"—is, in Angel's case, literally true. "The more you live in this world, the more you see how apart from it you really are," the demon Whistler tells him in "Becoming, Part I," a second-season episode of *Buffy*.

Typically Whedonesque, *Angel* is acutely aware of its generic influences and revels in self-conscious allusions to noir. For example, in the third-season episode "Sleep Tight," Angel asks Wolfram + Hart attorney Lilah Morgan (Stephanie Romanov): "Don't you ever get tired of the whole femme fatale act?" Lilah—young and beautiful, but icicle-cold and completely without scruples—is indeed a formidable femme fatale, beginning with her first appearance, in the first-season episode "Ring," in which she coolly spectates as enslaved demons pound each other to death in a boxing ring while frenzied gamblers cheer them on. Lilah later offers Angel—himself having been abducted and compelled to fight—freedom, but only if he agrees to toil for Wolfram + Hart (no deal). In a story arc straddling seasons three and four, Lilah and Wesley Wyndam-Pryce (Alex Denisof), another Buffy alumnus who joins Angel Investigations, become lovers, and in true noir fashion Lilah first approaches Wesley in a bar, where he sits alone drinking after having been exiled from Angel's inner circle. (Scholar Jennifer Stoy has described Lilah's entrance as a "fairly direct visual allusion to Lauren Bacall's entrance into a very similar bar in *The Big Sleep*"). Feeling abandoned, and consumed by self-loathing, Wesley reluctantly responds to Lilah's overtures, even as she delights in ridiculing him. Presenting Wesley with a rare copy of Dante's "Inferno," Lilah asks if he can remember who occupies the worst spot in hell. Judas Iscariot, replies Wesley. "Right, so don't pretend you're too good to work for us," she says. Later, after a romp in the sack, Wesley boots Lilah out, and they continue their hard-boiled tête-à-tête:

"Don't be thinking about me when I'm gone," Lilah says.

"I wasn't thinking about you when you were here," Wesley responds.

Cherchez la femme

Of course, Angel's ultimate femme fatale is Darla, who not only sires Angelus but molds him, showering him with attention, arousing him with "gifts," inciting him to new heights of cruelty. At one point in their long history together, when Angelus and Darla are trapped in a barn under siege by vampire hunters, Darla flees on horseback, leaving Angelus to fend for himself, yet, once free, he roams continents to rejoin her. After the Gypsy curse, Darla deserts him again, repulsed by "his filthy soul," and while Angel tries desperately to go on without her, his despondency is so abject that he tracks her down halfway around the world in China, feigning soullessness again so that she will welcome him back. This is in the great noir tradition of *amour fou*, or mad love, so memorably depicted in films like Charles Vidor's *Gilda* (1946), in which Detective Maurice Obregon (Joseph Calleia), commenting on Johnny Farrell's (Glenn Ford) relationship with the title character (Rita Hayworth), tells him: "It's the most curious love-hate pattern I've ever had the privilege of witnessing, and as long as you're as sick in the head as you are about her you're not able to think about anything clearly." In the second season, Wolfram + Hart resurrects Darla, hoping she can lure Angel back to the dark side: "We don't want him dead. We want him dark, and there's no better way to a man's darkness than to awaken his nastier urges," says attorney Lindsey McDonald (Christian Kane). Now human, with a soul, Darla is dying of the syphilis she had contracted centuries earlier as a prostitute, before becoming a vampire, and she attempts to seduce Angel into granting her immortality, just as she had once done for him: "Before you got neutered you weren't just any vampire, you were a legend. Nobody could keep up with you, not even me. You don't learn that kind of darkness. It's innate." Angel refuses, but Drusilla happily obliges, and Angel becomes obsessed with hunting Darla down and killing her. As he trains for the task, he says: "I can still feel her, her pain, her need, her hope. I'm too close, too close to fight her." When Wesley tells him that he, Cordelia, and Charles Gunn (J. August Richards), the newest member of Angel's team, are "all that's standing between you and real darkness," Angel fires all three on the spot and embarks on a crusade to obliterate Wolfram + Hart. Lorne (Andy Hallett), the empathic-demon host of a karaoke bar, counsels Angel: "You went from helping the helpless to hunting down the guilty."

"You wanna know what my problem is?" Angel replies. "I'm screwed, that's my problem. I can't win. I'm trying to atone for a hundred years of unthinkable evil. News flash: I never can. Never gonna be enough."

Finally, in "Reprise," *Angel*—reeling from depression over his torment by Darla—beds her violently; the following morning, as Darla savors her conquest, Angel coolly informs her that his soul is intact because what he experienced was not perfect bliss, but perfect despair.

Angel leans, too, on noir's visual aesthetics, thanks largely to director of photography Herb Davis, who created what Rhonda V. Wilcox and David Lavery have called a "beautiful dark," involving a preponderance of night scenes (logical, since direct sunlight is fatal to vampires in Buffyverse) and frequent use of dark tunnels and alleyways (where Angel himself is first sired, and where, centuries later, Darla stakes herself to death while giving birth to Connor). In season four, L.A. is, for a time, literally pitch-black around the clock, after the Beast blots out the sun, transforming the city into a post-apocalyptic world where demons rule the streets. The city of L.A., home to so much classic noir, is crucial to *Angel*, beginning with the obvious connection to the protagonist's name. Producer Marti Noxon once referenced L.A. as a place "where a lot of lonely, isolated, and desperate people end up," in search of new identities and purpose; in *Angel*, this describes not just Angel Investigation's clients—Angel calls them "the weak ones lost in the night"—but also the principals themselves: Cordelia, who fled Sunnydale destitute and disgraced because of her father's tax fraud, flailing as an actress when she first hooks up with Angel in L.A.; Wesley, craving validation as a Watcher after his disastrous experiences on *Buffy*; Gunn, homeless, the product of a treacherous inner-city neighborhood, compelled to have staked his own sister to death after she was turned into a vampire; Fred (Amy Acker), brilliant but emotionally damaged after spending five years enslaved in an alternate dimension; Lorne, the gentlest of souls, living in self-imposed exile from a clan of warrior demons; and, of course, Angel himself: cursed, haunted, desperate for redemption, happiness, and romantic fulfillment—none of which he may ever be permitted.

Scholar Benjamin Jacob has dubbed *Angel*'s L.A. "Los Angelus"—"a place where the glittering skyscrapers of late twentieth-century wealth meet darkness, alienation and threat." This blanc-noir duality of the city—which parallels Angel's own divided self—is an integral part of Los Angeles's mythology. In *The Fragmented Metropolis: Los Angeles, 1850–1930*, Robert F. Fogelson quotes an itinerant Presbyterian minister writing in 1854: "The name of this city is in Spanish the city of Angels, but with much more truth might it be called at present the city of Demons. . . . If I am to stay here, may the Lord be with me." In "Los Angelus," the noir "underworld" references not just the labyrinthine tunnels and sewers that Angel traverses to avoid direct sunlight (much like Harry Lime in *The Third Man*), or even the criminals (both human and not) who prey upon the shadow people so near and dear to Angel's heart, but Hades itself, as Angel discovers in the episode "Reprise": accompanied by Manners, Angel descends via elevator to Wolfram + Hart's "home office," the locus of evil, only to find that when the doors open, they are looking out at people routinely going about their business in bright, sunny L.A. "See, we're in the hearts and minds of every single living being," Manners tells him. "And that, friend, is what's making things so difficult for you. See, the world doesn't work in spite of evil, Angel. It works with us. It works because of us." When Angel protests that this cannot possibly be hell, Manners begs to differ: "Well, you know it is. You know that better than anyone. The things you've seen. The things you've, well, done. You see, if there wasn't evil in every single one of them out there, why, they wouldn't be people. They'd all be angels."

As *Angel* progressed, the hard-boiled elements of the series receded, overtaken by fantasy, horror, and the superhero comic ethos—Angel is frequently compared to Batman, the Dark Knight: two morally conflicted superheroes struggling to balance their dark and light sides. By the final season, when Team Angel actually takes over Wolfram + Hart to combat evil from the inside out (and Spike, believed to have died in the series finale of *Buffy*, joins the team, initially as a ghost, but later corporeally), the series is almost unrecognizable as noir, though the final episode concludes in a way any noir buff would applaud, refusing to settle for tidy endings, or any ending at all, really. In the final scene, Angel and his soldiers gather in a dark, rain-drenched alleyway (yes, another dark alley), preparing to wage war one last time, against an overwhelming legion of minions from hell. "Let's go to work," Angel says, just before the screen goes black. The outcome of the battle is forever unknown (unless you count the comic books), which is exactly how it should be. For Angel, the battle—for his own redemption and for humanity's—goes on forever; what's important is not winning, but the fight itself. As Angel—the existentialist vampire detective—put it himself many episodes before: "If there's no great glorious end to all this, if nothing we do matters, then all that matters is what we do."

Angel: Season by Season

Season One

Angel, gumshoeing in L.A., hangs out a shingle: Angel Investigations, along with fellow *Buffy* alum Cordelia Chase, trying (and failing) to launch an acting career, and half-demon Allen Francis Doyle, a conduit for the cosmic Powers That Be, who feed him painful, premonitory visions of Angelinos in need of a champion. That would be Angel. On the other side of the aisle is Wolfram + Hart, nefarious interdimensional law firm representing the baddest of the bad, demons and humans alike, whose ranks include attorneys Lilah Morgan and Lindsey McDonald. LAPD Detective Kate Lockley pops in and out, sometimes helping Angel, sometimes hating him, sometimes flirting with him. Make up your mind, lady. Nine episodes in, Doyle perishes, sacrificing himself to save a shipload of fellow half-breed demons, though not before transferring those skull-shattering visions to Cordelia, via a kiss. Thanks, bro. Wesley Wyndham-Pryce, ex-Watcher, current "rogue demon hunter," joins the team. Upgrade? TBD. Also on board: Charles Gunn, L.A. gangbanger/vampire killer. Wolfram + Hart buses in rogue Slayer Faith Lehane, with the intent of bumping off Angel. How's that go? *Duh.* In the hectic season finale, AI headquarters are blown to smithereens; Wesley deciphers the Shanshu Prophecy, apparently foretelling that Angel becomes human again, once he "fulfills his destiny"; and W + H summons Darla, Angel's sire, back from the dead. Nifty cliffhanger, eh?

Season Two

No matter how rough things gets, there's always time for karaoke, which explains the presence of empath demon Krevlornswath ("You can call me Lorne") of the Deathwok Clan, who reads auras by listening to humans or demons sing, revealing, among other, possibly more crucial things, that Angel is a Barry Manilow fan. Oh, Mandy, tears are in our eyes, too. As for those other, more crucial things: Darla is now human, dying of syphilis, as she was centuries before when the Master sired her, and pleading with Angel to take a nip out of her, thereby re-granting her immortality. Seems Wolfram + Hart wants not to kill Angel, but to transform him back into Angelus. Angel isn't biting (*ugh*), but voluntarily undergoes mystical trials hoping to win Darla a second chance at life (he wins, but all for naught, since Darla already used up her second chance when W + H brought her back). W + H shifts to Plan B, roping in Drusilla to sire Darla—these guys must have an amazing e-mail directory. Angel totally flips out, firing his three amigos and bedding Darla. The twist: he's still Angel, having experienced not perfect bliss, but perfect despair. Team Angel makes up. Cordelia gets sucked through a magical portal, landing in the demon dimension of Pylea, Lorne's hometown, and the boys follow, rescuing not just Cordy but also a wispish Texas physicist named Winifred "Fred" Burkle, who had disappeared through the same portal five years earlier and been held as a slave in Pylea ever since, before finally returning to L.A., neither safe nor sound.

Season Three

Welcome centuries-old vampire hunter Daniel Holtz, who, through the intervention of the demon Sahjhan, is transported to present-day L.A., which is especially bad news for Angel and Darla, since they slaughtered his family two hundred years earlier. Holtz has one thing in mind: revenge. Darla returns to L.A. eight-and-a-half-months pregnant, thanks to that one-nighter with Angel. All agree it's a miracle that two undead vampires have created life, but . . . *hello?* This is *Angel*. Darla, afraid that she, as a vampire who basically wants to eat everyone she sees, will want to kill her own child, stakes herself, leaving behind her infant son, whom Angel names Connor. Everyone—and we mean everyone, Holtz, Sahjhan, Wolfram + Hart—wants a piece of this kid. Wesley too, having come across a prophecy (later proved false) that "the father will kill the child." Wes kidnaps Connor, but is ambushed by a Holtz minion, who turns the boy over to him. A showdown ensues among Angel, agents of W + H, and Holtz, who flees with the boy into a hell dimension, which immediately seals, making it impossible for Angel to follow. Dark days follow: Angel, despondent, boots Wes from the team, even tries to smother him with a pillow. Isolated, lonely, full of rage, Wesley canoodles with Lilah Morgan, Wolfram + Hart ice maiden. Connor returns, now eighteen, since time moves faster in the hell dimension (we would have suspected the opposite, really), with *huge* Daddy issues, determined to kill Angel for slaughtering Holtz's family. In the midst of all this turmoil, Angel and Cordy plan a rendezvous, at which, perhaps, each will profess his/her love for the other? My god, man, WWBS? (What Would Buffy Say?) Anyway, it never happens, because Connor kidnaps Daddy, chains him up in a casket, and drops him to the bottom of the ocean, which is ironic, since Cordy winds up trapped way *above* Earth, transformed into a higher being, which ranks as the second-worst creative decision ever made by the *Angel* writers. Wondering about the first? Read on.

Season Four

Wes, God bless him, tracks down Angel, and frees him. In a truly excruciating storyline, Cordy spends three months as a higher being, all glowy and disembodied, before mysteriously returning, her memory wiped clean. As bad as that is, what happens next is worse: she sleeps with Connor, sort of her surrogate son; yup, preggers. Gross, yuck, etc. A Neanderthal demon known as the Beast terrorizes L.A., blotting out the son, turning the city into the "Devil's oyster," though at least there's a reduction in brushfires. Also on the plus side: he wipes out the entire staff at Wolfram + Hart, with the exception of Lilah Morgan, who has more lives than a litter of cats. Since indications are the Beast and Angelus once palled around, Wesley—now back on the team— suggests extracting Angel's soul, so they can interrogate Angelus. Like that'll go well. Cordy, under the influence of whatever is growing inside her, frees Angelus, and his bottled-up soul mysteriously disappears. Angelus kills the Beast, restoring sunlight to L.A.—not that that was his intent. Thing-inside-Cordy kills Lilah. Wes, Faith (sprung from prison), and Willow (dropping in for a visit) restore Angel's soul. Cordelia gives birth to a higher being, who adopts the name Jasmine, whom everybody worships, even though she eats naked people and advances her purported agenda of world peace through spiritual enslavement, until Fred discovers the truth and enlightens the rest of the gang, which forms an underground resistance. Angel eventually destroys her by revealing her true name, which, *hello*, Rumpelstiltskin? We would share with you here except that it is unpronounceable by human tongue and we have no idea how to spell it. Cordy lapses into a coma. Lilah returns from the dead, briefly, with an invitation from the senior partners, to take over the newly re-staffed L.A. branch of Wolfram + Hart. Ridiculous? You bet. So let's do it! After all, paid holidays, including the anniversary of Lucifer's fall. Angel makes a deal, accepting the offer on the condition that Connor's memory is wiped clean and he is granted a "normal" life. Lucky kid gets to forget what the writers did to Cordelia.

Season Five

Team Angel takes the reigns at Wolfram + Hart's L.A. office, working with (temptress) Eve (no relation to *Buffy*'s Adam), liaison to the senior partners, who, it turns out, is double-crossing not just Angel but also the senior partners, with her paramour, Lindsey McDonald, who just won't go away. Still, gutsy move, Eve. Spike, last seen dying in *Buffy*, miraculously materializes at W + H, first as a ghost, but later corporeally, and joins the team, which leads to endless irritation for Angel, but also some of the season's best scenes.

"I'll be your mirror": two faces of the multifaceted Cordelia Chase (Charisma Carpenter).

WB/20th Century Fox/Photofest

Cordelia wakes from her coma, and praise the Powers (or, really, scripter David Fury): she's the old Cordy! Sadly, she sticks around just long enough to finally smack lips with Angel, in the process slipping him a clue as to the existence of the Circle of the Black Thorn, a top-secret cabal of evil demons working for the senior partners. Angel becomes a puppet—literally, a puppet—but just for an episode, though even then it complicates his budding relationship with Nina, a werewolf. Wes and Fred finally hook up, but Wes has the worst luck this side of Angel: Illyria, an ancient demon, returns to earth, possessing the body of Fred, who perishes in Wes's arms. Angel infiltrates the Circle of the Black Thorn, then stages a multifront operation eradicating the group all over L.A., but resulting in Wesley's death (think about it: Angel's fate, as a vampire, is to outlive every human to whom he ever becomes attached). Lorne shoots Lindsey dead, as instructed by Angel, who knew that in the end he would betray them, but the act of violence is too much for the gentle empath demon to bear, so he says *sayonara*. Angel's act of war vexes the senior partners, who unleash a legion of monsters on the city, including a dragon, Angel's favorite. The series ends just as Armageddon is about to begin; last words, from Angel: "Let's go to work," followed by fade to black.

> Cordelia did go down a path where the audience began to dislike her. And certainly the whole Angel-Connor-Cordelia triangle was very, very difficult for people to take. . . . I'm very grateful Joss gave me the opportunity to do "You're Welcome," which allowed me to send off Cordelia as the one we loved—the Cordelia that was loved in the beginning gets to go away, because before she went away, you know, we disliked her, the whole pregnancy thing, it just wasn't working. And it was really fun to work with Charisma. Joss was always very emotionally connected to these episodes—he'll be weeping as he writes, he'll watch them, he'll direct them, and he'll tear up, and I always thought that was kind of "Okay, that's sort of the sixteen-year-old girl again," and yet when I did "You're Welcome" and I wrote the scene between Cordelia and Angel at the end, before he gets the call and finds out she died, I was crying, I was weeping, I was doing exactly what Joss does, and I was like, "Okay, I get it now." I was really touched by it.
>
> —*David Fury*

Angel: Myth + Mythology

Angel, of course, unfolds in the same universe as *Buffy*, meaning the shows share a common mythology. Here's a selection of significant enhancements to that mythology as depicted over five seasons of *Angel*:

The Beast

Super-nasty demon dude who works the streets for the higher being known as Jasmine. The Beast eradicates Wolfram + Hart (only Lilah Morgan survives), including Mesektet, conduit to the satanic senior partners, which isn't a terrible thing, except that Kant would argue it's all about intent, and the Beast's—blotting out the sun to turn Los Angeles into a "demon playground"—probably isn't winning any community-service awards.

Circle of the Black Thorn

Elite ultra-secret society/earthbound branch of the Wolfram + Hart senior partners. The Black Thorns "make sure man's inhumanity to man keeps rolling along," as Lindsey McDonald puts it. Right, but what *exactly* do they do? "Starts with an 'a' and ends in 'pocalypse.'" Oh, now we get it. In the series finale, Angel orchestrates the annihilation of the Circle in a manner that would have made Michael Corleone proud. Downside? Armageddon.

Deeper Well

Mystical graveyard wherein lie thousands of sarcophaguses containing the essences of the Old Ones, a race of pure-breed evil demons who ruled Earth millions of years before the advent of humankind. The guardian of the Deeper Well, located in Cotswolds, England (and traveling straight through to the other side of the Earth), is a bloke named Drogyn the Battlebrand, a mystical warrior who had been granted eternal youth a thousand years earlier, and who was compelled to answer every question ever asked him truthfully, which never seemed to be a problem until Spike showed up.

Illyria

A pure-breed demon—one of the "Old Ones"—Illyria is resurrected when her sarcophagus is teleported out of the Deeper Well by a sycophantic acolyte named Knox, who works in the science lab at Wolfram + Hart. Science and religion—never a good match. This is bad news on so many levels, but especially on the Fred level, since it's her body that Illyria possesses, ending with her tragic death. Illyria wants to wash "humanity from the face of the world," but who doesn't? Turns out her entire army of doom, supposedly locked away in a time-frozen temple called Vahla ha'nesh, has been dusted, necessitating an abrupt policy redirection, so Illyria fights alongside Team

Angel in the battle against, first, the Circle of the Black Thorn and, then, the monster mash unleashed by the senior partners. As allies go, she's a keeper.

Jasmine

Jasmine is tricky, because how can you trust a pathological liar? Once reborn into the world (conceived by Connor and Cordelia, on the one occasion on which they mated), Jasmine tricks 99.99 percent of the world's population into believing she looks like Gina Torres, the strikingly beautiful actress who portrays her, when, in fact, her face is a rotting, worm-infested mess, as Fred discovers once their bloods mingle. Taken at her word, Jasmine is a renegade alum of the Powers That Be, a "great being" who walked the Earth millions of years before the coming of humankind but departed for greener pastures once the malevolent Old Ones grew stronger, converting the Earth into a demon realm. She never calls, she never writes, but apparently she never stopped caring, and finally, unable to bear all of the suffering back on Earth, she engineers a series of "miracles" that eventually results in her rebirth, at which point she purportedly plans to eradicate human suffering through spiritual enslavement of the entire world population—or at least those among it whom she doesn't eat first.

The Oracles

A pair of higher beings who serve as conduits to the Powers That Be. Angel visits them thrice, with mixed results: once, after a brief flirtation with mortality, to reverse time, allowing him to become a vampire again, so that he could be of some assistance to Buffy in the fight against evil (request granted); once to resurrect Doyle (request denied); and once to help Cordelia, after she was branded with the debilitating Mark of Vocah, a warrior demon who slays the Oracles before Angel arrives.

The Powers That Be

Cosmic force of good, possibly comprising what once, many millions of years ago, were benevolent entities that graced Earth before departing for safer environs when demonic forces began to assert control. Like their evil counterparts, the senior partners, the Powers That Be communicate through liaisons, like the Oracles, Doyle, and, later, Cordelia. Although the Powers are never mentioned by name on *Buffy*, many assume they play a role in crucial events of that series as well, like dispatching the demon Whistler to New York

City in 1996 to rouse Angel from his apathy, and later, in the third-season episode "Amends," gifting Sunnydale with a white Christmas in the middle of a heat wave.

Quor'toth

A "cesspool hell dimension," as Wolfram + Hart's inimitable Lilah Morgan puts it, Quor'toth is also known as "the darkest of the dark worlds," accessible only through a rip in the fabric of reality, which explains why Angel can't follow vampire hunter Daniel Holtz there in pursuit of his infant son Connor, whom Holtz has abducted. Time passes quickly in Quor'toth, so Connor ages at an accelerated pace and returns to Earth—just weeks later—eighteen years old, full of teen angst and piss and vinegar, though remarkably acne-free.

Sahjhan

Incredibly irritating Granok demon who recruits vampire hunter Daniel Holtz in his scheme to do away with Angel's son Connor, which makes sense, since the Nyazian Scrolls foretell that Connor will eventual kill him. Sneaky Sahjhan alters the prophecy to read: "The father will kill the son," leading Wesley to abduct Connor to protect him from Angel, which is just a disaster for everyone, all because of this meddling demon, who eventually gets what's coming to him anyway when Connor slices off his head.

Senior Partners

Biggest of the Big Bads, an ultra-secret, ultra-powerful cabal of ultra-evil demons who spend most of the series trying to woo Angel to the dark side, and, when that fails, unleash all hell on Los Angeles in the series finale. Illyria knows them as the Wolf, the Ram, and the Hart, and comments that back in the day "they were weak, barely above the vampire." Eventually driven from this dimension, they created Wolfram + Hart and the Circle of the Black Thorn to carry out their business on Earth.

Shanshu Prophecy

A *huge* deal, contained within the Scrolls of Aberjian, foretelling that a vampire with a soul will play a defining role in the coming apocalypse—for good or bad TBD—and, as a reward, become human. All along everyone assumes its Angel, but then Spike shows up, so all bets are off.

Tro-Clon

A confluence of events to bring about the purification and/or ruination (depending on whether you prefer the Aramaic, ancient Greece, or Ga-shundi translation) of mankind, as prophesied in the Nyazian Scrolls. If you choose to believe the demon Skip, another notorious liar, all of the major events over the first four seasons of *Angel* were manipulated to bring about the birth of Jasmine.

Wolfram + Hart

Nefarious law firm that, as a front for the senior partners, represents the scum of the Earth and every other known dimension in the universe, and harasses Angel (mostly through the personages of attorneys Lilah Morgan and Lindsey McDonald) over the first four seasons of the series, until Team Angel finally assumes control of the firm in season five, hoping that fighting evil from within will be easier than from without (not).

Must-See Angel: A Baker's Dozen

1. "I Will Remember You" (Season One, Episode Eight, by David Greenwalt + Jeannine Renshaw): Arguably the most heart-wrenching episode ever—of *Angel* or *Buffy*.
2. "Hero" (Season One, Episode Nine, by Howard Gordon + Tim Minear): If you're going to watch just one Doyle episode, this is it.
3. "The Prodigal" (Season One, Episode Fifteen, by Tim Minear: The siring of Angelus.
4. "Sanctuary" (Season One, Episode Nineteen, by Tim Minear + Joss Whedon): Angel and Buffy duke it out over Faith.
5. "Are You Now or Have You Ever Been" (Season Two, Episode Two, by Tim Minear): McCarthy-era betrayal.
6. "Reunion" (Season Two, Episode Ten, by Tim Minear + Shawn Ryan): Mass firings at Angel Investigations, as Angel—not Angelus—flirts with the dark side.
7. "Lullaby" (Season Three, Episode Nine, by Tim Minear): A child is born; a vampire dies.
8. "Spin the Bottle" (Season Four, Episode Six, by Joss Whedon): Sort of Angel's take on "Tabula Rasa," for those who miss the old Cordy (and who doesn't?). Possibly the funniest Wesley Wyndham-Pryce ever, which is saying a lot.
9. "Destiny" (Season Five, Episode Eight, by David Fury + Steven S. DeKnight): For all you shippers out there: Angel and Spike vie for the right to be

Shanshu-prophesied vampire with a soul who plays a pivotal role in the apocalypse, though we all know what they're really fighting for.

10. "Damage" (Season Five, Episode Eleven, by Steven S. DeKnight + Drew Goddard): Qu'est-ce que c'est? Psycho Slayer Dana unhands Spike, though Tom Lenk steals the show as Andrew (those Goldfish!).

11. "You're Welcome" (Season Five, Episode Twelve, by David Fury): God bless David Fury for giving us back the old Cordy, if only to take her away again, dammit!

12. "Smile Time" (Season Five, Episode Fourteen, story by Joss Whedon + Ben Edlund, teleplay by Edlund): In which the single ordeal heretofore never unleashed upon Angel in a century of torment and despair finally happens: he becomes a puppet.

13. "Not Fade Away" (Season Five, Episode Twenty-Two, by Jeffrey Bell + Joss Whedon)

And Whedon said, "Let there be darkness."

The Spinoffs That Never Were

Angel was the only *Buffy* television spinoff ever to come to fruition, but not the only one ever under consideration. None of the following ever made it to air.

"Grampire" (1998)

Dean Batali, a staff writer on the first two seasons of *Buffy*, recalls that Howard Gordon's toddler son called the offices one night and left a message for Pops, also a writer on the show, saying, "I hope you come home soon from writing 'Buffy the Grampire,'" Kids say the darndest things. Whedon drew a picture of dentures in a cup, with fangs, on the whiteboard, and wound up pitching the concept to FOX as a movie, to be scripted by five of the *Buffy* writers. Pretty funny, right? Except that FOX bought it (an actual contract was signed). The plan was to break the story over a week at a rented beach condo. Never happened.

"Ripper" (2001)

Rupert Giles–centric BBC TV project, alternately proposed as a series, miniseries, and TV movie, with Anthony Stewart Head reprising his *Buffy* role, focusing on his life in England following *Buffy*. Numerous explanations have surfaced over the years as to why the project never took off, including funding, rights issues, and the busy schedules of Whedon and Head.

"Buffy, the Animated Series" (2002)

Greenlighted by 20th Century Fox, but exec producers Whedon and Jeph Loeb couldn't find a network. Several *Buffy* cast members signed on to provide voices, though not Sarah Michelle Gellar. A three-plus-minute unaired presentation lives on YouTube.

"Faith the Vampire Slayer" (2003)

Described by *Angel* showrunner Tim Minear as "Faith meets *Kung Fu*. . . . It would have been Faith, probably on a motorcycle, crossing the earth, trying to find her place in the world." However, Eliza Dushku opted for FOX's *Tru Calling* instead, telling IGN it was too soon after *Buffy*, and "I kind of just wanted to try something else."

"Slayer School" (2003)

Would have included Potentials from season seven, plus maybe Willow, but never got very far; according to writer-producer Jane Espenson, Whedon never got behind it.

"Spike" TV Movie (2004)

Per published reports, this post-*Angel* idea starred James Marsters reprising his *Buffy* and *Angel* role, with Amy Acker (Fred/Illyria) and Alyson Hannigan (Willow). Minear was set to direct. The concept was pitched, but Whedon couldn't sell it, and Marsters's script became the basis of the 2014 Dark Horse comic *Spike: Into the Light*.

21

There's a Slayer Handbook?

Academia + Fandom

Willow: Everything seems normal. Not a snake, not a wasp.

Cordelia: Yep. School can open again tomorrow.

Xander: Explain to me again how that's a good thing?

—*"I Only Have Eyes for You,"* Buffy the Vampire Slayer

Myth-making . . . is simultaneously a psychological and social activity. The myth is articulated by individual artists and has its effect on the mind of each individual participant, but its function is to reconcile and unite these individualities to a collective identity."

—*Richard Slotkin*, Regeneration through Violence: The Mythology of the American Frontier, 1600–1860.

In 2012, the online magazine *Slate* explored which of the following film or television series had generated the most academic writing, all selected because they were judged to be "pop culture favorites known to have provided plenty of PhD fodder over the last couple decades": *Alien* (quadrilogy), *The Simpsons*, *Buffy the Vampire Slayer*, *The Wire*, and *The Matrix* (trilogy). In deference to the intelligence of our readers, we'll cut right to the chase: *Buffy* won, decisively. Whereas *Alien* finished second with eighty-six academic papers, essays, and books, *Slate* found over two hundred titles on *Buffy*, at which point it stopped counting.

We refuse to let this dampen our enthusiasm for the show.

Kidding! Some of our best friends are college professors.

Honestly, though, not surprised. *Buffy* may be the only show in television history with both a scholarly journal and recurring academic conference created in its honor, so that educators can excavate the myriad interdisciplinary pedagogical issues lurking beneath its generic trappings, including—and trust us, this is a *very* abbreviated list—genre, race, community, otherness, good versus evil, fandom, sexuality, and, of course, the ever-popular gender, because what academic isn't jazzed by that?

Both the journal and the conference are titled *Slayage*, and have been expanded since their inception to embrace the entire Whedonverse, including the television shows *Firefly* and *Dollhouse*, the Internet series *Dr. Horrible's Sing-Along Blog*, and numerous feature films (the journal is now officially named *Slayage: The Journal of Whedon Studies*, and a second publication, *Watcher Junior: The Undergraduate Journal of Whedon Studies*, has been added). They are produced by the Whedon Studies Association, a nonprofit, international association of scholars devoted to the study of Whedon's works.

The first Buffy academic conference, "Blood, Text, and Fears: Reading Around Buffy the Vampire Slayer," was presented in 2002—the same year the series started its seventh and final season—when four professors from the University of East Anglia at Norwich, England, hosted about 160 scholars from around the world, followed later that year by a symposium at the University of Melbourne in Australia. The first Slayage gathering—attended by four hundred scholars—took place two years later, in 2004, in Nashville, convened by David Lavery, an English professor at Middle Tennessee State University and something of a rock star in pop-culture academia, who passed away in 2016, and Rhonda V. Wilcox, also an English professor, and Dickens specialist, at Gordon State College in Barnesville, Georgia. Editing a collection of essays for *Fighting the Forces: What's at Stake in Buffy the Vampire Slayer* (2002), they had received over 140 submissions, and discovered that two additional anthologies of *Buffy* essays were in the works.

The notion of dissecting television shows in collegiate classrooms seems common enough now, but Lavery, Wilcox, and their Buffyology cohorts were out there marching in the vanguard, make no mistake about it, opening the floodgates for all of the programs that have followed, which means we have *Buffy* to thank for such courses as Mad Men: Media, Gender (yup), Historiography at Whitman College in Walla Walla, Washington (final exam: answer one of the following questions: Who is Don Draper? Who is Peggy Olson?).

According to Wilcox, many scholars—herself included—were initially drawn to *Buffy* through Willow Rosenberg, especially in the early years, "because of feeling like the unaccepted smart kid" themselves. The character undergoes a radical transformation over the course of the series, becoming both a lesbian and an extremely powerful witch, and in one of the most acclaimed episodes, season four's oneiric "Restless," she is consumed by the fear that this earlier, more timid and alienated iteration will be exposed as her true identity. "That's one of the things that the show repeatedly warns against and recognizes in young people, and heck it's not just young people, that self-hatred and self-doubt," Wilcox says. "I'm thinking about the episode ['Who Are You'] in which Faith has switched bodies with Buffy and she's punching her own face, she's punching herself, because she hates herself so much. And yeah, in 'Restless' Willow shows that same doubt of self, and I think it's part of the emotional realism that [cultural theorist] Ien Ang talks about. It's the idea that even if you're dealing with magical actions in the narrative, if the emotions of the characters seem believable then we can relate to them. I think that is something that Whedon is an absolute master at."

Rhonda Wilcox

FAQ: Was *Buffy* a pioneering show in terms of the academic world embracing it?

Rhonda Wilcox: In many ways it was a pioneer, in terms of being a clearly feminist series that was embraced by the academic world, but I also think that there were other series beforehand that were making a difference, and one of them was *Twin Peaks*, and *The X-Files*. And also I think there has never stopped being an underlying prejudice against fantasy and science fiction in taking things seriously, so that although there are many, many academics who value *Buffy* highly, there are also people who still get a curl to their lip. I also think it was at the beginning of a great wave of television that was so good that even doubters could not ignore the success anymore, and many of those programs were from a more traditional, realistic background when I think about it in literary terms, like *The Sopranos*, for example, which is just a wonderful thing, and which had less trouble, I think, getting respect across the board because it wasn't part of fantasy.

FAQ: So, *The Sopranos* premiered two years after *Buffy*. Do you consider them contemporaneous in terms of academic attention?

RW: Yes, and there was, and there still is, a lot of attention paid to *The Sopranos* and a great deal of respect given to *The Sopranos*, which is definitely deserved, but people have more to say about *Buffy*, I think, and I think that has to do with not only its aesthetic qualities but also its social symbolism.

FAQ: Social symbolism?

RW: The most famous example probably is an instance that comes in the second season that many people refer to, that fans relate to, and that is the episode ["Surprise"] in which *Buffy* and *Angel*, her beloved vampire, make love for the first time, and when she wakes up he has turned into a monster, and young women across the world shouted, "That happened to me!" That's one example of something that was symbolic but also socially significant. It was significant in part because the show does not shame her for it. People in the show treat her with respect and affection, and, of course, I also have to acknowledge that people also note when you do have sex in *Buffy* it's often a very dangerous enterprise, so that the subtext may be a little bit more warning than the text, but the show in which Buffy and Angel make love for the first time—one of the things that I noticed about it is that there's never a mention of the idea, there's never the use of the phrase "She lost her virginity." It's not presented as a situation where she has done something shameful or wrong. It's presented as a situation in which she has a tragic, miserable encounter, but it is not presented as a shaming of the woman, and I think that's a really important bit of social symbolism. And, of course, just the very basic idea of the person who looks helpless but stands up for herself with furious power is something that many, many people related to.

FAQ: So, you've taught *Buffy* in the context of English. Is that typically where you'd find it at a college, in the English department? Or would you find it in the film department or the media department?

RW: Communications studies often will be a place that you would find it, but people squeeze it in wherever they can.

FAQ: In all your years at Slayage, what sorts of professors have attended?

RW: We've had historians, we've had mathematicians, we've had quite a number of sociologists, gender studies, women studies, literature professors, musicologists do a wonderful job with it too, religious studies.

FAQ: You said in your book [*Why Buffy Matters: The Art of Buffy the Vampire Slayer,* 2005] that someday you hoped to explore in-depth the similarities between Whedon and Dickens. Now's your chance.

RW: There's loads and loads of them. First of all, the fact that each of them took a medium that was not highly respected and made people give it more serious attention, because Dickens was writing serialized novels, what were called shilling numbers, that came out regularly and in parts so that people could buy cheaply each little bit of it. Some of them came out once a month, some of them came out once a week, but those were looked down on compared to the three-decker novels that came out in bigger chunks, which, of course, you'd have to have more money to be able to buy. And I think that's comparable to what Whedon was doing by being one of the great explorers, innovators, he just knows how to use television really well, just as Dickens knew how to use the novel really well, that was coming out in that serialized form. They also both used social symbolism. If you think about the fog in *Bleak House* and how it symbolizes the fog of immorality and also the disease that connects people and a society that wants to think of itself as having people above who are untouchable and people below who are not worth touching, and yet we see that they are all connected, and, of course, we've already talked about the way that Whedon uses social symbolism. . . . I do also think that in Buffy the whole idea of community and family is terribly important to many, many people, and no matter what your situation really is in the world, I think almost everyone thinks of himself or herself as an outsider, and this is a group of outsiders who band together and because of banding together manage to make the world better and find an emotional home for themselves,

A moody ink-and-brush study of star-crossed soulmates Buffy and Angel by Aaron Minier.

Art by Aaron Minier

and I think that that's something that scholars as well as fans really love to dwell on. And I think it's really wonderful that both of them [Dickens and Whedon] are able to combine great tragedy and emotional dynamics with humor. They are both famous for being very funny guys and became popular because of that and yet at the same time had really wonderfully memorable characters, and they are both absolutely inimitable in terms of their language. Dickens's nickname was "The Inimitable Boz," and you know that his language was such that he's now considered to be one of the greatest writers in the English language. If you know Dickens you can recognize his style. There is that adjective, Dickensian, and Whedon is also somebody who is stylistically inimitable. Michael Adams wrote a book called *Slayer Slang* for Oxford University Press—the whole book is analyzing Whedon Speak, or Slayer Speak, as people sometimes call it. I could probably go on, but those are some of the big things I see as similarities between the two of them. They both really, really wanted their work to make a difference in the world.

FAQ: Now you've got us going because we're comparing Sidney Carton [from *A Tale of Two Cities*] to Buffy at the end of season five [when she sacrifices her own life, to save her sister's].

RW: Oh, yes, yay! See what I mean? I think it definitely can be a book.

FAQ: When I was first reading your book I was getting the sense that you were an *Angel* shipper, but then, as you started to get into the whole discussion of the Joseph Campbell monomyth and you started to talk about its application to Spike as well as Buffy I started to doubt myself. So, Rhonda Wilcox, I'm putting you on the spot: Which shipper are you?

RW: Definitely Spuffy.

FAQ: Really? So you're with Joss on that and not Sarah Michelle Gellar?

RW: I saw that recently and I was just delighted! It took me a long time to warm up to *Angel.* David Boreanaz is really beautiful, he got to display more and more acting skill and depth of character as he went on, and I could understand now why somebody would be a *Buffy-Angel* shipper, but I just love the character of Spike so much. I love his bad Victorian poetry and his suffering, and it's kind of like an English major's fantasy because you start out as the person trying to write poetry and then you get to be a real badass, right? After you go through all of the humiliation. And I just think there's so many wonderful scenes showing him to be an extraordinarily perceptive character who's also willing to put himself out there emotionally. Don't get me started on Spike.

To help clarify the scope of interdisciplinary studies within Buffyology: papers presented that first year at Slayage included "'Selfless': Locating Female Identity in Anya/Anyanka through Prostitution" (James Francis Jr.), "Music, Subtexts and Foreshadowings: Contextual Roles of Popular Music in

Buffy the Vampire Slayer, 1997–2003" (Kathryn Hill), "On Escherian Dualism and the Metaphysics of the Middle Way: Interpreting the Spatial Architecture of *Angel* the Series" (Mara Schiffren), and "When Ontologies Collide: The Essential Confusion of Existence in the Buffyverse" (Susan Stuart).

Happily, *Buffy* scholars have a sense of humor—they're *Buffy* fans, aren't they?—even bawdy at times, as evidenced by the titles of such first-year papers as "'Size Doesn't Matter?': The Disembodied Miniature in *Buffy the Vampire Slayer*" (Amy L. Montz) and "'Who Died and Made You John Wayne?' or, Why Riley Finn Could Never Be a Scooby" (Jennifer Stokes)—the latter arguing that Riley was an attempt to "normalize" Buffy, which we all kind of knew anyway, though how many of us went to the trouble of producing a twenty-six-page paper with fifteen works cited to argue it?

The WSA's "Whedonology: An Academic Whedon Studies Bibliography," compiled by Alysa Hornick, includes over two hundred pages of entries, a great many of them devoted to *Buffy* and/or the spinoff series *Angel*.

Whedon's take on all this: thumbs up. "I think it's always important for academics to study popular culture, even if the thing they are studying is idiotic," he told the *New York Times* in 2003. "If it's successful or made a dent in culture, then it is worthy of study to find out why. 'Buffy,' on the other hand is, I hope, not idiotic."

One of the more divergent applications of *Buffy* studies is "Biological Warfare and the 'Buffy Paradigm,'" issued on September 29, 2001—eighteen days after the terrorist attacks—in which Anthony H. Cordesman, Arleigh A. Burke chair in strategy at a D.C. think tank called the Center for Strategic and International Studies, urges decision-makers to "think about biological warfare in terms of a TV show called 'Buffy the Vampire Slayer,' that you think about the world of biological weapons in terms of the 'Buffy Paradigm,' and that you think about many of the problems in the proposed solutions as part of the 'Buffy Syndrome.'" Cordesman's thesis: that Buffy, like the United States itself, "lives in a world of unpredictable threats where each series of crises only becomes predictable when it is over and is followed by a new and unfamiliar one." Kind of like adolescence, which was the whole point of the show, right?

Does *Buffy* possess some intangible quality that renders it especially seductive to scholars—after all, weren't shows like *The Twilight Zone* and *Star Trek* attempting similar allegorical messaging decades earlier? Presented with that question, Cynthia Burkhead, chair of the English department at the University of North Alabama and Whedon Studies Association president, chuckles: "Intangible quality? That's kind of funny, because as academics of course we want to name everything. I think for me, and I think for many others, it's from that very first moment of the show, where the genre conventions got twisted, you know that very first moment—it's not going to be the bad boy wanting sex who's going to be evil, it's going to be the good little Catholic-school-looking girl who's really the vampire, and that entire twist. I think as a woman, and I would argue that most Whedon scholars, male or female, are feminists, I think that its celebration of the woman, the sweet little blonde who looks like she can't lift a feather, being empowered in this world—on a passionate, emotional level, that's what gets them."

Interesting: scholars connecting to *Buffy* on a "passionate, emotional level." Doesn't that make them "fans"? Yes, college professors are human, too (most, anyway), but emotion versus intellect is, for some, a traditional demarcation between scholar and fan. In *Buffy*, the boundaries are less clear. Chronology plays a role: *Buffy* premiered early on in the development of Internet fan culture, with instant interactivity—among fans, yes, but also between fans and scholars. The term "acafan" now identifies academics who also proudly consider themselves fans; conversely, "fan-scholars" are non-scholars who apply academic methodologies to their analyses of the show and are able to "publish" their thoughts due to the democratization of content distribution. Rabid fandom is itself a fertile field of study within Buffyology.

Thomas Hill, professor of English at Cornell University, was attracted to *Buffy* as a teaching tool because of parallels to medieval romance, but proudly relates to it as a fan as well. "I'll tell you a story," he says. "A few years ago I said to the class, 'Look, if you don't know *Buffy*, I'll put on a couple of episodes for you so you can watch it and see what you think. So I put on the last two episodes of season two ["Becoming, Parts 1–2"], you know, the business about where Angel's transformed and Buffy has to kill him. So we watched that, and I don't know, under ten but more than five students showed up and they watched those two episodes, and at the end of it some of them were crying. I do pretty good lectures on *Beowulf*, I think, but no one's ever cried in my class. And I was like, 'Wow! This is a powerful story.'"

Angel or Spike, Professor Hill?

"I don't have much to offer as a medievalist—very few medieval romances deal with or discuss the problem of two boyfriends and how to choose. But as a fan I am wholly on the side of Spike—he is funny, and, after all, he is around for a lot longer. This is maybe not fair to Angel, since he is supposed to be dark and broody, and dark and broody is not as amusing as what Spike is, but that is my opinion."

Clearly, Spike rules the academic kingdom, and we can't help wondering what he would have to say about it.

"Bollocks"?

Cynthia Burkhead

FAQ: What exactly happens at a Slayage conference?

Cynthia Burkhead: It's a full three-day conference, very scholarly. I've had people confuse what we do with a fan convention. We're not dressing up in costumes. We conduct our conference like any other academic conference.

FAQ: So, for people who don't know what an academic conference is like?

CB: Papers are presented, mostly twenty-minute scholarly papers. People submit proposals. We have people who will vet those proposals, so it is juried. . . . We also have keynote speakers. Jeanine Basinger, who was Joss Whedon's film professor [at Wesleyan] joined us one year and did a brilliant and fun keynote address. She was actually permitted [by Whedon] to read from some of his undergraduate papers to us.

FAQ: Have you ever had anyone from the Buffy creative team attend?

CB: We have not, yet. We have had, for instance, a taped message from [writer/producer] Jane Espenson one year. We would love to have anybody associated with Whedon's cause, but we want to make sure also that we are framing it in a scholarly framework.

FAQ: Do we have any way of knowing how many professors are out there teaching Joss Whedon in one form or another?

CB: In the association, we may have two hundred at a conference, but we probably fluctuate between four and five hundred as far as membership. And I'm just pulling that number off the top of my head.

FAQ: What do Whedon scholars like to do for fun at night, after the sessions?

CB: We do touristy things. We sit in each other's hotel rooms and watch fan vids or play Whedon board games. We drink (responsibly, of course). We have a banquet where we sing the entire score to "Once More with Feeling." And we laugh and eat. [Quoting Whedon] "Humor keeps us alive. Humor and food. Don't forget food. You can go a week without laughing."

FAQ: Is there anything we haven't discussed that would help us better understand the academic community's appreciation of Whedon?

CB: I would also perhaps add that the degree to which Whedon scholars are serious about doing this scholarship might be proven by the fact that many of them may have had their colleagues in their department rolling their eyes at them. You take a risk.

FAQ: Is there really a lot of that?

CB: I think that in the early days there was probably more of it, but I think that not only for Slayage but many, many other scholarly organizations with pop culture association. There has been so much Whedon scholarship that our colleagues who are not studying what we're studying are seeing it at least being taken seriously by other academics, so I think that it's become easier.

FAQ: Last question: Angel or Spike?

CB: To me, Spike has the most interesting development arc. He comes so damn far in rehumanizing, even though it is not fully possible. Knowing full well that Angel's re-souling was a curse, Spike goes after it for himself—because he loved! Angel and Buffy had no choice about what they were, but Spike did, and he made a good choice (finally, after being such a miserably evil vamp for so long). I love a good redemption. So yes, Spike/Buffy—but only after the redemption!

The "Buffy Musical Big Screen Extravaganza"

Film programmer Clinton McClung helped pioneer the *Buffy* singalong, building participatory events around theatrical screenings of the musical episode "Once More With Feeling," as far back as 1999, at the Coolidge Corner Theatre in Boston, an independent nonprofit arthouse. He scheduled the screenings for midnight, and recruited burlesque performers and puppeteers to enhance the experience.

Clinton McClung: I can't remember the year, but *The Sound of Music* singalongs started out and were touring around the country and were a huge thing and came to our theater for two weeks and sold-out audiences. I was like, "This is really cool, this is really interesting." They gave away goody bags, they encouraged people to sing along, they had a host, and the only thing I didn't like about it was the movie, *The Sound of Music* . . . . So around that same time the musical episode of *Buffy* had aired, and I was living with six girls at the time, we all shared this huge apartment in Boston, and they were all obsessed with *Buffy the Vampire Slayer*, and when I had moved in initially I was sort of like, "Oh, that show's okay," and then they got me really hooked on it. Every Tuesday night turned into a party at our house, where we'd all watch the previous *Buffy* episode and then the one that aired that night, and then we'd talk about it for four hours, and then we'd watch it again, so *Buffy* was a huge thing in my house, so it was kind of a natural progression for me to think, "This musical episode's amazing; we should do a singalong version and encourage everyone to sing along." So that was kind of the germ of the idea. And then in October 2004 I went to a play in Boston by this group called Queer Soup, which was an underground queer theater group, and they did a play called "Buffy the Vampire Slayer's High School Reunion," which was sort of a parody of *Buffy* and all of the characters and what would happen with them coming together ten years later and how they changed. And it was really funny, and there were musical numbers in it. They did a version of

"Bye Bye Bye" by *NSYNC. So, after the show I approached them and I said, "Hey, I've been having this idea, I'd like to have a singalong of 'Once More with Feeling' in my theater, and would you guys like to collaborate with me on that?" So, they came up with a live intro, I worked on putting together goody bags by watching the show and coming up with different ideas, and ways to participate in it, and we did it as a one-night-only midnight event. There wasn't really a way to clear the theatrical rights to a TV series, that's always been a really hard thing to do in the cinema world, so we just did it as a free show. As a nonprofit, the Coolidge had a blanket license to do free screenings of television shows or different movies, so we did it for free and six hundred people showed up, and we were all kind of blown away.

FAQ: How did the screenings go off? What songs would you say the fans really enjoyed? Was there a moment in the episode that went over super big?

CM: I think the great thing about that episode in particular is that it opens so strong, it opens right out of the gate with one of the catchiest songs in the show that sets up the whole premise for the episode and what's going on, puts you right in the headspace that Buffy's in at that time, and is one that's super fun to sing along with. It was also really great to do that one in front of an audience because as soon as the first chords start up—"I was going through the motions" starts kicking in—people get really excited and start cheering. Everybody knew the first line as soon as it started, and it ends with that great moment of her singing "I just wanna be alive" and stabbing a vampire and the vampire exploding into dust. At that moment I would usually shoot off a confetti cannon over the audience and everyone would just lose their mind and it was just such the perfect way to start the show. It brought the energy level up to just that right level, and everyone was so excited by the time that Buffy was done, and, honestly, if all I ever did was show up and set off a confetti cannon on "Going Through the Motions" I could just walk out of the theater for the rest of the show and people would just go nuts and do it themselves.

FAQ: What else did you do to make it interactive? How did it evolve over time?

CM: The first show that we did we basically planned for the opening act, which was the folks from Queer Soup did a number, and then I just gave people instruction sheets and let the audience sort of play it themselves, and I got up and did a little intro and told everybody how excited we were and all that. And then, between 2004 and 2006, I did, like, three shows at the Coolidge, and each one evolved just a little bit more, like I learned at the first show that people loved the goody bags and interactive props that we gave them. We gave them vampire teeth, we gave them a little bag of tissues for when Giles sings his going-away song, we gave people packets of mustard, which turned out to be a terrible idea. I never did that again.

FAQ: Because, later, you couldn't get the mustard out, right?

CM: Yeah, later, we could not get the mustard out. I gave people bubbles to blow during Dawn's ballet, because that was the one part of the show where you can't really sing along or participate unless you wanna get up and try to do ballet, so we gave people bubbles, which filled the theater

Some Sweet audience participation at the IFC Center in New York for the *Buffy* sing-along.   *Courtesy of Clinton McClung*

with this sort of fantastical air, which played really well with that number. My favorite thing was the kazoos, which honestly I only included in the goody bags because I had a ton of plastic kazoos sitting around from another show, and I was like, "What do we do with these?" So we gave them to the audience and instructed them to use them during the song "Something to Sing About" at the end when Buffy sings that emotional line about how she was in heaven, and she's so emotional that I think on purpose she wavers off tune a little bit just to show that she really means it right now, and I told everybody to blow their kazoos during that line in tune with what she was singing, and that was one of the funnest things. Kazoos make this heartbreaking wail, especially if there's two hundred of them going off at the same time. In a weird way, it made that moment even more powerful, but also made us all laugh a little bit. It was really beautiful. So anyway, each show that we would do I would sort of watch what the audience was responding to and what they liked and then sort of tweak it a little bit for the next show, and then when what I did at the first show at the IFC Center in New York in 2006, then it turned into a totally different thing.

FAQ: What kind of reaction did you get from any of the cast or creators?

CM: I had the honor of doing the show at the L.A. Film Festival, and, to my surprise, and unannounced beforehand, Marti Noxon and Joss Whedon were both in the audience and came up to do a little Q+A—

FAQ: Wow!

CM: I know! At the end of the show the programmer came up to me and I was gonna do the closing announcements after the show was over and said, "We have a couple of guests, would you mind announcing them?" and I said, "Sure," he was like, "It's Marti Noxon!" and I was like, "Oh, my God!" So I announced Marti Noxon and she came up to the front and talked to the audience and then said, "Oh, I'm sorry, we're burying the lead, there's someone else here," and Joss Whedon came up. So I had an opportunity to do a little Q+A with him on stage and talk to him briefly about it. And also MTV News filmed one of our shows in New York City and did a little piece on it and they interviewed him and some of the cast as well, and from what I could tell people were just delighted that fans were coming together and participating in the show and singing along and having such a good time. The only critique I got from Joss Whedon is, "Why do you guys hate Dawn so much?"

FAQ: How did he know that?

CM: That actually came up because when we first did the show and they were very audience driven, there was a huge vocal contingent of audience members that, especially in this episode, because Dawn's character is sort of

Many times more, with feeling: *Buffy* sing-along at the Michigan Theater.

Courtesy of Clinton McClung

the one who is the catalyst for all of the bad things happening. Every time she says something it leads to, you know, Tara finds out that Willow put a spell on her, or Sweet knows that the Slayer's in town and she's got to bring her to him; Dawn is like a typical young girl, you know, spills the beans too often, but the audience, the first couple of shows, were very visceral about this and every time Dawn would come on the screen would start yelling "Shut up" at her and I was like, "Okay, this is something people are responding to," but I didn't want the *Buffy* singalong to become like *Rocky Horror,* where people were yelling at the screen all the time. I wanted it to be a celebration of the show, so it wasn't that people had to follow the rules, but it was, like, if you gave people some very basic rules to follow they would stick within that and then have their own things but not feel the need to sort of invent the show as it's going along. So when people started yelling, "Shut up, Dawn" at the screen, and it started getting a little out of hand, I was like, "Okay, how do we reign this in a little bit?" So, I made it an official part of the show, because it wasn't really anything official before, and picked three moments where you're allowed to yell, "Shut up, Dawn." And the best part was, in New York, we had a cast that came out and performed live on stage in front of the screen during the musical numbers, and the girl that we had playing Dawn was so funny and cute and engaged, like people loved our live Dawn, and she would come out and hold up a little cue card that said, "Shut up, Dawn" on it, and everyone would yell it at her and she would bow her head and cry a little bit and people would love this.

FAQ: Did any other cast or creative team members ever engage with you in any way by showing up or sending e-mails, for example?

CM: A couple of times. Tom Lenk was at the L.A. Film Festival screening, and he approached me afterward and told me how much he loved it and how he had such a good time and how he was excited to finally be able to come and see it. And then a couple of years ago, I work with the Seattle International Film Festival now and a couple of years ago we premiered Joss Whedon's *Much Ado About Nothing* and his whole cast came out and Alexis Denisof came out as well and he happens to be married to Alyson Hannigan, who came with him, and she agreed to appear the next night at sort of a secret, for-free *Buffy* singalong screening, and I was able to do a really long intro and Q+A with her and talk a little about the show, and they sat down and watched the singalong. She'd never experienced it before, and I think they had a great time.

FAQ: Alyson Hannigan has very little singing in the episode, because she wasn't confident about her singing. Did she talk at all about that?

CM: She did. She definitely asked to have her role in that episode reduced a little bit, so she specifically did not want a huge production number, because she was afraid of—she's not a good singer, and she didn't want to be put on the spot. But what Joss did that I think was really, really clever was, there was one line in the musical that was actually written for Willow—it's during "Walk Through the Fire," where she sings, "I think this line's mostly filler"—that was an ad lib by Alyson. The original line was "I think this guy's mostly fear." She was talking about the demon, and Alyson actually turned to Joss at one point and said, "I think this is just filler, like you just gave me a line so I would have at least one line in this song," and he rewrote the line to be "I think this line's mostly filler."

FAQ: Is there anything in the way that fans have reacted during the screenings that has struck you as unexpected or remarkable?

CM: I think the parking ticket song, where Marti Noxon comes out and she has that line, that song that sort of fades out as the camera's panning away and you don't hear the last line of the song because it's only on the soundtrack CD, when the last line of the song is, "Hey, I'm not wearing underwear." *Everybody* in the audience sang that; they went the whole way through the song and they kept going and they sang that last line that you can only hear on the soundtrack, and that was one of the eye-opening moments for me, where I was like, "People are living this show; they're not just watching it." And not only that, but there was this core group of people that starting bringing underwear and throwing it at the screen during that song.

FAQ: Were there other characters who stood out to you, in terms of fan reaction during the sing-alongs?

CM: Two moments really stood out to me. When Spike first shows up in this episode, when he's coming out of his crypt, right before he starts singing "Rest in Peace," I remember people would go absolutely nuts when Spike first appeared. There were a lot of Spike fans. It's interesting, because he's a character they put through a lot of different permutations, and he's not a good guy. He's a vampire, who sort of found love and found a soul through this passion of his, but seeing the fan response to him was pretty fun. In fact, we worked that into the show: whenever Spike first shows up people just start yelling, "Hotness!" and freaking out. And then there's the love scene between Willow and Tara, which was a wonderful scene a) because it was one of the first lesbian kisses—well, that was in "The Body," but once "The Body" happened they could come out with this relationship in a beautiful, exciting way—but what was really interesting about the fan reaction to Willow and Tara's singalong is that the subtext of that song is not very subtextual. At that moment where the sharp cut happens, we gave people party poppers, which were little confetti poppers, so right at that moment of orgasm, if you will, we set up this confetti cannon that would fill the theater with confetti, and also filled the theater with the scent of burning smoke, because they give off that scent, and pretty much right after that there's a scene where there's a guy dancing and he's set on fire. It just played together really well. But mostly it was just fun to watch how excited people were to react to that cut at the end of that song. People couldn't help just hooting and hollering.

Selected Bibliography

Books

Buffy the Vampire Slayer: Panel to Panel. Milwaukie, OR: Dark Horse Books, 2015.

Buffy the Vampire Slayer: Tales of the Slayers. Milwaukie, OR: Dark Horse Books, 2011.

Adams, Michael. *Slayer Slang: A Buffy the Vampire Slayer Lexicon.* New York: Oxford University Press, 2003.

Chandler, Raymond. *The Long Goodbye.* New York: Houghton Mifflin, 1953.

———. *The Simple Art of Murder.* New York: Houghton Mifflin, 1950.

Crusie, Jennifer. "The Assassination of Cordelia Chase." *Five Seasons of Angel: Science Fiction and Fantasy Writers Discuss Their Favorite Vampire*, edited by Glenn Yeffeth. Dallas, TX: BenBella Books, 2004.

Fogelson, Robert M. *The Fragmented Metropolis: Los Angeles, 1850–1930.* Berkeley/Los Angeles/London: University of California Press, 1967.

Golden, Christopher, and Nancy Holder. *The Watcher's Guide.* New York: Pocket Books, 1998.

Havens, Candace. *Joss Whedon: The Genius Behind Buffy.* Dallas, TX: BenBella Books, 2003.

Jacob, Benjamin. "Los Angelus: The City of Angel." *Reading Angel: The TV Spin-Off with a Soul*, edited by Stacey Abbott. London/New York: I. B. Tauris, 2005.

Miller, Elizabeth. *Dracula: Sense & Nonsense.* United Kingdom: Desert Island Books, 2000.

Pascale, Amy. *Joss Whedon: The Biography.* Chicago: Chicago Review Press, 2014.

Stoker, Bram. *Dracula.* United Kingdom: Archibald Constable and Company, 1897.

Stoy, Jennifer. "'And Her Tears Flowed Like Wind': Wesley/Lilah and the Complicated(?) Role of the Female Agent on *Angel*." *Reading Angel: The TV Spin-Off with a Soul*, edited by Stacey Abbott. London/New York: I. B. Tauris, 2005.

Stuller, Jennifer K. *Fan Phenomena: Buffy the Vampire Slayer.* Chicago: Intellect Books, 2013.

Topping, Keith. *Hollywood Vampire: The Unofficial and Unauthorized Guide to Angel* (3rd edition). London: Virgin Books, 2004.

Wilcox, Rhonda V., and David Lavery. "Afterword: The Depths of *Angel* and the Birth of *Angel* Studies." *Reading Angel: The TV Spin-Off with a Soul*, edited by Stacey Abbott. London/New York: I. B. Tauris, 2005.

Whedon, Joss. *Fray*. Milwaukie, OR: Dark Horse Comics, 2003.

Wilcox, Rhonda. *Why Buffy Matters: The Art of Buffy the Vampire Slayer*. London/New York: I. B. Tauris, 2005.

Periodicals

"10 Questions for Joss Whedon." *New York Times*, May 16, 2003.

Bianco, Robert. "Producers Pour Souls into City of 'Angel.'" *USA Today*, July 20, 1999.

———. "'Buffy' Network Switch Means 'Angel' Has to Fly on Its Own." *USA Today*, October 22, 2001.

Broeske, Pat H. "Hollywood Goes Batty for Vampires." *New York Times*, April 26, 1992.

Canby, Vincent. "'Night of the Comet,' Adventure in California." *New York Times*, November 16, 1984.

Counts, Kyle. "The Changing Faces of Buffy the Vampire Slayer." *Fangoria*, September 1992. Emerson, Jim. "Films for Teen-agers Strive for Reality." *Orange County Register*, June 7, 1992.

Gerard, Emily. "Transylvania Superstitions." *The Nineteenth Century*, 1885.

Goodman, Walter. "In 'Tokyo Pop,' Youth Cultures Clash." *New York Times*, April 15, 1988.

Gustines, George Gene. "Experimenting in Bed When Not After Vampires." *New York Times*, March 5, 2008.

Kehr, Dave. 'Buffy' Is, Like, So Campy, You Know?' *Chicago Tribune*, July 31, 1992.

King, Thomas R. "Movies: Hollywood Springs to Fast Summer but Faces Olympics and Other Hurdles." *Wall Street Journal*, July 14, 1992.

Leerhsen, Charles. "Buffy the Vampire Slayer," *Newsweek*, August 9, 1992.

Lovecraft, H. P. "The Call of Cthulhu." *Weird Tales*, February 1928.

———. "At the Mountains of Madness." *Astounding Stories*, February/March/April 1936.

Marx, Andy. "A Look Inside Hollywood and the Movies: Summertime Bruise: Who Dares Intrude During the Season of the Giants? Several Rock-Slinging Davids." *Los Angeles Times*, May 17, 1992.

Maslin, Janet. "She's Hunting Vampires, and on a School Night." *New York Times*, July 31, 1992.

Mathews, Jack. "'Buffy': "As Silly (But Clever) As It Sounds." *Newsday*, July 31, 1992. Millman, Joyce. "Lessons in Being Human." *New York Times*, September 23, 2001.

———. "Hail and Farewell: *Dawson's Creek, Buffy* and the Soul of the WB." *Portland Phoenix*, May 2–8, 2003.

Persons, Mitch. "Buffy, Vampire Slayer," *Cinefantastique*, March 1998.

———. "Buffy, Vampire Slayer," *Cinefantastique*, March 1999.

Rhodes, Joe. "Buffyhood Is Powerful." *Newsday*, July 28, 1992.

Siskel, Gene. "Effects-laden 'Death' Is Unbecoming to Its Stars." *Chicago Tribune*, July 31, 1992.

Tolkan, Robin. "The Claddagh Ring Amongst Hollywood." *Entertainment Weekly*, March 20, 1998.

Welkos, Robert W. "Why Three Didn't Live Up to High Hopes." *Los Angeles Times*, September 1, 1992.

Websites

"Kung Fu Faith." http://bbc.adactio.com/cult/news/buffy/2003/04/14/3812.shtml, April 14, 2003.

Allie, Scott. "From the Editor," https://www.darkhorse.com/Zones/Buffy/344, March 7, 2008.

Axmaker, Sean. "What's in Your DVD Player, Joss Whedon?" http://www.whedon.info/Joss-Whedon-Angel-Tv-Series-Comic,24626.html, November 4, 2007.

Geeks of Doom, "The 'Buffy the Vampire Slayer' Abortion Controversy," http://www.geeksofdoom.com/2012/03/23/the-buffy-the-vampire-slayer-abortion-controversy, March 23, 2012.

Hibberd, James. "Joss Whedon: The Definitive EW Interview," http://ew.com/article/2013/09/24/joss-whedon-interview/, September 24, 2013.

Jackal. "An Interview with Scott Allie," http://stakesandsalvation.blogspot.com/2007/05/interview-with-scott-allie.html, May 16, 2007.

Jozic, Mike. "Buffy Post-Mortem: The David Fury Interview," http://whedonesque.com/comments/8936, December 2005.

Kuhn, Sarah. "An Interview with Eliza Dushku," http://www.ign.com/articles/2003/05/28/an-interview-with-eliza-dushku, May 28, 2003.

Lametti, Daniel, Aisha Harris, Natasha Geiling, and Natalie Matthews-Ramo. "Which Pop Culture Property Do Academics Study the Most?" http://www.slate.com/blogs/browbeat/2012/06/11/pop_culture_studies_why_do_academics_study_buffy_the_vampire_slayer_more_than_the_wire_the_matrix_alien_and_the_simpsons_.html, June 11, 2012.

Morgan, David. "Wide Angle/Close-up: Conversations with Filmmakers by David Morgan: Director, Producer and Film Distributor Fran Rubel Kuzui," http://www.wideanglecloseup.com/kuzui.html, June 10, 1992.

Phegley, Kiel. "The Buffy/Angel Continuity Conundrum," http://www.cbr.com/the-buffyangel-continuity-conundrum/, January 11, 2010.

Plume, Ken. "An Interview with Joss Whedon," http://www.ign.com/articles/2003/06/23/an-interview-with-joss-whedon, June 23, 2003.

Robinson, Tasha. "Interview: Joss Whedon," http://www.avclub.com/article/joss-whedon-13730, http://www.whedon.info/Joss-Whedon-Angel-Tv-Series-Comic,24626.html, September 5, 2001.

Thompson, Kelly. "Buffy the Vampire Slayer Season 9 #6," http://www.cbr.com/buffy-the-vampire-slayer-season-9-6, February 8, 2012.

Vary, Adam B. "Joss Whedon Talks About the End of the 'Buffy the Vampire Slayer' Season 8 Comic, and the Future of Season 9," http://ew.com/article/2011/01/19/joss-whedon-buffy-season-8-comic-exclusive, January 19, 2011.

———. "Buffy Getting an Abortion: Joss Whedon on the Big Decision," http://ew.com/article/2012/02/08/buffy-season-9-joss-whedon/, February 8, 2012.

Index

THE FAQ SERIES

AC/DC FAQ
by Susan Masino
Backbeat Books
9781480394506................. $24.99

Armageddon Films FAQ
by Dale Sherman
Applause Books
9781617131196......................... $24.99

The Band FAQ
by Peter Aaron
Backbeat Books
9781617136139 ....$19.99

Baseball FAQ
by Tom DeMichael
Backbeat Books
9781617136061.......................... $24.99

The Beach Boys FAQ
by Jon Stebbins
Backbeat Books
9780879309879 ....$22.99

The Beat Generation FAQ
by Rich Weidman
Backbeat Books
9781617136016 ....$19.99

Beer FAQ
by Jeff Cioletti
Backbeat Books
9781617136115 .... $24.99

Black Sabbath FAQ
by Martin Popoff
Backbeat Books
9780879309572.....................$19.99

Bob Dylan FAQ
by Bruce Pollock
Backbeat Books
9781617136078 ....$19.99

Britcoms FAQ
by Dave Thompson
Applause Books
9781495018992 ....$19.99

Bruce Springsteen FAQ
by John D. Luerssen
Backbeat Books
9781617130939.......................$22.99

A Chorus Line FAQ
by Tom Rowan
Applause Books
9781480367548 ....$19.99

The Clash FAQ
by Gary J. Jucha
Backbeat Books
9781480364509 ....$19.99

Doctor Who FAQ
by Dave Thompson
Applause Books
9781557838544.....................$22.99

The Doors FAQ
by Rich Weidman
Backbeat Books
9781617130175 .... $24.99

Dracula FAQ
by Bruce Scivally
Backbeat Books
9781617136009 ....$19.99

The Eagles FAQ
by Andrew Vaughan
Backbeat Books
9781480385412 .... $24.99

Elvis Films FAQ
by Paul Simpson
Applause Books
9781557838582................... $24.99

Elvis Music FAQ
by Mike Eder
Backbeat Books
9781617130496...................... $24.99

Eric Clapton FAQ
by David Bowling
Backbeat Books
9781617134548 ....$22.99

Fab Four FAQ
*by Stuart Shea and
Robert Rodriguez*
Hal Leonard Books
9781423421382.......................$19.99

Fab Four FAQ 2.0
by Robert Rodriguez
Backbeat Books
9780879309688...................$19.99

Film Noir FAQ
by David J. Hogan
Applause Books
9781557838551....................$22.99

Football FAQ
by Dave Thompson
Backbeat Books
9781495007484 .... $24.99

Frank Zappa FAQ
by John Corcelli
Backbeat Books
9781617136030....................$19.99

Godzilla FAQ
by Brian Solomon
Applause Books
9781495045684 ....$19.99

The Grateful Dead FAQ
by Tony Sclafani
Backbeat Books
9781617130861...................... $24.99

Guns N' Roses FAQ
by Rich Weidman
Backbeat Books
9781495025884 ....$19.99

Haunted America FAQ
by Dave Thompson
Backbeat Books
9781480392625.....................$19.99

Horror Films FAQ
by John Kenneth Muir
Applause Books
9781557839503 ....$22.99

James Bond FAQ
by Tom DeMichael
Applause Books
9781557838568....................$22.99

Jimi Hendrix FAQ
by Gary J. Jucha
Backbeat Books
9781617130953.......................$22.99

Johnny Cash FAQ
by C. Eric Banister
Backbeat Books
9781480385405 .... $24.99

KISS FAQ
by Dale Sherman
Backbeat Books
9781617130915 .... $24.99

Led Zeppelin FAQ
by George Case
Backbeat Books
9781617130250 ....$22.99

Lucille Ball FAQ
*by James Sheridan
and Barry Monush*
Applause Books
9781617740824 ....$19.99

M.A.S.H. FAQ
by Dale Sherman
Applause Books
9781480355897 ....$19.99

Michael Jackson FAQ
by Kit O'Toole
Backbeat Books
9781480371064 ....$19.99

Modern Sci-Fi Films FAQ
by Tom DeMichael
Applause Books
9781480350618 .... $24.99

Monty Python FAQ
*by Chris Barsanti, Brian Cogan,
and Jeff Massey*
Applause Books
9781495049439 ....$19.99

Morrissey FAQ
by D. McKinney
Backbeat Books
9781480394483 .... $24.99

Neil Young FAQ
by Glen Boyd
Backbeat Books
9781617130373 ....$19.99

Nirvana FAQ
by John D. Luerssen
Backbeat Books
9781617134500 .... $24.99

Pearl Jam FAQ
*by Bernard M. Corbett and
Thomas Edward Harkins*
Backbeat Books
9781617136122 ....$19.99

Pink Floyd FAQ
by Stuart Shea
Backbeat Books
9780879309503 ....$19.99

Pro Wrestling FAQ
by Brian Solomon
Backbeat Books
9781617135996 .... $29.99

Prog Rock FAQ
by Will Romano
Backbeat Books
9781617135873 .... $24.99

Quentin Tarantino FAQ
by Dale Sherman
Applause Books
9781480355880 .... $24.99

Robin Hood FAQ
by Dave Thompson
Applause Books
9781495048227 ....$19.99

**The Rocky Horror
Picture Show FAQ**
by Dave Thompson
Applause Books
9781495007477 ....$19.99

Rush FAQ
by Max Mobley
Backbeat Books
9781617134517 ....$19.99

Saturday Night Live FAQ
by Stephen Tropiano
Applause Books
9781557839510 .... $24.99

Seinfeld FAQ
by Nicholas Nigro
Applause Books
9781557838575 .... $24.99

Sherlock Holmes FAQ
by Dave Thompson
Applause Books
9781480331495 .... $24.99

The Smiths FAQ
by John D. Luerssen
Backbeat Books
9781480394490 .... $24.99

Soccer FAQ
by Dave Thompson
Backbeat Books
9781617135989 .... $24.99

The Sound of Music FAQ
by Barry Monush
Applause Books
9781480360433 .... $27.99

South Park FAQ
by Dave Thompson
Applause Books
9781480350649 .... $24.99

Star Trek FAQ
(Unofficial and Unauthorized)
by Mark Clark
Applause Books
9781557837929 .... $19.99

Star Trek FAQ 2.0
(Unofficial and Unauthorized)
by Mark Clark
Applause Books
9781557837936 ....$22.99

Star Wars FAQ
by Mark Clark
Applause Books
9781480360181 .... $24.99

Steely Dan FAQ
by Anthony Robustelli
Backbeat Books
9781495025129 ....$19.99

Stephen King Films FAQ
by Scott Von Doviak
Applause Books
9781480355514 .... $24.99

Three Stooges FAQ
by David J. Hogan
Applause Books
9781557837882......................$22.99

TV Finales FAQ
*by Stephen Tropiano and
Holly Van Buren*
Applause Books
9781480391444 ....$19.99

The Twilight Zone FAQ
by Dave Thompson
Applause Books
9781480396180 ....$19.99

Twin Peaks FAQ
*by David Bushman and
Arthur Smith*
Applause Books
9781495015861 ....$19.99

UFO FAQ
by David J. Hogan
Backbeat Books
9781480393851 ....$19.99

Video Games FAQ
by Mark J.P. Wolf
Backbeat Books
9781617136306 ....$19.99

The Who FAQ
by Mike Segretto
Backbeat Books
9781480361034 .... $24.99

The Wizard of Oz FAQ
by David J. Hogan
Applause Books
9781480350625 .... $24.99

The X-Files FAQ
by John Kenneth Muir
Applause Books
9781480369740...................... $24.99

HAL•LEONARD®
PERFORMING ARTS
PUBLISHING GROUP

FAQ.halleonardbooks.com